Shakespeare's Virtuous Theatre

Edinburgh Critical Studies in Renaissance Culture

Series Editors: Lorna Hutson, Katherine Ibbett, Joe Moshenska and Kathryn Murphy

Visit the Edinburgh Critical Studies in Renaissance Culture website at www.edinburghuniversitypress.com/series/ECSRC

Shakespeare's Virtuous Theatre

Power, Capacity and the Good

Edited by

Kent Lehnhof, Julia Reinhard Lupton
and Carolyn Sale

EDINBURGH
University Press

Edinburgh University Press is one of the leading university presses in the UK. We publish academic books and journals in our selected subject areas across the humanities and social sciences, combining cutting-edge scholarship with high editorial and production values to produce academic works of lasting importance. For more information visit our website: edinburghuniversitypress.com

Edinburgh University Press Ltd
The Tun – Holyrood Road
12(2f) Jackson's Entry
Edinburgh EH8 8PJ

Typeset in 10.5/13 Adobe Sabon by
Cheshire Typesetting Ltd, Cuddington, Cheshire, and
printed and bound in Great Britain

A CIP record for this book is available from the British Library

ISBN 978 1 4744 9904 0 (hardback)
ISBN 978 1 4744 9906 4 (webready PDF)
ISBN 978 1 4744 9907 1 (epub)

Contents

Part III: Virtue in Transit

Part IV: Sustaining Virtue

Acknowledgements

This book emerged out of a seminar on 'Shakespeare and Virtue', convened by Julia Reinhard Lupton and Donovan Sherman, at the 2020 meeting of the Shakespeare Association of America. We would like to thank everyone who contributed to that seminar.

The New Swan Shakespeare Center at the University of California, Irvine assisted with manuscript preparation.

Kent Lehnhof's contribution revises and reprints material from his article 'Sweet Fooling: Ethical Humor in *King Lear* and Levinas', which appeared in *Shakespeare Quarterly* 71.3–4 (Fall–Winter 2020), 198–220. We are grateful to Oxford University Press for permission to republish it.

Series Editor's Preface

Edinburgh Critical Studies in Renaissance Culture may, as a series title, provoke some surprise. On the one hand, the choice of the word 'culture' (rather than, say, 'literature') suggests that writers in this series subscribe to the now widespread assumption that the 'literary' is not isolable, as a mode of signifying, from other signifying practices that make up what we call 'culture'. On the other hand, most of the critical work in English literary studies of the period 1500–1700 which endorses this idea has rejected the older identification of the period as 'the Renaissance', with its implicit homage to the myth of essential and universal Man coming to stand (in all his sovereign individuality) at the centre of a new world picture. In other words, the term 'culture' in the place of 'literature' leads us to expect the words 'early modern' in the place of 'Renaissance'. Why, then, 'Edinburgh Critical Studies in *Renaissance Culture*'?

The answer to that question lies at the heart of what distinguishes this critical series and defines its parameters. As Terence Cave has argued, the term 'early modern', though admirably egalitarian in conception, has had the unfortunate effect of essentialising the modern, that is, of positing 'the advent of a once-and-for-all modernity' which is the deictic 'here and now' from which we look back.[1] The phrase 'early modern', that is to say, forecloses the possibility of other modernities, other futures that might have arisen, narrowing the scope of what we may learn from the past by construing it as a narrative leading inevitably to Western modernity, to 'us'. *Edinburgh Critical Studies in Renaissance Culture* aims rather to shift the emphasis from a story of progress – early modern to modern – to a series of critical encounters and conversations with the past, which may reveal to us some surprising alternatives buried within texts familiarly construed as episodes on the way to certain identifying features of our endlessly fascinating modernity. In keeping

[1] Terence Cave, 'Locating the Early Modern', *Paragraph* 29.1 (2006), 12–26 (p. 14).

with one aspect of the etymology of 'Renaissance' or 'Rinascimento' as 'rebirth', moreover, this series features books that explore and interpret anew elements of the critical encounter between writers of the period 1500–1700 and texts of Greco-Roman literature, rhetoric, politics, law, oeconomics, *eros* and friendship.

The term 'culture', then, indicates a licence to study and scrutinise objects other than literary ones, and to be more inclusive about both the forms and the material and political stakes of making meaning both in the past and in the present. 'Culture' permits a realisation of the benefits to be reaped after two decades of interdisciplinary enrichment in the arts. No longer are historians naive about textual criticism, about rhetoric, literary theory or about readerships; likewise, literary critics trained in close reading now also turn easily to court archives, to legal texts, and to the historians' debates about the languages of political and religious thought. Social historians look at printed pamphlets with an eye for narrative structure; literary critics look at court records with awareness of the problems of authority, mediation and institutional procedure. Within these developments, modes of research that became unfashionable and discredited in the 1980s – for example, studies in classical or vernacular 'source texts', or studies of literary 'influence' across linguistic, confessional and geographical boundaries – have acquired a new critical edge and relevance as the convergence of the disciplines enables the unfolding of new cultural histories (that is to say, what was once studied merely as 'literary influence' may now be studied as a fraught cultural encounter). The term 'Renaissance' thus retains the relevance of the idea of consciousness and critique within these textual engagements of past and present, and, while it foregrounds the Western European experience, is intended to provoke comparativist study of wider global perspectives rather than to promote the 'universality' of a local, if far-reaching, historical phenomenon. Finally, as traditional pedagogic boundaries between 'Medieval' and 'Renaissance' are being called into question by cross-disciplinary work emphasising the 'reformation' of social and cultural forms, so this series, while foregrounding the encounter with the classical past, is self-conscious about the ways in which that past is assimilated to the projects of Reformation and Counter-Reformation, spiritual, political and domestic, that finally transformed Christendom into Europe.

Individual books in this series vary in methodology and approach, sometimes blending the sensitivity of close literary analysis with incisive, informed and urgent theoretical argument, at other times offering critiques of grand narratives of the period by their work in manuscript transmission, or in the archives of legal, social and architectural history, or by social histories of gender and childhood. What all these books have in common, however, is the capacity to offer compelling, well-documented and lucidly written critical accounts of how writers and thinkers in the period 1500–1700 reshaped, transformed and critiqued the texts and practices of their world, prompting new perspectives on what we think we have learned from them.

Lorna Hutson, Katherine Ibbett,
Joe Moshenska and Kathryn Murphy

Introduction

Kent Lehnhof, Julia Reinhard Lupton and Carolyn Sale

'Fair virtue's force'

In *A Midsummer Night's Dream*, the newly transformed Bottom, abandoned by his friends, comforts himself with a simple ditty that awakens Titania from her drugged sleep:

> I pray thee, gentle mortal, sing again.
> Mine ear is much enamored of thy note;
> So is mine eye enthrallèd to thy shape,
> And thy fair virtue's force perforce doth move me
> On the first view to say, to swear, I love thee. (3.1.121–5)[1]

The comedy of the encounter rests in the mismatch between Titania's heightened language and Bottom's asinine form: when she praises 'thy fair virtue's force', audience members likely note that hairy Bottom is neither fair nor especially virtuous. Yet the phrase speaks to the vitalist understanding of virtue that runs beneath and alongside more personal understandings of virtue in the classical tradition and helps infuse the fairy forest with animate agency. Titania's pairing of 'virtue' and 'force' indicates the roots of *virtus* in ideas of power, potentiality, virility and vitality that are tapped and disciplined in the individual exercise of ethical capacities such as courage and liberality.[2] Greek *arete*, like Roman *virtus*, could simply refer to 'the quality or proficiency of men,

---

[1] All references to Shakespeare come from *The Norton Shakespeare*, ed. Stephen Greenblatt et al., 3rd edn (New York: W. W. Norton, 2016).

[2] Holly Crocker, *The Matter of Virtue* (Philadelphia: University of Pennsylvania Press, 2019); Julia Reinhard Lupton and Donovan Sherman (eds), *Shakespeare and Virtue: A Handbook* (Cambridge: Cambridge University Press, 2022). See also Jessica Rosenberg, 'Poetic Language, Practical Handbooks, and the "vertues" of Plants', in *Ecological Approaches to Early Modern Texts: A Field Guide to Reading and Teaching*, ed. Jennifer Munroe, Edward J. Geisweidt and Lynne Bruckner (Abingdon: Routledge, 2016), pp. 61–9.

gods, animals and things. [In Homer,] there can be an *arete* of feet, of
fighting, of shoemaking, or of the mind'.[3] Indeed, the streaked flower
harvested by Puck is possessed of a 'virtuous property' (3.2.367), a
hidden efficacy, that is already acting upon Titania in this scene. We
might extend the phrase 'virtuous property' to any object wielded on
stage to build worlds and effect change.[4] The virtuous properties of
plants, books, skulls and swords are called forth by the skill and judgement of the persons who handle them, and both actor and actant subsist
within an environment of forces and factors, from the epidemiological
to the civic, that can stymie or amplify the actualisation of powers and
projects. Virtue encompasses the broadest possible range of potentiality, both human and non-human, with everything that entails for
Shakespearean drama, which so often witnesses one person's pursuit
of virtue in conflict with the projects of others, and sometimes supports
enterprises that are anything but virtuous.

Presenting Shakespeare's theatre as a place infused with fair virtue's
force, this collection offers new ecological, feminist and historical
thinking about virtue and addresses the virtues of performance. Like
Shakespeare and Moral Agency, edited by Michael Bristol, the essays
here presume the continuing importance of 'vernacular criticism' and
'the compelling interest we have in a Shakespeare character as a virtual
self, moving in the center of its moral actions'.[5] But unlike the more
recent *Shakespeare and Renaissance Ethics*, edited by Patrick Gray and
John Cox,[6] the essays here focus on these 'virtual selves' not simply in
relation to 'the freedom of the individual self (*autos*) to formulate his
or her own moral code (*nomos*)' but also in the struggle to exercise
forms of virtue whose conditions are communal. In our attention to the
communal dimensions of virtue, we aim to consider the affective dimension of playgoing, the intersubjective phenomenality of virtue, and the
transformative effects of wit and humour, along with the national and
transnational, the pedagogical and the disciplinary, and (as Karen Raber
notes in her essay) the 'commonalities and mutualities that knit human
and animal together'.

---

[3] E. E. Shelp (ed.), *Virtue and Medicine: Explorations in the Character of Medicine*,
Philosophy and Medicine 17 (Dordrecht: D. Reidel, 1985), p. ix.
[4] Julia Reinhard Lupton, 'Shakespeare's Virtuous Properties', in *Shakespeare's Things*,
ed. Brett Gamboa and Lawrence Switzky (New York: Routledge, 2019), pp. 109–22.
[5] Michael Bristol (ed.), *Shakespeare and Moral Agency* (New York: Bloomsbury
Academic, 2010), p. 5; Michael Bristol, Review of *Shakespeare and Renaissance Ethics*,
ed. Patrick Gray and John D. Cox (Cambridge: Cambridge University Press, 2014),
Shakespeare Quarterly 68.3 (2017), 301.
[6] Patrick Gray and John D. Cox (eds), *Shakespeare and Renaissance Ethics* (Cambridge:
Cambridge University Press, 2014).

Shakespearean drama participates in several traditions of thinking about virtue, including ancient virtue in its extra-moral sense, virtue ethics as the classical and medieval art of human cultivation, and ethics as an increasingly universalised sphere of philosophy in the modern period. *Virtue* in its broadest dimensions concerns the affordances and abilities of human and non-human actors to initiate change in the multiple intersecting environments they inhabit. The poison-seeking Queen in *Cymbeline* speaks this language when she tests the compounds of the natural world for 'their several virtues and effects' (1.5.23). Placing sheer potentiality in the service of human betterment, *virtue ethics* addresses the moral habits required to advance and sustain *eudaemonia* (happiness, flourishing). In this vein, Lucentio, the romantic hero of *The Taming of the Shrew*, declares his desire, upon arriving in Padua, to study 'Virtue, and that part of philosophy / . . . that treats of happiness / By virtue specially to be achieved' (1.1.18–20). Finally, the domain of virtue ethics belongs to ethics more broadly, which would eventually displace virtue as a foundational category, eschewing the bewildering plurality and skills-based genesis of the virtues for more systematic and universalisable maxims and principles.[7] The essays collected here track the feedback loops between virtue's physics, flowing among diverse beings and faculties, and virtue's ethics, focused on individual dispositions and aptitudes, as their dance gestures outward towards the transcendental projects of ethical thinking as such.

The virtue ethics that Shakespeare received from antiquity and scholasticism took flight from the four cardinal virtues: justice, judgement, courage and temperance. This quartet of capacities, with courage as their ground and justice as their aim, appears across ancient philosophy, from Plato and Aristotle to the Christian, Jewish and Muslim philosophers who renovated classical ideas within new theological frameworks and geopolitical realities. In *Coriolanus*, Cominius declares that 'valor is the chiefest virtue' (2.2.81), and *Measure for Measure*'s Duke Vincentio tells Isabella, 'Virtue is bold, and goodness never fearful' (3.1.202). Courage, surging out of a visceral spiritedness or *thymus* in classical psychology, exemplifies the primal movement of the cardinal virtues between passion and reason, the former releasing energy and motivation and the latter providing order and oversight.[8] The word 'cardinal' means hinge: these four virtues reinforce each other and offer a foundation for other ethical comportments such as magnanimity, friendship, wittiness and

---

[7] See, for example, *The Routledge Companion to Virtue Ethics*, ed. Lorraine Besser-Jones and Michael Slate (New York: Routledge, 2015).
[8] Paul Tillich, *The Courage to Be*, 2nd edn (New Haven, CT: Yale University Press, 2000), pp. 3–5.

truthfulness. The four cardinal virtues were supplemented by the three theological virtues of hope, faith and charity in the Christian Middle Ages.[9] Whereas the cardinal virtues focus on human capacities for self-development in relation to a common good identified with the polis, the theological virtues suffuse the soul with grace, placing the disposition for action beyond the human will and supplementing worldly happiness with otherworldly salvation. When the Captain in *Twelfth Night* praises the 'courage and hope' practised by the shipwrecked Sebastian, he is coupling virtues with different provenances (1.2.13): courage is a cardinal virtue that responds to danger, pain, hardship and opportunity in the present under the guidance of reason, while hope is a theological virtue that expresses love in and for the future beyond rational calculation.

The virtues understood as dynamic capacities for thought and action provided an ideational infrastructure for ethics and pedagogy from the classical through the early modern era. Shakespeare inherited this world-view but also witnessed the rising challenges to it. Echoing Aristotle, Hamlet addresses virtue as a habit to be learned through practice when he urges Gertrude to 'Assume a virtue if you have it not' (3.4.161).[10] Elsewhere, though, Hamlet is more sceptical about virtue's capacity to guide human action; thus he warns Ophelia that 'virtue cannot so inoculate our old stock but we shall relish of it' (3.1.115–16). Lines like these indicate Hamlet's Lutheran outlook, which emphasised the limits of the sinful will to effect meaningful change in the world.[11] Mining the same dark view of human nature, the great secularisers Niccolò Machiavelli and Thomas Hobbes divorced individual virtues from a shared purpose and reduced them to alibis for the weak and cynical ruses for the strong. In the words of Iago, 'Virtue? A fig! 'Tis in ourselves that we are thus, or thus' (1.3.302). By the end of the seventeenth century, responding to the new realities of reformation, secularisation, capitalism and liberalism, virtue ethics were in disarray, to be eclipsed by the duty-based ethics of Immanuel Kant and the utilitarianism of John Stuart Mill and Jeremy Bentham. Drained of their earlier scope and vitality as responsive

[9] See entries in Lupton and Sherman, *Shakespeare and Virtue: A Handbook*: Kevin Curran, 'The Four Cardinal Virtues', pp. 113–23; Sarah Beckwith, 'The Three Theological Virtues', pp. 125–36; Stephanie Shirilan, 'Shakespeare's Rabbinic Virtues', pp. 279–89; and Yasin Basaran, 'Islamic Virtues: Ethics in the Premodern Ottoman Empire', pp. 291–98.

[10] See Kate Narveson, 'Hexis (Habit)', in Lupton and Sherman, *Shakespeare and Virtue: A Handbook*, pp. 61–2.

[11] Jennifer Herdt, *Putting on Virtue: The Legacy of the Splendid Vices* (Chicago: University of Chicago Press, 2008); David Aers, 'Calvinist Versions of God: A Revolution in Medieval Traditions', *Journal of Medieval and Early Modern Studies* 52.3 (2022), 445–82.

capacities rooted in interdependent lifeworlds suffused with grace, the virtues faded into the paler concepts of altruism, benevolence and sexual propriety, where they continue to languish in Sunday schools, advice columns and 'virtue signaling'.[12]

Though still a tertiary branch of modern ethics, virtue ethics was revived by analytic philosopher Elizabeth Anscombe, moralist and novelist Iris Murdoch, conservative philosopher Alasdair MacIntyre and liberal philosopher Martha Nussbaum, among others.[13] In *The Fragility of Goodness* (1986), Nussbaum drew on the idea of moral luck from Bernard Williams in order to bring out the context- and status-bound constraints that shape the individual exercise of virtue. Aristotle asserts that ethics belongs to politics, not only because virtuous actions aim at building a common good (1094b), but because the particular polis in which people live shapes their possibilities for action and their capacities for flourishing. Nussbaum repurposes the aristocratic *arete* of Aristotle into a democratic view of the human person 'as a being both capable and vulnerable, in need of a rich plurality of life activities'.[14] Feminists such as Lisa Tessman, environmental thinkers such as Philip Cafaro, and epistemologists such as Julia Annas have contributed new themes to virtue ethics.[15] Shakespeare studies have passed through these revivals and renewals, yielding both neo-scholastic defences of traditional character criticism (David Beauregard) and feminist and ecological renderings of virtues as powers nourished by attitudes of kindness and stunted by patterns of inequity (Holly Crocker, Jessica Rosenberg).[16]

Shakespeare's dramatic responses to the powers, limits and ambiguities of *arete* are as varied and plastic as virtue itself. Moving from the arable landscapes of the early comedies to the more intractable matter of plays like *Measure for Measure, Hamlet, King Lear* and *Troilus*

---

[12] Alasdair MacIntyre, *A Very Short History of Ethics* (New York: Macmillan, 1966); Alasdair MacIntyre, *After Virtue: A Study in Moral Theory*, 3rd edn (Notre Dame, IN: University of Notre Dame Press, 2007).

[13] G. E. M. Anscombe, 'Modern Moral Philosophy', *Philosophy* 33:124 (1958), 1–19; Iris Murdoch, *The Sovereignty of Good* (London: Routledge, 1970); and Martha Nussbaum, *The Fragility of Goodness: Luck and Ethics in Greek Tragedy and Philosophy*, 2nd edn (New York: Cambridge University Press, 2001).

[14] Nussbaum, *Fragility of Goodness*, p. xviii.

[15] Lisa Tessman, *Burdened Virtues: Virtue Ethics for Liberatory Struggles* (New York: Oxford University Press, 2005); Ronald Sandler and Philip Cafaro (eds), *Environmental Virtue Ethics* (Lanham, MD: Rowman & Littlefield, 2005); and Julia Annas, *Intelligent Virtue* (Oxford: Oxford University Press, 2011).

[16] David Beauregard, *Virtue's Own Feature: Shakespeare and the Virtue Ethics Tradition* (Newark, DE: University of Delaware Press, 1995); Crocker, *The Matter of Virtue*; and Jessica Rosenberg, *Botanical Poetics: Early Modern Plant Books and the Husbandry of Print* (Philadelphia: University of Pennsylvania Press, 2022).

and Cressida, Shakespeare increasingly found himself caught between Aristotle and Augustine, *eudaemonia* and original sin. In these middle plays, the efficacy of 'fair virtue's force' is adulterated, though never obliterated, by the fatal attractions of violence, incest, exploitation, resentment and greed in a proto-Hobbesian world in which man is wolf to man. Following these existential challenges to the scope of virtue, Shakespeare's late romances are, in Jesse M. Lander's phrase in this volume, 'virtue-centric'. In *Cymbeline, Pericles* and *The Winter's Tale*, Shakespeare renovates the cardinal and theological virtues in experimental inquiries into courage, constancy, fidelity and hope, comportments tempered by forgiveness and leavened by trust.[17] These and other virtues – received, confounded, battered, abandoned, untangled and amended – resonate within and across Shakespeare's works as renewable resources for ethical thought.

'The living voice'

The title of this volume, *Shakespeare's Virtuous Theatre*, calls attention to the deep relation between virtue and performance that shapes virtue ethics as a pedagogy and life practice from its earliest articulations. Initiating what virtue ethicists call 'the skill analogy', Aristotle frequently compares virtue to the expertise of a musician acquired through diligent practice:

> Every virtue both comes into being and is destroyed, as is similarly the case also with an art. For it is as a result of playing the cithara that both good and bad cithara players arise . . . So too in the case of the virtues: by doing things in our interactions with human beings, some of us become just, others unjust; and by doing things in terrifying circumstances and by being habituated to feel fear or confidence, some of us become courageous, others cowards.[18]

Aristotle's reference to music affiliates the virtuous person with the performing artist, a link that resonates in the term *virtuoso* and ripples through the semantics that affiliate 'action', 'acting' and 'actor'.[19] Aristotle

---

[17] For variations on this narrative, see for example Sarah Beckwith, *Shakespeare and the Grammar of Forgiveness* (Ithaca, NY: Cornell University Press, 2013); and Hugh Grady, *Shakespeare's Dialectic of Hope: From the Political to the Utopian* (Cambridge: Cambridge University Press, 2022).

[18] Aristotle, *Nicomachean Ethics*, trans. Robert C. Bartlett and Susan D. Collins (Chicago: University of Chicago Press, 2011), 1103b.

[19] Eduardo Côrte-Real and Susana Oliveira, 'From Alberti's *virtù* to the *virtuoso* Michelangelo', *Rivista di estetica* 47 (2011), 83–93.

captures the punctual and transient quality of virtuous performances as well as the iterative building of habits over time in settings that always involve 'interactions with human beings' as well as the instruments and environments of particular arts. Philosopher Julia Annas writes, 'We find the important similarity of virtue to skill in skills where two things are united: the *need to learn* and the *drive to aspire*.'[20] Both virtue and skill require practice, draw on tacit and embodied knowledge, take aim in relation to goals, and live and die through their performance. Learning higher-level skills (playing an instrument, suturing a wound, reading a literary text, staging a fight scene) requires care, judgement, vigilance, patience, generosity, attention and trust. It takes virtue to acquire skills, and skills themselves continue to orchestrate an ensemble of virtues when they are put into practice. Music, shipbuilding, medicine and statecraft are Aristotle's examples; weaving, carpentry, bellows-mending, and theatre count among Shakespeare's. Travelling among human and non-human as well as natural and cultural carriers, 'fair virtue's force' activates the circuits connecting beings and things in the world.

When, for example, Bottom, like a small child or a captive animal, uses rhythmic movement and vocalisation to still his panic and muster courage in the strange circumstances in which he finds himself – 'I will walk up and down here, and I will sing, that they shall hear I am not afraid' (3.1.108–09) – he exercises the courage that Hannah Arendt will later characterise as the movement into the dramatic field of self-disclosure, in which agents entrust the impact and import of their deeds to others: 'The connotation of courage, which we now feel to be an indispensable quality of the hero, is in fact already present in a willingness to act and speak at all, to insert one's self into the world and begin a story of one's own.'[21] Arendt is tapping virtue's passage in Aristotle from potential (*dynamis*) into actuality (*energeia*), a process that both Arendt and Aristotle associate with the performing arts. The action of acting manifests and reorganises the source of the actor's art – their *dynamis*, their powers or capacities – through skilled and intentional exercise. Compare Nussbaum:

> Activity, *energeia*, is the coming-forth of that good condition from its state of concealment or mere potentiality; it is its flourishing or blooming. Without that, the good condition is seriously incomplete. Like an actor who is always waiting in the wings and never gets a chance to appear on the stage, it is not doing its job, and in consequence, is only in a shadowy way itself.[22]

---

[20] Annas, *Intelligent Virtue*, p. 16.
[21] Hannah Arendt, *The Human Condition* (Chicago: University of Chicago Press, 1957), p. 186.
[22] Nussbaum, *Fragility of Goodness*, p. 324.

The pursuit of virtue sounds the actor's abilities and aspirations in an environment fraught by imbalances of power and the real risks of recognition. The result is a thick, ambivalent, multi-sensory virtue that grounds the virtual theatre of sound and light in a kinetic theatre of touch, taste and smell.

In early modern England, it was a humanist commonplace to consider literature as the source of actions to be imitated in the pursuit of virtue; but in furnishing such actions, the theatre's literary arts had an advantage over literary material to be read. While granting that 'more examples for imitation can be obtained from reading', Erasmus contends that 'fuller nourishment comes from the living voice, especially the voice of the teacher'.[23] He cites Seneca to suggest that the exercise of the 'living voice' in the theatre has something curative about it: 'The living voice and the intimacy of a common life will help you more than the written word.'[24] Theatrical practice brings together players and playgoers in the common house of the theatre in a collaboration, fleeting, ephemeral and evanescent, that may have all kinds of effects, a virtuous yield or harvest, outside the theatre's walls. In Shakespeare's theatre we watch a 'sharing of communicative and cognitive abilities'[25] – 'I see a voice', says Bottom as Pyramus in *Dream*'s final act (5.1.190) – that may spur the sharing of such abilities elsewhere in acts for which the activity of the players may be both model and inspiration. 'A conversation is a dramatic work', writes MacIntyre, and the artificial representation of fictional conversations in the space of the theatre, via the expressive mechanism of the 'living voice', may prepare us for the virtue-making prospectively at stake in any conversation even as the fictional circumstances of the Shakespearean drama offer us intellectual and emotional rehearsal for eventualities we cannot predict which will test our capacity for 'right action'.[26] We therefore keep alive here obsolete and rare meanings of 'virtuosity' as 'moral goodness; virtuousness' and 'strength or excellence of character', but also extend the sense of the word to the theatrical practice as a courageous one in Arendt's sense. Regardless of the genre of the play being performed, the playgoing experience invites audience members to occupy together, even if only temporarily, a space within which they experience a form of 'common life', with the contemplative

---

[23] Erasmus, *Adages*, in *The Collected Works of Erasmus*, vol. 2, lil to lv100, trans. Margaret Mann Phillips, annotations by R. A. B. Mynors (Toronto: University of Toronto Press, 1982), p. 162.

[24] Ibid.

[25] Paolo Virno, *Grammar of the Multitude*, trans. Isabella Bertoletti, James Cascaito and Andrea Casson (Los Angeles: Semiotext(e), 2004), p. 67.

[26] MacIntyre, *After Virtue*, p. 211.

activity that can take place there assisting them in the support of a state of virtuous well-being or *eudaemonia* ('blessedness, happiness, prosperity'[27]) that may be not only individual but collective.

As MacIntyre noted in *After Virtue*, virtue in its collective aspect is oriented to 'political community' as a 'common project'.[28] His book, first published in 1981, took as one of its pressing concerns the view that this orientation was 'alien to the modern liberal individualist world'.[29] It is arguably more alien now, decades later, on a planet beset with the emergency predicaments that neoliberalism has wrought. We agree with Hillary Eklund and Wendy Hyman, in their introduction to *Teaching Social Justice Through Shakespeare* (2019), that humanists must counter the forces that . . . threaten humane values'.[30] The essays in this collection address Shakespeare's theatre as an arena for the representation of the struggles of 'virtual selves' to be virtuous, but also as the home of a practice, that of the theatrical company, whose actorly labours make possible the recreational potential of the playgoing experience. *Dream*, the most metatheatrical of Shakespeare's plays, is also a touchstone in this respect – not only, as Lander notes in his essay, because it provides us with explicit language for virtue as an intersubjective phenomenon, but also because it spotlights the virtuous capacity of the actors. As Peter Quince's stuttering delivery of his prologue informs us, we are to 'repent' that 'the actors are at hand' (5.1.115–16). Depending on the genre of the play being performed, the 'repentance' required of us may be light-hearted or severe. As Paolo Virno notes, citing Arendt, all action in theatre depends on the virtuosity of the actors, who need 'an audience to show their virtuosity, just as acting men need the presence of others before whom they can appear; both need a publicly organized space for their "work"'.[31]

Shakespeare's Virtuous Theatre explores the environments of virtue – cognitive, physical, psychic, social, theatrical – sounded by the living voices of Shakespearean drama. We aim to demonstrate how Shakespeare's virtuous theatre enlists ancient virtues and shapes modern ones in complex scenarios that test virtues for their continuing value and emergent affordances. We approach the virtues as a source of imaginative, affective and intellectual nourishment, asking what Shakespearean

---

[27] Ibid., p. 148.
[28] Ibid., p. 156.
[29] Ibid.
[30] Hillary Eklund and Wendy Beth Hyman, eds., *Teaching Social Justice Through Shakespeare: Why Renaissance Literature Matters Now* (Edinburgh: Edinburgh University Press, 2019), p. 2.
[31] Virno, *Grammar of the Multitude*, pp. 52–3.

drama contributes to the project of weighing what may need to be abandoned, revivified or reinvented in traditional virtue ethics in order to build a virtuous sociality today.

For both Aristotle and the Stoics, human beings shared an ensemble of natural virtues with other animals, including perception, understanding, memory and the capacity for social attachment (5888b28–589a5).[32] Ancient virtue discourses also avoid mind–body dualism, thanks to virtue's links to the tacit and embodied knowledge of the artisan and performer and virtue's alliance with the passions. For Shakespeare and the ancient philosophers who inspired him, virtue – embodied, responsive, energetic and dynamic – harnesses the skills and capacities that engage minds, bodies, passions and worlds in principled action and the furthering of shared worlds. Exploring Shakespeare's virtues in tragic, comic and romance modes and from ethical, theatrical and political perspectives, this volume establishes virtue as a framework for a socially, environmentally and spiritually renewed literary criticism. Whether the focus is on ecology (Carolyn Sale and Karen Raber), global wisdom (Unhae Park Langis) or humanist pedagogy (Michael Bristol, Thomas Moretti), the essays assembled here balance historical depth and philosophical insight with the art of close reading, which is exercised in the dynamic field of virtue as it ebbs and flows across time and space and in the entangled lives and troubled circumstances of Shakespeare's characters.

This volume also invites readers to observe the complex moral ecologies in which we are all embedded and to consider what forms of life we wish to cultivate. This often means reflecting upon the antagonisms between different virtues and the tensions that can arise around the pursuit of virtue. Chastity, for example, has been used both to discipline the desires and capacities of women and to stake out a region of feminine autonomy and self-determination beyond marriage and procreation (Kristina Sutherland on *Much Ado About Nothing*). Chastity can allegorise the purity of the nation, but it can also yield transnational models of cultural interdependence and exchange (Michael Gadaleto on *Cymbeline*). Constancy asserts the absolute value of maintaining one's identity over time, but can also make room for accommodation and adjustment, especially when constancy becomes a defining virtue for female moral actors in interpersonal spaces of love, fidelity and care

---

[32] James G. Lennox, 'Aristotle on the Biological Roots of Virtue', in *Bridging the Gap Between Aristotle's Science and Ethics*, ed. Devin Henry and Karen Margrethe Nielsen (Cambridge: Cambridge University Press, 2015), pp. 193–213 (p. 206). See also Jacob Klein, 'The Stoic Argument from Oikeosis', *Oxford Studies in Ancient Philosophy* 50 (2016), 143–200.

(Lander on *Cymbeline*). Identifying the complex dramas of virtue in the Shakespearean drama, this collection challenges readers to recognise when an individual's commitment to a given virtue may put them into conflict with others or where a seeming virtue may transmute into a vice, as Sale argues happens to Kent's loyalty in *King Lear*.

We are also interested in how any virtue invariably gets caught up in questions of power. A virtue such as courage, with its strong masculinist and aristocratic bias, is unevenly apportioned among classes, genders and races, vulnerable to manipulation and misuse, easily co-opted for self-aggrandising projects, and difficult to achieve, as Daniel Juan Gil and Thomas Moretti contend in their essays on *Hamlet* and *Macbeth* respectively. Who gets to decide, then, what constitutes a virtue or where or how a seeming virtue must be upheld? When are codes of conduct potentially oppressive, and which virtues help us resist such codes to ensure that one person's exercise of virtue does not become the source of another person's oppression? And where does virtue need to be oriented to the communal as well as the individual, and sometimes the communal over the individual, to support collective goods? This collection shows how Shakespeare's dramas invite audiences to experience and evaluate both the benefits and the dangers of virtue with the aim of orienting audiences to virtues that bend towards justice.

These essays also present Shakespeare's theatre as a virtuous practice that uses embodied performance to make us experience our own capacities in ways that expand our sense of what it is to be human. The plea at the end of *King Lear* to 'speak what we feel, not what we ought to say' is ultimately a call to reinvest words with their virtuous force by reforming the arts and environments of speech, as Katie Adkison demonstrates in her essay. Apparently negative comportments such as grief and complaint become virtues when handled with a sense of dignity and shared purpose, as explored by Emily Shortslef and Michael Bristol, while wit and humour reveal their ethical import in essays by Ian Munro and Kent Lehnhof. In his Afterword, Kevin Curran locates virtue in an 'everyday dramaturgy' that supports 'the applied craft of making a world'. Attending to what Shakespearean drama furnishes by way of experience in the time and space of playgoing, these essays show us how theatre exercises the capacity of audiences and readers to think, deliberate, judge and feel. By elaborating virtue's affective dimensions in the time and space of performance, these essays find the virtues of Shakespeare's drama not only in the efforts at self-fashioning that separate individuals from each other, but also in the acts and attitudes of kindness, empathy and trust that assert interdependence among various forms of life as they muster the courage to be seen and heard. The essays here are historicist insofar as they turn back to ancient and early modern lexicons of virtue and to cultural conceptions of particular virtues, such as chastity, courage and constancy, whose meanings have changed over time. These essays are also presentist in that they ask readers to consider how Shakespeare's representations of virtuous capacities relate to goals for living together now. Probing the full scope of virtue in Shakespearean drama, we offer a vocabulary for talking about virtue in theatre, inviting readers to consider the dispositions, capacities and conceptions of the good that might best serve human aspirations in the twenty-first century.

Ecologies of Virtue

Part I investigates the vibrant zone between virtue's moral and extra-moral as well as human and non-human dimensions. In the field hospital near Dover, Cordelia bids 'All blest secrets, / All you unpublished virtues of the earth' to 'be aidant and remediate' to her father's distress (F 4.3.14–16). Cordelia's search for a pharmacy capable of healing her father depicts Earth as a repository of latent powers and imagines humans as remediating figures actively seeking not the extraction but the release of material and immaterial resources to one another. It is no accident that Cordelia speaks these words to an unnamed Doctor; in Aristotle's virtue ethics, medicine is a source and a metaphor for the skilled actualisation of the 'unpublished' latencies that Cordelia's prayer invokes. MacIntyre derives virtue from skilled social practices (*After Virtue*, 1981), and Nussbaum has mapped the reach of the medical analogy in ancient philosophy (*Therapy of Desire*, 1994),[33] disclosing theatre as a virtuous ecology in which actors discover, distribute and redistribute sensory and cognitive gifts among each other, their audiences and the setting of performance. Shakespeare's virtuous theatre affirms both inherited and new-created forms of kinship – with other human beings and with creatures in the natural world, guided by skilled practices and by philosophical ideas and ideals. This kind of creative thinking helps us increase our world-making capacity – that is, our ability to imagine the coordination of 'virtues' not just across species, but also across the animate and inanimate realms.

In 'Cordelia's Fire', Carolyn Sale presents Cordelia as a remediating figure and considers the theatrical ecology of the play as itself a 'publishing' of virtues. Sale takes on a variety of problems, starting

---

[33] MacIntyre, *After Virtue*; Martha C. Nussbaum, *The Therapy of Desire: Theory and Practice in Hellenistic Ethics*. Princeton, NJ: Princeton University Press, 1994; 2018.

with Aristotle's willingness to make virtue the experience of only some (masters and not slaves), as well as the critical tradition, which finds the play's virtues in all the wrong places. Sale argues that Shakespeare's tragedy enlists the stripping-down of *autopoietic* or self-aggrandising figures as part of the audience's participation in a *sympoietic* experience, or a making-with others in which they undergo the experience of being and making kin. One of the essay's most important figures for *sympoietic* experience is Gloucester, who carries a torch that blazes kindness as he tries to bring warmth to Lear on the storm-blasted heath. Gloucester's 'walking fire' enacts the play's consideration of the uneven distribution of warmth, both physical and empathetic, among creaturely communities. But the essay also considers what happens by way of virtuous affective experience for the audience during the scene at Dover cliff. According to Sale, the theatre is a kind of social hearth, a gathering place where humans work in concert with their environment to be brought into relation with one another to practise kinship and kindness.

In 'Voice, Virtue, Veritas: On Truth and Vocal Feeling in *King Lear*', Katie Adkison continues Sale's discussion of embodied and environed virtue by presenting Shakespeare's theatre as an experience of voice in which we are taught what it means to hear the voices of others long before we hit the play's explicit appeal, in its closing lines, that we 'speak what we feel, not what we ought to say'. Instead of rejecting the play's final plea as trite and naive, Adkison asks us to consider what speaking actually feels like: how passionate, intentional speech activates bodily and musical rhythms in an art of environmental attunement. Adkison's discussion draws on Hannah Arendt, Adriana Caverero and Sarah Beckwith to map Shakespeare's theatre as a place where voice may be at its most powerful when it bears – as in Lear's howls – no semantic content at all. The advent of voice in Shakespeare's virtuous theatre places us into more compassionate relationship with others across dramatic encounters with bodies, affects and sounds in a theatrical undertaking that is its own good.

In 'Reading Virtues: Shakespeare's Animals', Karen Raber explores kinship among human and animal creatures in *As You Like It*. She argues that the play's apparent affirmation of patriarchy is actually queered and feminised by exchanges between people and animals and asks what difference animal cultures might make for the social worlds of Shakespeare's plays. Like Sale, she mounts a *sympoietic* reading of human–animal relationships that takes animal capacities and relationships themselves, including creaturely styles of communication, attachment and listening, as the starting point of analysis. Building on the work of philosopher of science Vinciane Despret, Raber offers politeness, understood as the comportment of getting to know what the other is all about, as the guiding virtue of a new hermeneutic of reading Shakespeare's animals and the linked propensities for care and violence that humans and animals share. Tending the failing Adam, gentle Orlando turns bellicose, just as the lioness milked dry by her starving cub later crouches to attack the sleeping Oliver. Male and female and human and animal virtues flow freely among different kinds of living actors in the forest ecology of *As You Like It*, whose actions 'make even' the brute oppositions between genders and species that simplify so much mental experience (5.4.100). Raber's final considerations turn on the little-read *Two Noble Kinsmen*, where failures of animal–human communication lead not only to Arcite's untimely death but also to the testing of an alternative ethics of 'tolerance, accommodation and grace'.

Virtue's Performances

The essays in Part II build on those in Part I to show how Shakespeare's dramas of virtue expose us to something transformative in the time and space of playgoing. 'The purpose of playing', Hamlet tells the players, is to 'show virtue her feature' (3.2.19, 21). This showing is not merely mimetic but involves the unexpected manifestation or bodying forth of who one is through the contingency of significant speech and action. 'Feature' means face or form; in Hamlet's metaphor, virtue is looking at herself in the mirror provided by drama. 'Feature' also means a distinctive trait or characteristic, a particular capacity that is elicited in the course of a new action. The human actor proves herself courageous or cowardly, just or exploitative, when she ventures a judgement or makes a choice, and theatre is a record of these showings. Virtue, in its link to exercise, practice, habit and actualisation, is always performative, manifesting or publishing what is latent, implicit or unborn in a context of skilled practice and concerted enterprises shared with and broadcast to others. Virtuosity, as Paolo Virno has argued in *Grammar of the Multitude*, amplifies the performative core of virtue into an image of activity performed for its own sake, whether as art, work or labour. The experience of the Shakespearean drama rehearses the kinds of virtue that sustain communities, sometimes by directing our attention to those that do not. The very expression of certain virtues in the theatrical space is often an act of disclosure in which characters and the actors playing them make themselves vulnerable in order to bring forth an idea of what might be good to life.

The theatre's propositional character and its world-making potential are heightened to the extent that we leave the theatre already altered by what we have witnessed. Our agreement to participate in theatre is a crucial part of the theatre's virtuous practice. As the essays in this section show, Shakespeare's virtuous theatre depends upon us as we lend our bodies and our imaginative and intellective capacities to the unfolding of a performance in time and space. In asking us to respond to a range of expression from fictional others, Shakespeare's drama attunes us to the various dimensions of a virtuous sociality, which begins with recognising the needs of others and our shared status as equals, what Arendt called the plurality of the human condition.[34] The essays in this section pay special attention to the performative dimensions of virtue and to theatre as an immanent apprehension of virtue in the course of a play's performance.

In 'Shakespeare and the Virtue in Complaining', Emily Shortslef finds the Shakespearean drama staging a particular type of virtuous performance in choreographing the passionate speech and action of female complaints. Although the Stoics present complaining as the antithesis of virtue, Shortslef argues that Shakespeare follows Aristotle in taking a more generous approach to appropriate anger. *Richard III* and *Measure for Measure* are test cases for the rational public exercise of righteous distress by moral agents who are generally not afforded equal access to virtue's capacity-building resources, namely women. In these plays female characters achieve positive outcomes for themselves in 'interceptive action': the staging of scenes in which they challenge offences against virtue. This essay launches a line of consideration that other essays in the collection pursue: how does the Shakespearean drama deal with women's different relations to virtue and the special challenges they face in finding ways to identify and help drive change to social practices that stand in the way of a virtuous sociality?

In 'Masculine *Virtù* and Feminine Virtue in *Much Ado About Nothing*', Kristina Sutherland further addresses the gender dimensions of virtue by exploring the conflict between two traditional virtue concepts. She demonstrates that Italianate notions of *virtù*, with *vir* at its centre and as a practice to be enacted by men, enjoyed a broader, more active, set of meanings and preferred behaviours than feminine virtue, which tended to be identified with sexual chastity and was deeply vulnerable to public opinion and social appearances. *Much Ado's* Hero, as her name suggests, is an exemplar of virtue, but a virtue narrowly conceived: as a female 'hero', she is held to one criterion, that she be chaste. The

---

[34] Arendt, *The Human Condition*, p. 7.

play's great comic heroine, Beatrice, on the other hand, insists on her right to engage in a more elastic set of virtuous practices and attitudes. She does so for Hero, who tries to emulate her bolder cousin; for the audience, who get to enjoy her heightened sense of autonomy and wit; and for Benedick, who learns from her example how to move beyond his purely chivalric or military *virtù* in order to practise a more humane and inclusive kind of virtue that Sutherland names 'virtue *virtuosa*'. According to Sutherland, the play's comedic resolution comes about as Beatrice moves the men of Messina to embrace this more nuanced model of conduct that tempers the violent tendencies of *virtù* and validates the virtues of women. As Beatrice pursues her sense of what is good and necessary, she offers to the audience a liberatory sense of women's contributions to the shaping of virtuous communities.

In 'The Virtue of Humour in *King Lear*', Kent Lehnhof considers how the Fool in *Lear* might fulfil an analogous function, using his wit and humour to encourage more virtuous ways of relating to oneself and others. Rooted in the writings of Levinas and in recent work delving into the role of humour in Levinas's radical ethical philosophy, Lehnhof's essay demonstrates that the Fool's wit is profoundly virtuous in that it invites the king to laugh: both at himself (in a self-critical act of ethical abdication) and with others (in a generative opening towards interrelation). Although the king struggles to accept these invitations, the Fool relentlessly pushes the play in virtuous directions by using humour to place himself before others in a posture of vulnerability and exposure that Levinas sees as the foundation of all ethics. According to Lehnhof, the tragedy underscores the virtuous potentiality of wit, humour and fooling by showing how it can interrupt our egoism, abstract us from ourselves, impel us to consider other viewpoints, and open us to a more authentic connection with others.

In the final essay in this section, '*Vita Energetica*: *Love's Labour's Lost* and Shakespeare's Maculate Theatre', Ian Munro deepens the discussion of wit and humour by probing the virtues and possible failings of Gabriel Harvey's comic theory in relation to *Love's Labour's Lost*. In Harvey's comic theory, art, virtue, skilful action and social performativity converge in the ideal of the *vita energetica* – a life of *energeia* or 'being-in-action'. What does it mean, Munro asks, for virtue to be associated with mastery, whether over materials, oneself or others? According to Munro, such an attitude leads to wit's failure in Harvey's pamphlet war with Thomas Nashe: in his view, Harvey quite simply fails at being funny in his attempts to 'school' Nashe in 'decorum'. This observation informs Munro's reading of *Love's Labour's Lost*, the Shakespeare play in which characters most strenuously strive to outdo one another in displays of wit. Munro argues that while Harvey approaches humour as a metaphysical project tied to the pursuit of a perfected *telos*, Shakespeare liberates humour from final ends in a rhizomatic entertainment that finds its virtue in unfettered wit.

Taken together, these essays suggest that the Shakespearean drama is a special resource for representing the capacity for action that may shape a virtuous sociality. In both comedy and tragedy, characters use their voices to take aim at social dynamics and ideologies that would limit or inhibit the virtuous capacities of individuals and communities. By way of wit, complaint or other forms of self-expression and self-actualisation, these characters spur growth and development. In this way, they affirm our ability to establish the virtues that matter to us either in action or in a relationship to language in which we exploit its kinesis, or its potential to help us transform one kind of sociality into another.

Virtue in Transit

The essays in Part III explore what we might think of as virtue's constitutional dimensions, with various implications for the founding and sustaining of families, institutions, nations and transnational or global cultures. In all three of these essays, virtue is crucially interpersonal, and the representation of its complex transits between persons and places reveals virtue's role in the shaping of communities, starting with the community of the couple. Shakespeare's late plays, *Cymbeline* and *Othello*, test the virtuous capacities of their characters even more sorely than *Much Ado* and *Measure for Measure*. In *Cymbeline* and *Othello*, humour and wit alone are insufficient to save the central characters. Whereas Posthumus, Imogen[35] and Desdemona manage to draw on additional virtues, Othello notably falls short. His shortcomings bring about a tragic catastrophe that contrasts with the romantic reunion of Posthumus and Imogen, but the transits of these two fictional couples, whether across the ancient landscape of Britain in *Cymbeline*, or between temporal and spiritual planes in *Othello*, encourage deliberations about the kinds of virtues and the forms of love upon which cultures committed to a virtuous sociality depend.

[35] The Arden 3rd series of the play follows the *Oxford Shakespeare* in amending the character's name to 'Innogen'. The editors of this volume have elected to retain the spelling of the First Folio and refer to the character as 'Imogen'. William Shakespeare, *The Oxford Shakespeare: The Complete Works*, ed. Stanley Wells and Gary Taylor (Oxford: Oxford University Press, 1986).

In 'Constancy in *Cymbeline*', Jesse M. Lander turns to *Cymbeline* to address a virtue that was widely admired in the Renaissance but rarely considered in ethics today, constancy. Lander proposes that our continual revision of what constitutes a virtue may help us recover and renovate a virtue that we tend not to think of as 'modern'. Shakespeare's use of the 'virtue-centric' genre of romance invites audiences to reflect on the affective bonds of a fictional couple as a conceptual model for the bonds required amongst members of virtuous communities. Posthumus's and Imogen's struggles to exist in virtuous relation despite their belief that the other has betrayed them makes their experience of constancy an intersubjective phenomenon that tests their capacity to adapt to changing circumstances, placing the virtues in a matrix of interpersonal relations.

In '*Cymbeline* and the "Swan's Nest" of Britain: Insularity, Chastity and Imogen's Greater Transnational Virtues', Michael Gadaleto continues the collection's discussion of Shakespeare's late romance by bringing the dialectic of masculine *virtus* and feminine virtue introduced by Sutherland in Part II to bear upon *Cymbeline*'s contribution to an evolving understanding of 'Britain' under James I. In Gadaleto's reading, the complex allegory through which *Cymbeline* represents the virtues of England as an 'island nation' deliberates between two ways of understanding national virtue. The play's early emphasis on the importance of Imogen's purity and chastity suggests an insular view of Britain that transmutes over the play in relation to a conception of the nation's virtues as paradoxically transnational. Building on Lander's characterisation of romance as 'virtue-centric', Gadaleto demonstrates that the virtues that communities need – from the national and transnational to the global – find their touchstone in the couple at the heart of the romance. Imogen's talk of Britain as a 'swan's nest' (related to but crucially different from John of Gaunt's idea of England as a 'water-wallèd bulwark' in *Richard II*) is a sign for both the play's sense of the virtuous nation and the space in which its action plays out, with the play suggesting that hybridity and openness to worlds beyond the self are virtues necessary to the constitution of nations.

The final essay in this section, Unhae Park Langis's 'Sufi Theoeroticism, the Sophianic Feminine and Desdemona's Tragic Heroism', invites us to think of Desdemona in an entirely new way, as 'a female archetype of virtue' whose 'tragic heroism' is grounded in Sufi-Christian spirituality. In Desdemona and Othello's marriage we have a 'wedding of wisdom traditions' in which Desdemona's quest for 'perfect soul' involves a striving towards the good to be understood in the terms of Sufi theoeroticism. Othello's ability to join Desdemona in 'the theoerotic aim of harmonising divine and profane love in the contingent world they inhabit' is grotesquely undermined by Iago, whose project of turning virtue into vice is construed in new terms in Langis's reading. Langis offers a fresh reading of Desdemona's willow song and its transformation of the theatrical space into spiritual space, modelling the kind of virtue that playgoers may find in the playgoing experience of *Othello*.

Sustaining Virtues

The essays in Part IV of *Shakespeare's Virtuous Theatre* concern virtue as an attitude of conservation, preservation, curation, endurance and defence by turning to those virtues that assist with the *longue durée* of suffering, survival and cultural transmission. In *After Virtue*, MacIntyre notes that 'the courage required to sustain the household or a military expedition' remained central to the lived ethical life of feudal society.[36] As the humanities are responsible for sustaining literary and philosophical traditions through research, teaching and public work, the essays in this section ask which virtues, including grief and courage, are geared towards individual, cultural and institutional endurance. These essays consider how Shakespeare builds upon and breaks with Aristotelian virtue and where Shakespeare serves as a guide for thinking about concepts and practices of virtue now.

In 'Enduring the Eventual: A Virtuous Way of Reading Shakespeare', Thomas J. Moretti makes the case that Shakespeare's works are especially well suited to the cultivation of virtues on account of the intersubjective opportunities they afford, as well as the concentrated appeal they make to the interdependent human faculties of reason, emotion, imagination and instinct. According to Moretti, Shakespeare's plays repeatedly invite us to test our capacity for goodness in low-stakes acts of interpretation that make art a medium for ethics. In close readings of *Othello* and *Macbeth* Moretti finds the plays representing different ways of dealing with sudden crises – a public display of domestic abuse; an overwhelming urge to pursue some horror for a selfish, narrow *telos*; or a sudden expression of vulnerability from a falling tyrant – that require courage and prudence from the characters and may make possible for us a more flexible, hopeful and humble orientation towards the future. In the end, Moretti emphasises the ethical potential afforded by Shakespeare's plays and advocates for self-critical engagements that practise and habituate virtuous responses to unforeseen predicaments.

---

[36] MacIntyre, *After Virtue*, p. 166.

In 'Sustaining Courage in the Humanities: The Example of *Hamlet*', Daniel Juan Gil draws on MacIntyre's discussion of the 'sustaining courage' required to support organisational units such as households, expeditions or armies to consider how this kind of virtue might model what is needed to sustain Shakespeare studies and the humanities today. For Gil, this is an urgent matter, inasmuch as he believes that the humanities are at risk of becoming unmoored, in practice, from the transcendental virtues or goods that are their end. To impress upon us the dangers of this disconnect, Gil reads *Hamlet* as a loose allegory, with the despondent prince standing in for the academician who can no longer articulate the ultimate purpose that would confer meaning on his day-to-day academic activities. For Gil, the malaise, melancholy and immobility that afflict Hamlet warn us of what awaits, in the absence of sustaining courage. To encourage disciplinary persistence, Gil advances his sense of the objectives and virtues we can draw on as we strive to keep Shakespeare studies alive.

Finally, in 'On the Virtue of Grief', Michael Bristol returns us to virtue's affective dimensions, asking us to consider how Shakespeare's representations of a seeming vice – grief as the indulgence of passion – may in fact belong to a virtuous theatrical practice. Approaching *Richard II* as an inquiry into the resources of mourning, Bristol argues that the staging of grief over the course of the play opens up and recommends the capacity to mourn as a virtuous activity. Grief itself is not 'a task to be completed' but rather a hermeneutic accumulation of regrets and grievances whose virtue lies in challenging any fantasies we might harbour about self-determination. To grieve, we discover, may be to experience the magnanimity or greatness of soul that loss and regret can breed in those who bear it with care, making the expression of grief one of our most powerful means of putting ourselves into relation with one another.

Taken together, the essays in this collection consider a wide range of virtues that shape our social relations. In his *Complaint of Peace*, Erasmus indicates that these virtues are not exclusive to human actors. According to Erasmus, values like sympathy and *sympoiesis* are also evident in creaturely cultures of care:

> Animals, though they lack the faculty of reason, live together peacefully and harmoniously according to the norms of their different species ... You can find friendliness in trees and plants ... Nothing could be so insensible as a stone, and yet you could say that stones too have a sense of peace and concord; thus the magnet draws iron to itself and holds it when attracted.[37]

---

[37] Erasmus, 'Complaint of Peace', in *The Erasmus Reader*, ed. Erika Rummel (Toronto: University of Toronto Press, 1990), location 5173.

Finding sermons in stones and wisdom in howling, this volume presents the Shakespearean theatre as an ecology of skills, vitalities and capacities. The essays assembled here suggest that the experience and evaluation of virtues in the course of playgoing invite audiences to seek cultures that are more virtuous, or more just, because they take as their premise the need for humans to consider all of their actions, and all of their supposed virtues, in relation to the social and natural world. 'Our virtues / Lie in th'interpretation of the time', remarks Aufidius to Coriolanus (4.7.49–50). Virtues change meaning over time, and virtues are themselves interpretive acts that adjudicate the demands of the situation in which action is called for. In the Aristotelian tradition, judgement (*phronesis*) is not just one virtue among others, but the necessary cognitive accompaniment to all virtuous exercise. Now, more than ever, the need to act with judgement is pressing. With an eye to our increasingly challenging futures, in which our continuing existence and that of all life forms on Earth will almost certainly depend upon our reinvigorating old forms of virtuous relation and inaugurating new ones, we offer up these essays as exercises in *phronesis* in and beyond the world of Shakespeare's virtuous theatre.

Part I

Ecologies of Virtue

Chapter 1

Cordelia's Fire

Carolyn Sale

'I'll able them'[1]

In *King Lear*, virtue is something that can be 'tasted' (1.2.45). It is also something that can be faked: one can be a 'simular man of virtue' while in fact being an 'incestuous caitiff' (3.2.54–5) as Edmund demonstrates in the opening act of the play when his forged letter so easily convinces Gloucester that Edgar might wish to kill him. This kind of viciousness derives from and drives a culture of division that severs 'nature's' bonds or the bonds of kinship, as Lear does in the opening scene when he 'unfriends' Cordelia and tells her it would have been better had she not been born 'than not t'have pleas'd [him] better' (1.1.234). The play's dire opening scene implies that we are to find virtue in conduct that is the opposite of Lear's: in those who make bonds, rather than break them, or those who seek to make kin with others, and not just within any family unit. Lear's narcissism, which would require others to supply him with a 'kind nursery' even as he refuses all reciprocal obligations, makes him a destructive *autopoietic* figure: a person focused, that is, on the making of the self to the exclusion of the need to meet reciprocal obligations in processes of what Donna Haraway calls *sympoiesis*, or a making-with others.[2] Pitting those who would sow division against those who would resist it, the play pursues an idea of virtue that is not about the making of the excellent self or the *autopoietic*, but the making of kin or the *sympoietic*.

In Haraway's terms, the Shakespearean drama, at least in the form of this play, is 'tentacular': it seeks to create filiations that support forms of

---

[1] All references to *King Lear* are to the *Riverside Shakespeare*, 2nd edn, ed. G. Blakemore Evans, (Boston: Houghton Mifflin, 1997) and will be provided in the text. This line of Lear's falls at 4.6.168.
[2] Donna Haraway, *Staying with the Trouble: Making Kin in the Chthulucene* (Durham, NC: Duke University Press, 2016), pp. 58–61.

virtue that are not merely individual, but always also urgently oriented to the interdependence of life forms. As Alasdair MacIntyre notes in *After Virtue*, in Aristotle's conception, '[t]he virtues are precisely those qualities the possession of which will enable an individual to achieve *eduaimonia* ['blessedness, happiness, prosperity'] and the lack of which will frustrate his movement toward that *telos*'.[3] It is, however, 'the *telos* of man as a species which determines what human qualities are virtuous'. As several of the other essays in this collection in different ways suggest, virtue is not properly virtue unless its ends are communal or oriented to a shared flourishing. The *autopoietic* orientation (that is, the pursuit and maintenance of one's own virtues) is not necessarily in conflict with the *sympoietic* (forms of 'making with' that support the flourishing of life in its interconnectedness). But as Haraway notes, we must beware the 'bounded' individualism that threatens to lead 'us down deadly paths', for the '*autopoietic*, self-making man' can produce 'tragic system failure'.[4] The *autopoietic* striving towards virtue must be set within the infinite complexity of *sympoietic* making with others if the individual's pursuit of virtue is not to be destructive to others.

Haraway claims that it is Shakespeare's punning on 'kin' and 'kind' in *Hamlet* that set her on the path of thinking about the forms of *sympoiesis* that support the individual pursuit of virtue while holding in check the dangers of those whose orientation would otherwise be exclusively *autopoietic*. Haraway's interest is in a kin-making that comprehends all species. I take that as inspiration here as this essay grapples with the question of how *Lear* tests our capacity for virtue and exemplifies the virtuosity of Shakespeare's theatre.

This essay's presumption is that we have in playgoing a special kind of 'practice' in MacIntyre's terms, one in which virtues have an 'arena' in which they can be 'exhibited', with this exhibition constituting an 'extension of human powers' that 'transforms and enriches' our capacity for virtue.[5] The forged letter that Edmund pretends to have Gloucester believe is merely Edgar's means of 'essaying' or 'tasting' his virtue is a synecdoche for Shakespeare's script, which gives us a fiction in which characters conspicuously fail at being virtuous so that we may have the opportunity to 'taste' our sense of what virtue is. 'Essay', in a now obsolete meaning, is metallurgical: you could 'essay' or 'assay' a metal either with a cupel, a small vessel with a hole in the middle, placed over

---

[3] Alasdair MacIntyre, *After Virtue* (Notre Dame, IN: University of Notre Dame Press, 1981; 3rd edn, 2007), p. 148.
[4] Haraway, *Staying with the Trouble*, pp. 33 and 47 respectively.
[5] MacIntyre, *After Virtue*, pp. 187 and 193.

a flame, or a 'test', the 'movable hearth of the reverberatory furnace in which silver is separated from lead by cupellation'.[6] Shakespeare's metallurgical imagination is well in evidence in other plays,[7] but in *Lear* the metaphor is lashed to the very nature of the theatrical experience. Lear is metaphorically bound on his 'wheel of fire' but it is we who are assayed in a theatrical experience that so powerfully answers back to the anti-theatrical pamphleteers who saw not virtue but viciousness in the recreation of playgoing. One of these pamphleteers, William Rankins, went so far as to contend that with their 'Torches', the players would 'inflame the harts and inkindle [the] myndes' of playgoers 'to contende with virtue, and wholy to be guided and lighted by vice'.[8] *Lear* plays with fire both literal and figurative to 'inflame' hearts and 'inkindle' myndes not to 'contende with virtue' but to realize it.

For John Rainolds, the prerogative of any such 'inkindling' lay with prophets and apostles, whose responsibility was to 'instill in souls a godly fire of desire for embracing virtue'.[9] The theatre was presumptuous when it dared to arrogate to itself any such role. But as Russ Leo reminds us, the public theatre had an important learned defender in Alberico Gentili, Regius professor of civil law at Oxford, who claimed that poets were doctors who 'cure[d] through the emotions in a powerful way'.[10] Drawing upon Aristotle's theory of catharsis, Gentili contended that the curative project of the theatre, which works 'by shows', often required both 'serviceable lies' and 'indecorous imitations'.[11] *Lear* takes the 'indecorous' to an extreme. But its theory of the theatre and its implicit promise that we will be assayed in order to be cured find expression in Edgar's generative metaphor that the 'art of known and feeling sorrows' may make us 'pregnant with pity' (4.6.222–3). 'Virtues', MacIntyre noted, 'are dispositions not only to act in certain ways, but also to feel in particular ways.'[12] What is it, then, of which we must be cured in order to be released into a way of feeling or being at play's end that is virtuous on the play's terms?

---

[6] *OED* 'essay' v. †2. To test the composition of (an ore, metal, salt, etc.) by chemical means; = ASSAY v. 4. *Obsolete*.

[7] See Carolyn Sale, '"The King is a Thing": The King's Prerogative and the Treasure of the Realm in Plowden's Report of the Case of Mines and Shakespeare's *Hamlet*', in *Shakespeare and the Law*, ed. Paul Raffield and Gary Watt (Oxford: Hart Publishing, 2008), pp. 137–58, esp. 150–1.

[8] *A mirrour of monsters wherein is plainely described the manifold vices, &c spotted enormities, that are caused by the infectious sight of plays* (1587), fol. 23r, sig. Giiir.

[9] Rainolds, as quoted in Russ Leo, *Tragedy as Philosophy in the Reformation World* (Oxford: Oxford University Press, 2019), p. 138.

[10] Leo, *Tragedy as Philosophy*, p. 128.

[11] Ibid., p. 129.

[12] MacIntyre, *After Virtue*, p. 149.

Aristotle takes the position that our experience of virtue is always differential. '[A] human being grows up with weapons for VIRTUE and PRACTICAL WISDOM to use', but these 'weapons' are not equally available to all; 'everything is defined by its TASK and by its capacity', with some persons, as masters, having the prerogative to determine the tasks that others must do.[13] '[A] piece of property is a tool for maintaining life', he writes, and some men are the tools for maintaining the lives of others.[14] And though he considers the proposition that 'the superior in virtue ought to rule, or be master' may be 'an interference with nature' or its 'violation', he nevertheless allows it: 'there are some people, some of whom are naturally free, others naturally slaves, for whom slavery is both just and beneficial'.[15] As Louis Leroy puts it in his late sixteenth-century edition of the *Politics*, 'Nature her selfe teach[es] vs by the proposed partes of a man, that it is a most iust thing, that the better should always haue preheminence and dominion ouer the worser.'[16] MacIntyre suggests that while these ideas may 'affront' us, 'these limitations in Aristotle's account of virtues do not necessarily injure his general scheme for understanding the place of the virtues in human life, let alone deform his multitude of more particular insights'.[17] I beg to differ.

In the previous century Erasmus had been scathing about the problem that the reception of Aristotle posed for the virtuous flourishing of Christian cultures. Declaring in his discussion of war in the *Adages* that Aristotelian thinking had been 'accepted into the heart of theology, and accepted to the extent that his authority was almost more sacred than that of Christ', Erasmus attempted to counter Aristotle's influence with his own assertion of the importance of Christ's 'commandment of love'.[18] 'Search the whole of [Christ's] teaching', he writes; 'nowhere will you find anything that does not breathe peace, that does not ring of friendship, that does not savour of love'.[19] In Christ's terms, '[b]lessed are those', he continues, 'who do good to everyone'.[20] The attempt 'to fuse together' Aristotle's 'decrees' with 'the teachings of Christ' was

---

[13] Aristotle, *Politics*, trans. C. D. C. Reeve (Indianapolis and Cambridge: Hackett Publishing, 1998), pp. 4–5. The capitals are as in the edition.

[14] Ibid., p. 15.

[15] Ibid., p. 9.

[16] Louis Leroy, *Aristotles politiques, or Discourses of gouernment* (London: Printed by Adam Islip, 1598), fol. 33, sig. Fiiir.

[17] MacIntyre, *After Virtue*, p. 160.

[18] Erasmus, *Adages*, in *The Collected Works of Erasmus*, vol. 6, IIivl to IVii100, trans. Denis L. Drysdall, ed. John N. Grant (Toronto: University of Toronto Press, 2005), pp. 419 and 416 respectively.

[19] Ibid., p. 417.

[20] Ibid.

not only, in his view, 'like mixing fire and water', but resulted in a situation in which Christ's precepts were treated as if they were 'utterly repugnant'.[21] Straddling a temporal Rubicon between its pre-Christian setting and the Christian culture of its early seventeenth-century audiences, Shakespeare's play puts Aristotle's philosophy on its legs in the theatrical space so that we may experience the wrong of a culture of difference and division in which some are masters and others the ruled as well as the virtue of a shared capacity that is comprehensive in its inclusion.

As my title suggests, Cordelia constitutes a shaping force whose loss we must mourn at the play's climax. But my discussion begins with Kent, for my proposition is that the Shakespearean drama tests our understandings of and capacity for virtue in part by making us experience conduct that is vicious. Our sense of the ideas of virtue that a play promotes will be affected by the extent to which we account for the play's representation of viciousness. As Jesse M. Lander notes later in this volume, virtue is not only 'situational'; 'in certain circumstances particular virtues are infelicitous'. With Kent we see that in certain circumstances an ostensible virtue may translate into conduct that is downright destructive. The representation of this destructiveness heightens our sense of the importance of the virtues we find elsewhere in the play, which have a strong theological dimension. At its most exciting, I argue, the play offers us an experience of virtue that is not merely intellectual but visceral as it tests our responsiveness to its representations.

Kent's Loyalty

'Men / Are as the time is', Edmund informs us (5.3.30–1) as he arranges for a nameless Captain to kill Cordelia and knows he can count on him to do it because the 'time' makes murder work for those who 'cannot draw a cart, nor eat dried oats' (5.3.38–9). Kent, too, agrees that men are to make themselves of use, in his case to the man that he calls master, with his very life nothing more than a 'pawn' to be 'waged' against Lear's 'enemies' (1.1.155–6). He declares this in Act 1 as he dares to speak truth to power in the hope of keeping Lear from acting on his declaration that he intends to 'disclaim all [his] paternal care' for Cordelia and make her a 'stranger' to his heart forever (1.1.113–15), and there is no question Kent's fearlessness in the face of Lear's narcissistic rage

---

[21] Ibid., p. 420.

in order to keep him from breaking the bonds of kinship is a virtue. But the 'plainness' that Kent exhibits when he declares to Lear that he does not fear to lose his life, '[Lear's] safety being the motive' (1.1.157), has another face in both 1.4 and 2.2, when he subjects Goneril's servant Oswald to a great deal of violence both verbal and physical.

In the first of these scenes Kent quite clearly seeks, as the newly adopted servant 'Caius', to demonstrate his loyalty to Lear. Caius's character is thus consistent with Kent's, and there is an obvious virtue in it: whatever his persona, Kent is prepared to put himself at the service of another. Strictly speaking, as the service is to the king, the service is to all those that the king has the duty to sustain. But unlike other Shakespeare characters who, as Lander notes, 'refuse the command of their liege lord in order to preserve a greater good', Kent assumes that what will please Lear and make 'Caius' seem a fitting servant to him is violence towards others. A knight has moments earlier suggested to Lear that he is experiencing, in Goneril's household, 'a great abatement of kindness' (1.4.60), a view Kent encourages by taking a crude revenge on Lear's behalf by tripping Oswald. Making a football of one man in order to please another, Kent participates in a culture that willingly degrades some men in order to venerate others; and by Aristotle's logic, the minute that Kent sticks out a foot to trip Oswald he degrades himself by proving himself a 'natural slave' – that is, someone who as the tool of another can have no virtue of his own. With such conduct Kent shows himself incapable of *phronesis*, the 'intellectual virtue' that prompts the exercises of judgment 'without which none of the virtues of character can be exercised'.[22]

Kent's conduct in 2.2 is worse. The verbal denigration there is much more extensive, and culminates in a threat of physical violence should Oswald dare to deny 'the least syllable' of an 'addition' in which Oswald is a 'whoreson Zed' and 'unnecessary letter' (2.2.64). Kent's metaphors may vary, but the upshot is the same: Oswald is to be treated as if he is of no value and disposable. When Oswald denounces Kent (rightly) as a 'monstrous fellow' (2.2.25) Kent draws his sword and we have to watch him beat Oswald. The intensity of this beating will be attenuated where either actor or director shies away from the ugliness of the behaviour being represented; but whatever happens in terms of stage action, the feigned beating must seem to be sufficiently vicious to justify Oswald's two lines calling for help in the face of his seeming murder.

When confronted by Cornwall and Regan, Kent attempts to justify his conduct as an instance of anger's 'privilege' (2.2.70). This is an

---

[22] MacIntyre, *After Virtue*, p. 154.

outrageous claim in the context of a popular text on anger published in several editions across the first decade of the seventeenth century, John Downame's 'Treatise on Anger', offered to the public with the end (as the title page declares) that 'men may see the dangerousnesse of this disease of the soule'. For Downame, anger is 'a turbulent affection that doth vex and torment like a raging fire'.[23] And while Downame acknowledges that anger may sometimes be justified, and sometimes even just, with Christ furnishing the supreme example when he 'looked angrily upon the Scribes and Pharisees' and then toppled the tables in the temple in a 'holy anger' driven by the sight of 'his fathers house turned into a market',[24] anger has no privilege that leaves any man free to topple or degrade another. It is, instead, to be resisted at all costs as a passion that 'extinguishes the love of God'. Downame urges his readers to do everything they can to control it so that 'he that should tast you' will 'finde you free fro[m] gaule'.[25]

Downame hopes that wise readers will meditate on human infirmities, including their own, and restrain themselves rather than engage in behaviour for which they might be condemned.[26] It is this kind of meditation that the play encourages. Kent's support for the man who has already proclaimed himself to be a 'dragon' and who will later threaten to subject others to the 'terrors of the earth' takes forms that cannot be deemed instances of virtue. Arguments such as Wendy Olmsted's that Shakespeare draws upon 'a Ciceronian belief in the constancy of the friend in adversity' to represent 'Kent as the stabilizing presence that reduces suffering' miss a crucial ethical consideration: what virtue is there, ever, in denigrating or harming another?[27] In exercising violence against Oswald to show that he is a friend to Lear, Kent is the epitome of a problem. It is true, as MacIntyre notes, that 'the bond of friendship and friendship is itself a virtue'. But as MacIntyre also notes, the 'type of friendship which Aristotle has in mind is that which is a shared recognition and pursuit of a good'.[28] Moreover, 'the exercise of the virtues requires ... a capacity to judge and to do the right thing in the right

---

[23] John Downame, *Spiritual physicke to cure the diseases of the soule, arising from superfluitie of choller, prescribed out of Gods word* (London, 1600), 36r.

[24] Ibid., 5r–5v.

[25] Ibid., 80v.

[26] Ibid., 62v–63r.

[27] Wendy Olmsted, 'To Plainess is Honour Bound: Deceptive Friendship in *King Lear*', in *Discourses and Representations of Friendship in Early Modern Europe, 1500–1700*, ed. Maritere López, Daniel T. Lochman and Lorna Hutson (London: Routledge, 2010), pp. 181–94 (p. 190).

[28] MacIntyre, *After Virtue*, p. 155.

place at the right time in the right way'.[29] Antagonism towards one in the name of friendship for another is not a virtue, and violence against another cannot be deemed right action.

But in the representation of vicious conduct as part of the play's programme of 'serviceable lies' we have the potential for the generation of virtue. Our capacity for *phronesis* is exercised when Kent declares that his project is to 'teach' Oswald 'differences' (1.4.89–90). The speech in which Kent expresses his desire to tread Oswald underfoot as an 'unbolted villain' who may be made into the 'mortar' with which he will 'daub the walls of a jakes' (2.2.65–7) invokes the lowest person in the feudal hierarchy, the *villein*, who was required to do the most degrading of tasks, 'carry out the donge and fylth of the lord vnto the land of his lord therto lay it, cast it, and sprede it abrode vpon the land'.[30] But the moral question of the scene turns on how Kent as Caius lets himself be employed. In Kent's grotesque fantasy, another man is mere matter to be 'bolted' and then used to decorate the space in which others defecate. We cannot ignore this. If we 'bolt' or sift the text in order to set aside those elements of the play that we find unpalatable, we are not in a position fully to appreciate what the play later offers us by way of virtue. Shakespeare's representation of Kent shows us the kind of ugliness that cascades downwards in a hierarchical culture in which sovereignty itself is grounded in violence.

It is certainly an irony that Oswald, saved from Kent's violence, will later claim that another man's 'eyeless head' was 'first framed flesh / To raise [his] fortunes' (4.7.227–8) and dies calling another man 'dunghill' (4.7.243). But Oswald's later viciousness does not excuse Kent's. Shakespeare is giving us a character portrait, one entirely incidental to the main action, whereby he heightens the stakes of what the tragedy might do, as purgative or curative force. When the Fool laughs at the sight of 'Caius' in the stocks – 'Hah, ha, ha, he wears cruel garters . . . When a man['s] overlusty at legs, then he wears wooden nether-stocks' (2.3.7–11) – we hear a fitting ethic: those who would use their body parts as weapons against others must be restrained if the culture for whom the play is performed is to find ways (as Haraway argues we must) to support our *sympoietic* flourishing. It is tragic that Kent's subscription to his master is so complete that Lear is not only the 'great patron thought of in [his] prayers' (1.1.142), but the possessor of the voice that Kent imagines hailing him into death at play's end: 'My master calls me, I must not say no' (5.3.323). Kent is as much a victim

---

[29] Ibid., p. 150.
[30] Thomas Littleton, *Tenures in Englishe* (London, 1556), 37r.

as anyone else in the play (including Lear) of the culture of 'differences' or 'degree' deriving from *lex corona*, which makes the king 'the most excellent person' and everyone else his inferior.[31]

Walking Fire

We find one important counterpoint to Kent in Gloucester, in relation to whom we experience an opposite trajectory. At first we see him committing the error of being too easily duped by Edmund, apparently because he is predisposed to believe that others wish to take from him his wealth, privilege and status. But Gloucester starts to redeem himself from this folly, even before his eyes are plucked out, when his kindness drives him out onto the heath in search of Lear, to bring him some kind of help: 'Though I die for it, as no less is threatened me, / the king my old master must be relieved' (3.3.17–19). Both Kent and Gloucester feel the imperative to serve the 'master', but Gloucester does so in ways that are fully peaceful and at genuine risk to his own life. For this he pays a terrible price. But when the actor playing him walks out on the stage serving as storm-blasted heath in Act 3 he transforms it, for he comes bearing a life-sustaining force.

The Fool has just referred to this force with a simile that likens the environmental predicament of those on the heath to the predicament of a lecher: 'Now a little fire in a wild field were like an old lecher's heart; a small spark, all the rest on's body cold' (3.4.111–13). The Fool's simile suggests not only the personal repercussions of a life of 'lechery', or a life (in the Fool's language elsewhere) of 'snatching', but also the immediate predicament for the little society attempting to sustain itself on the heath. The characters are 'cold' because we all are in a polity that does not distribute even warmth equally.

When the actor comes on stage bearing actual warmth – 'Look, here comes a walking fire', the Fool declares (3.4.114) – we have in Gloucester's torch one of the play's several signs for its functions, one that gives the lie to the anti-theatrical pamphleteers' characterisations of the public theatre. As 'walking fire' Gloucester blazes kindness. In the Globe in 1605 or 1606, the only bodies likely to have been close enough to the torch's flame to feel its warmth would have been those of the

---

[31] William Fleetwood links the culture of 'degree' to *lex corona* in the opening pages of his treatise on the royal forest (BL MS 26047), *A Treatise vpon the Charters Liberties Lawes and Customes of all Forrestes Parkes Chases and Free Warrens* (Harvard Law School, 1581). The latter phrase is from Plowden. See Sale, '"The King is a Thing"', pp. 140–1.

other actors or those standing closest to the stage.[32] The actor bearing the torch nevertheless presents the audience with matter (the burning wood and its flames) that lets fire briefly play a cameo role in which 'the real leaks out of the illusion' and what is shared out isn't just actual warmth but the theatre's capacity to bring playgoers into relation round a fictional fire that gives off real heat.[33] Playing with fire, the theatrical company signifies not just all the material resources at stake in social relations (all those 'germains', as it were, that Lear in his narcissistic rage would simply 'spill' [3.2.8–9]), but its own potential role in shaping those relations. We are all *virtuosos*, the Italian philosopher Paolo Virno contends, by virtue of our expressive capacity as speakers; but we need public places in which to be present to one another in order to feel our capacity to marshal our virtuosity to 'act in concert'.[34] The play makes a 'little fire' on the 'wild field' of its wooden stage to draw playgoers into a form of company that may spark their hearts with a desire for a different way of being than the lecher's.

We hear of another fire, one associated with a kindness more radical, in Cordelia's talk of fire in 4.7. Confronted with what her father has been subjected to, Cordelia declares:

> Mine enemy's dog,
> Though he had bit me, should have stood that night
> Against my fire; and wast thou fain, poor father,
> To hovel thee with swine, and rogues forlorn,
> In short and musty straw? (4.7.35–9)

We have in this speech a political philosophy that must be tied both to Lear's talk of the superflux in 3.4 and Gloucester's similar speech in 4.1. The political vision that glimmers in Lear's speech would turn on the redistribution of an expropriated surplus which Shakespeare's unusual word, 'superflux', suggests is to be associated not just with material wealth but with dynamism, movement and change, and a capacity that is no one person's alone. The implication is that a distribution of the superflux requires a scattering of generative potential as much as of

---

[32] I assume the use of an actual torch on the basis of scholarship on fire and pyrotechnics in the early modern theatre that includes Philip Butterworth's *Theatre of Fire* (The Society for Theatre Research, 1998); Gwilim Jones's '"This Much Show of Fire": Storm and Spectacle in the Opening of the Globe', in *The Spectacular in and Around Shakespeare*, ed. Pascale Drouet (Newcastle upon Tyne: Cambridge Scholars Publishing, 2005), pp. 3–16; and Ellen MacKay's *Persecution, Plague and Fire: Fugitive Histories of the Stage in Early Modern England* (Chicago: University of Chicago Press, 2011).

[33] Bert States as quoted in MacKay, *Persecution, Plague, and Fire*, p. 179.

[34] Paolo Virno, *A Grammar of the Multitude*, trans. Isabella Bertoletti, James Cascaito and Andrea Casson (Los Angeles: Semiotext(e), 2004), pp. 55–6.

things. In Lear's speech it is 'pomp' that must act. In Gloucester's variation it is the 'superfluous and lust-dieted man' whose actions must be transformed, and the desired distribution is not to be left either to an abstraction or to those who top a hierarchy; everyone is implicated not only in the problem (inasmuch as everyone succumbs to one 'lust' or another) but also the solution, or the 'distribution' into which everyone is subsumed and through which everyone is cared for.[35] Gloucester's more comprehensive vision involves the undoing of 'excess' that ensures 'each man' shall 'have enough' (4.1.70–1). In both speeches, however, the vision nevertheless remains abstracted. In Cordelia's speech, in contrast, the philosophy quite literally finds a place, the place to which anyone may come – even the dog of the enemy, and that dog even after it has bitten her. Cordelia's fire, then, is the sign of an all-embracing kindness, one of an inclusion so radical it makes nonsensical the impulses in which other characters in the play indulge as they seek to reduce others to something less than human. It marks the theatrical space as the site of a virtuosic capacity that springs from the players' art and grows with the audience's responsiveness, with the imaginative thought that all animals, not just those that speak, may be brought within its embrace.

In this, too, the play is a rejoinder to Aristotle. Aristotle contends that it is better for animals to be domesticated, for 'rule by humans' will 'secure their safety'.[36] But the play elsewhere suggests the price that animals pay for any such 'safety' when Lear refers to a farmer's dog barking at a beggar as a 'great image of authority' (4.6.155–8). When a dog joins its master in treating another creature as foe by helping to keep a beggar from the farmer's gate, humanity deforms not only itself but another species. No person is safe in a culture that protects one man at the expense of others and allows all kinds of violence in his name; and no form of life is safe where even animals are made to serve a human culture of division. Imagining a situation in which she is willing to risk further hurt to herself rather than exclude any creature from the sheltering warmth of her fire, Cordelia is a figure for the kind of philosophical cure desperately needed for a human culture of division, one that embraces species beyond the human. (Karen Raber takes the consideration of the human–animal relation further in her essay in this collection.)

We have an even more lavish figure for such a philosophy in the little drama that the Fool offers Lear in 2.4 when Lear complains that his heart rises at the sight of 'Caius' in the stocks:

---

[35] For a related discussion of the speech, see Richard Strier, '*King Lear* and Social Security', *Raritan* 40.2 (2020), 63–72, esp. pp. 69–70.
[36] Aristotle, *Politics*, p. 8.

> Cry to it, nuncle, as the cockney did to the eels when she put 'em i' the paste alive; she knapped 'em o' the coxcombs with a stick, and cried 'Down, wantons, down!' 'Twas her brother that, in pure kindness to his horse, buttered his hay. (2.4.122–6)

Craig Dionne suggests Shakespeare's use here of Erasmus's idea of the 'hunting of eels' as a metaphor for abusive political dominion.[37] Lear may recover the situation, by this logic, as the Fool at first seems to urge, by beating down his daughter and her husband. But the speech ends with a surprise, and the idea of another world, in the 'pure kindness' that leads the cockney's brother to butter his horse's hay. This is the only kind of 'excess' in which the play finds a virtue: the excess in which one gives to another creature (in this case, a member of another species) something sumptuous without expecting anything in return. Choosing the former course, Lear proceeds on his path of *autopoietic* self-destruction in which even his own tears seem to be the agents of his dissolution as they 'scald like molten lead' (4.7.47). But the audience has the chance to proceed on another course, as the play serves up the opportunity for playgoers to feel 'pure kindness' in the scene that Stephen Orgel has called 'a paradigm not simply for Shakespeare's stage but for all theater'.[38]

'Th'extreme verge'

As Julia Lupton has argued, there is a virtue inherent in the theatrical activity that makes possible the scene at Dover cliff.[39] The actors are engaged in a kind of blind man's bluff in which the actor playing Gloucester must trust the actor playing Edgar to lead him safely across the stage to the place which constitutes 'th'extreme verge' from which playgoers are asked to imagine that the actor playing Gloucester may chuck himself by 'leap[ing] upright' (4.6.27). It's a weird challenge for the actor, who must somehow fake a fall that is really not much of a fall at all, though it may nevertheless leave the actor bruised.

The challenge is great for the audience as well, as its imagination is being worked even more vigorously than the Chorus in *Henry V* calls

[37] Craig Dionne, *Posthuman Lear: Reading Shakespeare in the Anthropocene* (Santa Barbara, CA: Punctum Books, 2019), pp. 99–100.

[38] Stephen Orgel, 'Shakespeare Imagines a Theater', *Poetics Today* 5.3 (1984), 549–61 (p. 557).

[39] See the discussion from pp. 164–71, esp. 167–8, in Julia Lupton, 'Trust in the Theatre', in *The Palgrave Handbook of Affect Studies and Textual Criticism*, ed. Donald Wehrs and Thomas Blake (New York: Palgrave Macmillan, 2017), pp. 155–81.

for that play's audience to work theirs. *Lear*'s audience must imagine that they are ecstatically at Dover even as their experience of the actors, especially by those audience members closest to them, cannot help but 'leak the real' as much as Gloucester's torch. After the fall, Edgar will refer to Gloucester's 'heavy substance' when he remarks on the seeming 'miracle' of his having fallen without having 'shiver'd like an egg' (4.6.51). But the audience's encounter with that 'heavy substance' even as the blindfolded actor simply stands before them is a visceral experience heightening playgoers' sense of their embodied presence in the theatre: a flesh-and-blood man may be about to take a tumble, and of what kind we cannot be sure.

We earlier see one actor take a fall when Kent trips Oswald. Another has to drop to the stage when Cornwall kills the nameless servant of Gloucester's who dares to stand up against the plucking out of Gloucester's eyes and whose reward is to have his corpse chucked on a dunghill. This is a play that asks us to watch body after body fall as it builds towards the scene in which Lear must bear the 'heavy substance' of his 'best object', the dead Cordelia, in his arms as he stumbles on stage in 5.3 in imagery that has been likened to a reverse pietà.[40]

The setting is a pagan one, but the play is being performed for an audience whose members are (at least notionally) Christians. The implication of such readings is that the play asks audiences to see the play's tragedy as tied to the absence of a community still to come, one that refuses to make 'differences' between men and women but instead draws them into the loving interrelation of equals. The play works paradoxically by asking its audience to imagine they inhabit an imaginative world in which this community, inspired by 'a Galilean vision of humility' and 'pure kindness', does not yet exist, so that they may feel the community's vulnerability or precariousness, perhaps even its absence, in worlds outside the theatre's walls.[41]

A great deal has been written about the speech in which Edgar aims to create the sense for Gloucester that he is at a place from which he might successfully kill himself.[42] Not enough has been said, however,

---

[40] For a superb discussion of Lear-and-Cordelia as pietà and the play's relation to other liturgical rituals and forms, see Jason Crawford, 'Shakespeare's Liturgy of Assumption', *Journal of Medieval and Early Modern Studies* 49.1 (2019), 57–84.

[41] The phrase 'Galilean vision of humility' is Catherine Keller's in *Political Theology of the Earth: Our Planetary Emergency and the Struggle for a New Public* (New York: Columbia University Press, 2018), p. 137.

[42] For the most cited discussion see Jonathan Goldberg's 'Dover Cliff and the Conditions of Representation: *King Lear* 4.6 in Perspective', *Poetics Today* 5.3 (1984), 537–47. For the most lyrical, see Simon Palfrey, *Poor Tom: Living King Lear* (Chicago: University of Chicago Press, 2014), pp. 167–89.

about the figures that Edgar would have Gloucester believe that he sees there, or their relation to the audience. These include, '[h]alf way down' (4.6.14–15), a man clinging to the cliff and supposedly gathering samphire, a seaweed that was, in Shakespeare's lifetime, an aristocratic delicacy.[43] Its briny flavour explains its nickname, green salt. The word is an anglicised contraction of 'Saint Pierre', but its second syllable rhymes with 'fire'.[44] Edgar also asks Gloucester, and the actor, the audience before him, to imagine that on the beach below he can see fishermen. In both cases, the figures are symbolically diminished: the samphire gatherer 'seems no bigger than his head' (4.6.16) and the fishermen 'appear like mice' (4.6.18). These figures have, however, an outsized symbolic significance.

The samphire gatherer is, as Edgar notes, engaged in a 'dreadful trade' (4.6.15). To gather a weed worth a matter of pennies in early seventeenth-century England, a samphire gatherer had to risk their life.[45] Shakespeare's samphire gatherer is a figure for the lack of a just distribution at its most extreme. He is not on the 'verge' with Gloucester, but already over it, and trying to sustain life in dire circumstances. While clinging to the cliff, the man is, moreover, suspended from social relations: he is stranded and alone. As such, he needs to be set in relation to the play's many other representations of devalued and degraded persons, with these including Goneril, informed by Albany in 4.2 that she is 'not worth the dust which the rude wind / blows in her face' (30–1). This is a play that insists that we take note of how 'pomp' treats the greater part of humanity – as if its members were not just despicable, but disposable. In the case of the samphire gatherer, a man is a tool for acquisition of 'virtues of the earth' (4.4.16) for others who remain elsewhere, both absent and idle.

The samphire gatherer, while below Gloucester in Edgar's imaginative topography, joins Gloucester in another respect, for they are both above the fishermen oblivious to their fates who do not know that they will be called upon, in a theology-to-come, to be the fishers of men. But every member of Shakespeare's audience would understand that they are at an imaginary scene at which Gloucester needs to be saved in a form of redemption for which they know the terms. The samphire gatherer clings to the rock that symbolically sprouts Peter while those who move around the rock's base recall the apostolic community, several of whom

[43] Dionne, *Posthuman Lear*, p. 130.
[44] See https://blog.metmuseum.org/cloistersgardens/2012/09/07/rock-samphire/.
[45] Susan Sachon, *Shakespeare, Objects, Phenomenology: Daggers of the Mind* (New York: Palgrave Macmillan, 2020), p. 122.

were fishermen. In the scene's brilliant dramaturgy, the appeal of both Edgar's speech and then Gloucester's appeal to those audience members regarded as the 'least' – those who have paid a mere penny to get in at the gate – is to think of themselves as the 'murmuring surge' (4.6.20) and then the 'mighty gods' (4.6.34) important to Gloucester's fate.

In Christian terms, Gloucester's act of precipitating himself off the edge of the cliff is, as a result of Edgar's imagery, a symbolic flight downwards to the least (or in the play's language, the 'base'). It is also an act of symbolic *ascension* as Shakespeare's fictional beach at Dover serves as the symbolic site of the 'strange and sudden alteration to come' in which the 'last become first, and the lowest, highest'.[46] The audience's experience is caught up with the character's symbolic transformation.

In a sermon of 1609, John Rawlinson refers to the allegory of the apostles as the 'fishers of men' as one that 'spreads': 'not a metaphor thorowout the whole volume of Gods booke', he writes, 'that more willingly dilates and spreads it selfe into an allegory'.[47] We are all to be caught, Rawlinson continues, 'with the net of Gods word made of lines taken out of the text of scripture', and in that net be 'draw[n] to the shore of a better life . . . as members incorporate into the body of Christ'.[48] The imagery that Shakespeare crafts for our vicarious experience at Dover is one in which Gloucester's symbolic flight downwards is not only a flight into the embrace of the primitive church as he becomes 'incorporate into the body of Christ', but a flight downwards to the 'murmuring surge' of the audience. This is where things get exciting.[49] At the play's Dover, which is simultaneously a fictional place but also the actual space of the theatre, it is not just 'deficient sight' that may 'topple down headlong' but a living and breathing man – one that we, pebble-gods, may feel we need to surge forward to save.

In those moments in which the audience cannot be certain what the actor may do or what may be required of them, its members are being assayed. To the extent that the audience considers even fleetingly that the 'heavy substance' of one man might very well be about to meet the 'heavy substance' of others, the audience may be feel that they are called, or should at least be ready – ready to be the fishers of a flesh-and-blood man that might chuck himself into the net of their warm arms. In those

[46] John Rawlinson, *Fishermen, Fishers of Men. A sermon preached at Mercers Chapell on Mid-Lent Sunday the 26. of March 1609* (1609), fol. 19, sig. D2r.

[47] Ibid., fol. 7, sig. B4r.

[48] Ibid., fol. 9, sig. C1r and fol. 7, sig. B4r.

[49] In *Shakespeare and the Materiality of Performance* (New York: Palgrave Macmillan, 2012), Erika Lin notes that Shakespeare scholars tend to focus on 'the verbal aspects of plays at the expense of the evanescent experience of theatre' (p. 26).

moments the audience experiences virtue not merely as an idea but as something needing to be enacted, and what surges is a sense of the audience's capacity – their capacity as 'intercarnational' superflux to respond with an act of 'pure kindness' greater than that of the cockney's brother.[50]

'Fiend with a thousand noses'

I am arguing that in the experience of this play in the time and space of playgoing, playgoers have the opportunity to experience something unusual: a sense of their own potential to act not only in imagination, at the fictional scene, as if they were there, but at the sites of life's daily dramas, where they have the choice either to support a culture of division breaking them into friends and foes or to respond with one or another instance of *sympoietic* kindness. Inasmuch as the call to action is theological, it is a daunting one. As Terry Eagleton has noted of Christ, the man who was 'homeless, propertyless, celibate, peripatetic, socially marginal, disdainful of kinsfolk, without a trade, a friend of outcasts and pariahs, averse to material possessions, without fear for his own safety, careless about purity regulations, critical of traditional authority, a thorn in the side of the Establishment, and a scourge of the rich and powerful', makes 'ruthless demands' upon his followers, including that they 'feed the hungry, welcome the immigrants, visit the sick, [and] protect the poor, orphaned and widowed from the violence of the rich'.[51] On top of all of this, they must be 'ready to lay down [their lives] for a total stranger'.[52] But the play's appeal to playgoers is also the call of what Catherine Keller has called an 'amorous agonism' to which the very act of coming together, congregating, is essential: 'Against the friend/foe politics', she writes, 'we practice the political as the self-assembling of an insistent public at the edge of chaos' predicated on finding co-creative potential in plurality and difference.[53] Such a community can only be truly operative, however, where no one is treated as if they are superfluous; where everyone, instead, is made to understand that they are 'belov'd' (5.3.240), and finds the proof of that love not in others' deaths, as Edmund does at play's end, but in the actions of the living.

[50] Keller, *Political Theology of the Earth*, pp. 109, 116.
[51] Terry Eagleton, *Reason, Faith, and Revolution: Reflections on the God Debate* (New Haven, CT: Yale University Press, 2009), pp. 10 and 19.
[52] Ibid., p. 23.
[53] Keller, *Political Theology of the Earth*, p. 160.

Even as the hearts and blood of those nearest to the 'verge' may still be pumping with the anticipation of the role that they might have been called upon to play, 4.6 abruptly shifts away from its claims upon the audience's embodied experience to an experience of an entirely different kind as Edgar asks both Gloucester and us to imagine that we can now see, 'upon the crown o'th'cliff', a 'fiend' with 'a thousand noses' and eyes like 'two full moons' (4.6.70–2). Now it is our capacity (both individual and collective) to engage a symbolic order in the form of the phantasmatic that is worked. With Gloucester we have been moving along an incredible emotional trajectory, from the recognition that generates the political vision of need for a distribution that undoes excess downwards to utter abjection, and then upwards again into a symbolic rebirth when Edgar pretends Gloucester has floated light as 'goss'mer' into new life. Now we are asked, along with the character, to imagine that there is present something that neither he nor we can see, a 'fiend' that pitilessly drives others off the edge of cliffs. The play is here asking its audience to generate a symbolic image of the viciousness that must be purged from the theatrical community.

From the intellectual vantage point afforded by modernity's psychoanalytic hermeneutic, it is easy enough to construe the hyper-phallicism of this figure, with its 'thousand noses', as well as what it stands for in terms of a masculinist co-optation or expropriation of the feminine, with its eyes like 'two full moons'. The fiend is the grotesque supernumerary expropriating the superflux to itself. It is the figure of a political theology so distorted that the place marked as the 'crown' has been thoroughly taken over by the singular one with all of its supplements (including in the form of a retinue of a hundred knights), the one whose heartless 'addition' requires that many be rendered 'wretched' to produce its superfluous 'pomp'. With its 'thousand noses', the fiend is also a figure for the vice of anger. As Downame notes, the Hebrew word for anger, *aph*, is also the word for nose, and perhaps deemed apt for anger 'because in a mans anger the breath doth more vehementlie and often issue out of the nose, which is as it were the smoke issuing from the flame kindled about the hart'.[54] The angry man carries with him the wrong kind of fire, and deals in it like a weapon. Shakespeare's fiend with a thousand noses represents anger as by-product and symptom (flux, superfluity) of the insatiable demands of the *autopoietic*/supernumerary figure to which the fiction of king lends itself: 'Come not between the dragon and his wrath', Lear declares to Kent in 1.1. But the fiend is not just a figure for the kind of vices unleashed under the name of 'king'. In Lear's plaintive

[54] Downame, *Spiritual physicke*, 3r.

line, 'They told me I was everything' (4.6.104–5), responsibility for the creation of the fiend is shared out. The imaginary fiend confronts the audience with its members' own creative capacity darkly reflected back at them in a phantasmatic thing that they have helped to make in their every act as 'silly-ducking observants' (2.2.103) to any master even if they never directly encounter the king.

But the 'king' is not just a phantasmatic 'thing'.[55] The king has two bodies, and the actor that now walks on stage to represent Lear gives us the king as 'natural body' to assist in the tragedy's purgative project.[56] And what we witness after Lear enters is the madness of the vices unleashed not by the person who is Lear but the legal fiction that makes him what he is. Nothing in the rant about women that cascades from Lear's complaint about the 'simp'ring dame, / . . . / That minces virtue' (4.6.118–20) is news, as Lear has amply expressed his misogyny when condemning Goneril and Regan's attempts to restrain him. But here the misogyny is expressed in a far more intense register and generalised in a comprehensive vision of women as not fully human: 'Down from the waist they are centaurs / Though women all above' (4.6.124–5). Lear further renders female sexuality and generativity monstrous first by distorting the female body (a woman has a 'face' to be found between her 'forks' [119]) and then designating the place from which children issue as the 'sulphurous pit' (128). It is not, however, just the imagination of the character that needs an apothecary's civet to sweeten it.

Rawlinson writes that God's 'net' makes 'no distinction between *sexe*'.[57] Aristotle thinks otherwise: 'the relation of male to female is that of natural superior to natural inferior, and that of ruler to ruled'.[58] But Aristotle was himself simply drawing upon (and choosing not to resist) a tradition. Lear's crazed vision derives from and marks what Fredric Jameson has called 'the sedimentation and the virulent survival of forms of alienation specific to the oldest mode of production of human history', 'sexism and the patriarchal', and we are hard pressed to find a character in the play that does not succumb to it.[59] We hear equivalents from one of the nameless servants at the scene in which Gloucester loses his eyes, as well as from Albany, who declares in Act 4 that '[p]roper

[55] For my discussion of Hamlet's play with the concept, see Sale, '"The King is a Thing"', pp. 145–7.
[56] For the most famous explication of the legal fiction of the king's two bodies, see Ernst Kantorowicz's *The King's Two Bodies: A Study in Mediaeval Political Theology* (Oxford: Oxford University Press, 1957), esp. pp. 7–16.
[57] Rawlinson, *Fisherman, Fishers of Men*, fol. 27, sig. E2r.
[58] Aristotle, *Politics*, p. 8.
[59] Fredric Jameson, *The Political Unconscious: Narrative as a Socially Symbolic Act* (Ithaca, NY: Cornell University Press, 1981), pp. 99–100.

deformity seems not in the fiend / So horrid as in woman' (4.2.60–1). This statement should make it impossible for any critic to refer to 'the virtuous Albany'.[60] Misogyny is the original viciousness, as it were, that the play would cure.

In this light let us return imaginatively to the ugliest of the play's scenes. Whatever we may feel when witnessing Cornwall and Regan pluck out Gloucester's eyes, when we hear Lear's imagining of the 'sulphurous pit' several scenes later, we have a responsibility to construe the earlier scene as involving the acting out of the revenge of persons designated as 'vicious' not because of anything they have done but because of the category of human in which they have been placed. The nails that extract Gloucester's eyes are the tools of the dehumanised seeking their rehumanisation, tragically, in viciousness that has been learned. For Goneril, who proposes it, and Regan, who helps do it, the plucking out of Gloucester's eyes is participation in the cruel mathematics of a culture of 'snatching' in which one is fully human only to the extent that one is a supernumerary making assemblages of one's expropriations from others. Gloucester's eyes are the symbolic pay-back for the figurative stealing of women's 'moons' in imagery through which Shakespeare suggests how patriarchy's sexism disorders the cosmos. As the horror of the play deepens, even Edgar is presented to us as subject to the culture's dominant thematic of division and devaluation when he declares that the 'gods' were 'just' in what they did to Gloucester: 'The dark and vicious place where thee he got / Cost him his eyes' (5.3.173–4). The play has immense therapeutic work to do to convince its audiences that no one is superfluous, and no person, a place, even as the horrors of its ending leave not a single woman standing.

Remediate Tears

If the play succeeds at its boundary-pushing experiment in tragedy, we must feel for Lear as much as we feel for any other character. The structural brilliance of 4.6, already packed with so much, reaches its climax as we move through a series of oscillations in which Lear indulges in some of his worst behaviour even as he makes some of his most moving appeals to our sympathy. First, in one of the most narcissistic gestures imaginable, he offers to lend Gloucester his eyes so that

[60] Stephen Orgel, '*King Lear* and the Art of Forgetting', in Orgel, *Spectacular Performances: Essays on Theatre, Imagery, Books, and Selves in Early Modern England* (Manchester: Manchester University Press, 2011), pp. 101–8.

Gloucester may weep for him. Then, in the very next breath, he appeals to our ineradicable commonality when he makes us think of ourselves as all emerging into life wawling and crying. This image of humanity at its most vulnerable is immediately displaced, however, as he ricochets back to his necro-politics, first with a military thought ('It were a delicate stratagem, to shoe / A troop of horse with felt' [4.6.184–5]), and then with a descent into aggression so great he reduces himself to an expression of unadulterated murderousness: 'kill, kill, kill, kill, kill, kill!' (4.6.187). But then, with the hands of Cordelia's nameless gentleman laid upon him, he may elicit the most sympathetic response of all from us when, assuming that the gentleman is taking him prisoner, he asks, 'No seconds? All myself?' (4.6.194).

This is the emotional state to which the entire play has been building as it tracks its tragic route through acts of figurative and actual violence – acts of division, cutting and 'abatement' by which characters who seek to assert themselves over and against others, often through the grotesque acts of denigration in which others are notionally reduced to the status of 'dog' (1.4.81, 2.2.80, 3.7.75 and 4.3.45), are themselves in one way or another brought down. The man who believes himself to be the great *autopoietic* supernumerary must be made to feel utterly alone, with no one to come to his aid when someone treats him (he believes) as foe. His desolation is underscored by what may be the most extraordinary ecological metaphor in all Shakespeare:

> Why, this would make a man a man of salt
> To use his eyes for garden water-pots
> Ay, and laying autumn's dust. (4.6.195–7)

Lear's figurative transformation to a 'man of salt' would be a powerful thing if Lear's tears were a sign of his repentance for wrongs to others. 'As *brine* keepes fish from *putrefaction*', Rawlinson writes, 'so the *brackish,* and *brinish waters of repentance, (our paenitent teares)* are *Animae pro sale,* to the soule in stead of salt, to keepe it from the *corruption and tainture of sin.*'[61] Lear weeps, however, not for any wrong that he has done, but because he believes himself without 'seconds'. Salt does not preserve his soul; salt is all he is. But what matters to the success of the tragedy is not Lear's fictional tears but ours, for the task of managing the 'autumn's dust' in ways that support both the Earth's generativity and the well-being of all life cannot be the task or responsibility of any one person alone.

---

[61] Rawlinson, *Fisherman, Fishers of Men*, fols 10–11, sigs. C1v–C2r.

The curative power of tears has already been associated twice with Cordelia, first in 4.3, where her gentleman casts her within the frame of one of the culture's most common paradigms for virtue by declaring her 'a queen / Over her passion who, most rebel-like, / Sought to be king o'er her' (13–15). As the title page of Downame's book declares, 'He that is slow to anger is better then the mightie man; he that ruleth his own mind is better than he that wins a city.' The gentleman then refers to the tears that drop from her eyes at the news of what Lear has endured '[a]s pearls from diamonds dropp'd' (4.3.22). There is no question that the play is valorising Cordelia. As Kent Lehnhof notes, the play's 'treatment' of her is 'numinous'.[62] Cordelia is presented to us as a creative force potentially so powerful that her 'aidant and remediate' tears might make spring from the earth 'blest secrets' and 'unpublish'd virtues' (4.4.15–17).

The imagery of her tears bears directly upon our experience of the tragedy when we hear that the tears are 'guests . . . in her eyes' (4.3.21). We have not yet heard the speech in which we learn that she stands for a community all-embracing in its welcome, but in this speech Cordelia is already a figure of hospitality. This is a play that repeatedly asks us to consider where it is we may be accommodated, where it is we may find shelter. As Peggy Phelan has noted, the play's shelters include the 'hovel' on the heath which Lear enters with trepidation, asking 'Wilt break my heart?' (3.4.3).[63] *Lear* risks breaking hearts on the premise that some good may come of it. But if the hovel is one of the spaces through which Shakespeare's theatre represents itself, so, too, are Cordelia's eyes: in the play's iconographic imagination, Cordelia's eyes are the hospitable vessel from which her remediating tears spill to make her (and by extension the theatre) the host of a sympathetic flux that may cure. Cordelia can be this hostess for she herself, amidst a culture of expropriators, has expropriated nothing. As the medium/space of the gentle, generative reproduction that begins with sympathy and realises itself in what another Shakespeare play calls the 'flux of company', Cordelia's eyes spilling their remediating tears are a sign not just of the theatre's powers but what may come of our being guests there even as the character who most stands for the possibility of overcoming a culture of division must die.

---

[62] Kent Lehnhof, 'Theology, Phenomenology, and the Divine in *King Lear*', in *Of Levinas and Shakespeare*, ed. Moshe Gold, Sandor Goodhart and Kent Lehnhof (West Lafayette, IN: Purdue University Press, 2018), pp. 107–22 (p. 110).
[63] Peggy Phelan, 'Reconstructing Love: *King Lear* and Theatre Architecture', in *A Companion to Shakespeare and Performance*, ed. Barbara Hodgdon and William Worthen (Oxford: Wiley-Blackwell, 2005), pp. 13–35 (p. 30).

Cordelia's Breath

When we figuratively bend with Lear over Cordelia at play's end, we cannot be sure just how much pain we are going to be asked to bear. In the chronicle histories and *King Leir*, Cordelia's counterparts live. For a brief time we may share Lear's hope: we know that the actor does indeed breathe, but not whether we are permitted to believe that the character does. As a result, even as the play reaches its tragic climax with Cordelia's loss, there is again something happening in terms of embodied experience that may matter beyond the fiction.

Michael Witmore has suggested that 'Lear's pause over Cordelia . . . engag[es] the senses in ways that are at once ethically, socially, and existentially demanding'.[64] This is unsurprising, given that, as Lehnhof has noted, Cordelia is the character 'whose imperiled alterity arrests our egoism and ordains us to an exhausting ethical responsiveness'.[65] But something even more elemental is occurring. When the actor playing Lear bends over the actor playing Cordelia in search of her breath, we are enlivened to what Robin Kimmerer calls 'the privilege of breath' and Catherine Keller 'our shared animal breathiness'.[66] As Kimmerer argues, the challenge of any culture committed to the 'moral covenant of reciprocity' – a covenant that would reject what Albany suggests at play's end when he calls for 'All friends [to] taste / The wages of their virtue, and all foes / The cup of their deservings' (5.3.303–5) – is for its members to have 'hearts open enough to embrace' not just one another but also 'our more-than-human kin'.[67] Using the metaphor so important to the play, that of the heart as a sustaining fire, Kimmerer asks her readers to find an emblematic touchstone for each of our hearts in the *shkitagen*, the 'black knob' of the birch tree which when 'disbranched', as Shakespeare would say, and cut open, reveals an interior 'banded in glowing shades of gold and bronze, with the texture of spongy wood, all constructed of tiny threads and air-filled pores'.[68] The *shkitagen*'s 'burnt exterior and golden heart' suggest its proper use: 'once an ember meets *shkitagen* it will not go out but smolders slowly in the fungal matrix,

[64] Michael Witmore, 'Eventuality', in *Early Modern Theatricality*, ed. Henry Turner (Oxford: Oxford University Press, 2013), pp. 386–401 (p. 387).
[65] Lehnhof, 'Theology, Phenomenology, and the Divine', p. 111.
[66] Robin Kimmerer, *Braiding Sweetgrass: Indigenous Wisdom, Scientific Knowledge, and the Teachings of Plants* (Minneapolis, MN: Milkweed Editions, 2013), p. 384; and Keller, *Political Theology of the Earth*, p. 167.
[67] Kimmerer, *Braiding Sweetgrass*, p. 373.
[68] Ibid., p. 364.

holding its heat. Even the smallest spark, so fleeting and easily lost, will be held and nurtured if it lands on a cube of a *shkitagen*'.[69] The theatre gives us a place where we may be in the presence of others and experience the capacity to 'act in concert', and nowhere does this play more powerfully suggest our role than it does when it asks us to imagine that one of us – all of us? – might bend over Cordelia and offer the spark of breath that makes her live again.[70] In those moments, the audience may experience itself as a 'force field of speechless breathing bodies' with the capacity to fire a new world.[71]

From the kind of perspective that Robin Kimmerer offers (it pains her, she writes, the degree to which we lack 'ecological insight' and cannot identify the life forms around us), it may hurt to see how Lear continues to get things wrong, even as his death looms. Cordelia would not be 'dead as earth' if he had understood that no one is anyone else's 'best object'; had understood that earth is not dead, but alive;[72] and could stop making evaluative distinctions between forms of life as he does when he asks, 'Why should a dog, a horse, a rat, have life, / And thou no breath at all?' (5.3.306–7). These errors may make our hearts break. But ultimately it may be the death that we do not experience directly that exercises the greatest imaginative force for us, the death of Gloucester, whose heart is able to 'burst smilingly', exploding and perhaps igniting at the moment of his death because he has reached the understanding that Lear has not: that of our necessary interdependence. For Keller, the recognition of 'our interdependence with all that lives in the cycles of oxygen, carbon, nitrogen . . .' is a first step towards 'respir[ing] and conspir[ing] with the nonhumans in us and around us in order to salvage the precariously interdependent life of the planet'.[73] This is a recognition that may come to us both intellectually and emotionally, as part of our participation in this play's superflux. That superflux leaves the proof of its metaphysics not only in the salt that with our 'cadent tears' may 'fret channels in [our] cheeks' (1.4.285), but with the taste that it may leave upon our lips, as if we have eaten samphire – as if we, having endured so much across the play, may now number ourselves amongst 'virtues of the earth' freshly 'publish'd' because transformed, and in our

---

[69] Ibid.

[70] For my earlier discussion of breath in Shakespeare's theatre, see 'Eating Air, Feeling Smells: *Hamlet*'s Theory of Performance', *Renaissance Drama* 35 (2006), 145–68.

[71] Keller, *Political Theology of the Earth*, p. 16.

[72] As Kimmerer notes, it is possible to find 'soft black humus . . . so sweet and clean you could eat in by the spoonful' and in so doing eat all of the life with which it is filled. *Braiding Sweetgrass*, p. 234.

[73] Keller, *Political Theology of the Earth*, pp. 167–8.

transformation enlivened to a sense of the virtuous world that we might join others to make as we spill out of the theatre's doors, each of us a 'walking fire' or a travelling 'nursery' in search of a community in which no one and no thing is called 'master'.

Chapter 2

Voice, Virtue, Veritas: On Truth and Vocal Feeling in *King Lear*

Katie Adkison

At the end of William Shakespeare's *The Tragedy of King Lear*, Edgar surveys the devastation of the final act and offers what could be a personal reflection, a public elegy, a religious homily or the play's epilogue: 'The weight of this sad time we must obey, / Speak what we feel, not what we ought to say' (5.3.330–1).[1] Bruce R. Smith summarises the contrasting ways critics usually read these lines: either as a woefully inadequate conclusion to such consequential tragedy and loss or as emotionally truthful in all its inadequacy to what the experience of loss is.[2] Drawing out a middle ground in these readings 'between gesture and words, between feeling and saying', Smith traces the play's attention to the tactility of language for listeners and audiences and the interplay between the perception of touch and the cognitive sense that something is 'touching'.[3] Amanda Bailey further reads this moment as an expression of political sympathy, 'the shared acknowledgment that the juridical-political order is founded on the principle that one never affects without being affected'.[4] And, in his essay for this collection on the virtue of grief, Michael Bristol proposes that these 'enigmatic' lines are 'roughly equivalent to saying that we in the audience are among those who are bound to carry the burden of grief', a burden that Bristol understands as a 'duty' that 'asks us to undertake the task of mending

---

[1] All citations from the play are taken from the Pelican Shakespeare's *King Lear*, ed. Stephen Orgel (New York: Penguin Random House, 1999). Orgel's edition is a traditional conflated text which exhibits an implicit preference for the folio by distinguishing lines that appear only in the quarto in editorial brackets and leaving the folio text as the standard in this edition. In attributing these final lines to Edgar, I follow Orgel's edition as well as the preference for the folio text (Albany speaks these lines in the quarto).

[2] Bruce R. Smith, *Phenomenal Shakespeare* (Oxford: Wiley-Blackwell, 2010), pp. 174–6.

[3] Smith, *Phenomenal Shakespeare*, p. 175.

[4] Amanda Bailey, 'Speak What We Feel: Sympathy and Statecraft', in *Affect Theory and Early Modern Texts*, ed. Amanda Bailey and Mario DiGangi (New York: Palgrave Macmillan, 2017), pp. 27–46 (p. 38).

the torn fabric of our social life'. Each of these critics crucially theorises the potential at the heart of the tension between speaking and feeling, putting words to a collective sense at the end of the play that to speak of how we have been touched, of what it is to feel together, of the grief we carry, is politically urgent and emotionally vital – even as we sense that any words we might have will not be enough. Truly, in forcing an audience to grapple with the ever-entangled and yet never-quite-aligned relationship between vocalised language and embodied sensation, Edgar's speech appears to posit an unresolvable problem. If the feeling that something is beyond words paradoxically compels us to tangle with that something in language, and if, as Brian Massumi observes, one cannot speak of a feeling without changing its felt quality, then how can we reconcile speech and feeling in order to 'speak what we feel'?[5] How in the world are we to speak what we feel if to speak is to feel that we have failed?

I want to build on these readings and the questions to which they give rise by examining *Lear*'s attention to the phenomenal experience of speech for the speaker, as well as those for the listener and audience, as embodied experiences with the potential to facilitate more virtuous interaction. Edgar's words are an appeal for the future, but they also reflect back on the play's attention to voice as a feeling experience from its opening scene, asking us to reckon with what it means to not be able to reconcile certain concepts, feelings, words as a necessary path to social reconciliation. Indeed, *Lear* is concerned throughout with what I am calling vocal feeling: the expressive, experiential, embodied qualities of speech that necessarily exceed the semantic meaning that speech articulates. Not only Edgar, but also Cordelia (especially) and Lear (eventually) confront the possibilities located in vocal sounds, sensations, vibrations, rhythms and resonances by exploring the residuals of voice beyond language. The play refuses to reconcile this too-much-ness of the voice and instead calls attention to speech as an equation that will necessarily result in a remainder, in vocal excess beyond words. In dwelling on the felt qualities of the voice that enable language but are not reducible to language, I will argue, the play treats such a vocal capacity in a manner suggestive of the virtuous mean, a crucial structure within Aristotelian virtue ethics. Positioning the feeling voice as a crux between Aristotelian poetics, politics and virtue ethics, Shakespeare also places it within a wider epistemological debate about the relationship between reason, sensory knowledge and meaning. In this essay,

---

[5] Brian Massumi, *Parables for the Virtual: Movement, Affect, Sensation* (Durham, NC: Duke University Press, 2002), pp. 24–26.

I contend that Shakespeare does so in order to depict vocal feeling as a sensory-like capacity – an ethically crucial way of holding, knowing and shaping the speaker's (and audience's) relationship to self, to other, to world.

To understand the voice in this way – as an experience that feels like something – is to change one's orientation towards truthful communication and expression. It is to understand that what can be spoken is always informed by what it feels like to speak in a given situation, to orient oneself towards the ever-unfolding environment a situation of speech enacts. It is to better understand both what is possible or impossible to say and which possibilities might be foreclosed or brought into being by the circumstances of speech. Drawing on philosophies of the phenomenal voice, from Michel de Montaigne to Adriana Cavarero, I hold that the play imagines vocal feeling not only as a sensory-like capacity, but also as a virtue itself: an experience that, when we attune ourselves to its resonances, might enable further action towards 'the good'. I claim, too, that the play imagines the stage as a privileged space for confronting this virtuous capacity of the voice. The multifaceted positionalities of character, actor and audience member open up a testing-site within the theatre for exploring the way that vocal feeling could better index the tensions we experience between speaking and feeling, expressing and meaning, knowing and understanding.

In other words, there is something nascent in the voice's feeling capacity that we overlook when we focus only on the words spoken by a voice, but to which we could hone an attunement. Becoming better attuned to this facility in ours and others' lungs, throats and mouths, furthermore, might help us better open our ears, minds and hearts. As the editors of our collection note in their introduction, there is a close relationship between virtue and the honing of a skill: 'Both virtue and skill require practice, draw on tacit and embodied knowledge, . . . and live and die through their performance.' Insofar as it is masked by the frequency with which most of us use our voices to speak (too often unthinkingly), the sensations of vocalisation might be a strange experience to think of as a skill or a virtue. Yet, *Lear* opens with what we might think of as an extended parable about vocal feeling, only to return again and again to the felt experience of giving voice emphasised by the opening scene. In doing so, *Lear* asks its audience to reconsider the experience of vocal feeling as a worthwhile virtue, to probe the depths of an experience so quotidian for most adults that we might otherwise be inured to its potential. Ultimately, the play suggests that an attunement and responsiveness to this experience might enable a more truthful and virtuous relationship to meaning and interpretation; it indicates this, moreover, by also avowing that vocal feeling is nothing less than the very condition through which it becomes possible for humanity to speak at all.

The Mean of Meaning

Though Edgar's final lines are the culmination of the play's attention to speaking and feeling, it is Cordelia who first emphasises this tension through the felt materiality of the voice. When Lear demands that his daughters speak their love, Cordelia's first words are an aside: 'What shall Cordelia speak? Love and be silent' (1.1.61). Tellingly attuned to the interplay between words and the act of speech, Cordelia's question flags a slippage between speaking and what is said, a slippage between action and meaning.[6] She reveals Lear's real desire – to strip speech of the virtuous potential in the qualities that surpass its language – for it is not truth Lear wants, but mere performance: daughters like puppets who will move their mouths as he opens his hands. As Stanley Cavell has it, Lear's test is actually about the 'avoidance of love' – that is, it is about Lear's desire to not have to be known, seen, acknowledged.[7] In Cavell's influential reading, Cordelia attempts to give Lear what he seeks (or, better put: to not give Lear what he is afraid of), recognising correctly that he does not want to have to confront real love, but misrecognising that the best way to give him his desire is to speak nothing at all.

Though I follow Cavell's interpretation of Lear's desire and the vital role of acknowledgement in the play, I differ with him in my reading of Cordelia, and her sense of what meaning means. Rather than a mis-recognition of how to give her father what he wants, I see Cordelia's response as an attempt to change the course of the exchange by calling attention to the felt quality of her voice. Akin to what Emmanuel Levinas calls 'Saying' – an ethical act of care attuned to the meaning of expression that surpasses one's language – Cordelia's attempt offers her father a middle ground between the act of speaking and the words

---

[6] She thus resonates with the distinction Emmanuel Levinas draws between the Said versus the act of Saying. See *Otherwise than Being or Beyond Essence,* trans. Alphonso Lingis (Pittsburgh, PA: Duquesne University Press, 1998), p. 17. Adriana Cavarero, whom I discuss more extensively than Levinas here, also draws on this distinction. See Adriana Cavarero, *For More than One Voice: Toward a Philosophy of Vocal Expression,* trans. Paul Kottman (Stanford, CA: Stanford University Press, 2005), esp. pp. 26–32, for her discussion of Levinas. For further discussion of the way that *Lear* performs something akin to a Levinasian ethics of 'otherwise than being', see Kent Lehnhof's essay in this collection, 'The Virtue of Humour in *King Lear*'.

[7] See Stanley Cavell's chapter 'The Avoidance of Love', in Cavell, *Must We Mean What We Say?,* updated edn (Cambridge: Cambridge University Press, 2002), pp. 246–325.

said.[8] This middle ground is the place of virtue. In Aristotelian virtue ethics, a given virtue occupies the middle space, or mean, between the extremity of two vices.[9] Yet this mean is not exactly the average of the two vices; rather, it is conceptually equidistant between them. Thus, a virtuous mean does not reconcile the two vices in the mathematical sense implied through the process of dividing the sum of a number set by the quantity of numbers in the set, for it is not reducible to either of the two opposite traits.[10] Instead, the virtuous mean holds the tendencies of either extreme in balance, becoming more than the sum (or average) of their parts. Cordelia turns to vocal feeling as this middle ground because her aside cannot set her love aside. Even as she vows silence, pledging love by not speaking too much, by not being too much, her words slip past the line's iambic pentameter. An extra, eleventh syllable in 'silent' seeps out of Cordelia's mouth, itself leaking meaning even as Cordelia seems to denounce trying to mean. On its own, this extra syllable could be more of a happy accident than a deliberate rhetorical appeal, a rather lovely poetic glitch that simply resonates with the impossibility of speaking her love in words her father can hear. However, the subsequent exchange between father and daughter becomes more and more attuned to syllables and measures and metrics. It evolves into an exchange that blends the discourse of vocal feeling and rhythm with the discourse of arithmetic in such a way as to suggest that the extra syllable is no accident – happy, or (as Cordelia otherwise insists) deeply 'unhappy'.

When Cordelia speaks 'nothing', she sets into motion a dialogue that aligns words with numbers and implies that linguistic meaning might have to have an interpretive middle ground, a virtuous mean. As a response to Lear's request, in fact, Cordelia's 'nothing' begins by trying to occupy that mean:

---

[8] Although Cavell sees Cordelia as trying to 'love by being silent', Cordelia is not exactly silent. If she realises that 'to pretend to love, where you really do love, is not obviously possible', her public response goes well beyond saying 'nothing'. Cavell, 'The Avoidance of Love', p. 267.

[9] 'It follows then, since moral virtue is a mean and is always concerned with pleasures and pains, whereas vice lies in excess or deficiency and is concerned with the same matters as virtue, that moral virtue is a state tending to choose the mean in relation to us in things pleasant and painful', writes Aristotle in the *Eudemian Ethics*. *Writings from the Complete Works*, ed. Jonathan Barnes and Anthony Kenny (Princeton, NJ: Princeton University Press, 2016), 1227b 5–9. See definition II.7.a for 'mean, n.' in the *OED* for the word's meaning derived from Aristotelian ethics.

[10] In the *Nicomachean Ethics*, Aristotle clarifies that the mean of any virtue is 'midway according to arithmetical proportion', or is the number that remains, that is precisely equidistant, between two other numbers. *Writings from the Complete Works*, 1106a, 29–35. In contemporary statistical language, it is what we would call the 'median', whereas 'mean' has come to serve as a synonym for 'average'. See definition II.10.a for 'mean, n.' in the *OED* for its evolving meaning in mathematics.

```
LEAR:                    – Now our joy,
   Although our last and least, to whose young love
   The vines of France and milk of Burgundy
   Strive to be interested, what can you say to draw
   A third more opulent than your sisters? Speak.
CORDELIA: Nothing, my lord.
LEAR: Nothing?
CORDELIA: Nothing.
LEAR: Nothing will come of nothing. Speak again. (1.1.82–90)
```

Cordelia's answer is true in the most literal sense: having already divided the kingdom in thirds, Lear has not left Cordelia with room to 'draw' anything he has not already set aside for her. Rigged from the get-go, the love test is not really a competition to 'love [him] most' (1.1.51). Lear's demand warps the relationship between speaking and meaning, so Cordelia attempts to split the difference between semantics and performance. She does 'speak', obeying her father's actual command, and she does answer his question. There is simply nothing she 'can say' to win a different kingdom. Nullifying Lear's plan, her 'nothing' throws off her father's division of sovereign power.

Her father's response, 'Nothing will come of nothing', further cements the mathematical tone of the exchange. Though Cordelia provides an answer that 'solves' her father's problem, Lear disputes it, asks her to show her work, commands her to rethink the relationship between his apportioned kingdom and the zero she offers to divide it by. Critics have long read the king's reassertion of his demand as an echo of the Aristotelian *ex nihilio nihil fit*, or the belief that in the material universe 'nothing can come out of nothing', and Mary Thomas Crane demonstrates how the new science and 'new forms of nothing' inform Lear's reply.[11] The possibility of infinite divisibility and of void space introduced by the new science, Crane shows, helps to develop the play's central anxiety: an existential dread that accompanies knowledge of material nothingness.[12] In addition to bespeaking concerns that circulated about material existence, however, Lear's point of clarification also evokes the principle that it is impossible to divide by zero. While early modern mathematics, following Zeno, would have made room for infinite divisibility and conceptions of smallness beyond comprehension,

---

[11] Mary Thomas Crane, *Losing Touch with Nature: Literature & the New Science in 16th-Century England* (Baltimore, MD: Johns Hopkins University Press, 2014), p. 123.
[12] Early modern knowledge, she observes, was beginning to grapple with what it feels like to exist in a world in which one's embodied knowledge of the universe could not fathom scientific findings too small to be experienced. Crane, *Losing Touch with Nature*, pp. 132–3.

this infinite smallness still could not be divided by nothing. If Cordelia is to offer her love as the divisor for the dividend of the kingdom – for Lear's demand is a request to help him complete his division – to present Lear's dividend with 'nothing' is to launch Lear's plan into the realm of impossibility. He cannot divide the something of his kingdom by 'nothing', and so Cordelia receives what might as well be an error code: 'Speak again'.

At first glance, Cordelia's subsequent response appears to resemble the zero-sum game that Lear would have love and power be:

> Unhappy that I am, I cannot heave
> My heart into my mouth. I love your majesty
> According to my bond, no more nor less. (1.1.90–2)

However, although she refers to her love as a 'bond' that sounds like either a legal or economic contract, she does so after insisting that her words simply cannot hold the weight of her love. Additionally, Cordelia's seeming self-description – 'Unhappy that I am' – contains a pun on the formal metre, the iamb, in which Cordelia and her father mostly speak, a pun that renders the notion of explaining love in legalese into a moot point. By punning her psychic state with the rhythm of her lines, she doubles down on the problem of divvying love as if it were a monetary inheritance with a set quantity, or even a kingdom. Indeed, Cordelia's pun is also potentially deictic, gesturing to her following line, which includes an extra iamb – 'unhappy' as a metric foot, perhaps, because it is as out of step with the pentameter as she is with her father's demands. Even as she asserts that her affection for her father is 'no more nor less' than is due, her assertion of love nevertheless exceeds the standard measure: My heart' in·to' my mouth'. I love' your ma'jes·ty'. 'Unhappy', she seems to say, 'that you insist that I contain the uncontainable. Unhappy, that little iamb that highlights how un-metric I am, how excessive is my love.' Despite her words, her rhythm rejects the zero-sum logic of her father's love test. Self-reflexively gesturing to the broken rules of iambic pentameter in her assertion of love and describing her experience of speaking these very words as an effort that surpasses her strength, she reveals that the truth of her love will always exceed the rules or bounds of any test, of any measure.

Cordelia's punning on 'iamb' and 'I am' suggests that the relationship between poetic metre and numerical proportion informs Cordelia's appeal. Sixteenth-century English poets exhaustingly debated whether to embrace syllabic counting, which measured a line by its 'weight' (the length of vowels and time it took to speak), or the counting of rhythmic feet.[13] Just as Cordelia's concern with language is one of feeling, fit and weight, the terms of the measure debate revolved around which unit of measurement provided the best-felt 'fit' for English voices. Should English dance to traditional quantitative rhythm, or was it doomed to trip and stumble trying to keep time with something it simply could not be?[14] Intervening in this debate of numbers and feeling, George Puttenham attempts to square the circle in his *Arte of English Poesie* by embracing the facility English poets had to be playful, to choose to follow poetic rules when and how best suited their purpose.[15] Toying (inaccurately) with the supposedly related etymologies of rhythm, rhyme and arithmetic, Puttenham implies their inherent relationship. He characterises rhythm as 'a certain musical numerositie in utterance'.[16] A 'musical' arithmetic or a mathematical 'utterance': Puttenham's chiasmic logic insinuates a natural connection between numbers and sound, syllabic counting and rhythmic feet. He purports that the meaning of metre lies in a felt mean, the conceptual middle ground between the numerical and the sonic. To think of rhythm properly one must hold quantity in tension with quality, making space for both measures without entirely reconciling one to the other. One must feel to mean and one must mean to feel.

Just as Puttenham understands rhythm to be a 'musical numerositie in utterance', Shakespeare follows this precedent, similarly using Cordelia's rhythmic arithmetic to complicate the relationship between love, language, feeling, knowing and division that is at stake in the scene:

> Haply when I shall wed,
> That lord whose hand must take my plight shall carry

---

[13] This is to say nothing of disputes about whether metre or rhyme was preferable as the foundation of poetic verse. Paula Blank describes the search for an English metre as one harbouring the anxiety that 'the English language itself was unfit for true measure'; see *Shakespeare and the Mismeasure of Renaissance Man* (Ithaca, NY: Cornell University Press, 2006), p. 54.

[14] Roger Ascham describes Surrey's iambic pentameter as clumsy feet: 'feete without joyntes, that is to say, not distinct by trew quantitie of sillables'. *The Scholemaster* (London: Printed by Iohn Daye, 1570), p. 314. Gabriel Harvey provides the opposite objection to Edmund Spenser's desire to measure verse by syllables, protesting that changing the accent of a word in English to fit a classical metrical pattern is tantamount to despotism, a method that 'tyrannize[s]' the English language's 'quiet companie of words'. See Catherine Nicholson for a discussion of this debate: *Uncommon Tongues: Eloquence and Eccentricity in the English Renaissance* (Philadelphia: University of Pennsylvania Press, 2014). Harvey quoted in Nicholson, *Uncommon Tongues*, p. 128.

[15] George Puttenham, *The Arte of English Poesie* (London: Printed by Richard Field, 1589), p. 3. He contends that English possesses 'twentie other curious points in that skill more then they ever had, by reason of our rime and tunable concords or simphonie'.

[16] Ibid., p. 57.

Half my love with him, half my care and duty.
Sure I shall never marry like my sisters,
To love my father all. (1.1.100–4)

It is telling, perhaps, that critics are often divided on what these lines about division mean. Cavell reads this moment as Cordelia's final attempt to appease her father: 'She is trying to conceal him; and to do that, she cuts herself in two'.[17] For her part, Crane sees Cordelia as possessing 'a mental model of the universe [that] is clearly more constrained than that of her sisters', whom Crane understands to be embracing possibilities of infinity and endless divisibility.[18] Differently still, Carolyn Sale movingly interprets 'Cordelia's Fire' (also in this collection) as a rebuke of any kind of hierarchical division, seeking instead to 'preserve ways of being and making that division would violently preclude'.[19] But what I want to advocate here is that we read these lines as directly informed by Cordelia's previous punning on 'iamb' and 'I am', and within the context of these debates about quantitative versus qualitative verse that this pun and her arrhythmic speech call to mind. For the logic of what she says is undercut by the rhythm in which she speaks. Even as she claims her love can be divided neatly, cleanly, in 'half', lines 101–3 contain eleven syllables, indicating that there is nothing cleanly divisible about either her love or her language. Any attempt to divide her love, like the attempt to divide her language from her vocal feeling, like Lear's attempt to divide the kingdom into thirds, will result in remainders and residuals.

Cordelia refers to the feeling capacity of her voice by thus naming – and then defying – the rhythm of her speech in what can only be an elliptical attempt at virtuously redirecting her father's understanding of love and language. Blending mathematical means, the virtuous mean, and the question of spoken meaning together in the play's weightiest verbal exchange, Shakespeare positions vocal feeling as something like a golden mean of spoken language: the mean of meaning. Vocal feeling is the middle ground between what is said and the act of speaking, the virtuous mean that holds semantics in tension with action. In

---

[17] Cavell, 'The Avoidance of Love', p. 269.
[18] Crane, *Losing Touch with Nature*, p. 139.
[19] For Sale, Cordelia's reference to fire in 4.7.37, in which she would invite even her enemy's dog to warm himself from the cold, represents a kind of radically inclusive care: the fire that the play imagines here is a 'place to which anyone may come – even the dog of the enemy, and that dog even after it has bitten her. Cordelia's fire, then, is the sign of an all-embracing kindness, one of an inclusion so radical it makes nonsensical the impulses in which other characters in the play indulge as they seek to reduce others to something less than human.'

reducing meaning neither to linguistic content nor to the mere fact of attempted speech, vocal feeling understands meaning to be a function of an attempt at producing language, the language actually produced, and the experiential tensions between these realities – an irreducible remainder that reveals the inherent flaws in Lear's quest for division. Thus, Cordelia's vocal feeling cannot be reconciled to either what Lear wants or what Cordelia says. This is why her claim to love her father '[a]ccording to [her] bond, no more nor less' both reiterates a truth and belies that truth. Though her 'bond' may evoke the language of law and economy, it is also indicative of a relational tie that cannot be contained in any contract. In psychoanalytic terms, their bond is more than both of them. It is what Jessica Benjamin calls 'the third'.[20] It is the destabilising self-object hybrid conjured in the connection between two people. To love according to this bond is to know that such love is always beyond even one's self. You might have such love, and yet that does not mean it belongs to you. Of course, Cordelia cannot say this to her father outright, so she gestures desperately to her voice. She is improvising and part of her strategy is to reveal that she is improvising: to speak in such a way as to call attention to the situation of her speaking. It therefore makes some sense for her to name the iambs of the dialogue, for the iamb's role in the playfulness of English poetry is important. Widely observed to be the rhythmic foot most suited to English voices, the iamb is also taken to be a foundational rhythm out of which one can improvise others.[21] The iamb, in other words, offers a vocal rhythm that defies its own enumeration; it is a rhythm that can both keep time and ad lib as necessary. When Cordelia gesticulates to her iambic rhythm, to the ways that she is off-rhythm, she is trying to tell her father that the virtue of her speech lies in the feeling of her voice, that this inexpressible remainder called into being by her experience of expression is the best representative of her love. Her claim of having balanced the equation – 'no more nor less' – is undermined by metric remainders not because Cordelia seeks to lie, but because she is aware of the impossibility of rendering love into nothing but display when the situation of her speech can only put love on display. Calculating syllables, Cordelia's self-referential language is anxious to keep count

---

[20] See Jessica Benjamin, *Beyond Doer and Done To: Recognition Theory, Subjectivity, and the Third* (New York: Routledge, 2017).

[21] Thomas Campion, for example, remarks that the iamb 'fall[s] out so naturally in our tongue' that most prose English is iambic. He further calls a trochee 'but an iambe turn'd over and over', and out of these two rhythms, he insists, 'we may easily derive other forms'. Thomas Campion, *Observations in the art of English Poesie* (London: Printed by Richard Field, 1602), p. 9.

of itself even as she seems to know there is no way to account for itself.

In her masterful study, *Shakespeare and the Grammar of Forgiveness*, Sarah Beckwith calls on Cavell's interpretation of Lear's 'avoidance of love' in order to show how the king's 'repudiation of language as a public form' is reimagined in *Pericles* where 'it is the agency of the human voice that is the medium of redemption'.[22] According to Beckwith, Shakespeare transforms the tragedy of *Lear* into the reconciliation of romance in *Pericles* by staging a 'recovery of voice' that 'will allow [Shakespeare] to perform acknowledgment itself as forgiveness' in his final plays.[23] I want to build on Beckwith's vital reading to suggest that the kernels of voice's recovery were sown in *Lear* not merely in the king's refusal of acknowledgement, but also in his daughter's virtuous offering: naming her embodied, deeply felt experience of giving voice in order to call her father to a more benevolent treatment not only of his family, but also of his sense of his own love. When we witness Pericles and his daughter Marina find each other through the 'mutual attunement'[24] of self-disclosure, then, we see the fulfilment of *Lear*'s parable of vocal feeling. More virtuous still: even as Cordelia seems to realise her attempt will not work, she refuses to give up on the goodness *in potentia* of vocal feeling. Her persistence in locating love in the irreducible feeling of her speech is the condition of possibility that facilitates Lear's course-correction later in the play – catastrophically late though it will be. Therefore, I wish to nuance Cavell's sense that she fails because she gives Lear what she thinks he wants. Rather, Cordelia here recognises and names the inevitability of her failure. She knows she will fail, can only fail, not because her father will misrecognise her offer, but because the singularity of her voice, its deeply felt entanglement with her love and with her father, was always too much to succeed in what he asks – to become, as it were, only words.

For Adriana Cavarero, it is precisely this resonant, phenomenal excess that might make the voice the occasion for a different approach to politics and ethics. In Cavarero's philosophy, the uniqueness of each individual voice forbids the perfect reconciliation of language with speech because spoken language cannot be separated from the phenomenological quality of its voice. The 'vocal phenomenology of uniqueness' that marks the voice of every speaker is 'essentially relational' and necessarily embodied, and the key to understanding the voice's politico-ethical

---

[22] Sarah Beckwith, *Shakespeare and the Grammar of Forgiveness* (Ithaca, NY: Cornell University Press, 2011), pp. 88 and 92 respectively.
[23] Ibid., p. 103.
[24] Ibid.

potential lies in the connection between its relationality and singular embodiment.[25] To understand the phenomenal voice as a virtue worth honing, then, is to attune ourselves to the way that the experience of vocal feeling articulates the ever-unfolding contingencies of our situations. It is to attempt to direct spoken responses not merely to the words of the other, nor merely to the being of the other, but to the enmeshment of our words with the bond of speech itself. The bond of speech is an experiential bond that is always in process – changing both self and other even as we speak. To this end, Cavarero concludes her vocal philosophy through an extended engagement with Jacques Derrida's treatment of the voice in his work on *différance*.[26] Where Derrida reads the experience of 'hearing-oneself-speak' as one that too easily erases the trace of *différance*, that sign of hetero-affection that he offers to deconstruct a metaphysics of presence, Cavarero avows that the experience of speaking itself contains a powerful form of *différance*.[27] In its excess beyond language, the voice's sound may refer to the uniqueness of any speaker, but it also articulates that this embodied singularity is relational from the start, entangled with the voices, words, feelings, beings of others. To be able to speak at all is to already have felt and experienced others' voices.[28]

If there is a key difference between Cavarero and Cordelia, who share a larger concern about the relationship of our voices with others', it is this: whereas Cavarero attunes herself primarily to the unique sound of the voice in order to philosophically negotiate how the singularity of personhood is a factor of the individual's infinite entanglements with the world, Cordelia dwells on rhythm and vocal feeling in an oratorical attempt, in real time, to stop the momentum of division in the play's opening scene. If we read the opening scene as a type of parable and use it as a hermeneutic for voice in the rest of the play, as I want to argue that we should, then we must attune ourselves to the ways that vocal feeling might help us more virtuously confront the self's spoken relation

---

[25] Cavarero, *For More than One Voice*, pp. 7–8.

[26] See Cavarero's 'Appendix: Dedicated to Derrida', in Cavarero, *For More than One Voice*, pp. 213–41. For Derrida's own discussion, see *Voice and Phenomenon*, trans. Leonard Lawlor (Evanston, IL: Northwestern University Press, 2011), esp. pp. 64–7.

[27] Cavarero, *For More than One Voice*, pp. 223–5.

[28] Engaging with Cavarero's work on narrative, Judith Butler writes: 'The moment I realize that the terms by which I confer recognition are not mine alone, that I did not single-handedly devise or craft them, I am, as it were, dispossessed by the language that I offer', a dispossession that leads to an ethical question: how can it be that 'the account of myself that I give in discourse never fully expresses or carries this living self?' Judith Butler, *Giving an Account of Oneself* (New York: Fordham University Press, 2005), pp. 26 and 36 respectively.

to the other: as an ever-shifting matrix, an ever-unfolding mean(ing) of relationalities. As Ian Munro notes in his essay here on *eutrepalia*, 'existence is flux', and any sense of self that insists on pure, stable identity is a misperception. Vocal feeling is not unlike virtuous wit. It is an energetic, deft capacity of speech. Knowing that the serious work of meaning requires a playful attunement to the flux of life, it offers a potentially ethical mode for both experiencing and expressing how we find ourselves to be intertwined with those to whom we speak – for helping us understand that experience and expression are constitutive of each other.

In this regard, it also resembles the space of the theatre. A space between reality and fantasy, theatrical mimesis allows an audience to recognise not only that speech is an embodied action, but also that there is a recursive experience that accompanies the witnessing of another's experience of speech. For an audience to feel the weight of Cordelia's appeal in the play's opening scene – even if the puns and the rhythmic ruptures are not consciously perceived – is for an audience to be with her in asserting that the meaning of her voice will always be more than mere semantics. For an audience member's heart to break when Cordelia cannot heave hers into her mouth is for them to know beyond her words that her response to Lear's demand was never 'nothing'. In this way, the play's opening scene primes the audience to seek out the middle grounds of spoken discourse throughout the rest of the show, to pay particular attention to the way that the truth and meaning, the virtue, of human language will necessarily exceed language itself.

Hence, if a speaker (or an actor-as-speaker) attempts to reduce the meaning of their vocal expression to mere language, they do not gain clarity, power or recognition. They lose themselves entirely. It is this knowledge that both Edgar and Lear will confront on the English heath.

'We came crying hither'

Philosophising about rock bottom – 'To be worst, / The lowest and most dejected thing of fortune, / Stands still in esperance, lives not in fear' (4.1.2–4) – Edgar runs into his recently blinded father in Act 4. This sight of unbearable grief, just as Edgar was hoping after hope, causes Edgar to rethink the question of 'the worst', making it a problem of expression:

> [*Aside*] O gods! Who is't can say 'I am at the worst'?
> I am worse than e'er I was [. . .]

And worse I may be yet. The worst is not
So long as we can say 'This is the worst'. (4.1.26–9)

Edgar comes to see his ability to produce speech as proof that he has
not been reduced to 'the worst'. To a degree, this is quite literally about
retaining one's humanity, and, according to Laurie Shannon, the status
of humanity in *Lear* is the key question of the play. Reading *Lear*
as offering a critique of the philosophical tradition that valorises the
human above other animals, Shannon asserts that the play's view of the
human is that of 'negative-exceptionalist man [. . .] a creature without
properties [. . .] a natural-historical oxymoron'.[29] For Michael Clody,
the play's attunement to animal voices, reaching its apotheosis in Lear's
'Howl, howl, howl!' (5.3.263), tests the limits of representation as the
limits of humanity, 'the expressive consequences of an effaced distinction between man and animal'.[30] In his reading of the play, the sonic,
animalistic qualities of speech continue to haunt the realm of representation and are a 'productive negativity' that contrasts, as animal need,
with language and reason.[31] I want to press on these crucial readings,
though, by taking seriously that the pre-linguistic voice is more than a
negative category contrasting with language and the human, for it is also
an experience with a meaningful feeling that could direct us towards the
more humane treatment of each other and the world. Truly, Edgar confronts his position in the world not quite through a semantic meaning/
sonic meaninglessness binary, but through vocal feeling that gives him
access to self-perception. More than the Derridean 'hearing-oneself-
speak', however, Edgar's vocal feeling is a decidedly social experience.
It is his, but it is his because it is also his father's. Hearing his father
miss him aloud – 'O dear son Edgar [. . .] Might I but live to see thee
in my touch / I'd say I had eyes again' (4.1.21–4) – is what tips Edgar

---

[29] Laurie Shannon, *The Accommodated Animal: Cosmopolity in Shakespearean Locales*
(Chicago: University of Chicago Press, 2013), p. 173.
[30] Michael Clody, 'The Mirror and the Feather: Tragedy and Animal Voice in *King Lear*',
ELH 80 (2013), 661–80 (p. 662).
[31] Clody, 'The Mirror and the Feather', pp. 663 and 673 respectively. In this regard,
Clody's reading comes closest to my own, especially when he suggests that the animal
voice in *Lear* troubles the very distinctions of human and animal, reason and need,
speech and language of which it is ostensibly exemplary. The potential that he sees in the
'productive negativity' of animal voice, however, is one that I want to resist reading as a
negativity, for I see in voice, and in the play's attention to vocal feeling, not the underside
of language that must be erased to enable speech or 'that which discourse must leave
behind' (p. 674) but a positivity that remains in the voice when it carries language, a need
that may be animalistic, but is no less human for being so. Indeed, I will attempt to posit
that the play is inviting its audience not to identify with Lear's orientation towards speech
and voice, but instead to see in the king's tragedy a critique of philosophies that hold too
tightly to these distinctions.

from lamentation into his evaluation of his own speech. In this regard, Edgar's evaluation of what it feels like to speak resonates well with Maurice Merleau-Ponty's concept of 'the flesh'.

For Merleau-Ponty, 'the flesh' is a chiasm, or 'reversibility', of perception that extends the sensing mind/body beyond itself.[32] Coming to know the world through sense-perception thus flags an experience of unknowability that is less a negation than it is an affirmation of what it is possible to know.[33] Merleau-Ponty concludes his theorisation of flesh by suggesting that speech operates in a homologous way, becoming a 'paradox of expression':[34]

> I hear my own vibration from within; as Malraux said, I hear myself with my throat. In this, as he also has said, I am incomparable; my voice is bound to the mass of my own life as is the voice of no one else. But if I am close enough to the other who speaks to hear his breath and feel his effervescence and his fatigue, I almost witness, in him as in myself, the awesome birth of vociferation. As there is a reflexivity of the touch, of sight, and of the touch–vision system, there is a reflexivity of the movements of phonation and of hearing [. . .] This new reversibility and the emergence of the flesh as expression are the point of insertion of speaking and thinking in the world of silence.[35]

This synesthetic voice, a tactile–sonic vibration, is not reducible, either, to a metaphysics of presence, for Merleau-Ponty emphasises that these feelings enable a 'reflexivity' not only between body and voice, but also between self and other. The reversibility of speech as sensory experience, 'the emergence of flesh as expression', is what allows a person to speak at all – it is 'the point of insertion of speaking and thinking in the world of silence'.[36] If something in the body's vocal capacity perceives that it can speak, feeling this potentiality in the mouth and throat even as the ears hear, so too does something in the voice's bodily capacity determine what it can say, assessing what is possible for the self through others'

---

[32] Maurice Merleau-Ponty, *The Visible and the Invisible*, trans. Alphonso Lingis (Evanston, IL: Northwestern University Press, 1968).

[33] Ibid., pp. 133–4.

[34] Ibid., p. 155.

[35] Ibid., pp. 144–5.

[36] It is worth noting that Merleau-Ponty's notion of the 'intertwining' that occurs in speech seems to make a brief appearance in Derrida's *Voice and Phenomenon*. Merleau-Ponty's essay was published originally in 1964, preceding Derrida's three books on *différance*; though he never directly cites Merleau-Ponty, Derrida does grapple with the 'intertwining' of semantic meaning and a 'sense' that is 'pre-expressive': 'Just as expression does not come to be added on as a "stratum" to the presence of a pre-expressive sense, the outside of indication does not come to affect accidentally the inside of expression. Their interweaving is originary. The intertwining is not the kind of contingent association that methodical care and a patient reduction could undo.' Derrida, *Voice and Phenomenon*, p. 74.

'breath and [. . .] effervescence'. What Edgar realises here is that speech is proof not merely of humanity, but of a vocal facility enabled by a fundamentally communal, feeling body. As James Kearney proposes, Edgar's experiences as Poor Tom resemble a Levinasian ethics; they emphasise our infinite ethical responsibility to others. This responsibility is a duty that can never be perfectly fulfilled, but that, in its imperfection and its infinity, is precisely what may make ethics possible.[37]

If we understand that the voice tarries at the limits of the expressible (at the limits, perhaps, of the possible), and that its threshold is that of self and other as much as it is body and self, *Lear* asks, then how might we begin to rethink the role of a feeling, embodied voice? When Lear finally finds himself confronting his experience of voice, it requires the mutual recognition of another, and it leads to one of the most infamous moments of Lear's philosophising. Encountering Edgar and Gloucester, Lear couples a meditation on voice with a meditation on the nakedness that is humanity's lot from birth:

> If thou wilt weep my fortunes, take my eyes.
> I know thee well enough; thy name is Gloucester.
> Thou must be patient. We came crying hither;
> Thou know'st, the first time we smell the air
> We wawl and cry. I will preach to thee. Mark.
> [. . .]
> When we are born, we cry that we are come
> To this great stage of fools. (4.6.177–83)

The voice extracted from language thus becomes the sign of both unique pain – a single babe, thrust into the world naked – and universal pain: we all 'wawl and cry' at our entrance to a world we do not understand. But if this moment appears to align natural and political philosophy in the Aristotelian sense, making the languageless 'mere voice' a sign of creatureliness, Shakespeare's source for these lines complicates this alignment.[38]

Shakespeare adapts these lines from Michel de Montaigne's 'Apologie for Raymond Sebond', from the section in which Montaigne contests man's supposed distinction from other animals. Disputing the philosophical tradition that Shannon calls man's 'negative-exceptionalism', Montaigne quotes Lucretius on the nakedness of man –

---

[37] James Kearney, '"This is above all strangeness": *King Lear*, Ethics, and the Phenomenology of Recognition', *Criticism* 54.3 (2012), 455–67.
[38] Aristotle, *Politics*. *Writings from the Complete Works*, ed. Jonathan Barnes (Princeton, NJ: Princeton University Press, 2016), 1253a 1–16.

An infant, like a shipwracke ship-boy cast from seas,
Lies naked on the ground and speechlesse, wanting all
The helpes of vitall spirit, when nature with small ease
Of throes, to see first light, from her wombe lets him fall,
Then, as is meet, with mournfull cries he fils the place,
For whom so many ils remaine in his lives race –

only to then argue that Lucretius has it wrong: 'Such complaints are false'.[39] As with all beasts, Montaigne affirms, the skin we have, the instincts we have, the voices we have – all are bestowed upon us by nature. So, if we 'accommodate' ourselves with clothes, weapons, language or other tools, we are not working against nature. It is nature that has given us the instincts to do so. As Shannon demonstrates, Montaigne holds that man is neither better nor worse off than other animals.[40] To build on Shannon's analysis, I want to home in on the ways that voice plays a vitally distinct role in Montaigne's philosophy from that of Aristotle, Plato, Pliny and so on. Like Aristotle, Montaigne notes that 'our whining, our puling, and our weeping is common to most creatures'.[41] Unlike Aristotle, who declares that the removal of this 'mere voice' is the very thing that enables politics and makes man the only 'political animal', Montaigne insists on a signifying capacity in animal voices, too.[42] The consequences of acknowledging a signifying voice in other animals for political philosophy are large, but the most salient point for Lear's echoing of the 'Apologie' is Montaigne's claim that man's spoken language develops not out of a desire for rational signification, but instead out of an embodied craving to first express sound and feeling.

The too-much-ness of the voice – in other words, the 'whining', the 'puling' and the 'weeping' that Aristotle relegates to language-silencing excess – is precisely what allows for language to exist at all. This seems to be where Montaigne agrees with Lucretius. Though he does not

---

[39] Michel de Montaigne, 'An Apologie for Raymond Sebond', *The Essays of Michaell de Montaigne*, trans. John Florio (London: Printed for Edward Blount, 1603), pp. 262–3.

[40] Indeed, if there is a hero of Shannon's *The Accommodated Animal*, it is Montaigne, and Shannon crucially analyses Montaigne's orientation towards the human as one that resists the tradition of negative-exceptionality. She contends, though, that '*King Lear* gives man no such quarter' (p. 150).

[41] Montaigne, 'Apologie for Raymond Sebond', p. 263.

[42] Aristotle writes: 'Now, that man is more of a political animal than bees or any other gregarious animals is evident [. . .] man is the only animal who has the gift of speech. And whereas mere voice is but an indication of pleasure or pain, and is therefore found in other animals (for their nature attains to the perception of pleasure and pain and the intimation of them to one another, and no further), the power of speech is intended to set forth the experience and the inexpedient, and therefore likewise the just and the unjust'. *Politics*, 1253a 1–16.

see man as creaturely in the negative, exposed way Lucretius does, he follows Lucretius in maintaining that language did not evolve out of a teleological desire to communicate, but instead developed out of curious, sensory experimentation with the self: 'In such sort as what we speake we must first speake it unto our selves, and before we utter and send the same forth to strangers we make it inwardly to sound unto our eares.'[43] Imagining that even a child that grew up entirely alone would still 'no doubt have some kinde of words to expresse, and speech to utter his conceits' because the expression of sound is a corporeal, human need, Montaigne shortly goes on to acknowledge that the experience of the senses, experiences like that of the feeling voice, often appear to defy reason.[44] Rather than elevate reason in order to make an exception of humankind, then, Montaigne professes that if reason and the senses cannot always be perfectly reconciled, this is not a failure of human exceptionalism; it is instead a meaningful experience to be embraced as a crucial quality – one might say a virtue – of what it is to be human.[45] Therefore, though I agree with Shannon that King Lear, the character, seems to understand humanity's place within the world under the terms of negative-exceptionalism, I want to propose that *King Lear*, the play, is using its tragic hero to imagine that humankind could be otherwise.

It is doing so, moreover, by using something like Aristotelian virtue ethics to position the voice differently than in Aristotelian political philosophy. Instead of excluding the voice in favour of pure *logos*, the play attends to the feeling, phenomenological qualities of the voice as the only things that enable *logos*, as fundamentally the place where spoken meaning unites language with voice, semantics with action, to become something irreducible to either. Not a human exception, vocal feeling precedes language and implicates human politics in the natural world. Hence, David Kleinberg-Levin's observation that Merleau-Ponty's philosophy of voice must be read as 'always already eco-logical: ecologically generated, ecologically attuned, ecologically indebted', might also be made about *Lear*'s treatment of voice.[46] Given that both Shakespeare

---

[43] Montaigne, 'Apologie for Raymond Sebond', p. 264. In *De Rerum Natura*, Lucretius articulates the Epicurean theory of language that, like all things, it developed out of embodied sensation and was thus an instinctual response to the corporeal feelings of the voice: 'As for the various sounds of speech, it was nature that prompted human beings to utter them, and it was utility that coined the names of things.' *On the Nature of Things*, trans. Martin Ferguson Smith (Indianapolis, IN: Hackett Publishing, 1969), 5.1028–32, pp. 164–5. For the section on the shipwrecked infant, see 5.223–35, p. 143.

[44] Montaigne, 'Apologie for Raymond Sebond', p. 264.

[45] Ibid., pp. 347–51.

[46] David Kleinberg-Levin, *Before the Voice of Reason: Echoes of Responsibility in Merleau-Ponty's Ecology and Levinas's Ethics* (Albany: State University of New York

and Merleau-Ponty appear to draw on Montaigne to construct their treatments of voice, it makes sense that they would reach a similar conclusion.[47] Both emphasise the voice's pre-linguistic, feeling expression as that which gives way to – not that which stifles – speech.[48] When he perceives that 'we cry that we are come / To this great stage of fools', Lear harks back to the Fool's claim that Lear has 'given away' 'all [his] other titles', but the 'title' of 'fool' he 'wast born with' (1.4.146–7). Brian Sheerin notes that the Fool is playing, here, on the etymology of the word 'fool' (derived from the Latin for 'bellows') and teasing his king that Lear is now 'one filled with nothing but air'.[49] But as much as this wordplay certainly invites Lear to consider a greater humility, it also invites the audience to consider this air with which we are all filled: it is hardly nothing. The stuff of life itself, that which enables us to conspire with other beings through speech and feeling, the little bellows of the voice does not snuff out our fire.[50] It helps to ignite it.

To cry out at life, to cry out at a world full of crying fools, is for the cry to inform all subsequent spoken language. The expression of sound is thus a squeezing out ('express' is from the Latin *expresser*, 'to press out') of need first, and then reason after.[51] If Lear's 'O reason not the need!' correctly understands Regan's and Goneril's cruelty as a stripping down of his humanity, he nonetheless misunderstands reason and need as opposites (2.4.264). In a Montaignian view, all needs are reasonable. Attuning ourselves through vocal feeling to these needs, both in ourselves and in others, would thus be both a virtue unto itself and an action that can enable other virtues. Hence, excesses and accommodations are not unnatural expressions of human nakedness or frailty; they are instead the expression of our capacity to be more humane. In truth, a human capacity to act in a humane way necessarily requires us

---

Press, 2008), p. 17. Many thanks to Kent Lehnhof for recommending Kleinberg-Levin's book.

[47] For some of the ways that Merleau-Ponty echoes Montaigne, see Kleinberg-Levin, *Before the Voice of Reason*, pp. 39–42.

[48] Writes Kleinberg-Levin, 'Language must acknowledge its mimetic origin in nature – and its need for a continuing relationship to nature. Is it not true, after all, that, when we were children, our voices were solicited and educed by the sounds of nature, sounds we found immeasurable pleasure in responsively learning to imitate?' *Before the Voice of Reason*, p. 14.

[49] Brian Sheerin, 'Making Use of Nothing: The Sovereignties of *King Lear*', *Studies in Philology* 110.4 (2013), 789–811 (p. 805).

[50] In addition to the spark that would be ignited by a bellows in the imagery implied by the Fool's etymological wordplay, I mean very much to invoke Sale's magisterial reading of what 'Cordelia's fire' symbolises: an emblem of 'community in which no one and no thing is called "master"'. See Chapter 1 in this collection for her full discussion.

[51] *OED* 'express, v.' Etymology.

to decentre humanity as a proof or measure of virtue. Our ability to choose to care about the way that we are imbricated with human and non-human others, *Lear* uses the voice to suggest, entails feeling out the non-semantic quality entailed within the experience of giving voice that has otherwise been disavowed by political philosophy. If the feeling voice is an embodied remainder that politics would prefer to exclude as if human language should be treated as a problem of long division, then the reclamation of this virtue provides us with one avenue for imagining a politics that makes room for the uneasy remainders of existence – the excesses and accommodations that make life not only liveable, but meaningful.

And these excesses and accommodations include the theatre. In this regard, we might reread Lear's 'Howl, howl, howl', as more than the breakdown of human language into animalistic keen, more, even, than the threshold between an excruciating, unanswerable question – 'how, how, how' – and an impossible imperative directed at the audience, a demand an audience can hardly answer by standing and howling, too. Instead, Lear's self-echoing howls occupy their own unending potentiality. All those things that his cry could signify – animal wail, human sob, storming wind, question, demand, reverberation within theatrical space – ricochet back through each other, transforming the space of the theatre, if only momentarily, into the bellows of the voice itself. The moment's excess of theatricality thus becomes one of the accommodations that humankind needs to process its needs. Theatrical performance offers a space where voice can act out its sensory experiments in order to make new language. This space is a privileged one precisely because there is an audience within it to witness these sensory experiments as the multiply inflected experience that all vocal feeling is. If, too, this virtuous capacity of the voice is better witnessed in the space of the theatre than in our quotidian existence due to the elevated aesthetic of mimesis, then this only strengthens the case for why we need the stage. If we can recognise some things about ourselves more clearly when we are not those speaking, suffering, acting, then the theatre provides us a space for honing our ability not only to witness for others, but also to account for the experiential knowledge that witness provides us when we are the ones taking action. We came crying hither – to the stage – to process the meaning from, and speak back with meaning to, all the world. A virtuous theatre, indeed.

Perhaps, however, this is also what makes the play so unbearable for so many. The play forces its audience to confront these extremes of grief even after Lear does recognise the virtue Cordelia held out to him, even after their reconciliation, even after she grants him her forgiveness.[52] Indeed, it seems that Shakespeare fulfils the Aristotelian definition of tragic anagnorisis by making it Aristotle's own folly in suppressing 'mere voice' that his king recognises too late. After Lear and Cordelia meet again in Act 4, Lear will spend the remainder of the play seeking the resonant qualities of his child's voice, 'ever soft, gentle, and low' (5.3.278–9). Hope exists for Lear even if they both must 'sing like birds i' th' cage' (5.3.9), and it is a hope that resides in the situation of speaking together, or, better yet, of singing together. Forgiveness given again and again is tied to blessings spoken again and again. Voice resonates in the potentiality of the relations it sutures back together; community forms not so much upon the words such speech contains, but upon the felt spaces that voice makes possible when 'pray[ing], and sing[ing], and tell[ing] old tales, and laugh[ing] / At gilded butterflies' (5.3.10–13). Arguably, Lear even overcorrects, running the risk of reducing Cordelia to the qualities of her voice. His desperation to hold on to heightened vocal feelings, especially those of song and laughter, could index an attempt to erase the tragedy of his errors, an attempt to overleap a negotiation with the meaning of his own words and actions. Certainly, Cordelia is gentler with her father than the play is with its audience; one of the conundrums of the play seems to be that Cordelia has a greater capacity for forgiveness than we might. I have no great interest here in defending or questioning Cordelia's forgiveness of her father. It wrenches my heart and it troubles me, as it seems to trouble many critics, students, audiences. But, however we read the fact of Cordelia's forgiveness – whether virtuous, unjust, full of grace, maybe all of these things – it is notable that it follows a moment of resonance with the opening scene's attention to vocal feeling.

'Do not laugh at me', Lear says when he finally recognises his daughter, 'For, as I am a man, I think this lady / To be my child Cordelia (4.7.70–2). Speaking what she feels, Cordelia echoes her initial invitation to imagine a more virtuous language that does not strip itself of the truths enabled through vocal feeling: 'And so I am! I am!' (4.7.73).[53]

---

52 For a crucial reading of Shakespeare's development of the theme of forgiveness, in this play and others, see Beckwith, *Shakespeare and the Grammar of Forgiveness.*
53 I am grateful to Julia Reinhard Lupton for her observation that Cordelia's words resonate with, and perhaps echo, Abraham's answer to God's call in the Hebrew Bible: 'Here I am', from the Hebrew *'Hineni'*. Abraham answers God's call in this way twice: first, when God instructs him to take his son, Isaac, to Moriah as a sacrifice; and, second, when God stops him from sacrificing his bound son (Genesis 22:1 and 22:11).

Chapter 3

Reading Virtues: Shakespeare's Animals

Karen Raber

In Shakespeare's *As You Like It* Orlando violently invades the Duke's camp in Act 2 to steal food for himself and his servant Adam. Calmed by the Duke's gracious generosity, Orlando climbs down from his rage-fuelled threats, and asks only that the party wait a little before sharing their bounty with him: 'Then but forbear your food a little while, / Whiles like a doe I go to find my fawn, / And give it food' (2.7.128–30).[1] Orlando's 'fawn' is, of course, old Adam, his servant, left fainting from hunger under a bush. Like the foraging doe, Orlando has ventured afield while hiding his vulnerable infant from predators. Topsell mentions this practice in his *History of Four-footed Beasts*, noting that does 'lodge [their young] in a stable fit for them of their own making, either in some rock, or other bushy inaccessible place; covering them'.[2] Deer hide their young in this way especially during the two weeks after birth, when the fawn cannot run from predators, and they may continue to hide fawns for several months during summer. Anyone who has hiked or ridden in forests or fields has quite likely passed a resting fawn without seeing it – their camouflage is so effective and they are so preternaturally still unless accidentally flushed from the spot. Indeed, recent public service announcements from animal rescue groups and other organisations have repeatedly tried to inform Americans that they should never remove a fawn discovered in this fashion, since the doe will return to it; moving it will often guarantee it dies without its mother to nurse it.[3]

Orlando's characterisation of Adam as his fawn and himself as a nurturing doe reflects his turn away from violence and towards virtue, which

---

[1] *As You Like It*, ed. Juliet Dusinberre (London: Bloomsbury/Arden, 2006, repr. 2014); all references to this play are to this edition by act, scene and line numbers.

[2] Edward Topsell, *The History of Four-Footed Beasts* (London, 1658), p. 102.

[3] See for example these two websites offering public service announcements about moving fawns: https://deerassociation.com/dont-move-that-fawn/ and https://www.dnr.sc.gov/news/2019/apr/apr9_deerfawns.php.

is here imagined as moral action leading to mutual support, or what in Shakespeare's world might be called friendship. That word could have a more capacious meaning for early moderns than perhaps it has in our own time: friendship establishes a kind of generalised kinship, a disposition of amity towards others, the embrace of accord or alliance.[4] At the same time Orlando's image registers the gender, class and age inversions and conversions involved in his relationship with Adam, which involves unexpectedly mutual charity – just as Adam, in a gesture that deviates from the expectation that an older servant would be the dependent in this relationship, contributes his life savings to Orlando's support, so Orlando in turn commits himself to rescuing his faithful but weakened companion. Peter Erickson has observed that Orlando's identity is built on the need to identify with and as his own father: it is this that motivates his rage at Oliver, who by feeding him 'husks' and denying him the 'feeding' and 'manage' that he grants his horses (1.1.1–23), disinherits Orlando.[5] Adam, as the namesake of the original father of humankind, becomes one substitute for the absent Roland de Boys, a surrogate who opens his 'foster-nurse' (that is, his purse, 2.3.39–40) to the younger and poorer man.

The Duke emerges as another surrogate father figure when, in Act 2, scene 7, he turns Orlando away from theft and 'savage' acts, and towards 'recovery of patriarchal lineage' through the communal feast that the Duke provides.[6] When Orlando bursts in on the exiled court and threatens Jaques, the Duke intervenes to save his courtier, but he also restores Orlando to the path of 'reason' (2.7.101). The Duke encourages Orlando to see how virtue succeeds where vice cannot:

> True is it that we have seen better days,
> And have with holy bell been knolled to church,
> And sat at good men's feasts, and wiped our eyes
> Of drops that sacred pity hath engendered;
> And therefore sit you down to gentleness
> And take upon command what help we have
> That to your wanting may be ministered. (2.7.212–27)

---

[4] The language of disposition, accord and alliance can be found in *OED* definitions of friendship 2a and 2b. For more on the idea of how disposition aligns with virtue, see Alasdair MacIntyre, who argues that virtue is not limited to action, but involves the 'disposition' of emotion or feeling. *After Virtue: A Study in Moral Theory*, 2nd edn (Notre Dame, IN: University of Notre Dame Press, 1984), esp. p. 149.

[5] Peter B. Erickson, 'Sexual Politics and the Social Structure in *As You like It*', *The Massachusetts Review* 23.1 (1982), 65–83.

[6] Erickson, 'Sexual Politics', p. 74.

Orlando can minister to Adam's needs because the Duke ministers to Orlando's, both physical and spiritual. In this moment, Rosalind's young lover emerges as a character whose willingness and ability to transgress gender binaries, playing the nurturing role of the doe despite his initial masculine aggression, ensures that he will help engender a more caring, loving version of the play's world. While Erickson argues that what Orlando permits is the establishment of a 'self-sustaining patriarchal system' in which 'the men take over the traditional female prerogative of material nurturance', subsequent generations of feminist and queer scholars have questioned the absolute status of patriarchy in Shakespeare's plays, imagining other possibilities opened by actions like Orlando's.[7] Perhaps, then, we can allow the virtues represented by Orlando's doe to circulate more transformationally in the play.[8]

This conversion scene happens amidst an array of animal references that seem to map onto a simple grid in which some animals can instruct humans in virtue, while others encourage humans to vice. It can be tempting to affirm that grid when analysing the idea of animal virtue, to divide Shakespeare's animals according to which ones display the capacity for virtue, and which represent vice. Early treatments of animals often do exactly this: consider Caroline Spurgeon's *Shakespeare's Imagery*, which groups animal references into 'low type[s]' versus those of a 'certain dignity', or Audrey Yoder's mid-twentieth-century work discussing the Aesopian tradition in the plays in terms of 'villains' as opposed to 'sympathetic' portraits.[9]

Shakespeare's animals are not usually understood to be virtuous in themselves and *for themselves*. No sense of animal culture, ethics or morality usually attends their creation or reception. Rather they are

---

[7] Erickson, 'Sexual Politics', p. 75; for examples of feminist and queer approaches, see Valerie Traub, 'The Homoerotics of Shakespearean Comedy', in *Shakespeare, Feminism and Gender*, ed. Kate Chedgzoy (London: Palgrave Macmillan, 2001), pp. 135–60; or Cynthia Lewis, 'Horns, the Dream-Work, and Female Potency in *As You like It*', *South Atlantic Review* 66.4 (2001), 45–69.

[8] Feminist analyses of patriarchy's self-perpetuation vie with critical responses to overlooked or more subtle opportunities provided by language and characterisation in Shakespeare's works in ways that often map onto Eve Sedgwick's description of paranoid versus reparative reading, something that some might consider a rubric for my analysis here. See Sedgwick, 'Paranoid Reading and Reparative Reading: Or, You're So Paranoid You Probably Think This Essay Is About You', in *Touching Feeling: Affect, Pedagogy, Performativity*, ed. Michèle Barale, Jonathan Goldberg, Michael Moon and Eve Kosofsky Sedgwick (Durham, NC: Duke University Press, 2002), pp. 123–51.

[9] Caroline Spurgeon, *Shakespeare's Imagery and What It Tells Us* (Cambridge: Cambridge University Press, 1966), 336; and Audrey Yoder, *Animal Analogy in Shakespeare's Character Portrayal* (New York: Columbia University Press, 1947), chapter titles for part II, chapter ii and iv.

anthropocentrically positioned to inspire or illustrate virtues in human beings, to provide the matter on which human virtues may be exercised, or to provide didactic exemplars via proverbs and fables. The virtues animals embody range from bodily qualities like strength or noble bearing to virtues of temperament like discipline or chastity; rarely, animals might be credited with what appear to be spiritual virtues like mercy or charity, although the most common such virtue is, not surprisingly, humility.[10] Any of Shakespeare's exemplary animals can, of course, be used ironically or deconstructed in specific instances, but such moves rely on the audience's instant understanding of what virtues the animal is traditionally reputed to represent. And in most instances, the lauding of animal virtues is designed to *naturalise* certain moral actions or qualities, thus contributing to their ideological location in a hierarchised, blood- and lineage-based, often racialising and misogynistic system.

As You Like It seems to conform to the dichotomised use of good and bad animals. In contrast to the gentle doe of Act 2, we have the lion and serpent that later threaten Oliver in Act 4, leading to Orlando's display of physical and ethical virtue defending his brother. What the lion and snake share with all the other animals I've named, however, is that they are primarily used to construct distinction, either between humans and animals or between different sorts of humans. That explains their lack of what early theologians and philosophers would consider consistent, rational, prospective and fully moral or ethical virtues. Topsell, for instance, notes that the 'virtuous' actions of the doe in protecting her fawn can coexist with dangerous folly brought on by the same behaviour:

> Many times the young Calf is the cause of the taking of his Dam: for the Hunter early in the morning before day light, watcheth the Hinde where she layeth her young one, until she go and refresh herself with pasture; when he hast seen this, then doth he let loose his Dogs, and maketh to the place where the Hind-Calf was left by his mother . . . The silly Calf lyeth immoveable as if he were fastened to the earth, and so never stirring, but bleating and braying suffereth himself to be taken . . . The Hinde, both hearing and seeing the thraldom of her poor son, cometh to relieve him, without dread of Hound or Hunter, but all in vain for with his dart he also possesseth himself of her, comes to rescue and is taken as well.[11]

---

[10] Examples of animal virtues lauded or referenced in the plays are legion; for a full account, see Karen Raber and Karen Edwards, *Shakespeare and Animals: A Dictionary* (London: Bloomsbury, 2022).

[11] Topsell, *History*, p. 106.

What seems unproblematically a case of motherly protection in Orlando's analogy becomes in the natural history an instance of cervine stupidity, of instinct that dooms the animal but which it cannot change because it lacks reason. There is 'virtue' in instinct, to be sure, but it is the kind of embodied, irrational virtue that allows humans to dismiss or demote animals and other humans for lacking 'true' virtue – that founded on reason and choice.[12] An animal may offer motherly succor to its off-spring, but that natural compulsion is without the component of reasoned volition that makes Orlando's actions moral and humane. Instead of being endowed with intrinsic, essential, intransitive virtue, animal virtues in Shakespeare's plays are instrumentalised. Virtuous animals exist primarily for their metaphorical, emblematic or material ability to move *human beings* to better behaviour and action. That instrumentality is easily mustered to illustrate distinctions within human communities meant to illustrate the superiority of some – based on class status, race or gender – and the inferiority of others. Like Orlando marking his innately greater value as a human by devaluing oxen, horses and *hinds* (that is, servants, 1.1.10–18), animals are merely there to instruct audiences in what humans should do to be clearly human and not bestial.

And yet. This seems to me an unsatisfying conclusion about Shakespeare's or anyone's representations of animals and virtue, not only because I have always found Shakespeare yields more than we might expect when we fully engage with the plays and poems, but also because writing off Shakespeare's animal virtues as I've outlined them above means turning away from their potential influence on any exploration of how virtue itself can be differently thought. I propose that we can benefit from asking different questions about does and fawns or lions and snakes, different questions about many of the literary animals who seem only to be employed to represent human merits or inspire humans to be less bestial. Rather than pinning Shakespeare's animals to a reading of *animal* virtue in the plays (a reading that inevitably leads us back to human self-conception), therefore, I want to change the focus of our discussion – or, rather, the *disposition* of our discussion,

---

[12] Two of the main touchstones for Renaissance ideas about virtue are Aristotle's *Nicomachean Ethics* and Thomas Aquinas's *Summa Theologiae*; however, I am not especially interested in any debates over Christian versus classical virtues or the definitions of virtues offered by either (although I have noted Aquinas's concept of practical wisdom in passing): these debates are likely more relevant and covered in more detail by others in this volume. Holly Crocker usefully summarises the ways medieval and early modern theories of virtue excluded women (along with those of the lower classes, non-white humans and animals) in *The Matter of Virtue: Women's Ethical Action from Chaucer to Shakespeare* (Philadelphia: University of Pennsylvania Press, 2019), esp. pp. 10–14 and 140–3.

from the Latin *disposito*, meaning 'arrangement', which suggests that our insights and conclusions are determined about how we position ourselves as well as others. I cannot promise to offer anything fundamentally anti-anthropocentric, since the concept of virtue is unavoidably anthropocentric. But I can go some way to addressing the lamenesses, the blockages, the asininities and *bêtises* potentially involved in reading animal virtues.[13] The remainder of this essay is governed by one question: how can we look beyond the limitations of history, of Shakespeare, of our culture's past assumptions – and often our own – to recover some alternative concept of virtue that does not repeat past blindnesses and erasures? To engage with this question I will follow the example of ethologist Vinciane Despret, and instead of discussing the virtues of Shakespeare's animals I will embrace what she calls the 'virtue of politeness that allows animals to be interesting' by adopting a different mode of critical, readerly and scholarly engagement with early modern literary animals. I align with Despret in my interpretation of animal virtue not by ignoring or sidestepping the predicament of anthropocentrism, but by acknowledging it in order to see beyond its limits. To borrow the language Carolyn Sale uses in her essay for this volume, I am interested in the virtue of making 'kin' over the virtue of making the human 'self', *sympoiesis* over *autopoiesis* – in other words, in seeking a definition of virtue that interrogates human entitlement, the siren call of autonomy, individual will and disciplinary rigour, and instead emphasises the commonalities and mutualities that knit human and animal together in a virtuous circle.[14]

Asking Polite Questions

Philosopher of science Vinciane Despret's work has most often focused on the role of the observer in interpreting animal behaviour. As she puts it, what she does is an ethology of ethologists, the goal of which is

[13] The assertion of an unbridgeable abyss between human and animal is what Derrida calls a 'bêtise', the beastly folly or 'asininity' at the root of a long history of oppression and philosophical erasure; see Jacques Derrida, *The Animal That Therefore I Am*, ed. Marie-Louis Mallet, trans. David Wills (New York: Fordham University Press, 2008), p. 18. The incapacities that make such asininity possible in the first place ironically locate us in community with Isabella's beetle as well as Topsell's doe.

[14] These terms crop up in Donna Haraway's *Staying With the Trouble: Making Kin in the Chthulucene* (Durham, NC: Duke University Press, 2016); *sympoiesis* simply indicates 'making with' rather than making by oneself, but as Sale points out, Haraway turns to Shakespeare for examples of the way this indicates the making of kinship via plays on kin/kind.

summarised in the title of her most recent book, *What Would Animals Say if We Asked the Right Questions.*[15] For instance, Despret recounts the attempts of early twentieth-century scientists to understand the case of Clever Hans, a horse that was celebrated for being able to perform miraculous feats of intellect. Clever Hans was one of a series of animals made to entertain audiences with human-like or even superhuman acts of cognition.[16] At the time, psychologist Oscar Pfungst 'proved' that Hans was no genius or telepath: rather, he was a surpassingly subtle reader of human bodily reactions, willing to engage in the human-invented game of counting, and even capable of influencing his questioners. Despret notes that 'Hans [could] read human bodies' at a level humans themselves could not; Hans could educate his questioners to show him 'trust and interest' to succeed.[17] Yet after Pfungst's extraordinary findings were made public, Hans's case was only invoked by other scientists to 'impoverish the range of explanations' of animal behaviour – to demonstrate that the animal is never a genius, never capable of surprising capacities. To ensure that conclusion, Despret points out, investigators had to overlook the 'miracle' of animal attunement.[18] An animal like Hans is thus never asked more than the narrow range of questions that will confirm its intellectual inferiority or its conformation to predetermined human expectations. 'At every turn Sultan is driven to think the less interesting thought', says Elizabeth Costello, J. M. Coetzee's fictional animal advocate, recounting Wolfgang Köhler's experiments on apes in the early twentieth century: 'Although his entire history . . . leads him to ask questions about the justice of the universe . . . a carefully plotted psychological regimen conducts him away from ethics and metaphysics toward the humbler reaches of practical reason.'[19] This is the dominant pattern for making animals less interesting.

In a later essay, 'Sheep Do Have Opinions', Despret follows Thelma Rowell, a primatologist turned student of sheep behaviour, who observes the reactions of her twenty-two sheep at feeding time by setting

---

[15] Vinciane Despret, *What Would Animals Say if We Asked the Right Questions?*, trans. Brett Buchanan (Minneapolis: University of Minnesota Press, 2016).
[16] See Vinciane Despret, 'The Body We Care For: Figures of Anthropo-zoo-genesis', *Body & Society* 10.2–3 (2004), 111–34. The list of such animals would include the early modern case of Morocco, another 'counting' horse, as well as very recent 'genius' animals like Washoe, the chimpanzee taught American Sign Language by Allen and Beatrix Gardner.
[17] Ibid., p. 115.
[18] Ibid., pp. 116 and 125.
[19] J. M. Coetzee, *The Lives of Animals* (Princeton, NJ: Princeton University Press, 1999), p. 29.

out a twenty-third bowl.[20] With this bowl Rowell rejects the usual structures for thinking about herd behaviour, which eternally repeat the paradigm of competition and hierarchy (Rowell calls it the 'hierarchical scandal' in primatology). The usual experimental structure would require setting twenty-one bowls of food for twenty-two sheep in order to elicit competitive feeding behaviour. Normally, ethologists would find in food scenarios an easy means of observing social behaviours in more complex animals. Sheep register quite low on the ladder of expectations for intelligence or social graces, certainly lower than primates or other honorary primates like dolphins, which makes sheep unlikely candidates for such ethological investigation. Rowell, however, believes that studying food competition alone ignores other subtle but important influences on animal lives, like predation, and on this count sheep may actually be quite smart. 'From the point of view of predation, sheep-like behavior, which in our political metaphors seems to be emblematic of their stupidity', results in 'a strategy of coordination and cohesion that protects them from predators'.[21]

Given the extra bowl, Rowell's sheep are also given choices that, in addition to showing how predation shapes their reactions to their environment, reveal their relationships with one another, the changes in their behaviour traceable to gender, season and familial bonds. The social organisation of ewes is distinct from that of rams, for example, while ewes with lambs interact according to other patterns than those without. Sheep have friends with whom they fight less vigorously than they do with enemies. They engage in complex bodily communications with one another. All this information is only observable if a narrow ethological interest in food and competition is replaced with something more generous, less restrictive. In Donna Haraway's words, the bowl 'is the open, the space of what is not yet and may or may not ever be; it is a making available to events; it is asking the sheep and the scientists to be smart in their exchanges by making something unexpected happen'.[22] Despret deems Rowell's decision about the extra bowl a virtue:

> The fact that I have chosen such a trivial and concrete element to start that reconstruction is not irrelevant. It attests to a particular epistemological position to which I am committed, *one that I call a virtue: the virtue of politeness.* I try to acquire this virtue during my work in which, as an ethologist, I study

---

[20] Vinciane Despret, 'Sheep Do Have Opinions', in *Making Things Public: Atmospheres of Democracy*, ed. Bruno Latour and Peter Weibel (Cambridge, MA: MIT Press, 2006), pp. 360–70.

[21] Ibid., p. 366.

[22] Donna Haraway, *When Species Meet* (Minneapolis: University of Minnesota Press, 2008), p. 34.

the work of other ethologists, and it is in contact with them that I learn it. As primatologist Shirley Strum would have put it, this politeness forces me, as far as possible, to avoid 'constructing knowledge behind the backs of those I am studying'. In Strum's practice, the questions she puts to baboons are always subordinate to 'what counts for them'. This politeness of 'getting to know' has proved itself sufficiently for me to propose adhering to it myself.[23]

While it is a staple of etiquette and so tangentially related to ethics, 'politeness' is not generally considered a virtue – manners may be socially important, but neither classical nor Christian virtues revolve around the respect politeness grants another. Yet hiding in the term is what for Despret is a foundational ethics: although etymologically politeness derives from the Latin *polire*, to smooth or polish, the word also resonates with 'polity', or the civil order of the polis.[24] This fruitful slippage becomes important when Despret argues that making animals interesting goes hand in hand with principles of inclusivity:

> It is no coincidence that this twenty-third bowl enables me to group together ravens, babblers and primates, Bernd Heinrich, Amotz Zahavi and primatologists, under the sign of a common intelligence. All have experienced – some more recently – interesting evolutions that enabled them to break away from their position in the hierarchy – ours this time. All, to some degree, attest to what the political role of ethology can be: 'making things public' is not only making them known, it is also exploring conditions for new ways of organizing ourselves. The role of this ethology is legible in this emblematic twenty-third bowl: it is responsible for inventing, with the generosity of intelligence, polite ways of entering into relationships with nonhumans.[25]

Politeness requires us to ask more interesting questions, which in turn result in more interesting knowledge, knowledge that enables us to embrace a wider range of relationships to non-human (and other human) beings – in other words, we expand the polis, the body politic. In doing so, we also expand not just what and how we humans know animals, but we expand our obligations, our embodied interdependences, our communal interests.

But what does the virtue of politeness look like when we turn to early modern texts? After all, we literary critics are not ethologists – we cannot do fieldwork and offer up a twenty-third bowl to a flock of sheep. While we cannot directly pose questions through the reorganisation of a feeding practice, what we can do as scholars, critics and reflec-

---

[23] Despret, 'Sheep Do Have Opinions', p. 360, my italics.
[24] Laurie Shannon, playing on the same concept of 'polity', addresses animal zoopolity and their 'cosmopolity' with humans in *The Accommodated Animal: Cosmopolity in Shakespearean Locales* (Chicago: University of Chicago Press, 2013).
[25] Despret, 'Sheep Do Have Opinions', p. 368.

tive writers is choose to discover different kinds of questions we can ask of Shakespeare's virtuous animals than have been asked in the past. Ironically, it is often through impertinent or deliberately naive questions, questions deemed speculative, ahistorical, inconsistent, un-rigorous or antagonistic with regard to the disciplinary values we inherit, that scholarship discovers unexpected dimensions of animal 'life' in the plays. Sometimes it is enough to discover that the paralysing and ungenerous questions that are asked of animals can be rethought and reframed; sometimes we might find that virtue inheres merely in giving animals more time to 'speak' beyond the obvious readings. Sometimes all we might be seeking is minimal traces of other ethical *dispositions* in the stereotypical uses that pepper the plays.

Virtuous Reading

Recent scholarship has not ignored the problem of how to understand the virtues of early modern animals. Peter Harrison traces in early modern depictions of animal virtues the decline of an enchanted view of the world and nature, gradually replaced in the seventeenth century by growing scientism. Through the Middle Ages and into the Renaissance, 'Animals not only taught important moral lessons but also served as symbolic representations of important theological truths', notes Harrison; they provided a 'living pageant' of human passions, vices, virtues, 'accessible to the meanest minds'.[26] But by the latter part of the seventeenth century, scientific method undid this worldview, something we observe most clearly in the creation of Descartes' beast-machine (the idea that animals lacked not only reason, but mind and soul as well, and therefore operated mechanically): 'The Cartesian approach . . . spelled an end to the marriage between natural history and ethics' and resulted, Harrison argues, in the removal of moral animals to the pages of literary texts rather than natural histories or philosophy.[27] For Robert N. Watson, however, animals were lynchpins in turning Protestant, especially Calvinist, sentiments against animal cruelty.[28] Watson examines debates among Puritans about animal suffering and finds that, accusations of antipathy towards human pleasure aside, '[f]or many Reformers . . . enjoying the torment of our fellow creatures was

---

[26] Peter Harrison, 'The Virtues of Animals in Seventeenth-Century Thought', *Journal of the History of Ideas* 59.3 (1998), 463–84 (pp. 465 and 468).

[27] Harrison, 'The Virtues of Animals', p. 482.

[28] Robert N. Watson, 'Protestant Animals: Puritan Sects and English Animal-protection Sentiment, 1550–1650', *ELH* 81.4 (2014), 1111–48.

wrong in ways that other pleasure was not, and so wrong that it actually marked human beings as spiritually inferior to those supposedly lesser creatures'.[29] Compassion rather than cruelty was more than a passing consideration for Puritans: treading roughly the same time and territory as Harrison, Watson instead finds that 'a new kind of respect for natural life . . . accompanied the emergent empirical sciences of the late Renaissance', which emphasised the role of human embodied engagement with phenomena, among other things.[30] That in turn helped link human with animal experiences of the world. Kindness to animals, he argues, ultimately became a theological and a political commitment that would provide the grist for subsequent animal protection movements: 'As bodily experience weighed ever more heavily, human pride sank, and found some non-human kin.'[31]

These two brilliant studies of the virtues of animals and the virtues of human behaviour towards animals nevertheless do not fully engage with the ways that Shakespeare's animals might be read beyond or against anthropocentric ends. In one respect, namely their commitment to historicising animal virtues, both Harrison and Watson remain constrained in the questions they can ask. So how might a virtuously polite reading of Shakespeare's animals proceed differently? To answer that question, I turn to two readings by other critics before offering my own example.

After becoming a motherly doe in Act 2, Orlando intervenes selflessly on his brother's behalf in Act 4 of the play, effecting a transformation in Oliver and the reconciliation of the brothers:

> A wretched ragged man, o'ergrown with hair,
> Lay sleeping on his back; about his neck
> A green and gilded snake had wreathed itself,
> Who with her head, nimble in threats, approached
> The opening of his mouth. But suddenly
> Seeing Orlando, it unlinked itself
> And with indented glides did slip away
> Into a bush; under which bush's shade
> A lioness, with udders all drawn dry,
> Lay couching, head on ground, with catlike watch
> When that the sleeping man should stir. (4.3.105–15)

Once he has frightened away the serpent, Orlando wrestles with the lioness to save his brother's life. Both serpent and lioness are meant to be agents of violence, not innocent victims. Yet, like the doe in Act 2, and again in instrumental fashion, they are employed here to provide

---

[29] Ibid., p. 1116.
[30] Ibid., p. 1119.
[31] Ibid., p. 1141.

occasion for human virtue. The serpent represents many things: the paradox of the beauty and lurking dangers of the forest; the sinuous persistence of sin; the confusion of phallic and feminine that makes Oliver a 'feminized object of male aggression and the *ef*feminzed object of female desire'.[32] Likewise the starved nursing lioness may be 'an aged maternal figure',[33] or an analogue of the Nemean lion about to be dispatched by the Herculean Orlando; or it may be the biblical beast of the Psalms ('Thou shalt set thy foot upon the Lion and Adder; the young lion and the Dragon thou shalt tread under thy feet', 91:13), which makes Orlando in turn a Christian knight.[34]

Edward Berry, however, has a very different interpretation of this scene and its animals. He argues that the serpent and the lion, along with others like the doe and the hunted stag of Act 2, '[tie] human and animal life together in bonds that include both violence and kindness' and demonstrate Shakespeare's 'complex and unsentimental awareness of animal and human worlds as implicated in both nurturing and killing'.[35] As Berry notes, while humans are presumed to act out of reason – the practical wisdom that Thomists, for instance, insist is necessary for actions to rise to the level of virtue – in contrast to animal instinct, these two sources of action are difficult to keep separate, especially where the challenge of protecting a child, or a parental figure or one's companions is at stake. Berry's work is thoroughly and insightfully historicist, and his conclusions are made even more remarkable in that it is not especially informed by recent critical animal studies or theory. In chasing the 'variable and conflicting set of practices, symbols, and attitudes' mobilised in Shakespeare's hunting imagery, he nevertheless approaches for a moment a piercing critique of anthropocentrism via a reading that makes the animals of the play more than merely figures for human qualities, ideals or desires.[36] His reading forges a bond between humans and animals who share a world that renders them vulnerable even as they strike out at one another: 'although the play as a whole implies an acceptance of man's role as a killer, it does so . . . by implying a mutuality in the relationship between man and nature . . . [Shakespeare's metaphors] imply a community among humans and animals'.[37] Lion and doe

[32] Traub, 'Homoerotics', p. 142.
[33] Ibid.
[34] On Orlando as a Christian Knight, see Dusinberre's note in the Arden *As You Like It*, 301, n.113. The Nemean lion's relevance for the play is discussed in Richard Knowles, 'Myth and Type in *As You Like It*', *ELH* 33 (1966), 5–6.
[35] Edward Berry, *Shakespeare and the Hunt: A Cultural and Social Study* (Cambridge: Cambridge University Press, 2001), p. 186.
[36] Ibid., p. 37.
[37] Ibid., pp. 187 and 188 respectively.

share their need to succour their young, despite the weight of lore that casts the lioness as wild and violent, the doe as meek and gentle, and both share with the forest's humans, and especially with Orlando, the experiences of hunger and the pressure to find food for dependents.[38] Simple moral codes do not measure their being – all are amalgams of virtues and vices.

What if we extend this more inclusive and generous reading of the mutual fate of humans and animals to Orlando's first speech in the play? Why is a pig, an ox, or a horse less worthy than a human being? Why isn't the way all humans treat oxen, pigs and even horses equally as reprehensible as Oliver's mistreatment of Orlando? 'He lets me feed with his hinds', complains Orlando; 'Shall I keep your hogs and eat husks with them?' (1.1.18, 35). Orlando is convinced that association with both animals 'bars [me] the place of a brother' (1.1.17), by which he means the proper training and remunerated employment the son of a noble should enjoy. But 'the place of a brother' can, as the play ultimately demonstrates, mean something quite different, namely the embrace of unexpected beings as one's fellows. Both the Arden and Bevington editions gloss 'hinds' in Orlando's speech here as 'servants or farmhands': the *OED* derives this meaning from Old and Middle English terms meaning members of a family or household, which definition already invites us to consider how the word reflects invidious decline from familial union to class-based disunion.[39] Yet a 'hind' is of course also a female deer, the exemplar of virtuous nurturance in Act 2. Why must we choose one definition over the others? What hinders us as readers from allowing hinds, does and faithful servants like Adam to share their inherent moral value, even if the characters of the play resist such a levelling? The potential linguistic overlap of hinds and does suggests that the lesson Orlando needs to learn in the woods involves a different sense of brotherhood, one not contingent upon rank and blood *or species*, but one that embraces both the keeping-with of hogs and the kindnesses of dukes and female deer and Adamic hinds.

---

[38] The lion crouches under a bush, connecting it to the place Adam chooses to rest while fainting from hunger, and thus to Orlando's willingness to show vulnerability via the image of the nursing doe.

[39] See Dusinberre's note, p. 150 n.18; David Bevington in *The Complete Works of Shakespeare*, 5th edn (New York: Pearson, 2004) simply notes 'farm hands ' (p. 298, n.19); meanwhile the *OED* gives the etymology for hind (n.2) as 'Middle English *hine* singular, from earlier Old English (north midlands) and Middle English *híne* plural; apparently developed < *hína*, *hígna* genitive plural of *hígan*, *híwan*, in Old Northumbrian *hígu*, *hígo*, 'members of a family or household, domestics' and that for hind simply as Old English *hynde* for female deer. Yet by Shakespeare's time, the word was identical for both meanings.

Two Noble Horses, Alike in Dignity

In *Richard II*, the deposed king hears from his groom the report that his beloved horse has failed to toss off its new usurping rider:

> So proud that Bolingbroke was on his back!
> That jade hath eat bread from my royal hand;
> This hand hath made him proud with clapping him.
> Would he not stumble? would he not fall down, –
> Since pride must have a fall, – and break the neck
> Of that proud man that did usurp his back?
> Forgiveness, horse! Why do I rail on thee,
> Since thou, created to be aw'd by man,
> Wast born to bear? I was not made a horse;
> And yet I bear a burden like an ass,
> Spur-gall'd and tir'd by jauncing Bolingbroke.[40]

Richard first excoriates his mount for accepting the hand of a new master, then corrects his mistaken application of blame. Instead, Richard acknowledges that the virtues of a horse do not include the capacity for rebellion against those whom, he believes, God and nature created the horse to serve. To be a horse is to demonstrate a naturally given 'awe' for one's rider, whereas to be human is to accept responsibility for one's failure to lead.

Richard would have good reason to expect that his horse would dethrone Bolingbroke based on the many accounts of loyal horses in the period's natural histories of animals. Pliny, for instance, mentions that Bucephalus famously refused to allow any but Alexander to mount him; likewise he says that 'the horse that belonged to Caesar the Dictator is said to have refused to let anyone else mount it'.[41] Moreover, Pliny reports, a Scythian chieftain was killed in a duel, 'and when his adversary came to stript his body of its armour, his horse kicked him and bit him till he died' while an ostler was 'savaged by a horse for the same reason'. 'For horses understand the ties of relationship', Pliny concludes.[42] Topsell adds the case of the horse of a captain to Charles the Great whose horse would 'never suffer any to come on his back, except his Master'.[43] Such instances are, for Topsell, demonstrations of 'the

---

[40] *Richard II*, ed. Charles A. Forger (London: Bloomsbury/Arden, 2002; repr. 2014), 5.5.84–94.
[41] Pliny, *Natural History*, trans. H. Rackham (Cambridge, MA: Harvard University Press, 1940; repr. 1997), 8:63, p. 109.
[42] Ibid., p. 111.
[43] Topsell, *History*, p. 243.

wonderful work of God in the creation of this Beast, enduing it with . . . a noble spirit, the principal whereof is a loving and dutiful inclination to the service of Man'.[44] But such accounts emphasise something more akin to innate or inborn instinct rather than a reasoned exercise of will. That renders equine faithfulness, like the nurturing aspect of Orlando's doe, more of a reminder to humans that they have something to live up to, rather than necessarily demonstrating virtues inherent to horses as a species or as individuals.

Erica Fudge has persuasively argued for a very different interpretation of Richard's speech than is available in the prior critical and scholarly literature on it, different even from those invested in early modern animal studies. She sees in Richard's pivot to humble apology to his former mount ('Forgiveness, horse!') a moment of kinship between human and animal 'in which order, and the exercise of power it is based upon, is suspended, in which fellowship rather than dominion is possible'.[45] Fudge links the moment to horror at the barbarity of war. Richard's horse is forced to participate in a victory parade celebrating triumph in war at the cost of the animal's own – and the populace's – capacity for moral choices. Richard's assassination and the play's announcement of the violent ends of his allies register the brutal costs of war. For Fudge, then, the words 'forgiveness, horse' can also open up a possibility the play may not unequivocally assert, but which is fleetingly available nonetheless: an 'act of standing-down rather than a call to action'.[46] Fudge's reading suggests that the horse's virtue lies in the animal's ability to trigger self-reflection in king and audience, and a recognition of human moral flaws that lead to the constant resurgence of militarised aggression. In effect, Fudge rescues this animal from readings that emphasise historicist arguments about a shift towards scientific disenchantment or the place Shakespeare's plays might hold in a pre- versus post-Cartesian cosmos.[47] Instead, although Richard's speech may express ideas of animal submission, and seems to validate hierarchies of creation and authority, it does involve recognising that the individual animal and its limited (by humans) options can be read by an audience

[44] Ibid., p. 220.
[45] Erica Fudge, '"Forgiveness, Horse!": The Barbaric World of *Richard II*', in *The Routledge Handbook of Shakespeare and Animals*, ed. Karen Raber and Holly Dugan (New York: Routledge, 2020), pp. 292–306 (p. 303).
[46] Ibid., p. 304.
[47] Fudge takes note at length of prior readings of Richard's horse, including Bruce Boehrer's in his *Animal Characters: Nonhuman Beings in Early Modern Literature* (Philadelphia: University of Pennsylvania Press, 2010) and my own in 'Equeer: Human-Equine Erotics in *1 Henry IV*', in *The Oxford Handbook of Shakespeare and Embodiment*, ed. Valerie Traub (Oxford: Oxford University Press, 2016), pp. 347–66.

as a plea to reject war's brutality. In recognising a certain kinship with his former mount, Richard acknowledges that virtue and vulnerability are shared among species.

Elsewhere, one of Shakespeare's horses does in fact unseat an arguably usurping rider. *Two Noble Kinsmen*, co-authored by Shakespeare and John Fletcher, takes its plot from Chaucer's 'Knight's Tale', which concerns the friendship of two young Thebans, Palamon and Arcite, who take reluctant arms against the Athenian Theseus and, though surpassingly courageous in their defence of their tyrannical ruler Creon, find themselves among the defeated. While they are imprisoned in Athens, they catch a glimpse of the Amazon Princess Emilia and fall madly in love with her. Repeating themes of Shakespeare's early play *Two Gentlemen of Verona*, *Two Noble Kinsmen* meditates on the nature and consequences of friendship, its stability, its ability to inculcate – or degrade – individual virtues. Palamon and Arcite must navigate the transition to adulthood that love for Emilia represents: their youthful attachment to one another is shaken by their desire for a woman. When Emilia pleads for the lives of both men, Theseus grants instead that they battle one another in a formal contest: whoever wins the day 'He shall enjoy her; th'other lose his head, and all his friends'.[48]

Having triumphed in the tournament organised by Theseus in Act 5, Arcite makes a Bolingbroke-like parade through the streets of Athens:

> Mounted upon a steed that Emily
> Did first bestow on him, a black one, owing
> Not a hair-worth of white, which some will say
> Weakens his price and many will not buy
> His goodness with this note – which superstition
> Here finds allowance – on this horse is Arcite
> Trotting the stones of Athens, which the calkins
> Did rather tell than trample; for the horse
> Would make his length a mile, if 't pleased his rider
> To put pride in him. (5.4.49–58)

Arcite's mount reminds us of the Dauphin's beloved noble animal in *Henry V*, which 'bounds from the earth', a 'cheval volant' who 'trots the air'.[49] Unlike the Dauphin's horse, however, which is a bright bay of reddish hue and thus an animal of fiery but admirable temperament, Arcite's gift-horse is black all over and, according to early modern

---

[48] *Two Noble Kinsmen*, ed. Lois Potter (London: Bloomsbury/Arden, 1997; rev. 2015), 3.6.296–7. All further references to this play are by act, scene and line number.
[49] *King Henry V*, ed. T. W. Craik (London: Bloomsbury/Arden, 1995, repr. 2016), 3.7.13–16.

theories of coat colour, consequently prone to misbehaviour.[50] Arcite indeed discovers this is a deadly difference:

> As he thus went counting
> The flinty pavement, dancing as 'twere to th' music
> His own hoofs made (for, as they say, from iron
> Came music's origin), what envious flint,
> Cold as old Saturn and, like him, possessed
> With fire malevolent, darted a spark,
> Or what fierce sulphur else, to this end made,
> I comment not. The hot horse, hot as fire,
> Took toy at this and fell to what disorder
> His power could give his will; bounds, comes on end,
> Forgets school-doing, being therein trained
> And of kind manage; pig-like he whines
> At the sharp rowell, which he frets at rather
> Than any jot obeys; seeks a foul means
> Of boist'rous and rough jad'ry to disseat
> His lord, that kept it bravely. When nought served –
> When neither curb would crack, girth break, nor diff'ring plunges
> Disroot his rider whence he grew, but that
> He kept him 'tween his legs – on his hind hoofs
> On end he stands,
> That Arcite's legs, begin higher than his head,
> Seemed with strange art to hang. His victor's wreath
> Even then fell off his head and presently
> Backward the jade comes o'er and his full poise
> Becomes the rider's load. (5.4.58–81)

This description is loaded with the same ideological analogising that can be found in many instances where Shakespeare describes horses: the rebellious animal shows its bestial nature by reacting violently to a mere spark, degenerating into a thorough brute, as indicated by his 'pig-squeal'. He forgets his 'school training' at the manage (the advanced equestrian arts) and ignores his rider's signals. Too good a rider to be unceremoniously dumped or 'disrooted' by this 'jade', Arcite instead hangs on, trying to dominate it, until he is crushed beneath the falling weight of the animal. Readers might interpret the moment as proof that in this romance, Arcite's relatively aggressive, warlike worship of Mars makes him less proficient in controlling his emotions to rule this unruly

---

[50] Dennis Britton addresses the racialising language in this play in 'From the *Knight's Tale* to *The Two Noble Kinsmen*: Rethinking Race, Class and Whiteness in Romance', *Postmedieval: A Journal of Medieval Cultural Studies* 6.1 (2015), 64–78. In his analysis, the many ways individuals are denoted with colour-based adjectives undermines any sense of the 'indivisibility of whiteness' (p. 66), setting undesirable white people against desirable ones.

steed and therefore less fit a match for Emilia than Palamon, Venus's adherent. Since Arcite in fact confesses that he was 'false' if not 'treacherous' (for lying about the fact that Palamon saw Emilia and loved her first), his qualifications to restore the order the play generally drives to establish are indeed suspect.[51]

Other readings might emphasise instead the erotic implications of the description: the 'spark' that sets off the bestial actions of the horse could be Emilia herself, the desire for whom has made Arcite (and in fairness, Palamon too) deviate from the standards of true noble virtue. If male friendship is the Platonic ideal repeatedly proposed in the play's two sets of relationships between Arcite and Palamon as well as between Theseus and Pirithous, then love for women intrudes sexual desire that threatens to erode that ideal. The centaur-like feat of riding Arcite here accomplishes then becomes not a case of reason (the human rider) controlling passion (the beast between his legs), but a sign of Arcite's mistaken commitment to sexual pleasure and conquest over the bonds he shares with Palamon. Peggy Simonds links Arcite's death to Plato's description of love as the charioteer that drives the soul with a brace of horses, one rational and beautiful, the other ugly and wild: 'Arcite's black horse and its behavior are clearly symbolic of the Theban prince's inability to control his sexual lust . . . He, rather than Palamon, is the true wild man.'[52] Dominated by lust, Arcite is unable to judge his mount's nature or capacity, and so ends up in a subordinated, sexualised position, bearing the horse's weight instead of riding atop it.[53]

These are, at least, the kinds of readings we seem meant to produce. In them, the black horse is anything and everything, but never itself. Arcite's riding is anything and everything except a choice about a relationship to a horse. What if, instead, we posed a different question of this horse and rider: what if we asked whether, in a play that is deeply concerned with human friendships, Arcite is *a good friend to his horse*?

Laurie Shannon has argued that what is usually overlooked about *Two Noble Kinsmen* is that, in addition to the bonds between male characters, it offers an alternative – the friendship between women,

---

[51] A thorough reading of the ways horses are used in the play to convey ideas about sexuality and social order is provided by Natália Pikli in 'Hybrid Creatures in Context: Centaurs, Hobby-horses and Sexualised Women (*Hamlet, King Lear, The Two Noble Kinsmen*)', *Actes des congrès de la Société française Shakespeare* 38 (2020), 1–18.

[52] Peggy Simonds, 'Platonic Horses in *The Two Noble Kinsmen*: From Passion to Temperance', *Renaissance Papers* (1998), 91–101 (p. 99).

[53] The role of the horse is an early modern commonplace for expressing human sexuality and revolves around the idea of who is 'riding' another and who is being 'ridden'; for more on this topic, see Karen Raber, *Animal Bodies, Renaissance Culture* (Philadelphia: University of Pennsylvania Press, 2013), pp. 75–101.

glimpses of which are available in Emilia's conversations with her fellow 'lady knight' Hippolyta in Act 1, scene 3.[54] Shannon points out that while for early modern audiences '[t]he non-subordinating relation of friendly equals represented a utopian alternative to the subordination without limits inflicted by the tyrannical ruler', *Two Noble Kinsmen* actually sets the two *women* against the male–male attachments between Palamon and Arcite and Theseus and Pirithous. Even the latter friendship, despite its more profound and unchanging character, is coloured by Theseus's assertions of law and will, leaving Emilia's report of a youthful friendship with another woman 'a fully developed articulation' of sisterhood.[55] The play also establishes that 'marriage is a (brutally) political institution' in the play, and casts Theseus in the mould of a tyrant not unlike the defeated Creon: forcing marriage on Emilia makes Theseus 'a boundary problem', as Shannon puts it, because he exceeds his own boundaries and violates the boundedness of others. Theseus collapses personal and political desires when he calls for the battle between Palamon and Arcite and offers up Emilia as their prize; he enforces his will on all three unilaterally and in violation of reason.[56] 'Emilia's consent, of course, is never given', notes Shannon. On the other hand, she points out, as the only 'politically unsubordinated character in the play, Theseus is able to make choices he considers consistent with maintaining what he calls "our human title"' (1.1.233).[57]

If having a 'human title' means mastery, dominance of others and the free exercise of will, then Arcite certainly has it too. Yet his death reveals that his (and Theseus's) conception of humanity goes hand in hand with a set of failures – the failure to be flexible, to respond to his horse with kindness and tolerance, to be willing to fall, to submit himself to the needs of another. Human, then, but inhumane, brutal, disrespectful of the bodily and spiritual integrity of others. Arcite is, by any contemporary early modern standard, a great rider; by the standards of his horse, he is a terrible one, pulling the animal down with him out of a commitment to coercion and domination. This black horse that literally stands *against* its rider's determined control thus also stands *for* something: for its own identity distinct from its rider's, for an interest in its material

---

[54] Laurie Shannon, *Sovereign Amity: Figures of Friendship in Shakespearean Contexts* (Chicago: University of Chicago Press, 2002), pp. 90–122. Alan Sinfield has also commented at length on the relative queerness of *Two Noble Kinsmen's* female community in 'Cultural Materialism and Intertextuality: The Limits of Queer Reading in *A Midsummer Night's Dream* and *Two Noble Kinsmen*', *Shakespeare Survey* 56 (2003), 67–78.

[55] Laurie Shannon, 'Emilia's Argument: Friendship and "Human Title" in *The Two Noble Kinsmen*', *ELH* 64.3 (1997), 657–82 (p. 659); Shannon, *Sovereign Amity*, p. 114.

[56] Shannon, *Sovereign Amity*, p. 108.

[57] Ibid., p. 112.

world that does not correspond with and can't be overwritten by what humans take interest in, and ultimately for the invitation to a fellow creature to acknowledge kinship through tolerance, accommodation and grace. Were Arcite able to respond differently, his actions might fulfil Donna Haraway's slogan 'Make Kin Not Babies!' by turning from the lure of sexual and other forms of dominion available to men in the play, towards modes of care that enable the flourishing of others beyond himself.[58] In my mind, the black horse that rears, 'bounds' beyond the bounds allowed it by the tyrannical rider, and falls on Arcite in a sexualised 'load' that kills him, also asks – not metaphorically or instrumentally but in mutual distress with his rider – that we imagine more, that we rear up against the constraints of history, of literary-critical practice, to resist paradigms that insist on only one kind of relationship between humans and animals. That is the highest form of virtue I think we will find in Shakespeare's animals.

---

[58] Haraway, *Staying With the Trouble*, p. 102. Haraway calls on feminists in particular who have undone 'the supposed natural necessity of ties between sex and gender, race and sex, race and nation, class and race, gender and morphology . . .' among other configurations of life and can effect 'multispecies justice' (p. 103).

Part II
Virtue's Performances

Chapter 4

Shakespeare and the Virtue in Complaining

Emily Shortslef

Complaining or Virtue

Patience unmoved! . . .
They can be meek that have no other cause.
A wretched soul, bruised with adversity,
We bid be quiet when we hear it cry;
But were we burdened with like weight of pain,
As much or more we should ourselves complain.[1]

In Act 2 of *The Comedy of Errors*, irritated by her husband's mysterious failure to return home at the expected hour, Adriana complains. 'Why should their liberty be more than ours?' she asks her sister Luciana, 'Look, when I serve him so, he takes it ill' (2.1.10, 12). Luciana first offers a rationale for this disparity (men's 'business . . . lies out o'door'; husbands have authority over their wives), then scolds Adriana for complaining about its consequences (2.1.11). To complain of a husband's unexplained absence, as if he were not free to go where he wishes when he wants, is to be an insufficiently submissive ('bridle[d]') wife: Antipholus is 'master of his liberty' and your lord, she reminds Adriana, and you must 'let your will attend' meekly and patiently on his, without griping (2.1.13, 7, 25). This response, with its echoing of the common-sense logic of patriarchal ideology, provokes Adriana's defence of complaining as a reflexive reaction to the painful psychophysiological pressure caused by 'adversity', a pressure figured in the hydraulic imagination of humoral theory as a weight released and thereby relieved in the outbursts of passionate speech. If the unwed Luciana were 'to live to see like right bereft', to find herself burdened by the constraints that bar

---

[1] William Shakespeare, *The Comedy of Errors*, 2.1.32–7. All quotations from Shakespeare's plays, henceforth cited parenthetically, are from *The Norton Shakespeare*, ed. Stephen Greenblatt et al., 3rd edn (New York: W. W. Norton, 2016).

women from the freedom that men enjoy, Adriana argues, she would know better than to speak as if 'urging helpless patience would relieve me' (2.1.40, 39). She would complain too.

This passage is exemplary of a broader phenomenon: the interweaving, across a variety of early modern discursive formations, of scenes of complaint with normative forms of ethical thought – including, as here, commonly held and culturally enforced beliefs about the immorality, irrationality and harmfulness of 'complaining'. (In this context, 'complaint' and 'complaining' refer to everyday utterances that express grief, grievance and discontentment, rather than to the formal poems or songs of mourning with which the word is frequently associated.) Indeed, the exchange between the Ephesian sisters, in which a complaint about x is met with a moralistic criticism of giving voice to grievance – and that criticism countered in turn by the complainer's insistence on the limits of moral philosophy and the limitations of human strength in the face of intense suffering – comprises a formulaic debate staged in many of the period's texts. Another Shakespearean iteration appears in *Much Ado About Nothing*, where Leonato, skilfully performing his role in the pretence of Hero's death, responds to his brother's observation that it is 'not wisdom' to lament so vehemently by insisting that he cannot help but do so:

> 'Tis all men's office to speak patience
> To those that wring under the load of sorrow,
> But no man's virtue nor sufficiency
> To be so moral when he shall endure
> The like himself. Therefore give me no counsel.
> My griefs cry louder than advertisement. (5.1.2, 27–32)

Like Adriana, Leonato argues that pain must cry out, regardless of what philosophy prescribes. This same commonplace propels Montaigne's cheeky argument, in an essay about the misery of his kidney stones, that philosophers should conceptualise 'voluntary complaints' as they do involuntary motions of the body: 'out of our control', and thus morally neutral.[2] The proposal's point of reference is the unequivocally negative valence of complaining, complaints and complainers in Stoic and Neostoic ethical discourse, whose well-known models of *consolatio* –such as Boethius's *De consolatione philosophiae* and Justus Lipsius's *De constantia* – feature plaintive narrators whose progress towards the good is measured precisely by the gradual quieting of their 'querulous'

---

[2] Michel de Montaigne, 'Of the Resemblance of Children to Fathers', II. 37, in *The Complete Essays of Montaigne*, trans. Donald M. Frame (Stanford, CA: Stanford University Press, 1998), pp. 574–98 (p. 576).

and 'whining complaints'.[3] The dialogic form of those narratives underscores the two general categories of responses to adversity recognised by what Michael Bristol, in this volume, calls 'vernacular' Stoic ethical discourse: complaining (the morally problematic and, even for its defenders, weak and passive reaction) and not complaining, the hallmark of patience, that valorised virtue defined by Lipsius as 'a voluntarie sufferance without grudging of all things whatsoever can happen to, or in a man'.[4] The claim that virtue – moral goodness and/or strength – is exercised and actualised in refusing to complain remains axiomatic in today's popular therapeutic and self-help discourses, in which 'complaining' is the antithesis of healthy and empowering responses to losses, injuries and pain: you can complain, or you can practise radical acceptance; you can complain, or you can take action and 'do something about it'. (In this vein, a post on the Instagram feed for dailystoic, which purports to offer 'Ancient Wisdom for Everyday Life' and currently has 1.2 million followers, featured an inspirational quotation attributed to Marcus Aurelius: 'Don't be heard complaining . . . not even to yourself'. The accompanying caption reads, 'Putting off our responsibilities is easy. Complaining is easy. Both are as natural to us as breathing. But what good has either ever done for anyone in the long run?'.)[5]

The assumption that virtue and complaining are mutually exclusive is so engrained in so many forms of ethical discourse as to seem almost intuitive. Yet this essay is premised on the contrary belief that complaining is potentially virtuous – that there are times when the act of complaining can do some good, and that there are cases in which it is good, in the ethical sense, to complain. The semantic negativity of complaining notwithstanding, this statement is likely to be uncontroversial, but at any rate, my focus will be less on testing the assumption that complaining is potentially virtuous than on exploring the ethical weight that the act of complaining bears, and tracing the virtue(s) for which I will argue it is a conduit, in two other Shakespearean scenes of complaint that foreground – and give a positive valence to – the ethical charge that complaining carries. These are Act 4, scene 4 of *Richard III*, in which the Duchess of York and Queen Elizabeth interrupt Richard's procession to

---

[3] [Justus Lipsius], *Two Bookes of Constancie*, trans. John Stradling (London, 1595), pp. 110 and 116.

[4] Lipsius, *Two Bookes of Constancie*, C1r.

[5] Daily Stoic. [Quotation from Marcus Aurelius]. Instagram, 27 July 2021. Available at https://www.instagram.com/p/CR1OA54sUVO/ (accessed 30 July 2021). It's fascinating to see how the formulaic dialogue against and in defense of complaining that repeats across classical, medieval, and early modern texts plays out on Instagram too, fostered by the medium's ability to let users comment on posts (see, for instance, the comment in which one dailystoic follower objects that 'this is an impossible standard').

accuse him of the murders of Clarence, the Queen's kinsmen, and the two young princes; and Act 5, scene 1 of *Measure for Measure*, in which Isabella brings a complaint against Angelo to the Duke as he 'returns' to the city.

Actualised in these dramatic scenes of complaint is a virtuous potential that I would suggest is articulated, tellingly, in the very accounts of complaining's putative unvirtuousness elaborated by Stoic and early modern Reformed writers, whose respective ethical paradigms converge in targeting complaining as a way of speaking that embodies a quarrelsome and thus insubordinate disposition towards the 'eternal law' of nature or the sovereign will of divine providence.[6] This transgressiveness with regard to the would-be complainer's proper bounds is a manifest preoccupation of Calvin's sermons on that famously plaintive work of Hebrew wisdom literature, the Book of Job. Describing what can 'be applied to our own use' from this story, Calvin suggests that Job's experience clearly shows that while 'there is not that man which cannot skill to complain' about his own particular misery, 'neverthelesse wee must abyde it quietly', unlike Job himself, who, in complaining, 'flingeth himself out of his bounds against God'.[7] In Job, the stock figures of the complainer and the patient man coexist in one person, afflicted to the point of losing his reason, until – chastened by the voice that speaks to him in the whirlwind and reminds him how finite a creature he is, and how powerful his creator is – he silences his complaints. The practical ethical knowledge that Calvin extrapolates from the text (in all adversities we must 'abstain from such excessive speeches as we see Job hath uttered here') follows logically, in his reading, from the conceptual knowledge driven home to Job in the whirlwind: 'power & dominion are in God . . . it is reason that he should dispose of his creatures at his owne pleasure'.[8] A virtuous person may fall into complaint, but when they recall this truth they will stop complaining – a conversion figured in the Book of Job through the metaphors of the bridle and the hand, which the chastised complainer chooses to place in or over their own mouth. Entangled as it is with fatalistic forms of

---

[6] Seneca, 'On Providence', in *The Workes of Lucius Annaeus Seneca, Both Morrall and Naturall*, trans. Thomas Lodge (London, 1614), p. 498. Of course there are considerable differences even between Stoic and Reformed accounts of passionate expression; Calvin and Luther both distinguish their own position from the Stoics and suggest that a certain degree of expression of grief is appropriate and only natural. On this see Richard Strier, *The Unrepentant Renaissance: From Petrarch to Shakespeare to Milton* (Chicago: University of Chicago Press, 2011).

[7] John Calvin, *Sermons of Maister John Calvin, Upon the Booke of Job*, trans. Arthur Golding (London, 1584), pp. 148, 148, 149 and 262 respectively.

[8] Calvin, *Sermons*, pp. 222 and 241 respectively.

thought, the importance of uncomplaining submission is most accentuated in Stoic and Neostoic and Reformed ethical discourses, yet much of the thought about ethos that circulated in early modern England, across a range of philosophical and theological frameworks, similarly assumes that to be a good person is to accept one's lot as beyond human control or question, and thus beyond the 'excesses' of complaint. Plutarch, for instance, explains that it is 'the propertie of a wise man and well brought up' to remember that 'in all our worldly affaires, we are to be content with our portion allotted unto us, and without grudging and complaint, gently to yield our selves obedient' to whatever our 'hap' happens to be, and suggests that complaining is characteristic of 'the worse sort of people', prone to irrationality and less capable of self-control (a group in which he predictably includes women and non-Greek 'barbarians').[9] Luciana's mini-sermon to Adriana, which weds the counsel not to complain about a husband's greater liberty with an account of a natural order in which every created thing 'hath his bound', with male members of each species having dominion over their female counterparts (2.1.17), perfectly encapsulates how this way of thinking lends itself to rationalising and maintaining the hierarchies of any given socio-political order. What makes complaining an instance of 'excessive' speech is not simply that it expresses passion in excess of reason, but more specifically that that expression constitutes a transgression, an overstepping of – and at least implicitly, a challenge to the reason that governs – one's assigned place in a structure. This querulousness with regard to things that are allegedly natural, divinely mandated, fated or matters of sheer necessity is also, to my mind, what makes complaining potentially virtuous, and what opens a relation between the act of complaining and a virtue that exists in considerable tension with patience: justice.

This way of conceptualising complaining, which is informed by the contemporary cultural theorist Sara Ahmed's notion of complaint as a feminist and antiracist practice, orients my analysis of the following scenes of complaint from *Richard III* and *Measure for Measure*.[10] It is not insignificant that in these scenes of intensified emotion and heightened dramatic tension, when characters are pressured to respond to

---

[9] Plutarch, *Consolatio ad Apollonium* in *The Philosophie, commonlie called, the Morals written by the learned philosopher Plutarch of Chaeronea*, trans. Philemon Holland (London, 1603), pp. 510 and 523. On the gendering of virtue, see Unhae Park Langis, *Passion, Prudence, and Virtue in Shakespearean* Drama (London: Bloomsbury, 2011). On the relation between discourses of self-improvement and racialised identity, see Patricia Akhimie, *Shakespeare and the Cultivation of Difference: Race and Conduct in the Early Modern World* (New York: Routledge, 2018).

[10] See Sara Ahmed, *Complaint!* (Durham, NC: Duke University Press, 2021).

threats to the endurance of their lives and ways of living, Shakespeare directly pushes against the current of early modern ethical thought I have been describing, reversing its typical binaries. In each case, a performance of complaint described by certain characters as an irruption of insubordinate, feminised impatience appears at the level of the play as a purposive action rather than a form of passive suffering, and is aligned with virtue rather than vice, which is instead associated with those who would criticise or silence complaint. These scenes of virtuous complaining thus would seem to give form to a note of dissonance in classical ethical discourses on the topic of passion and its vocalisation as speech. Consider Aristotle's brief but intriguing suggestion, in the *Ethics'* discussion of calmness – the virtue that reflects the mean with regard to anger – that there is a virtuous degree of anger that may in some cases 'prescribe' a certain amount of complaining:

> The person who is angry at the right things and towards the right people, and also in the right way, at the right time, and for the right length of time, is praised. ... [B]eing a calm person means being undisturbed, not led by feeling, but complaining wherever reason prescribes, and for the length of time it prescribes.[11]

One way of understanding the ethical dimensions of theatrical scenes of complaint is to see them as opportunities for audiences to consider the ethos and situation of complainers and, with regard to these particular fictive persons and scenarios, make the judgements about 'particular cases' that, for Aristotle, ethics continually requires (as he notes, there can be no set of rules detailing when, how and how long one should feel anger or complain: what 'reason prescribes' will necessarily depend on the singular situation at hand, as it is perceived by the singular person who has to make that judgement).[12] Certainly there are Shakespearean scenes – Adriana's frustrated outburst is a prime example – that court such judgements, that invite us to consider whether someone who is criticised for complaining should be blamed, praised or merely excused

---

[11] 1126a. Citations are from Aristotle, *Nicomachean Ethics*, trans. Terence Irwin, 3rd edn (Indianapolis: Hackett, 2019). Other translations use 'be[ing] cross' (Crisp, Cambridge Texts in the History of Philosophy, 2000) or 'indignant' (Thomson and Tredennick, Penguin) in place of 'complaining'. Aristotle seems also to recognise a certain link between complaining and insubordination, insofar as he suggests that the virtuous man errs more in a deficiency than an excess of anger, as excessive calmness implies a certain 'slavishness', whereas anger and complaint show that a man is able 'to defend himself'.

[12] 'It is hard to define how, against whom, about what, and how long we should be angry, and up to what point someone is acting correctly or in error. ... It is not easy to answer in a general account; for the judgment depends on particular cases, and we make it by perception.' 1126b.

for doing so, and in eliciting such questions, some of these scenes foster what Bristol eloquently describes in Chapter 13 as 'a more responsive conception of what is reasonable that respects the experience of living in a world conditioned by chance, by the fragility of our shared social systems and by our obligation to honour the lifelong attachments we form with others'. But in turning now to the complaints brought against Richard III and Angelo, I want to turn away from the question of judgement, from deliberations about whether these complainers' anger is reasonable or their complaining (un)virtuous – a turn that I would suggest these scenes themselves enact, precisely in their ethical clarity.[13] In doing so, they activate and call forth different capacities of theatrical drama for conceptualising virtue: namely, its capacity to present and thus locate particular acts, including the activity of complaining, in what Julia Reinhard Lupton calls a 'virtue ecology', or 'a setting for action composed of social, political, economic, and environmental formations that differently afford and constrain the capacities for self-realization and civic participation for a range of persons and other actors on the scene'.[14] As I will argue, by situating complaining in plots of interruption – coordinated and choreographed outbursts of passion that disrupt the timing and *teloi* of others' unjust plots – these scenes represent complaining not as a sign of a character's individual virtue, but rather as an action through and around which various social virtue(s) flows. Here we find no patient people, only acts of complaint that illuminate the virtue of impatience.

Virtuous Complaining

Act 4, scene 4 of *Richard III* marks a turning point in the fortunes of Richard and the House of York, a pregnant moment recognised in the opening speech of the Lancastrian Queen Margaret, with whose solo entrance the scene begins: 'So now prosperity begins to mellow / And

---

[13] This is not to flatten the general moral complexity of either of these plays (especially the considerably more ambivalent *Measure for Measure*), but merely to say that *Richard III* makes Richard a patent villain, and *Measure for Measure* represents Angelo as someone who (at the very least) has erred with regard to the demand he makes of Isabella, his retraction of his oath to Mariana, and his abuse of his power, and the complaints against each man are clearly just. In a longer version of this paper I would want to connect these scenes' sidelining of ethical judgement about complaining to the fact that the complaints in these scenes are rooted in forms of complaint sanctioned as an alternative to disorderly violence (e.g., legal complaint).

[14] Julia Reinhard Lupton, 'After Sovereignty / *After Virtue*', SEL 58.1 (2018), 205–17 (p. 209).

drop into the rotten mouth of death' (4.4.1–2). But this 'now' is also that of a breaking point for the Yorkist women who have suffered by Richard's hand, and whose laments have throughout the play served as strange complements to Margaret's curses. At the start of this scene, those complaints would seem to have come to a dead end, though they continue: when they take the stage (causing Margaret to recede to watch) Queen Elizabeth and the Duchess of York enter complaining, but with words that have become 'dull' (4.4.118). Elizabeth's plaints, addressed to a god whose (in)action she challenges, verge on the insubordination that Calvin warns against ('Wilt Thou, O God, fly from such gentle lambs, / And throw them in the entrails of the wolf? / When didst Thou sleep when such a deed was done?' [4.4.17–19]). The Duchess suggests that grief has finally depleted her capacity even to complain ('So many miseries have crazed my voice / That my woe-wearied tongue is mute and dumb' [4.4.29–30]). But Margaret, by stepping forward to gloat by reciting their losses, at once refuels their passion and redirects it to its cause, by reminding them of what – that is, who – they had 'till a Richard killed him' (4.4.39). Continually remembered and repeated aloud, 'woes', Margaret suggests, can make even dull words 'sharp, and pierce' (4.4.119).

The scene goes on to dramatise how the women's complaining words pierce: how, in deciding to bring their complaints about Richard against Richard, they make what the Duchess has earlier described as a 'scene of rude impatience' that cuts into ('intercepts') his plans – a coordinated plot of their own that Shakespeare stages here as a physical interruption of the king's march (2.2.38). I quote the confrontation in full to capture its interruptive quality:

DUCHESS: Why should calamity be full of words?
QUEEN ELIZABETH:
. . .
    Let them have scope, though what they will impart
    Help nothing else, yet do they ease the heart.
DUCHESS: If so, then be not tongue-tied. Go with me,
    And in the breath of bitter words let's smother
    My damned son, that thy two sweet sons smothered.
                    [*Trumpet sounds.*]
    The trumpet sounds. Be copious in exclaims.
Enter KING RICHARD and his Train [including CATESBY], marching with drums and trumpets.
KING RICHARD: Who intercepts me in my expedition?
DUCHESS: O, she that might have intercepted thee,
    By strangling thee in her accursed womb,
    From all the slaughters, wretch, that thou hast done.
QUEEN ELIZABETH: Hid'st thou that forehead with a golden crown

Where should be graven, if that right were right,
The slaughter of the prince that owed that crown
And the dire death of my two sons and brothers?
Tell me, thou villain slave, where are my children?
DUCHESS: Thou toad, thou toad, where is thy brother Clarence,
And little Ned Plantagenet his son?
QUEEN ELIZABETH: Where is the gentle Rivers, Vaughan, Grey?
DUCHESS: Where is kind Hastings?
KING RICHARD: A flourish, trumpets! Strike alarum, drums!
Let not the heavens hear these tell-tale women
Rail on the Lord's anointed. Strike, I say! *Flourish. Alarums.*
Either be patient and entreat me fair,
Or with the clamorous report of war
Thus will I drown your exclamations.
. . .
DUCHESS: Then patiently hear my impatience. (4.4.120–50)

This scene bears out Bonnie Honig's argument, in her reading of Greek tragic drama, that one of the most powerful effects of the speech act of lamentation is interruption, which she understands as itself a type of speech act whose 'effect is that of stopping the current speaker or redirecting unfolding events, or even just trying to do so'.[15] The complaints through which the women 'intercept' Richard's 'expedition' are interruptive not of Richard's actual words, but rather of the procession and the power that is spoken, as it were, through its sounds, the drums and trumpets that proclaim his authority. (Indeed, Honig suggests that as a political tactic, interruption is especially potent when it causes disruptions in the normal procedures and workings of power, including the theatrics that sustain authority.) Notice that Richard cannot bear to hear these 'tell-tale women' – or, more to the point, to let their complaints be heard. Refusing Richard's demand that she 'be patient' and speak to him with respect, the Duchess readily admits to her 'impatience', which she demands that he hear (4.4.145, 150).

The Duchess and Elizabeth do in fact embody the impatience that complainers are said to exemplify, but Shakespeare suggests that this is not a bad thing. On the contrary, the scene casts impatience as a virtue, to the extent that it is on the side of justice. As we see here, impatience can be resistance to an unjust authority figure, or a refusal to be silent in the face of injustice (or, for that matter, to have the tone of one's speech determined by someone else). Often cast as a deficit (a 'want of endurance' and a 'failure to bear suffering . . . with equanimity' are both among the definitions of the word), impatience involves a certain

---

[15] Bonnie Honig, *Antigone, Interrupted* (Cambridge: Cambridge University Press, 2013), p. 3.

excess energy too: an 'intolerance of delay', a 'restless longing or eagerness'.[16] Another way to put this is to say that impatience means a heightened sensitivity to the way that time adds weight to suffering. As a materialisation of impatience, the act of complaining may – as it does in this case – interrupt the 'normal' flow of time for the sake of hastening justice. It is that immediately interruptive force of complaining (and not necessarily its longer-term outcome or effect, a matter about which the play is famously ambiguous) that *Richard III* demonstrates so vividly.[17]

The scene of complaint that comprises the climactic final scene of *Measure for Measure* stages a similar interruption, also animated by an impatience for justice – an impatience that in this instance calls forth, in turn, the virtue of courage. The interruptive potential of complaining is rendered less literally here than in the scene of complaint from *Richard III*, but here Shakespeare draws a clearer causal connection between an interruptive act of complaint and a just end, for Isabella's complaint catalyses the public exposure of Angelo, shattering his reputation and revealing the truth that 'all his dressings, caracts, titles, forms' have given cover to (5.1.61), the shelter of his power that he thinks puts him beyond the law ('For my authority bears so far credent bulk / That no particular scandal once can touch / But it confounds the breather' [4.4.21–6]). It's also worth noting that this interruption is linked to a certain reparative end, when the complaints have been heard, Angelo has been exposed, and the Duke, having reassumed his authority, makes his judgments and decisions. (Reparative in a formal sense, at least: gestures towards resolution and new futures are made, though the actual arrangements themselves are of course rife with their own problems, as has often been observed about the play's conclusion.) What I am most interested in here, however, is not the way in which the scene ends, but rather how it shows the activity of complaining occurring in a present marked by the absence of such knowledge.

The whole scene is framed as a drama carefully choreographed by the Duke through his disguise as Friar Lodowick and his letter to Angelo, which creates the occasion for the action to occur (he instructs Angelo to 'proclaim it an hour before his [the Duke's] entering, that if any crave

---

[16] *OED* s.b. 'patience' n. 1a. 2a.

[17] Many critics have explored the causal efficacy of the various forms of complaint in the play (lament, curse, prayers to God, the ghosts' complaints) with regard to Richard's eventual defeat and death. See, for instance, Lynne Magnusson, 'Grammatical Theatricality in *Richard III*: Schoolroom Queens and Godly Optatives', *Shakespeare Quarterly* 64.1 (2013), 32–43 and Gina Bloom, *Voice in Motion: Staging Gender, Shaping Sound in Early Modern England* (Philadelphia: University of Pennsylvania Press, 2007).

redress of injustice, they should exhibit their petitions in the street', to 'have a dispatch of complaints' [4.4.7–9, 10–11]). But if the Duke is the architect of the plot, Isabella is its lead actor, and she knows only her own part. Enraged at the injustice of (what she believes was) Claudio's execution, and having rejected Friar Lodowick's counsel to 'Show your wisdom, daughter, in your close patience', she agrees to his scheme to bring a complaint against Angelo to the Duke as he enters the city gate (4.3.112). The success of the plot hinges on her trust in Friar Lodowick – a trust that is increasingly put to the test as the scene progresses – and her courage. Recall Angelo's expressed certainty that Isabella will not dare expose herself to shame by bringing a complaint against him:

> A deflowered maid,
> And by an eminent body that enforced
> The law against it? But that her tender shame
> Will not proclaim against her maiden loss,
> How might she tongue me? Yet reason dares her no (4.4.19–23)

Reason may say no, but impatience (a rejection of the counsel to be 'close') says yes. Act 5 begins with the entrance at last of the Duke and his retinue, including Angelo, surrounded by citizens. Isabella enters into this public scene. At the right time – cued by Friar Peter – she steps forward, falls to her knees, and speaks:

> PETER: Now is your time: speak loud, and kneel before him.
> ISABELLA: Justice, O royal Duke! vail your regard
>   Upon a wronged – I would fain have said a maid.
>   O worthy prince, dishonor not your eye
>   By throwing it on any other object
>   Till you have heard me in my true complaint
>   And given me justice, justice, justice, justice.
> DUKE: Relate your wrongs: in what, by whom? Be brief. (5.1.20–8)

The scene demonstrates the extent to which Angelo has underestimated Isabella's courage.[18] Having made her accusation, she is immediately dismissed: Angelo suggests her 'wits' to be 'not firm', and the Duke echoes his judgement, calling her a 'poor soul' who 'speaks this in th'infirmity of sense', a phrase that recalls defences as well as criticisms of complaint as merely outbursts of passion (5.1.36, 51, 52). Her anguished cry when she is arrested expresses despair for her apparent failure, tinged with faith in otherworldly justice:

---

[18] Here it's important to note that the complaint Isabella brings does in fact risk her honour, insofar as she suggests that it was she, rather than Mariana, who was in bed with Angelo.

> And is this all?
> Then, O you blessed ministers above,
> Keep me in patience, and with ripened time
> Unfold the evil which is here wrapped up
> In countenance! (5.1.120–4)

It is only now that Isabella embraces 'patience' – now, when she believes that this is all, that she has played her part to its conclusion and done all she can do. Her impatience has given her courage to go beyond what 'reason dares', and to seize the 'now' that is, as Friar Peter puts it, her time – the moment in which she can act. Insofar as the theatrical audience knows more than Isabella does, the backdrop of uncertainty against which her action unfolds is especially palpable: we watch her act without the assurance of knowing how exactly the events her complaint has set in motion will unfold, without any knowledge of how the story will end. That impatience can disrupt the processes of rational thought is one of its problems, its risks, but it can also be one of the virtues of this peculiar virtue.

Carolyn Sale suggests that in performance, a play effects 'its own distribution of resources, its own "publishing" of certain "virtues,"' virtues that audiences may carry with them out of the theatre. I have been exploring how Shakespearean scenes of complaint that showcase impatience also reveal and illuminate its virtuous kernel – the capacity of impatience to further justice, to foster courage, to speak the truth and, through its own irruptive quality, to interrupt time lines, rationales and plots that obstruct human flourishing. In complaining, dramatic characters give voice to what they care about, what they value, what they want. We might see complaining, then, not as a signifier of moral character, as it has often been said to be, but rather as an expression of longing that reflects an idea about what the good life is (and is not): though early modern texts often pit the figure of the impassioned complainer against a seemingly more disinterested figure who speaks on behalf of a moralising 'philosophy', a complaint, too, opens onto – embeds, reflects, shapes, galvanises – philosophy, at the levels both of abstract thought and lived experience. The desire and discontent articulated in the complaints that fill Shakespeare's plays – complaints about abuses of power, gender inequity, discrimination, the heaviness of grief – must surely have resonated with various early modern theatregoers, whose own impatience may have been intensified or even sparked by seeing it flare up on stage, simultaneously close and at a remove. And these scenes of complaint, many of which are affective flashpoints (think of Lear, howling; Shylock, protesting; Caliban, cursing; Lavinia, writing; the citizens of *Coriolanus*, agitating), continue to offer the opportunity for particular productions to speak to and cultivate the impatience of their particular audiences, to encourage them to consider the objects of their desire and the causes of their dissatisfaction, to make the concerns and crises – the cares – of a play or its characters feel urgent to us, whoever 'we' are.[19] Such possibilities, which are necessarily more than what is 'in' Shakespeare, are built into the virtue ecology – the field of potential for action – that is the play itself, in its situated performances. As theatrical set pieces that attune us to an everyday and an *everywhere* speech act, scenes of complaint are sites of possibility for the play to turn towards the world and its many arenas of complaint, theatres in which we might alternately and at different moments find ourselves called to play the role of witness, listener, judge, addressee or speaker.

---

[19] On the way in which US productions of *Measure for Measure* became charged with such meanings in the wake of the explosion of the #MeToo movement in 2017 and Christine Blasey Ford's testimony to Congress about Brett Kavanaugh in the fall of 2018, see Laura Kolb, 'The Very Modern Anger of Shakespeare's Women', *Electric Literature*, 6 February 2019, available at https://electricliterature.com/the-very-modern-anger-of -shakespeares-women/ (accessed 16 January 2023). Criticism, too, is a site of making these connections; for example, see Jessica Walker's discussion of the parallels between Shylock's complaints and Black Lives Matter protests, '"What Should His Sufferance Be?" Protesting Injustice in Shakespeare's Venice and the Age of Black Lives Matter', *Journal of American Studies* 54.1 (2020), 44–50.

Chapter 5

Masculine *Virtù* and Feminine Virtue in *Much Ado About Nothing*

Kristina Sutherland

The enduring popularity of *Much Ado About Nothing* suggests that we, the public, make much of Shakespeare's characters indeed. The play can easily be considered one of Shakespeare's top ten scripts, and the castings of Benedick and Beatrice suggest that they are part of the play's success.[1] With A-list actors such as Kenneth Branagh and Emma Thompson or television stars David Tennant and Catherine Tate portraying these bantering lovers, one gets a sense of not only the importance of these characters, but also their popularity.[2] Despite the brutal depiction of the consequences of the cult of chastity, in which a villain's word can bring dishonour and death to a virtuous woman, audiences still delight in the 'kind of merry war betwixt' the two avowed bachelors (1.1.57). It is not star power alone that brings spectators to these performances of Shakespeare's witty couple on stage and film, but the depiction of something greater, a love story founded in what I will term 'virtue *virtuosa*' – a performance of ingenuity, strength and fidelity that transcends and transforms the stifling patriarchal structure of Messina.

The engagement of Hero and Claudio highlights the tension inherent in the social conditions of court life by contrasting the behaviours that early modern society idealised for each gender: latent virtues such as chastity, modesty, obedience and fidelity for women, and the more

---

[1] Eric Minton, 'Shakespeare Plays Popularity Index', Shakespearances.com, available at http://www.shakespeareances.com/wherewill/Play_Popularity_Index.html. Minton ranks the bard's work according to live production frequency, and showed *Much Ado* tied in sixth place with *As You Like It* for performances between 2012 and 25 May 2020. All references to Shakespeare's work come from *The Complete Works*, ed. Stephen Orgel and A. R. Braunmuller, The New Pelican Text (New York: Penguin, 2002), Internet Archive: Kahle/Austin Foundation, available at https://archive.org/details/completewor ks0000shak_b3y7.

[2] Kenneth Branagh, *Much Ado About Nothing* (Culver City, CA: Samuel Goldwyn Company, in association with American Playhouse Theatrical Films, 1993); Josie Rourke, *Much Ado About Nothing* (filmed at Wyndham Theatre, London; Digital Theatre, 2011).

active quality of *virtù*, a combination of strength, ingenuity, talent and other abilities for men. Early modern social constructs did not restrict all these qualities to one gender or the other, but certain aspects were deemed more important for women than men, and vice versa. For women, the virtue of chastity was elevated above all else. The priority of chastity as the primary feminine virtue is seen in Juan Luis Vives's chapter 'On Virginity' in *The Education of a Christian Woman*, as well as Baldassare Castiglione's *The Book of the Courtier*, where it is alluded to using the Italian terms 'onestà' (honesty) and 'continenzia' (temperance or self-restraint).[3] Though Castiglione's work does not call for the female courtier to remain silent, the ideal behaviour ascribed to women is described in terms of restrictions:

> her serene and modest behaviour, and the candour that ought to inform all her actions, should be accompanied by a quick and vivacious spirit by which she shows her freedom from boorishness; but with such a virtuous manner that she makes herself thought no less chaste, prudent and benign than she is pleasing, witty and discreet. Thus she must observe a certain difficult mean, composed as it were of contrasting qualities, and take care not to stray beyond certain fixed limits.[4]

Other qualities Vives considers important are obedience, modesty, humility, domestic industry and especially silence or restraint in speech.[5] In other words, while women were expected to be witty and lively, they still needed to cultivate an image of meekness and mildness. Latent traits like chastity, obedience, modesty and fidelity were thus part of the ideal behaviour for women.

In general, more patent or active qualities like strength, talent and ingenuity were more essential to the male courtier. As early modern courts developed, so too did the concept of what the behaviour of an elite man should entail. Before, the standard of masculine conduct was the Roman concept of *virtus*, 'i.e. the sum of all the corporeal or mental excellences of man, strength, vigor; bravery, courage; aptness, capacity; worth, excellence, virtue, etc.'.[6] In Italy, this ideal masculinity expanded

---

[3] Juan Luis Vives, 'On Virginity,' in *The Education of a Christian Woman: A Sixteenth-Century Manual*, ed. and trans. Charles Fantazzi (Chicago: University of Chicago Press, 2000), pp. 80–6; Baldassare Castiglione, *Il libro del Cortegiano*, 2nd edn, ed. Ettore Bonora and Paolo Zoccola (Milan: Mursia, 1976), pp. 196–204, pp. 212–14, p. 216, p. 240, pp. 244–5, pp. 247–53 and p. 263.

[4] Baldassare Castiglione, *The Book of the Courtier*, trans. George Bull, rev. edn (London: Penguin, 1976), p. 212.

[5] See, for instance, Vives, *Education of a Christian Woman*, pp. 70–3, 113–18 and 132–3.

[6] Charlton T. Lewis and Charles Short, *A Latin Dictionary* (Oxford: Clarendon Press, 1879), s.v. 'virtūs, ūtis'.

in the fourteenth, fifteenth and sixteenth centuries into the concept of *virtù*, defined simplest as 'Merit, Excellence of good quality'.[7] This concept combines the strength and ability already found in *virtus* with prowess, decisiveness, ruthlessness and cunning.[8] Ingenuity, cleverness and talent likewise became aspects of *virtù*.[9] As texts like *The Courtier* became available outside of Italy, the concept of *virtù* spread throughout Europe. While such works discussed the importance of various behaviours for men, they emphasised employing the characteristics of *virtù* in an active manner, such as demonstrating battle prowess and, more so because of its greater frequency, participation in civil conversation. Modesty and discretion were important, but more important was demonstrating one's aptness for guiding one's ruler to choose honourable actions and eschew vice.[10] As this was, according to Castiglione, 'the best end of all' for the efforts of a courtier, the use of *virtù* at court should be viewed as the praxis of the humanist doctrine of *vita activa* (active life), or elite participation in social reform as a politician, diplomat or royal adviser.[11]

Shakespeare's bride and groom are the embodiments of these traits. Hero has perfected her performance as the ideal lady. She is generally quiet in mixed company but not unsociable, and submissive and obedient to her father even when his desire for a princely son-in-law crosses her own preference for Claudio. Similarly, her groom is the very semblance of *virtù*, achieving in the recent war 'the feats of a lion' despite his youth and contributing to the prince's matchmaking scheme with his own sharp wits (1.1.15). Yet the crux of this relationship demonstrates the power differential found in the patriarchal construct of early modern conduct. Claudio and Don John employ their *virtù* to preserve their own honour by turning Hero's virtue against her and sacrificing her at the marital altar. The confrontation emphasises the ways in which early modern gendered standards of conduct restrict women's behaviour as well as their agency while enabling men to actively and

---

[7] Guido Ruggiero, *Machiavelli in Love: Sex, Self, and Society in the Italian Renaissance* (Baltimore, MD: Johns Hopkins University Press, 2007), pp. 86–7; Accademia della Crusca, *Vocabolario degli Accademici della Crusca*, 4th edn, 6 vols (Florence, 1729–38), s.v. 'virtù, virtude, e virtute'.

[8] Timo Airaksinen, 'Against All the Odds: Machiavelli on Fortune in Politics', in *Niccolò Machiavelli: History, Power, and Virtue*, ed. Leonidas Donskis (Amsterdam: Rodopi, 2011), pp. 3–14 (p. 13).

[9] Mark Musa, introduction to *The Prince*, by Niccolò Machiavelli, ed. and trans. Mark Musa (New York: St. Martin's Press, 1964), p. xv.

[10] Castiglione, *The Book of the Courtier*, pp. 284–5.

[11] Ibid., p. 285; Margo Todd, *Christian Humanism and the Puritan Social Order* (Cambridge: Cambridge University Press, 1987), pp. 33–43.

aggressively pursue their goals and defend their reputation, even at the cost of others.

Shakespeare offsets this cultural imbalance by bringing to the forefront his second couple, Beatrice and Benedick. His creation of Beatrice gives a feminine counter to the social problem of privileging honour to such a degree as to sanction violence. Outspoken yet courteous, assertive but not domineering, Beatrice is a woman of wit and strength – a lady of *virtù* – and a perfect match for Benedick, the one man determined enough to continuously engage with her in verbal spars. When Hero is slandered, Beatrice enlists Benedick to the bride's cause, effecting his transformation from misogynist to women's champion. Their courtship is a continuous act of virtuosity, in the sense detailed by Paolo Virno, as a performance of a *virtuoso*'s artistic capabilities which is by nature public and active, and therefore political.[12] Their acts subvert the social structures which imperil women through the veneration of chastity and sanction masculine aggression in the name of demonstrating *virtù* and defending honour. As they model a companionate relationship based on their status as rivals and equals, Beatrice and Benedick continue to perform the wit, strength and ingenuity for which they are known along with fidelity, humility and endurance. Furthermore, they seek to actively address the wrongs suffered by Hero. Beatrice and Benedick thus embody a virtue *virtuosa*, a radical standard of conduct capable of improving the community by tempering *virtù* through the valorisation of latent virtues traditionally emphasised as 'feminine' qualities, while also actively moderating and excising the violence caused by privileging men's honour and licensing masculine aggression.

'The poison of that'

It is entirely fitting that the man who disrupts the festive atmosphere of the play is himself of illegitimate issue, given that Don John uses the communal fear of women's inconstancy to poison the court. Yet it is not he alone who destroys the communal feeling, for he is aided by the very group which Harry Berger, Jr, refers to as 'the Men's Club of Messina'.[13] Don John does not create the imbalance between genders by influencing Don Pedro, Claudio and Leonato, for they already ascribe to the early

---

[12] Paolo Virno, *A Grammar of the Multitude: For an Analysis of Contemporary Forms of Life*, trans. Isabella Bertoletti, James Cascaito and Andrea Casson (Los Angeles: Semiotext(e), 2004), pp. 52–6.

[13] Harry Berger, Jr, 'Against the Sink-A-Pace: Sexual and Family Politics in *Much Ado About Nothing*', *Shakespeare Quarterly* 33.3 (1982), 302–13 (p. 305).

modern cult which venerates chastity above all other virtues in women. Like Vives, they too believe that 'the principal female virtue is chastity, and it is in itself the equal of all the others in moral worth. If this is present, one need not look for others, and if it is absent, one should disregard the others.'[14] The Men's Club is emblematic of the inherent problem of this cult. The prioritisation of chastity makes a woman with additional virtues a 'rich and precious gift', but even the appearance of incontinence renders her a 'rotten orange' (4.1.27, 31). Accordingly, conduct manuals suggest that women maintain their good reputation by controlling how others perceive them – as Castiglione puts it, one must act so 'that *she makes herself thought* no less chaste'.[15] The problem with public perception, however, is that it cannot be controlled by the person in question. It is not enough for Hero to successfully act both witty and reserved, for she is only as chaste as others perceive her to be. With such importance placed upon not only being chaste but also having the reputation of chastity, suspicion of incontinence is enough to corrupt.

Such an attitude practically justifies the responses seen when Claudio charges Hero with lascivious behaviour. Recounting both ancient and contemporary assaults against incontinent women, Vives states that

> It is not to be marveled at that such things are done by parents and close friends and that feelings of affection are suddenly changed into the most violent hatred, since these young women themselves, victims of a detestable and savage love, casting away all filial piety from their hearts, have shown hatred for their parents, brothers, even their children, not merely friends and relatives.[16]

Vives's perception of such filicides and sororicides suggests that the loss of a woman's chastity was seen as its own act of violence, and that the murder of a woman guilty of incontinence was an act of recompense and revenge for the familial loss of honour. The machinations of Don John rely on such social constructions which conflate chastity with honour and lasciviousness with a loss of reputation for the entire family. The false claim against Hero preys on the men's anxieties as the accusation, once accepted by the public, is not just a reflection on Hero herself. As Borachio well knows, the perception of wantonness in the bride will also harm the reputations of her suitor and his proxy. Knowing the significance which Don Pedro and Claudio place on their reputations, Borachio advises Don John to weaponise their concerns by appealing to the prince 'as, in love of your brother's honor, who hath made this

[14] Vives, *Education of a Christian Woman*, p. 116.
[15] Castiglione, *The Book of the Courtier*, p. 212. Emphasis mine.
[16] Vives, *Education of a Christian Woman*, p. 84.

match, and his friend's reputation, who is thus like to be cozened with the semblance of a maid' (2.2.33–6). Under this guise of consideration, Don John is thus able to lead his brother and Claudio to strike Hero down with slander to preserve their own reputations.

Though Leonato, Claudio and Don Pedro all prize chastity, they also ascribe to the belief voiced early on by Benedick that a married man is a cuckolded one. Early modern elite marriages, such as the one Claudio hopes to achieve, were typically 'arranged by families with a view to securing advantages or alliances, conforming to a patriarchal model. It was expected that aristocratic children would submit willingly to such marriages, happy to comply with paternal wishes'.[17] Negotiated by the families with concerns for reputation, status and future generations in mind, such an arrangement could not guarantee that the couple would form an emotional bond, let alone amity. Michel de Montaigne, for one, finds friendship and marriage quite incompatible:

> As for marriage, for one thing it is a bargain to which only the entrance is free – its continuance being constrained and forced, depending otherwise than on our will – and a bargain ordinarily made for other ends. For another, there supervene a thousand foreign tangles to unravel, enough to break the thread and trouble the course of a lively affection; whereas in friendship there are no dealings or business except with itself.[18]

Such negotiations could leave little room for companionship in a marriage where husband and wife were bound by their obligations to outside parties. This view of marriage as a commitment without the strong spiritual bond of friendship is part of the cultural construct which forms the views of the Men's Club. They believe that a married man 'will wear his cap with suspicion' of his wife's infidelity precisely because they do not believe that men and women form such a bond in marriage (1.1.189).

Her father, groom and matchmaker, Leonato, Claudio and Don Pedro, all rely on Hero's chastity as it reflects on their own honour, but her reputation and performance of virtue is not enough to defend her against their suspicions. Don John's snare therefore does the same work as Iago's traps in *Othello*. The accusation of unfaithfulness and the illusion produced with the help of Borachio 'turn [Hero's] virtue into pitch' by provoking the paranoia of the Men's Club (*Othello*, 2.3.348). Like Iago, Don John does not simply make the lady look dishonourable.

---

[17] B. J. Sokol and Mary Sokol, *Shakespeare, Law, and Marriage* (Cambridge: Cambridge University Press, 2003), p. 30.

[18] Michel de Montaigne, 'Of Friendship', in *The Complete Works: Essays, Travel Journal, Letters*, trans. Donald M. Frame (New York: Alfred A. Knopf, 2003), p. 164–76 (p. 167).

He alters the way in which the others assess her virtues. As with Desdemona's innocent concern for Cassio, Hero's chaste blushes and protestations cease to be signs of her goodness and instead become part of the framework that remodels her as guilty and deceptive. Her perfection of latent 'feminine' virtues thus becomes a weakness.

Just as virtue fails to protect Hero, so does *virtù*. The wit and strength of Claudio and Don Pedro are not enough to overcome their anxieties regarding their reputations and women's sexuality. They are both unable to answer as Orlando does in *As You Like It* that 'Virtue is no horn-maker' when Don John invites them to view misdeeds at Hero's window (4.1.58). Mistrust of women and personal concern for honour cause Claudio and Don Pedro to follow Don John's lead. Furthermore, the violence of the public denouncement is licensed by the very standards of conduct on which the men rely. A vital part of *virtù* includes the aggressive defence of one's reputation; honour was guarded vehemently and violence 'was often the only acceptable response' to threats and insults.[19] Once they decide to trust Don John rather than the virtuous Hero, Claudio and Don Pedro therefore also resolve to 'proceed accordingly', as the villain puts it (3.2.110). As their decision comes in anticipation of seeing a dishonourable act rather than in reaction to one, however, their actions are based less on the appearance of proof provided and more on their general mistrust of women. They resolve to act before confirming the need to do so because they decide the question of Hero's guilt when Don John approaches them, not when they see Borachio and Margaret. The deception merely serves to confirm their mistrust in Hero, when their wits should question their trust in Don John. Hero is thus undone by both her own virtue and 'the very bent of honor' (4.1.186). With the two war heroes defending themselves militantly and her own character so based in passive traits, the disgraced bride must wait for vindication and resolution from an outside source.

Shakespeare's Hero is not singular in her predicament, trapped as she is by the expectations of how virtuous women should act, the cultural suspicions that no women behave virtuously in private, and the desperate acts of men of *virtù* seeking to maintain their reputations at all costs. Two similar tales depict women of exceeding virtue brought down by illusions like the one orchestrated by Don John and Borachio. In the portion of *Orlando Furioso* considered to be one source for Shakespeare's story, Ludovico Ariosto's lover Ariodante originally finds security in the word of Princess Guinevere that she will marry him or marry no one due to her chastity:

[19] Ruggiero, *Machiavelli in Love*, p. 94.

He had no other proofs or need
for any. He had expected none from a soul
as pure and fine as hers.[20]

In Giovan Battista Della Porta's theatrical version of this spurned bride tale, the lover Don Ignazio is rebuked by his beloved's aunt when she believes him to be seducing rather than wooing:

> Know that even if my niece Carizia is young, she hides ripe virtue under her green age, hoary wisdom under that blonde hair, mature counsel under that young breast; and though she is poor in gold, her honor prevents her feeling any want, for she thinks herself rich in honor and integrity; within her chastity are enclosed her treasure and her dowry.[21]

Carizia's sensibilities and virtues inspire such a deep protectiveness that her aunt is reluctant to speak to Don Ignazio or allow him to speak to his beloved. Yet such virtuous women are not immune to false accusations and subsequent abandonment. Struck with the semblance of Guinevere's incontinence, Ariodante seemingly kills himself. His brother's grief leads him to disclose what he and Ariodante believed they saw at Guinevere's window, which in turn puts her in mortal danger due to local law. Carizia is undone by masculine rivalry as Don Ignazio's own brother accuses the bride of being a sex worker and produces stolen clothing and jewellery as proof. The result of Don Ignazio's refusal of Carizia is much the same as at Hero's wedding, with attempted filicide and the shame of such slander nearly killing the bride.

'She were an excellent wife for Benedick'

While Guinevere and Carizia find themselves belied and abandoned, Hero has a defender in place from the beginning. Shakespeare's creations of Beatrice and her counterpart Benedick not only serve as a comedic focus of the play, but also act as a counter to the cultural imbalance Don John utilises to create disorder in his princely brother's court. Though Hero is eventually vindicated by the 'dissembly' of the watch, the play does not rely on the letter of the law to condemn the men's excessive use of aggression (4.2.1). Just as the extreme adherence to the patriarchal constructs of behaviour make possible the betrayal of Hero, the courtship of Beatrice and Benedick propagates the play's comic conclusion

---

[20] Ludovico Ariosto, *Orlando Furioso*, trans. David R. Slavitt (Cambridge, MA: The Belknap Press, 2009), 5.35 (p. 72). For her promise, see 5.32–3 (p. 71).
[21] Giovan Battista Della Porta, *Gli duoi fratelli rivali: The Two Rival Brothers*, ed. and trans. Louise George Clubb (Berkeley: University of California Press, 1980), 2.2 (p. 101).

by providing a more nuanced model of conduct, a virtue *virtuosa* which rejects the masculine violence of *virtù* and actively validates women through public support.

Beatrice provides the first paradigm of this virtue *virtuosa*. Obviously not content to play the same part as her cousin, that of the silent and modest potential bride, she seizes the rights and *virtù* naturally granted to men at court for herself without losing the reputation of a virtuous woman. Carol Cook writes that Beatrice 'refuses the subjection of femininity, of castration, by placing herself among the men and wielding phallic wit as aggressively as they'.[22] Beatrice asserts her own agency, holding on to her unmarried status despite her family's concerns, and employs her ingenuity to assert herself. Just as Don Pedro and Claudio use metaphors of war to speak of wooing, so too do the characters describe Beatrice's wit as 'a kind of merry war', with Benedick especially complaining of her martial spirit (1.1.56–7). He says her jests left him 'like a man at a mark, with a whole army shooting at me. She speaks poniards, and every word stabs' (2.1.233–5). Furthermore, he quips that she would domesticate Hercules and refers to her as 'the infernal Ate' (2.1.239–42). This last comparison makes her a goddess considered in some texts as 'an ancient Greek divinity, who led both gods and men to rash and inconsiderate actions and to suffering', but who is also depicted in tragedies as one who 'avenges evil deeds and inflicts just punishments upon the offenders and their posterity'.[23] Benedick means, of course, to complain about her usurping masculine power, and more so outperforming him in demonstrating *virtù*, but these comparisons mark Beatrice as not only possessing *virtù* but also effectively wielding it.

Further proof of Beatrice's *virtù* appears as Don Pedro and his companions implement their elaborate jest, the Herculean task of fooling the two wittiest people in Messina so that they fall in love with each other. To some extent, when Don Pedro, Claudio and Leonato give evidence of Beatrice's valorous struggle with affection, one must remember that the actions they report are fictitious. Beatrice has not yet allowed herself to succumb. Their depiction, however, is not one of women's love sickness, often termed 'green sickness' in the early modern age. The symptoms of this supposedly female disease were inactivity and weakness – 'they grow lazy, and idle, and will hardly stir; their pulse beats little and

[22] Carol Cook, '"The sign and semblance of her honor": Reading Gender Differences in *Much Ado About Nothing*', *PMLA* 101.2 (1986), 186–202 (p. 190).
[23] William Smith (ed.), *A Dictionary of Greek and Roman Biography and Mythology* (London, c. 1873), s.v. 'Ate'.

faint'.[24] Instead, the men paint a portrait of a martial Beatrice, who, though they thought her 'invincible against all assaults of affection', is yet so tormented that she feels 'enraged affection' and may 'do a desperate outrage to herself' (2.3.113–14, 100, 148–9). What gives verisimilitude to the deception, then, is not a caricature of 'feminine' love, but a basis in Beatrice's publicly known *virtù*.

This fictional portrait of love successfully begins the transformation of Benedick. Rather than cling to his prior imagery of Beatrice as a 'harpy', that mythical creature of feminine looks and demonic behaviour, Benedick drops all misogynistic imagery and confirms his friends' appraisal of Beatrice's character:

> They say the lady is fair – 'tis a truth, I can bear them witness; and virtuous – 'tis so, I cannot reprove it; and wise, but for loving me – by my troth, it is no addition to her wit, nor no great argument of her folly, for I will be horribly in love with her. (2.1.256; 2.3.219–23)

Benedick also discards his pride, adopting the passive virtues of humility and endurance. Rather than take offence at the accusations that he 'hath a contemptible spirit' and would 'torment the poor lady', he focuses on reformation: 'I must not seem proud. Happy are they that hear their detractions and can put them to mending' (2.3.175, 153, 217–19). He also chooses to do what he has been unable to do thus far in the play. Until this moment, he has been incapable of taking quips of criticism in his stride. As Benedick determines to enter the state of matrimony despite his previous contempt of married men, he now resigns himself to the very sort of cutting remarks he himself only recently used against Claudio:

> I may chance have some odd quirks and remnants of wit broken on me because I have railed so long against marriage. But doth not the appetite alter? A man loves the meat in his youth that he cannot endure in his age. Shall quips and sentences and these paper bullets of the brain awe a man from the career of his humor? No, the world must be peopled. (2.3.223–30)

Confirming that Beatrice is a worthy lady of virtue and *virtù*, Benedick places his pride aside in consideration of her supposed feelings of love. He turns his compassion for her reported pain into his own passion and humour, and elects to endure rather than verbally spar with those who will mock him. This conversion is sudden but considerable.

The significance of Benedick's transformation doubles as Hero and Margaret enact the second trap to the same ends. Hearing herself

---

[24] Jane Sharp, *The Midwives Book, or, The Whole Art of Midwifry Discovered* (London, 1671), p. 258.

described as 'too disdainful' and accused of 'never giv[ing] to truth and virtue that / Which simpleness and merit purchaseth', Beatrice too drops her pride and scorn (3.1.34, 69–70). Bidding 'Contempt, farewell! and maiden pride, adieu!', Beatrice determines, as Benedick did, to love her former enemy (3.1.109). The doubled conversion from proud bachelor to compassionate lover marks the beginning of a companionate court-ship, a new construction of marriage founded not only in love but also in friendship, a meeting of equals rather than two people separated by different standards of conduct. This alternative to the portrayal of early modern marriage painted by Montaigne is not, in fact, dependent upon the independence of the two parties involved. Though Beatrice has no father present to direct her in her choice of spouse and Benedick has no kinsmen to negotiate the financial terms of a marriage, it is not this supposed freedom from outside interests that makes their match differ from that of Hero and Claudio. Rather, what sets Beatrice and Benedick apart is their resolve to change and embrace the other with understand-ing, which leads to the spiritual bonding which Montaigne reserved for friendships.

The idea of a companionate marriage, the blending of the union of bodies with the union of souls, was not entirely alien to early modern Europe, but neither was it widely practised. Erasmus's 'deliberately unconventional' treatise on *The Institution of Christian Matrimony* gives advice on how to enter and conduct a marriage in such a way as to have the deep spiritual bond of friendship between spouses.[25] For him, a true marriage was not the legal transaction described by Montaigne, 'but one that is cemented between equals in virtue by true affection; a union founded on moral qualities will very rarely fall apart'.[26] Erasmus advises potential spouses – or their families – to ensure that the bride and groom are suitable and have 'a temperament that will make for a harmonious union'.[27] Beatrice and Benedick are a fit match, and fol-lowing the admonishments of their friends, they are more than willing to do as Erasmus advises newlyweds, namely to 'lay aside that aggres-siveness which is so characteristic of inexperienced young women and hot-blooded adolescents and [. . .] take up the common yoke with docil-ity and make allowances for the other'.[28] Just as Benedick decides to

---

[25] Michael Heath, introduction to Desiderius Erasmus, *The Institution of Christian Matrimony*, trans. Michael Heath, in *Spiritualia and Pastoralia*, ed. John W. O'Malley and Louis A. Perraud, *Collected Works of Erasmus*, vol. 69 (Toronto: University of Toronto Press, 1999), 204–13 (p. 204).
[26] Erasmus, *The Institution of Christian Matrimony*, p. 227.
[27] Ibid., p. 311.
[28] Ibid., p. 335.

mend his faults, so Beatrice too declares 'I will requite thee, / Taming my wild heart to thy loving hand' (3.1.111–12). So resolved, the 'merry war' begins to form a new model by which spiritual coupling promises security from infidelity and tragedy in wedlock.

'Enough, I am engaged'

The transformation of Benedick and Beatrice continues as the public disgrace of Hero prompts Benedick to demonstrate his new alliance. Whereas the accusations of Don Pedro and Claudio emphasise the imbalance of power between the sexes, the scene which follows them shows the more just approach of virtue *virtuosa* in which *virtù* is used to support rather than dominate feminine virtue. At the wedding Benedick is not merely a discerning guest concerned for all parties, but a man who actively allies himself with the feminine. He avoids the conventional trap of believing all women guilty of lasciviousness and continues to display his newly found virtues of humility and endurance. Though his friendship with Don Pedro and Claudio means his reputation is also at stake, Benedick does not accept the report of Hero's dishonour even at the word of such esteemed men. He instead watches the scene unfold, taking in the details of the story as well as the reactions to it. With such circumspection, Benedick discerns rather quickly the source of the problem:

> Two of them have the very bent of honor;
> And if their wisdoms be misled in this,
> The practice of it lives in John the Bastard. (4.1.186–8)

Benedick proves his alliance by remaining with the ladies, inquiring after Hero, pacifying Leonato, and prompting Beatrice to help testify about her cousin's chastity. Although a military man, he takes on roles traditionally assigned to women as he becomes caregiver and peacemaker. This is part of his virtue *virtuosa*, as he uses his *virtù* to help persuade the enraged and humiliated Leonato of his daughter's innocence. He also offers private recompense:

> . . . by mine honor, I will deal in this
> As secretly and justly as your soul
> Should with your body. (4.1.247–9)

Though this seems like a plan for secretive action, we may imagine that Benedick plans another act of virtuosity, that of using his talents to convince his friends of the villainy of Don John and the virtue of Hero. Though his audience would be but two people, it would nevertheless be an effort to correct the political imbalance between the genders caused by the false accusations. Private acts of virtuosity do not seem to be enough for the early modern setting, as the play itself insists on communal redemption for Hero.

As Benedick and Beatrice begin to speak alone, slowly revealing their newfound affection for each other, they continue to develop this model of virtue *virtuosa* in a scene which calls attention to the need for virtuosity, that is, public action, in the face of injustice. Benedick voices his concern for Beatrice's feelings and the honour of her cousin, and for her part, she begins to cautiously invite Benedick to prove himself:

> BENEDICK: Surely I do believe your fair cousin is wronged.
> BEATRICE: Ah, how much might the man deserve of me that would right her!
> BENEDICK: Is there any way to show such friendship?
> BEATRICE: A very even way, but no such friend.
> BENEDICK: May a man do it?
> BEATRICE: It is a man's office, but not yours. (4.1.259–66)

Beatrice proposes that Benedick 'right' Hero while admitting that she has no rights to demand such action from him. Benedick's response is not to protest that he is a man, nor that it is his office, but to reveal his love to Beatrice as an offer in kind. He grants her the right to request his aid by professing, 'I do love nothing in the world so well as you' (4.1.267). Benedick's offer is all the more virtuous as it comes without obligation; as they are not yet amorously involved, there is no standard of duty which requires him to support her cousin in this way. He gives this aid freely out of love and admiration for Beatrice. Moreover, he commits to use his *virtù* selflessly, taking up this 'man's office' in open, and therefore political, action to correct societal imbalances for women (4.1.266).

For Beatrice and Hero, such action is necessary. It would not be enough to convince Don Pedro and Claudio that Don John lied and orchestrated an illusion because the act of defamation was public. The ignominy from such a scene 'usually remains forever and is not erased except by clear proofs of [the accused woman's] chastity and wisdom', according to Vives.[29] On the early modern stage at least, a man who stood to lose his reputation through the lack or apparent lack of chastity in a woman could be justified in calling for recompense for such offences through violence. In Spanish tragedies, men are pressed to revenge themselves upon wives and fiancées, feeling that 'there is no way

---

[29] Vives, *Education of a Christian Woman*, p. 125.

to undo the shameful situation, and no amount of compensating virtue will eliminate the identity of the shame with the person as a whole'.[30] As Unhae Park Langis demonstrates in this collection, Shakespeare's own Othello submits to this impulse to blot out the stain on his reputation with the blood of his Desdemona, failing to discard his ego and the corrupted world in favour of the sublime perfection. Beatrice longs for such revenge herself, but as a woman she can only bid Benedick, 'Kill Claudio' (4.1.288).

This is perhaps the crucial moment for this newly forged love, as we are well aware of the bonds of friendship binding Benedick to Claudio. In a generous light, Beatrice's call to arms can be seen as the same response that Giuliano de' Medici of *The Courtier* would have to Hero's plight, as he calls for courtiers 'to take up arms in defence of the truth, and especially when he hears a woman falsely accused of being unchaste'.[31] Yet Benedick knows, and has said to Beatrice, her cousin, her uncle and the friar, that the true mastermind of the denouncement was Don John. It is no wonder that, given his shrewd assessment of the situation and his bond with Claudio, his initial response is 'not for the wide world!' (4.1.289). The vehemence of Beatrice's desire stems not only from her loyalty to her cousin, but also from her sense of the severity of what has happened to Hero. Benedick questions her hostility with 'Is Claudio thine enemy?' (4.1.299). Her passionate response emphasises the active role the count played in denouncing Hero:

> Is [he] not approved in the height a villain, that hath slandered, scorned, dishonored my kinswoman? O that I were a man! What? bear her in hand until they come to take hands, and then with public accusation, uncovered slander, unmitigated rancor – O God, that I were a man! I would eat his heart in the marketplace. (4.1.300–5)

Beatrice's desperation and frustration stems from her outrage at the injustice done as well as her inability to act against those 'Princes and counties' responsible (4.1.313). Claudio's culpability is first and foremost in her mind, for although Don John may have made Hero seem unchaste, he did not force the groom to break with his bride in such a public and theatrical fashion.

Though Beatrice herself speaks for women's agency in choosing husbands, she is still bound by early modern gender roles which exclude women from taking up swords. According to *Hic Mulier: Or, The Man-*

---

[30] Matthew D. Stroud, *Fatal Union: A Pluralistic Approach to the Spanish Wife-Murder Comedias* (Lewisburg, PA: Bucknell University Press and Associated University Presses, 1990), p. 108.

[31] Castiglione, *The Book of the Courtier*, p. 242.

Woman, even the woman who takes up arms for a just cause 'shall lose all the charmes of womens naturall perfections, have no presence to winne respect, no beauty to inchaunt mens hearts, nor no bashfulnesse to excuse the vildest imputations'.[32] Notably, the response in *Hæc-Vir: Or The Womanish-Man* seems to agree with this assessment as there is no attempt to defend the use of swords by women, only the wearing of them.[33] As a woman of early modern virtue, Beatrice is therefore restricted from showing her *virtù* through the use of arms. She can only lament, 'O that I were a man for his sake! or that I had any friend would be a man for my sake!' (4.1.315–16). For Beatrice, the injustice is such that her cousin cannot recover her honour without a champion and Beatrice herself is so upset she feels she 'will die a woman with grieving' (4.1.321). Struck by the force of her feelings, Benedick asks her to confirm her sense of Claudio's responsibility:

> BENEDICK: Think you in your soul the Count Claudio hath wronged Hero?
> BEATRICE: Yea, as sure as I have a thought or a soul. (4.1.326–8)

With her unequivocal answer, he commits himself with the double engagement, the marital commitment to Beatrice and the martial commitment to challenge Claudio. Accepting this assessment of Claudio as the agent of Hero's downfall and taking Beatrice's enemy as his own, Benedick demonstrates his commitment to virtue *virtuosa* by pledging his sword to the public support of Hero and thereby declaring that no man, not even a prestigious count and one's 'new sworn brother', should be exempt from rectification when he has grievously harmed a woman (1.1.67).

'Those that slew thy virgin knight'

Despite Beatrice's wishes and Benedick's vows, the play does not end with the attempt to redress the defamation with blood. Rather, Shakespeare offers a development of chastity similar to that which Mike Gadaleto explores in this volume regarding *Cymbeline*, one which reconsiders the ethics of *virtù* and virtue to emphasise the need for a more dynamic concept of conduct. By circumventing this trial by combat, the resolution of the play takes virtue *virtuosa* to the community of Messina. The

---

[32] *Hic Mulier: Or, The Man-Woman: Being a Medicine to cure the Coltish Disease of the Staggers in the Masculine-Feminines of our Times* (London, 1620), B3v.
[33] *Hæc-Vir: Or The Womanish-Man: Being an Answere to a late Booke intituled Hic-Mulier* (London, 1620).

problem is not merely a personal one to be resolved amongst a group of friends or even simply within the court. It is a wider issue of standards of conduct that affects the commonwealth. The defamation of Hero portends wider discord than that at court. As Leonato stands as Governor of Messina, the connection between himself and the Prince, and therefore between the city and the ruling state, is as broken as the nuptials. The virtue *virtuosa* first modelled by Beatrice and Benedick is therefore a communal necessity. Their virtuosity delegitimises the use of aggression and assault in the name of chastity, honour or other virtues and openly defends the vulnerable from such abuse.

The spread of virtue *virtuosa* is both facilitated and symbolised by the involvement of Dogberry and the Watch. While this group of men appear to be fools whose language conveys next to nothing, they are quick to spot dishonesty when Borachio reveals the truth of Don John's production to Conrad. They bring the truth of the matter to the community they represent. They may appear 'desertless', as Dogberry mistakenly proclaims his Second Watchman George Seacoal to be, but despite their malapropisms and instructions to avoid interactions with knaves, drunks and thieves, they still 'preserve the wellbeing of the community' by apprehending Don John's accomplices (3.3.9).[34] Appropriately, Dogberry and his group are the mechanism by which justice comes to Messina. As the Watch, they symbolise community self-sustainment, a way for the city itself to prevent and correct local misdeeds. As an assembly that cannot comprehend its own shortcomings, Dogberry and his men are certainly 'the gross exemplar of an attitude which is endemic [in Messina]', for the elite Men's Club lacks self-awareness and the ability to see when a villain hides behind his elite status.[35] The involvement of the Watch therefore reminds us of our duties to ourselves and our communities to be circumspect in our observations of society so that justice can prevail despite human shortcomings.

By securing the confession of Borachio, the Watch supplies the catalyst which allows the play to rehabilitate Claudio and Don Pedro, a reconciliation which cannot be achieved by the lethal tradition of Beatrice's chosen course of action. The exposure of villainy cuts through the self-assurance of these two men who have rested secure in their own observations, killing their pride:

---

[34] Phoebe S. Spinrad, 'Dogberry Hero: Shakespeare's Comic Constables in Their Communal Context', *Studies in Philology* 89.2 (1992), 161–78 (p. 170).
[35] John A. Allen, 'Dogberry', *Shakespeare Quarterly* 24.1 (1973), 35–53 (p. 37). For more on Dogberry as a reflection of the 'Men's Club', see Carl Dennis, 'Wit and Wisdom in *Much Ado About Nothing*', *Studies in English Literature, 1500–1900* 13.2 (1973), 223–37.

PEDRO: Runs not this speech like iron through your blood?
CLAUDIO: I have drunk poison whiles he uttered it. (5.1.235–7)

This news has the effect foretold by the friar, as it restores Hero's 'rare semblance' in her groom's eyes (5.1.243). This restored love furthermore begins to convert Claudio much as Beatrice's love has for Benedick, as he submits to Leonato:

I know not how to pray your patience;
Yet I must speak. Choose your revenge yourself;
Impose me to what penance your invention
Can lay upon my sin. (5.1.262–5)

Although Claudio and Don Pedro still profess innocence in 'mistaking' Hero to be wanton – or more literally, in their mistaking Margaret for Hero – this moment is a significant turning point (5.1.266). Claudio here undertakes the timidity, humility and obedience formerly prescribed as Hero's role in life, and the men's penance demonstrates a newfound commitment to reassess the inherent imbalance of the status quo symbolised by their use of *virtù* against virtue. Through their reparation they acknowledge their abuse of social privileges which enabled them to denounce Hero and thereby deny women the ability to be virtuous on their own terms and thus defend themselves against such attacks.

The atonement, stylised and ritualistic though it is, proclaims to the community at large that virtue is *virtuosa* as it valorises the latent virtues traditionally ascribed to women and associates them with skilled performance. Claudio's epitaph and the 'hymn' which follows do not simply lament the loss of Hero and attest to her innocence (5.3.11). Both poetic works rewrite the virtue of her life as action, proclaiming her chastity as synonymous with *virtù* and virtuosity. Claudio proclaims that his lost bride 'Lives in death with glorious fame', while the song of praise more explicitly portrays Hero as a hero, Diana's 'virgin knight' (5.3.8, 13). Just as important is the reclassification of their actions. Though they first believed their denouncement to be the proper response, Claudio declares that Death now makes Hero famous in recompense 'of her wrongs' (that is, the wrongs done to her), and begs pardon from Diana as one would beg from a judge and jury (5.3.5, 12). Though short, the scene is significant. The act is public for the community of Messina and the theatrical audience. Both sets of spectators are directly shown the penance of Claudio and Don Pedro and may judge for themselves – rather than relying on second-hand information as so many do in this play – the verity of their repentance. Spectators thus become eyewitnesses to the efforts of these men to show submissiveness, remorse and a changed attitude towards feminine virtue. The verses are

not borrowed from a source, but are handcrafted at Leonato's charge
that Claudio, if he

> Can labor aught in sad invention,
> Hang [Hero's] epitaph upon her tomb,
> And sing it to her bones. (5.1.274–6)

These verses of heroic chastity from the groom show an acknowledgement of the imbalance created when Claudio and Don Pedro privileged
virtù over virtue. His vow to undertake the ritual yearly likewise signals
a commitment to a reformation in which neither concept is privileged to
the point of tyranny.

It may be hard for viewers to forgive Claudio in the way that Hero
does, given that he still seems to struggle with humility in the final scene.
Claudio attempts joviality at Benedick's expense but becomes churlish
when he finds himself figuratively wounded by Benedick's response. He
is impatient to 'seize upon' his veiled bride and his reluctant reconciliation with Benedick following the ceremony is emblematic of the fragility
of the newfound peace at court (5.4.53). But if we are put off by these
moments of pride, Claudio still resolves to take his bride veiled and
unknown, an act of submission to Leonato's will. In determining to
marry the bride he is given, Claudio forgoes his claim to a match which
would please or benefit him through either the lady's looks, manners or
status. Claudio submits to his new father-in-law in bride-like fashion
as Hero is given to him a second time. Rather than rejoicing in the fate
which has gifted him his bride again, Claudio beholds his new wife in
wonder with only the statement 'Another Hero!' (5.4.62). He listens in
silence as she and her father declare her virtue without again protesting
his own innocence in believing Don John, and remains quiet until his
interference seems necessary to ensure the marriage of Benedick and
Beatrice. Even if we cannot quite forgive Claudio for his earlier treatment of Hero, there is still evidence of his commitment to virtue *virtuosa*
as he accepts responsibility for his actions, submits himself to Leonato's
will with humility, and then acts with his bride as part of the nuptials of
Benedick and Beatrice.

'In friendly recompense'

If spectators harbour uncertainty regarding Claudio, they do not when
it comes to the affection of Beatrice and Benedick, as they continuously demonstrate virtue *virtuosa* in the form of their companionable
courtship. This may seem like a private matter between the two former

bachelors rather than a political act. The acts discussed so far as examples of virtuosity have been singular events – Benedick's offer to Leonato to deal with Hero's problem, his commitment to Beatrice to engage Claudio in a duel, and Claudio's own acts of repentance at Hero's tomb and then the altar. The private bond between their two hearts becomes political as they adapt their public behaviour to that of friends and lovers, giving Messina an example of a different style of marriage. Benedick and Beatrice's conversation before the second wedding is an act of virtuosity as much as their strange nuptials in front of the gentry of Messina are. These scenes are virtue *virtuosa* in action, giving both audiences and the court at Messina an exposition of spiritual bonding in wedlock which can cure the insecurities of men and prevent the tyranny of suspicion that threatens women.

This bonding is indicated through the cessation of arms in the 'merry war'. Though Beatrice and Benedick continue to match wits, their conversations are more a game than an altercation. Benedick admits as much when he agrees with Margaret that his wit is now 'as blunt as the fencer's foils, which hit but hurt not' (5.1.13–14). Beatrice also holds her own weapon in check, as Don Pedro reports that 'did she an hour together transshape thy particular virtues. Yet at last she concluded with a sigh, thou was the properest man in Italy' (5.1.165–8). This alteration of Benedick's *virtù* into a harmless, small, yet double-dealing wit is erased completely with Beatrice's assessment of his superior suitability and respectability. Knowing that she is in love, we can see her turns of Don Pedro's praises for Benedick as an attempt to hide the truth. With Benedick, to whom she has disclosed her feelings, her wit at his expense is merely a continuation of his own light-hearted banter:

> BENEDICK: And I pray thee now tell me, for which of my bad parts
>   didst thou first fall in love with me?
> BEATRICE: For them all together, which maintained so
>   politic a state of evil that they will not admit any good
>   part to intermingle with them. But for which of my
>   good parts did you first suffer love for me? (5.2.57–62)

As Benedick here attempts to elicit praise from his beloved, Beatrice humours herself instead by answering him in kind rather than enumerating his goodness. Just as the 'merry war' indicates that these two people are evenly matched, here they are like-minded individuals of wit and gentle humour, an example of friendship as 'a general and universal warmth, moderate and even, besides, a constant and settled warmth, all gentleness and smoothness, with nothing bitter and stinging about it'.[36] With the closing of open hostilities, the exchanges of Beatrice and Benedick become 'all gentleness and smoothness', and though they are in love, they do not act tempestuously but in a temperate manner that foreshadows a pleasant, companionable marriage.

Though Beatrice and Benedick joke, their feelings are not withheld from each other. When he quips that he loves her unwillingly, she answers, 'In spite of your heart, I think. Alas, poor heart! If you spite it for my sake, I will spite it for yours, for I will never love that which my friend hates' (5.2.65–7). Her tender response shows her devotion. Although in love with Benedick and thus his heart as well, their companionship is such that his emotions are hers, even if they run contrary to her affection. These lines point to a merging of wills, an amity like that of Montaigne for his own dearest friend: 'If you press me to tell why I loved him, I feel that this cannot be expressed, except by answering: Because it was he, because it was I.'[37] Taking Benedick's concerns for her own suggests the merging of minds which Montaigne sees as the indication of deep and true friendship, the sacred and unbreakable bond which he himself finds incompatible with marriage but which Erasmus would have in every marriage. We may also see Benedick's friendship as the very connection Beatrice desired when she desired a champion for Hero. When the second wedding is arranged, he confesses that he is glad, 'being else by faith enforced / To call young Claudio to a reckoning', yet maintains the emotional distance separating him from his former friend until after the second ceremonial rites are completed (5.4.8–9). Having engaged himself, Benedick takes Claudio as his own enemy because the count is Beatrice's enemy; once Claudio is Hero's husband and Beatrice's kinsman, Benedick accepts the count as an ally for he himself is allied with these women.

The importance of this companionable match can be seen in Shakespeare's arrangement of the double wedding, as it is not the rehabilitation of Hero which closes the play, but the celebration of nuptials between Beatrice and Benedick, a jovial match which lightens the solemnity of the restoration rites. During this highly anticipated moment, they once again cross foils in one last merry fight which again shows that they are highly suited to one another. Though they approach the altar with a verbal spar, it is only a ruse, and their true feelings are quickly revealed in the sonnets picked from their pockets. Their game is thus another moment of virtuosity, a display of friendship and love which serves as the play's final show of marriage.

---

[36] Montaigne, 'Of Friendship', p.167.
[37] Ibid., p. 169.

As they prepare to cross the threshold from bachelorhood to married life, Beatrice and Benedick thus give this final demonstration of virtue *virtuosa*. Their public announcement of commitment, enacted as a moment of play, is nevertheless a serious show of friendship and love, a moment of companionate courtship which models a subversive new mode of marriage. Rather than demonstrating the qualities of virtue and *virtù* that their counterparts Hero and Claudio embody, Beatrice and Benedick enter wedlock as equals, matching wits and hearts before the court in Messina. This continued display of strength, ingenuity and fidelity to each other – the conduct of virtue *virtuosa* – once again denounces the power differential which so threatened the life of Hero and the peace of the court. Man may be a 'giddy thing', as Benedick says, but through companionate marriage and virtue *virtuosa*, he may be a happy one as well (5.4.106).

Chapter 6

The Virtue of Humour in *King Lear*

Kent Lehnhof

As the essays in this volume by Carolyn Sale and Katie Adkison clearly demonstrate, *King Lear* is centrally concerned with virtue. France makes it a priority when choosing Cordelia for his wife, telling her 'Thee and thy virtues here I seize upon' (1.1.250).[1] Similarly, Cornwall cites Edmund's 'virtue and obedience' when deciding to 'seize on' Edmund as his own (2.1.115, 118). The fact that characters as opposite as Cordelia and Edmund are alike 'seized' upon on account of their virtue underscores how difficult it can be to determine who and what is truly virtuous. Lear highlights this very problem when he frets and rages about the 'simular [man] of virtue' who is actually perjurious and incestuous, as well as the 'simp'ring dame' who 'minces virtue' but goes to it with 'riotous appetite' (3.2.54; 4.5.116, 118, 121).[2] At the end of the play, Albany raises hopes that the problem of virtue's indeterminacy will be fully and finally sorted when he optimistically announces that 'All friends shall / Taste the wages of their virtue and all foes / The cup of their deservings' (5.3.278–80). Of course, these hopes are dashed almost instantly by the death of Lear, leading to widespread disappointment at the play's dramatisation of virtue. This was one of the chief concerns motivating Nahum Tate to revise the play in 1681. In Tate's rewrite, both Lear and Cordelia survive the conflict, and in the play's last lines Edgar offers up a pat moral message. Gesturing to Cordelia, Edgar exclaims: 'Thy bright Example shall convince the World / (Whatever Storms of Fortune are decreed) / That Truth and Vertue shall at last succeed' (5.6.159–61).[3] This virtue-rewarded ending was preferred by

---

[1] All references to Shakespeare, cited parenthetically throughout, come from *The Norton Shakespeare*, ed. Stephen Greenblatt et al., 3rd edn (New York and London: W. W. Norton, 2016). *The Norton Shakespeare* reprints both the Q and F editions of *King Lear*. Unless noted otherwise, all quotations from *Lear* come from F.

[2] Q has 'simular man of virtue', while F has 'simular of virtue'.

[3] Nahum Tate, *The History of King Lear* (1681), reprinted in *Five Restoration*

English audiences, and for nearly 150 years Tate's version was the only *Lear* to be performed. By the middle of the nineteenth century, however, Shakespeare's version had retaken the stage, once more challenging us with its unflinching moral and ethical vision and forcing us to think long and hard about virtue: what it is, what it does, and what it demands of us.

In my own consideration of these questions, I have found it helpful to draw on the writings of Emmanuel Levinas (1905–95), the French philosopher who has emphasised the way the Other summons the 'I' into virtuous and ethical relation by confronting it with that which cannot be assimilated or made same-as-me. The Other, Levinas says, exceeds my grasp at every moment, and this radical alterity arrests all of my self-serving pursuits.[4] Faced with one who cannot be reduced or totalised, the 'I' finds it hard to persist in its egoistic path and instead feels ordained to address itself to the nudity, neediness and vulnerability of the one before it by practising virtues like hospitality, generosity and care. According to Levinas, the absolute exposure of the Other para-doxically commands as a master commands, imposing ethical demands that are utterly exorbitant; hence, the difficulty – and trauma – of truly acknowledging the Other and submitting one's self to their needs.

To my way of thinking, Shakespeare's *Lear* anticipates and enacts in dramatic form many of the ideas that Levinas explores in philosophi-cal form. When Shakespeare's play begins, the old King is doing just what Levinas says the solitary ego does: he is seeking his own interests, maintaining his own existence, and trying to assimilate all unto himself – as when he tells his daughter, 'Better thou hadst / Not been born than not t'have pleased me better' (1.1.231–2). As Sale aptly remarks earlier in this volume, Lear operates in the opening scenes as 'a destruc-tive *autopoietic* figure', focused on making and preserving the self. Nevertheless, Lear's reductive, totalising approach proves difficult to sustain. Time and again, the King is brought face to face with individuals who resist assimilation. Their alterity checks the King's egoism and calls him into question. These upright others, as Levinas would say, depose Lear's sovereign ego and impose on him an obligation not merely to be but to be for the other. As the play progresses, Lear struggles mightily to accept this responsibility, but to the degree that he does, he can be seen to escape the horrors of solitary being, achieve authentic subjectivity/

Adaptations of Shakespeare, ed. Christopher Spencer (Urbana: University of Illinois Press, 1965), pp. 201–73.

[4] See Emmanuel Levinas, *Totality and Infinity: An Essay on Exteriority*, trans. Alphonso Lingis (Pittsburgh, PA: Duquesne University Press, 1994), esp. p. 39.

exteriority, and move towards that form of ethical transcendence that Levinas terms the 'otherwise than being'.[5]

Virtue-minded critics who have written about Lear's arduous and erratic journey towards transcendence have paid particular attention to the pivotal role played by characters who help him along his way as both a goad and a guide: characters like Cordelia (who exemplifies the Judeo-Christian virtues of love and forgiveness), Kent (who embodies the classical virtues of loyalty and stoicism) and Edgar (who enacts the creative virtues of the imagination and the theatre itself). In what follows, I wish to take this discussion of virtue in a different direction by concentrating on the character of the Fool.[6] By focusing on the role of the Fool in Shakespeare's tragedy – and by using Levinas's ethical philosophy to reflect on this role – I aim to examine the virtues of humour and laughter. Such an approach might seem odd at first, for few people would associate the tragedy of *King Lear* or the philosophy of Emmanuel Levinas with anything funny. To the contrary, these works feel sombre, weighty and serious. In the past couple of years, however, a number of scholars have attempted to find a place for humour in Levinas's ethics, most notably in the groundbreaking essay collection *Comedy Begins with Our Simplest Gestures: Levinas, Ethics, and Humor*. Applying this work to *Lear* can sharpen our sense of humour's virtuous capacity, not just in this play but also in Shakespearean drama more generally.

In his contribution to *Comedy Begins with Our Simplest Gestures*, Sol Neely makes much of the desacralising effects of humour: the way humour can combat the self-aggrandising impulses of the ego by rendering them risible. This type of humour, Neely says, takes aim at self-assuredness, idolatry and domination 'with a frankness and veracity that Levinas attributes to signification'.[7] Levinas develops his ideas

---

[5] For a fuller treatment of these themes, see Kent R. Lehnhof, 'Relation and Responsibility: A Levinasian Reading of *King Lear*', *Modern Philology* 111 (2014), 485–509. For another reading of *Lear* along these same lines, see James Kearney, '"This is above all strangeness": *King Lear*, Ethics, and the Phenomenology of Recognition', *Criticism* 54 (2012), 455–67.

[6] In addition to the scholarship cited in this essay, other notable readings of Lear's Fool include William Empson, 'Fool in *Lear*', *Sewanee Review* 57 (1949), 177–214; Thomas B. Stroup, 'Cordelia and the Fool', *Shakespeare Quarterly* 12 (1961), 127–32; Lawrence D. Green, '"Where's My Fool?": Some Consequences of the Omission of the Fool in Tate's *Lear*', *SEL* 12 (1972), 259–74; H. F. Lippincott, '*King Lear* and the Fools of Robert Armin', *Shakespeare Quarterly* 26 (1975), 243–53; Jonathan Bate, 'Shakespeare's Foolosophy', in *Shakespeare Performed: Essays in Honor of R. A. Foakes*, ed. Grace Ioppolo (Newark: University of Delaware Press, 2000), pp. 17–32; Robert D. Hornback, 'The Fool in Quarto and Folio *King Lear*', *English Literary Renaissance* 34 (2004), 306–38; and David Hershinow, 'Diogenes the Cynic and Shakespeare's Bitter Fool: The Politics and Aesthetics of Free Speech', *Criticism* 56 (2014), 807–35.

[7] Sol Neely, 'Toward a Critical Theory of Laughter', in *Comedy Begins with Our*

about 'signification' in connection with the expressivity of the other, which he sees as overflowing all measure. According to Levinas, the expressivity of the other encompasses not only the semantic content they communicate by way of words – which Levinas calls 'the said' (*le dit*) – but also the personal approach they enact by way of breath and discourse – which Levinas calls 'the saying' (*le dire*). And while 'the said' can be false or falsified, 'the saying' remains profoundly frank, for in the act of saying, Levinas maintains, the other surpasses the use of signs and becomes a sign themselves, delivering themselves up in an attitude of openness and exposure that Levinas calls 'the very signifyingness of signification'.[8] This kind of self-delivery is intensely disruptive. It tears apart my egoistic totality and knocks me off my perch. As Neely sees it, desacralising humour does much the same thing. Like Levinas's 'signification', desacralising humour is ethically anarchic: it overthrows idols by introducing and activating surplus meanings that resist incorporation within their master narratives and make a mockery of their grand pretensions.

This kind of humour bears some relation to the 'cultured insolence', or *pepaideumene hubris*, that Aristotle discusses in his *Rhetoric* and the witty virtue of *eutrapelia* that Gabriel Harvey obsesses about in his marginalia. In this marginalia, as Ian Munro notes in his contribution to this collection, Harvey documents his strong desire 'To do this before all; to speak living barbs'. In many regards, Lear's Fool fulfils Harvey's fantasy. Comically and consistently, the Fool bursts Lear's bubble, using witty barbs to puncture his inflated self-image. As Susan Snyder points out, 'The Fool has the clown-habit of pulling the grandly remote down to the physical and near.' His faltering doggerel puts the brakes on Lear's rolling verse, and his references to small and ordinary things contract Lear's sweeping, apocalyptic invocations.[9] Repeatedly, the Fool's ripostes strip the King of his exalted status and make him the butt of the joke:

LEAR: Dost thou call me fool, boy?
FOOL: All thy other titles thou hast given away; that thou wast born with.
    (Q 1.4.136–8 only)

Simplest Gestures: Levinas, Ethics, and Humor, ed. Brian Bergen-Aurand (Pittsburgh, PA: Duquesne University Press, 2017), pp. 99–121 (p. 103).
[8] Emmanuel Levinas, *Otherwise than Being: Or Beyond Essence*, trans. Alphonso Lingis (Pittsburgh, PA: Duquesne University Press, 2008), p. 5. In her contribution to this volume, Katie Adkison draws on Levinas's distinction between the saying and the said to discuss Cordelia's comportment in the love contest.
[9] Susan Snyder, *The Comic Matrix of Shakespeare's Tragedies* (Princeton, NJ: Princeton University Press, 1979), p. 162.

Echoing from the margins, the Fool's mockery runs athwart of Lear's ego-flattering efforts to thematise himself as a majestic god, a tragic hero or a sacred victim. This seems to be what Neely has in mind when he talks about the desacralising virtue of humour. It also seems to be what Lear has in mind when he says that the Fool is 'a pestilent gall to me' (1.4.104).[10]

In his role as galling humourist, the Fool seizes every opportunity to afflict Lear, and he displays a particular talent for turning seemingly benign situations into something more biting. Repeatedly, the Fool is asked a simple question or poses a generic riddle – and then twists the answer into a trenchant reminder of Lear's past folly and present pain:

> LEAR: When were you wont to be so full of songs, sirrah?
> FOOL: I have used it, nuncle, ever since thou mad'st thy daughters thy mothers. For [then] thou gav'st them the rod and putt'st down thine own breeches (1.4.140–3)

> FOOL: Canst tell how an oyster makes his shell?
> LEAR: No.
> FOOL: Nor I, neither, but I can tell why a snail has a house.
> LEAR: Why?
> FOOL: Why, to put 's head in, not to give it away to his daughters and leave his horns without a case. (1.5.21–6)

> FOOL: Nuncle, give me an egg, and I'll give thee two crowns.
> LEAR: What two crowns shall they be?
> FOOL: Why, after I have cut the egg i'th' middle and ate up the meat, the two crowns of the egg. When thou clovest thy crown i'th' middle and gav'st away both parts, thou bor'st thy ass on thy back o'er the dirt. Thou hadst little wit in thy bald crown when thou gav'st thy golden one away. (1.4.128–34)

Time and again, the Fool finds a way to convert amusement into embarrassment. As he does so, he practises a form of humour quite unlike that imagined by Kant in his *Critique of Judgment* (1790). In that work, Kant ties laughter to 'the sudden transformation of a strained expectation into nothing'.[11] As Kant sees it, the set-up of a joke creates tensions that the punchline instantly dissolves, causing us to laugh in a state of comic relief. The Fool's gibes, however, move in the opposite direction. Instead of alleviating distress, they intensify it. The Fool starts with something trivial and non-threatening (songs, oysters, snails, eggs), but the jest – instead of evaporating into nothingness – suddenly condenses

---

[10] Q has 'pestilent gull' (Q 1.4.104).
[11] Immanuel Kant, *The Critique of Judgment*, trans. J. H. Bernard, 2nd edn rev. (London: Macmillan, 1914), Part I, Div. 1, §54.

into an alarming indictment. Humour like this does not conform to Kant's theory of humour, but as Neely advises, it just might mesh with Levinas's notion of signification. Like signification, this sort of humour has ethical value, to the extent that it interrupts Lear's egoistic world-view, enforces a measure of humility, and overburdens him with a sense of guilt and responsibility.

Of course, the Fool's wit is not only or merely galling. Though it is true that the Fool uses humour to overthrow and afflict (as Harvey sought to do in his war with Nashe), he also uses it to express affection and invite connection. This can be seen in the Fool's whimsical term of address for Lear: 'nuncle'. The epithet is undoubtedly deflationary, in that it ignores the King's sovereign status and refuses to feed his fantasies of royal authority. But the pet name does not just take Lear down a peg or two; it also draws him near, positioning him as a close, familiar relation. With the epithet, the Fool endeavours to 'make kin' with Lear, in the sense articulated by Carolyn Sale's earlier essay, where it indexes a virtuous attempt to forge interpersonal bonds. Thus, the Fool's 'nuncle' is richly multivalent, like almost everything the Fool says to Lear. His gibes undermine, but they also edify: they are equal parts slap and caress. As Mehrdad Bidgoli demonstrates, the Fool both browbeats and revitalises, interweaving strands of the tragic 'said' with strands of equivocal, comic and ironic 'saying'.[12] In so doing, the Fool skilfully enacts the virtues of prudence and temperance. The judgement he displays in knowing when to press and when to retreat stands in stark contrast to Cordelia's austere honesty and Kent's 'unmannerly' courage, which will not give ground (1.1.142). The Fool's practical wisdom is on full display in 1.4, where he repeatedly touches Lear to the quick and then – before things become unbearable – relieves the pressure by whimsically changing subjects or posing a new riddle. As the Fool alternately inflicts pain and offers pleasure, the King's responses yo-yo between anger and affection. With one breath, he is addressing the Fool tenderly as 'my pretty knave' and 'my boy', but with the very next breath he is referring to the Fool resentfully as 'a pestilent gall' and 'a bitter fool' (1.4.88, 90, 104, 124). The more we consider the mixed, ambivalent nature of the Fool's humour, the harder it becomes to answer the question he puts to Lear – 'Dost thou know the difference . . . between a bitter fool and a sweet one?' – because the categories of 'bitter' and 'sweet' interinvolve (1.4.125–6). By teasing out the 'sweeter' aspects of the Fool's humour, though, we can deepen our sense of its ethical virtues, both in this play and beyond.

[12] See Mehrdad Bidgoli, 'Ethical Comicality and the Fool', *Comedy Studies* 11 (2020), 208–22, esp. p. 212.

To envision how humour can do more than just deflate or decimate, it is useful to look at the way Levinas uses humour in his Talmudic commentaries, which are surprisingly playful. This levity, however, does not aim to desacralise. As Annette Aronowicz explains:

> The humor in the Talmudic commentaries is not in the least opposed to the seriousness of what Levinas is saying. Rather, it is a sudden catapulting to the fore of his subjectivity, often in the form of irony, which reveals the distance, the heterogeneity, between the text and its interpreter at the same time that it reveals the relationship between the two. Examples of this kind of humor abound, and they depend on the sudden breaking of the rhythm of the discourse.[13]

This kind of humour is not an attempt to disparage or trivialise. To the contrary, it is a way of making an approach while also acknowledging the alterity of what is being approached. Tinged with irony and self-deprecation, this kind of humour allows Levinas to draw near the sacred text without taking on airs or pretending to be its master. In the absolutist court of King Lear, an analogous approach is advisable. Kent, however, cannot pull it off. He takes himself and his office too seriously and ends up offending. The King feels disrespected because Kent presumes to know and dares to lecture. The Fool's touch is softer, which is to say, less grave. Like Levinas in the Talmudic commentaries, the Fool uses humour to strike a delicate balance between familiarity/approach and difference/deference. Sometimes he leans in, and sometimes he pulls back. His jocular play with 'nuncle Lear' is a complicated combination of distance and relation – the very things that inform Levinas's idea of ethical interaction.

Yet even as the Fool's humour expresses a measure of regard, it remains disruptive. Like Levinas's wry humour in the Talmudic commentaries, the Fool's humour catapults his subjectivity to the fore and breaks up the rhythm of the discourse. As Bidgoli writes, 'interruptions' are most certainly one aspect of the Fool's sensibility towards Lear.[14] What the Fool says usually comes out of nowhere: we are unclear how it pertains, where it will lead, or what it all means. His enigmatic anecdotes, riddles, songs, sayings and prophecies interrupt what Levinas would call 'the play of the same' and confront the King with an alterity that cries out for consideration. Granted, a great many characters confront the King with alterity, but most of them do so more starkly, like Kent and Cordelia. At least at first, Lear cannot abide such overt displays and uses all possible

---

[13] Emmanuel Levinas, *Nine Talmudic Readings*, trans. and intro. Annette Aronowicz (Bloomington: Indiana University Press, 1994), p. xv.
[14] Bidgoli, 'Ethical Comicality and the Fool', p. 214.

means to avoid them; however, the comedic alterity of the Fool works differently. In the play's opening acts, the Fool's humorous impertinence does what Kent's and Cordelia's plain opposition cannot: it provokes productive dialogue. Whereas Kent and Cordelia are shut down and sent away, the Fool is entertained and interrogated. He is invited to teach:

> FOOL: Dost thou know the difference, my boy, between a bitter fool and a sweet one?
> LEAR: No, lad, teach me. (1.4.125–7)

The Fool disrupts and perplexes – but in a way that opens discourse. In this regard, the Fool's judicious humour can be said to do more than just deflate or desacralise. It can also be said to draw the ego outside of itself, teaching it to look on the world with other eyes.

Both Simon Critchley and Brian Bergen-Aurand spotlight this perspective-shifting potential in their own efforts to situate humour within a Levinasian ethics. Each emphasises the way humour can alter our outlook by breaking into our thoughts and causing us to consider new possibilities and points of view. According to Critchley, humour can benefit us by 'changing the situation in which we find ourselves', which it does by 'defeat[ing] our expectations' and 'producing a novel actuality'.[15] Bergen-Aurand makes a related claim. He explains that jokes and humour prompt us to take a fresh look at things we have taken for granted:

> Jokes show me the other sides of things. . . . And, in gaining a different angle or shot of something, . . . I am opened to different points of viewing the situation. Jokes slow me down and speed me up. They displace me, and in doing so, they replace me.[16]

This effect is readily observable in *Lear*. Although Lear is highly enamoured of his royal status at the start of the play, the Fool's jokes persistently impress upon him a different perspective of himself and his standing, one that accentuates frailty and folly instead of dignity and authority:

> FOOL: If thou wert my fool, nuncle, I'd have thee beaten for being old before thy time.
> LEAR: How's that?
> FOOL: Thou shouldst not have been old till thou hadst been wise. (1.5.34–8)

---

[15] Simon Critchley, *On Humour* (London and New York: Routledge, 2002), p. 1.
[16] Brian Bergen-Aurand, 'Knock, Knock / Who's There? / Here I Am, Exposed . . .', in *Comedy Begins with Our Simplest Gestures*, pp. 83–97 (p. 87).

At first, Lear bristles at these types of jokes ('Dost thou call me fool, boy?'), but the jokes take hold. In due course, Lear leaves off insisting on his own grandeur and echoes his fool in identifying himself as aged and unwise. By the time we get to Act 4, the alteration is obvious. What was once the Fool's recurring joke (you are old and foolish) has become the King's heartfelt refrain:

> LEAR: Pray do not mock me.
> I am a very foolish, fond old man. (4.6.55–6)

> LEAR: You must bear with me.
> Pray you now, forget and forgive.
> I am old and foolish. (4.6.78–80)

A great many things account for this change in Lear, but it is not insignificant that in his most humble moments, Lear echoes ideas initially articulated by his fool. As these lines indicate, the Fool's sayings resonate with Lear, not only interrupting his thoughts but also shifting his point of view, helping him heed the Act 1 injunction to 'See better, Lear' (1.1.156).

As Lear gradually comes to see differently and better, one of the things he begins to perceive is the suffering of his fool. In the midst of the cataclysmic storm, the King suddenly takes notice of the Fool and says, 'How dost, my boy? Art cold?' (3.2.68). This is a significant turn in Lear's ethical journey, for it is the first time he expresses concern for the welfare of another. In F, it is followed by further solicitude. Lear arrives at the door of the hovel and uncharacteristically defers to the other, telling the Fool: 'In, boy, go first. You houseless poverty, / Nay, get thee in; I'll pray, and then I'll sleep' (3.4.27–8). It might be coincidence that the King's first expressions of altruism are directed at the Fool, but I am tempted to attribute this to the virtue of the jokes that have passed between them. In this notion, I am emboldened by Bergen-Aurand's belief that jokes foster connection:

> [Jokes] open a relation between my self and others, across our situations and our bodies. They dislodge me from my solitary dwelling because they resituate me among other people and things, other times and places, and in resituating me they lead me toward new perspectives of living human corporeality.[17]

If we envision the Fool's jokes as accomplishing these ends, then it makes sense for Lear to take notice of the Fool's discomfort first and foremost. The implication, it would seem, is that the Fool's humour has

[17] Ibid., p. 87.

helped the King to make connections. The Fool's jests have dislodged Lear from his solitary dwelling, resituated him among people and things, and given him new perspectives on living human corporeality. This new perspective prepares Lear to perceive – as if for the first time – the nudity and neediness of the other.

There is certainly a way in which the Fool's jokes prompt Lear to see himself in relation to others. Resisting the King's romantic idea of himself as singularly tragic or uniquely victimised, the Fool's jokes routinely compare him to common folk: the labourer who bore his ass over the dirt, the master who surrendered his rod and pulled down his breeches, the cook who beat down the eels in her pot, the ostler who buttered hay for his horse. The lesson on offer is that Lear is neither wiser nor more just than anyone else. He is not the solitary, exceptional figure he wishes to be.[18] To the contrary, Lear stands in relation to – and, hence, bears an obligation towards – everyone else who trips and stumbles through this world, this 'great stage of fools' that makes us cry (4.5.177). Lear's memorable metaphor for the world is a great Shakespearean soundbite, but it is also compelling evidence that the King's perspective has been altered by the Fool, since the sentiment is perceptibly Fool-ish.[19] After all, the Fool is the one who has insisted throughout the play on the universal folly of humankind. He is the one who has repeatedly offered his coxcomb to others (especially Lear) and who has satirically complained that he cannot keep a corner on foolery, on account of all the grasping lords and ladies: 'They will not let me have all the fool to myself; they'll be snatching' (Q 1.4.141–3 only). It is easy to draw a straight line between jesting remarks such as these and Lear's increasing acknowledgement of folly. And it is just as easy to connect Lear's increasing acknowledgement of folly with his most virtuous moment in the play: the scene in which he reconciles with Cordelia by kneeling before her and confessing his folly: 'Pray you now, forget and forgive. / I am old and foolish'.[20]

---

[18] Snyder makes a similar point in *The Comic Matrix of Shakespeare's Tragedies*, explaining that the Fool's humour 'hints subversively that [Lear] is not so different from everyone else. . . . His experience is not peculiar to royalty or uniquely his, but is common to other men and even to snails and hedge-sparrows' (p. 161).

[19] Abrams shows that Lear's use of the word 'fool' in the first half of the play is very literal-minded, but by the time we reach this scene the King's usage has become more metaphorical and expansive. According to Abrams, '*Lear*'s shifting "fool" references suggest how deeply the Fool has marked his master'. Richard Abrams, 'The Double Casting of Cordelia and Lear's Fool: A Theatrical View', *Texas Studies in Literature and Language* 27 (1985), 354–68 (p. 361).

[20] This connection is even easier to trace if the actor playing the role of the Fool also plays the role of Cordelia, as has become common in modern-day productions. For

It is apparent, in other words, that the Fool's gibes work to modify the mindset of the King. But do they make him laugh? And what is at stake in asking such a question? If we turn to the playtext for answers, we discover that Lear is meant to laugh out loud in Act 1, after a joke about kibes:

> FOOL: If a man's brains were in 's heels, were't not in danger of kibes?
> LEAR: Ay, boy.
> FOOL: Then, I prithee, be merry; thy wit shall not go slipshod.
> LEAR: Ha, ha, ha. (1.5.6–10)

Lear's laughter here suggests that he is not unappreciative of the Fool's humour. Nevertheless, this is the only place where the playtext explicitly indicates laughter on the part of Lear.[21] Assuredly, the absence of additional cues in the text does not mean that Lear cannot or should not laugh at other points in the play, for laughter is very much a performance choice. But whether Lear laughs more or less in a given performance remains a significant question, inasmuch as laughter can signal a great many things, including pleasure, self-surrender, interpersonal connection and – quite possibly – that form of ethical transcendence that Levinas terms 'excendence'.[22]

Robert Bernasconi makes the case for the last of these in his work on Levinas and laughter. He contends that though Levinas sounds dismissive or even disdainful of laughter in his philosophical writings, the command 'You've got to laugh' is one of the few moral imperatives in Levinas's ethics. This command does not apply to all forms of laughter, for there are ways of laughing unethically, but Bernasconi singles out for praise the laughter we direct at ourselves. When we laugh with others at our own mistakes, Bernasconi says, we 'take a distance' from ourselves and experience something akin to excendence. According to him, this kind of laughter converts shameful faults into something better:

---

a reading of the play attentive to the possibilities of double casting, see Abrams, 'The Double Casting of Cordelia and Lear's Fool'.

[21] Aside from Lear's laughter in 1.5, the only other cue for explicit laughter in the play is found in 2.2, when the Fool comes upon Kent in the stocks and says: 'Ha, ha, he wears cruel garters!' (2.2.190).

[22] As Robert Bernasconi advises, Levinas uses the term 'excendence' instead of the more common term 'transcendence' to make it clear that he is not describing an ecstatic surpassing of the finite, as might be associated with mystical, out-of-body experiences. For Levinas, excendence is not about escaping the world or the self. To the contrary, it is about gaining the world and the self: a world with true exteriority and a self with supreme dignity and inalienable identity. See Robert Bernasconi, 'You've Got to Laugh', in *Comedy Begins with Our Simplest Gestures*, pp. 21–32 (p. 27).

In shame I am reduced to the error or fault I have just committed, but when my shame is transformed (then or later) into laughter, I disengage from myself. I step out of the situation, take a distance from myself, from my ego. Not all laughter can be described as a relation analogous to excendence, but what I am calling Levinasian laughter is a form of excendence because it answers the need to escape without losing myself altogether.[23]

It does not take much to transpose this account of ethical laughter onto the plot of *King Lear*, given that Lear's errors and unkindness at the beginning of the play afflict him with what Kent calls 'sovereign shame' (Q 4.3.43 only) and given that the Fool jokes relentlessly about these shameful errors. If the actor playing Lear accepts the Fool's humorous invitations and begins to laugh at his own mistakes, this laughter might license an optimistic reading of the play in which the virtuous humour of the Fool helps Lear take a distance from himself and move in the direction of the 'otherwise than being'.

Lear's laughter, in this interpretation, would show that the King is moving outside of himself. But it would also show that the King is moving towards the other, for laughter is a mode of connection. This is a point made by a number of Levinas scholars, including Robert Bernasconi, who claims that shared laughter is 'a form of embrace' that 'creates a bond'; Brian Bergen-Aurand, who says that laughing with the other allows us to 'complete the relation' and 'close the encounter'; and William Paul Simmons, who suggests that laughing in solidarity with others gives us 'a more saturated experience with the other.[24] To demonstrate the degree to which laughter links us with and is linked to the other, Timothy Stock points out that we tend to laugh longer and harder when we are in the company of others than when we are alone. Moreover, we tend not to laugh at jokes we have already heard – unless we are telling them to individuals who have not heard them, in which case they make us laugh all over again. Observations such as these support the idea that humour is intensely intersubjective, leading Stock to characterise humour as 'the ethical presence of other people within the subject'. As he sees it, humour is a relation with 'the other under-the-skin', and laughter is a way to draw near this other. 'Laughter is a form of proximity', Stock writes. 'When I laugh I engage in an involuntary election to being myself before others, to proximity, or "being turned

---

[23] Ibid., p. 30.
[24] Bernasconi, 'You've Got to Laugh', p. 31; Bergen-Aurand, 'Knock, Knock / Who's There?', p. 88; and William Paul Simmons, 'Levinas's Divine Comedy and Archbishop Romero's Joyful Laughter', in *Comedy Begins with Our Simplest Gestures*, pp. 123–39 (p. 138).

inside out."'[25] Thus, if the actor playing Lear were to make the choice to laugh with the Fool, this laughter could be quite meaningful. It could indicate an ethical awakening wherein Lear not only suspends his ego but also embraces and approaches the other, involuntarily electing to be turned inside out by 'the other under-the-skin'.

Of course, the idea of laughter-as-approach might strike some as anachronistic to *King Lear*. Stuart Tave, for instance, claims that the notion of laughter as benevolent does not take shape until the eighteenth century, and Indira Ghose maintains that ancient and early modern views of laughter are all based on the assumption that laughter is an expression of contempt.[26] Moreover, laughter is often derisory in Shakespeare's works, as in *Titus Andronicus*, where Aaron almost breaks his heart with laughter to see Titus cut off his own hand (5.1.111–20); or in *Twelfth Night*, where Sir Toby and his associates laugh themselves into stitches at the gulling of Malvolio (3.2.59–60); or in *The Tempest*, where Sebastian and Antonio laugh mirthlessly at Gonzalo as he speaks idealistically of the isle (2.1.139–77). But not all laughter in Shakespeare is derogatory. In *The Merchant of Venice*, Bassanio intends sociality, not scorn, when he says to his friends, 'Good signors both, when shall we laugh? Say, when? / You grow exceeding strange! Must it be so?' (1.1.66–7). In this invitation, laughter connotes warmhearted bonhomie much more than it does aggressive derision. The same is true of Titania's reveries in *A Midsummer Night's Dream*. Remembering with fondness her Indian votaress, the Fairy Queen waxes nostalgic about the night they sat together on the yellow sands, 'Marking the embarkèd traders on the flood, / . . . [and] laughed to see the sails conceive / And grow big-bellied with the wanton wind' (2.1.127–9). In moments such as these, as Indira Ghose allows, Shakespeare's perspective on laughter differs strikingly from that of his contemporaries. Though Shakespeare does portray laughter negatively, as an instrument of aggression, he also depicts laughter positively, as a means of creating social cohesion and enabling community identity.[27] For Shakespeare – and for Lear –

---

[25] Timothy Stock, 'How Humor Holds Hostage: Exposure, Excession, and Enjoyment in a Levinas Beyond Laughter', in *Comedy Begins with Our Simplest Gestures*, pp. 61–81 (p. 67).
[26] See Stuart M. Tave, *The Amiable Humorist: A Study in the Comic Theory and Criticism of the Eighteenth and Early Nineteenth Centuries* (Chicago: University of Chicago Press, 1960), esp. pp. 3–15; and Indira Ghose, 'Shakespeare and the Ethics of Laughter', in *Shakespeare and Renaissance Ethics*, ed. Patrick Gray and John D. Cox (Cambridge: Cambridge University Press, 2014), pp. 56–75, esp. 60–6.
[27] See Ghose, 'Shakespeare and the Ethics of Laughter', esp. p. 73. On this point, see also Edward Berry, 'Laughing at "Others"', in *The Cambridge Companion to Shakespearean Comedy*, ed. Alexander Leggatt (Cambridge: Cambridge University Press, 2002),

laughter can be a way to create a bond, complete the encounter and close the relation.

But what if the actor playing Lear does not laugh, or does not laugh much? Must we then conclude that the Fool's humour has failed? If we take Simon Critchley at his word, the answer is yes, for he is convinced that 'a joke that does not get a laugh is not a joke – end of story'. 'If you do not laugh at my joke', Critchley continues, 'then something has gone wrong either with my joke or with my telling of it. Either way, it is a mistake.'[28] Bergen-Aurand, however, is not so sure. He suggests that a theory of humour that privileges laughter is not unlike a theory of sex that privileges orgasm or a theory of sadness that privileges weeping. Laughter, orgasm and weeping are obviously important events, but when we make them the priority, Bergen-Aurand explains, we overlook much of what happens in humour, sex and sorrow. Consequently, he urges us to slow down our consideration of jokes and humour, taking into account the plethora of things that occur up to and through the moment when laughter erupts (or fails to erupt).[29]

If we take this tack with *King Lear* and slow down to consider what happens as the Fool's jokes unfold, we return to the idea that the Fool's jokes break into Lear's thoughts, interrupting his totality. When the Fool poses a riddle or tells a story, he effectively pulls Lear outside of himself. His jests abstract Lear from his own interests and immediate cares, prompting the King to give himself over to the Fool, if only temporarily. For the duration of the joke, Lear puts himself at the Fool's mercy, intent on following his logic and parsing his meaning. Why does one's nose stand in the middle of one's face? What would the Fool do with two cox-combs and two daughters? How can two crowns be made out of a single egg? The momentary self-surrender occasioned by the Fool's jests has an analgesic effect on the King, in that it causes him to forget his sorrows, but it also has an ethical effect, in that it causes him to forget his ego. The analgesic effect is what the unnamed Gentleman alludes to when he states that the Fool follows the outcast Lear and 'labors to out-jest / His heart-struck injuries' (3.1.9–10). The ethical effect is what we see whenever Lear puts his own projects on hold and allows himself to be occupied by the other, awaiting the resolution of the Fool's jest in a state of openness and attentiveness that Levinas would approvingly call 'passivity'.

pp. 123–38. Berry distinguishes between two forms of laughter – a Hobbesian satiric laughter (wherein we laugh *at* others) and a Bakhtinian carnivalesque laughter (wherein we laugh *with* others) – and then asserts that Shakespeare's comedies routinely subordinate the former to the latter, encouraging an empathetic laughter that draws us together.

[28] Critchley, *On Humour*, pp. 80 and 86 respectively.

[29] Bergen-Aurand, 'Knock, Knock / Who's There?', pp. 89–90.

In Levinas's writings, 'passivity' does not indicate inaction or inert-ness. Rather, it names a readiness to be moved by the other, to be directed by him or her without anticipating or presuming to know the outcome.[30] Levinas typically associates passivity with the face-to-face encounter, where the nudity and neediness of the other commands the 'I' to put itself at the other's disposal. Bergen-Aurand, however, feels that this phenomenology of nudity and neediness is not inapplicable to joking. To demonstrate how this is so, Bergen-Aurand asks us to reflect on the experience of telling a joke. When we tell a joke, Bergen-Aurand explains, we make an object of ourselves before the other and expose ourselves to his or her appraisal. Our joke pleads for a response, but we cannot compel that response and are therefore left hanging, awaiting the other's reply. Our joke could meet with the closure of a laugh or a smile. It could meet with the closure of a groan or shudder. Or it could meet with 'the closure that does not close': a blank stare and an awkward silence.[31] From a comical point of view, this last response is a disaster ('a joke that does not get a laugh is not a joke'). But from a philosophical point of view, Bergen-Aurand argues, unfunny jokes not only work but perhaps even work better, as markers of the intersubjective distance/dif-ference between us. According to Bergen-Aurand, the joke that does not get a laugh is profoundly significant, inasmuch as it makes manifest the radical asymmetry between the self and the other that is the foundation for Levinas's ethics.[32]

By this measure, a Fool who does not get laughs – from Lear, from other characters, from the audience – is not a failure, even though he might feel like one. When Antony Sher played the part in an RSC pro-duction in 1982, he set as his primary goal 'making the audience actu-ally laugh out loud'. In the Stratford performances, Sher achieved this objective rather effortlessly. When the production moved to London, however, Sher found he could no longer evoke laughter, which he found 'personally upsetting'.[33] As a comic actor, he felt the need to be funny. But 'unfunniness' might be an important aspect of the Fool's role. After all, some of his jests seem more likely to produce a grimace

---

[30] I derive this definition of 'passivity' from Catherine Chalier, 'The Philosophy of Emmanuel Levinas and the Hebraic Tradition', in *Ethics as First Philosophy: The Significance of Emmanuel Levinas for Philosophy, Literature and Religion*, ed. Adriaan T. Peperzak (New York and London: Routledge, 1995), pp. 3–12 (p. 8).

[31] Bergen-Aurand, 'Knock, Knock / Who's There?', p. 95.

[32] Ibid., p. 92.

[33] Antony Sher, 'The Fool in *King Lear*', in *Players of Shakespeare 2: Further Essays in Shakespearean Performance by Players with the Royal Shakespeare Company*, ed. Russell Jackson and Robert Smallwood (Cambridge: Cambridge University Press, 1988), pp. 151–65 (p. 165).

than a grin. In this regard, the prophecy the Fool makes in F is representative. The speech is a puzzling mash-up of satire, utopianism, self-contradiction and anachronism (see 3.2.80–94). Editors with their footnotes and critics with their close readings have laboured mightily over the years to establish its meaning.[34] But even if we succeed in making sense of the speech, it is even more challenging to make it funny. But what if this is precisely the point? What if the speech is meant to make us groan? In her brilliant reading of the monologue, Margreta de Grazia points out how perversely dilatory it is. At nine different points, the Fool appears to be wrapping up – only to pick back up and carry on. The speech, de Grazia concludes, is not so much a prophecy, or even a parody of a prophecy, so much as it is 'a sublimely self-conscious protraction of an exit routine designed to delay the close of the scene'. We keep expecting the Fool to leave, but the longer he lingers, the more he exhausts our interest, 'push[ing] the audience's amusement to the limit, or beyond'.[35] His speech, it would seem, is not supposed to be funny. Instead of exiting to peals of laughter, the Fool is meant to shuffle off in awkward silence, an emblem of exposure and vulnerability. Unfunny exits, Bergen-Aurand assures, can do ethical work.

If we accept Bergen-Aurand's idea that humour – especially halting humour – can be ethically meaningful, then it becomes possible to imagine an ethical efficacy for the Fool that goes beyond speaking truth to Lear, or satirising his follies, or using humour to solace him. In this ampler understanding, the Fool plays a vital role in Lear's virtuous journey by repeatedly making of himself an object for his royal master, all in the name of humour. As I see it, Lear reaches his ethical apex when he kneels at Cordelia's feet, subjecting himself to her censure and making of himself an entire offering to her. Can we not trace this action back to the Fool, who has continually done something analogous, in the act of telling jokes? If we credit Bergen-Aurand's suggestion that 'all jokes expose us, whether we intend them to or not', then perhaps we ought to view the Fool as a virtuous mentor: one whose humour models

---

[34] For notable interpretations of the Fool's prophecy, see John Kerrigan, 'Revision, Adaptation, and the Fool in *King Lear*', in *The Division of the Kingdoms: Shakespeare's Two Versions of* King Lear, ed. Gary Taylor and Michael Warren (Oxford: Clarendon Press, 1986), pp. 195–239, esp. pp. 225–6; and William O. Scott, 'Self-undoing Paradox, Scepticism, and Lear's Abdication', in *Drama and Philosophy* 12, ed. James Redmond (Cambridge: Cambridge University Press, 1990), pp. 73–85.

[35] Margreta de Grazia, 'The Fool's Promised Exit', in *Shakespeare Up Close: Reading Early Modern Texts*, ed. Russ McDonald, Nicholas D. Nace and Travis D. Williams (London: Arden Shakespeare, 2012), pp. 177–80 (p. 180).

for Lear how to make himself bare before the other, exposing himself to the other in all his nudity and poverty.[36]

The Fool – famously enough – drops out of the play before it draws to a close. It is common to say that he disappears because he has completed his task: he has helped the King admit his folly, has impressed upon the King his personal responsibility, and has prepared the King to enter into meaningful relation.[37] His place at Lear's side is taken by Edgar, who is something of a jokester himself, as is seen in the prank he plays on his father at the supposed cliffs of Dover, a prank that is nevertheless intended as a virtuous intervention: a 'trifle' designed to heal Gloucester of his suicidal melancholy. 'Why I do trifle thus with his despair / Is done to cure it', Edgar says (4.5.35–6). In his assumed humour of Poor Tom, Edgar confronts the King with riddles, puzzles and enigmas and puts himself before the King in a posture of denuded vulnerability. He presents himself, in other words, much as the Fool has done, albeit with greater intensity. Antony Sher describes the weirdness of Poor Tom as a super-potent drug, delivering to the King 'a more powerful "hit"' than the 'relatively safe anarchy' offered by the Fool'.[38] Even in this formulation, however, the anarchic humour of the Fool remains the gateway drug, as it were, that gets Lear to engage with the astonishing strangeness of Poor Tom. Were it not for Lear's sustained exposure to the 'relatively safe' humour of the Fool in Acts 1 to 3, we might expect the King to respond to the extreme alterity of Poor Tom in the same way he responded to the extreme alterity of Kent and Cordelia at the start – not by acknowledging it but by attempting to exile and ignore it. Yet the King takes a very different approach with Poor Tom, submitting himself to the beggar's strangeness and seeking to learn from him: 'First let me talk with this philosopher'; 'I'll talk a word with this same learned Theban'; and 'With him / I will keep still, with my philosopher' (3.4.141, 145, 163–4). With Edgar as his new intimate, the King appears to move even closer to that state of responsibility and self-sacrifice that Levinas terms the 'beyond being'.[39]

---

[36] Bergen-Aurand, 'Knock, Knock / Who's There?', p. 89.

[37] John Kerrigan and Mark Berge take a contrary position, proposing that the Fool recedes into the background because he realises that the King is irrecuperable and the situation remediless. See John Kerrigan, 'Revision, Adaptation, and the Fool', esp. p. 229; and Mark Berge, '"My Poor Fool is Hanged": Cordelia, the Fool, Silence and Irresolution in *King Lear*', in *Reclamations of Shakespeare*, ed. A. J. Hoenselaars (Amsterdam: Rodopi, 1994), pp. 211–22, esp. p. 220.

[38] Sher, 'The Fool in *King Lear*', p. 162.

[39] For discussions of Edgar's efficacy in helping Lear acknowledge otherness and embrace responsibility, see Kearney, '"This is above all strangeness"'; and Ann Astell, 'Girard and Levinas as Readers of *King Lear*', in *Of Levinas and Shakespeare: 'To See Another Thus'*,

Whether the King fully or finally breaks through remains a vexed question, for it is hard to read the play triumphally. The drama's final scene, in which Lear staggers onstage bearing the lifeless body of his daughter, gives us little cause for optimism or hope. For many, Samuel Johnson's distress is the most fitting response.[40] Yet as much as Johnson's gutted reaction might resonate with us, I would like to close my essay by reflecting on the response of another literary luminary, Leo Tolstoy, who reacted quite differently to this play and its concluding scene. Tolstoy did not think much of *Lear* and went through the tragedy scene by scene to highlight its failings. When Tolstoy arrived at the fifth act, he paraphrased the action as follows: 'After this enters Lear with the dead Cordelia in his arms, although he is more than eighty years old and ill. Again begins Lear's awful ravings, at which one feels ashamed, as at unsuccessful jokes.'[41] Tolstoy's reference to unsuccessful jokes, in the context of everything above, crackles with meaning. Tolstoy dislikes the play because it does not afford Lear tragic dignity at the end; rather, it compels Lear to lay himself bare before us, like a bad comedian. From Tolstoy's point of view, this is an affront. But from a Levinasian point of view, it looks quite different. From this perspective, Lear's awkward state of exposure serves as a bright reminder of our intersubjective asymmetry. The shame we feel in the face of Lear's grief originates in and attests to our incapacity to fully comprehend the other. But Lear's exposure is also a kind of salutary self-opening. In the same way that those who tell jokes make of themselves objects for the other, Lear in his 'awful ravings' makes of himself an object for the audience. He asks us to 'howl' and rage with him, much as the jokester asks us to smile and laugh, but the King cannot force this reaction any more than the jokester can (5.3.231). Lear can do no more than place himself before us – denuded and vulnerable – and await a response he can neither coerce nor control. In other words, Lear can do no more in the end than what he has seen the Fool do throughout.

ed. Moshe Gold and Sandor Goodhart with Kent Lehnhof (West Lafayette, IN: Purdue University Press, 2018), pp. 85–105, esp. pp. 100–2.

[40] In his preface to *Lear*, Johnson discloses, 'I was many years ago so shocked by *Cordelia's* death that I know not whether I ever endured to read again the last scenes of the play till I undertook to revise them as an editor.' Samuel Johnson, *The Yale Edition of the Works of Samuel Johnson*, 15 vols, ed. Arthur Sherbo (New Haven, CT and London: Yale University Press, 1968), 7:704.

[41] Leo Tolstoy, *Tolstoy on Shakespeare: A Critical Essay on Shakespeare*, trans. V. Tchertkoff and I. F. M. (New York and London: Funk & Wagnalls, 1906), p. 44. Qtd in George Orwell, 'Lear, Tolstoy, and the Fool', in Orwell, *Shooting an Elephant: And Other Essays* (New York: Harcourt, Brace and Company, 1950), pp. 32–52 (p. 37).

Tolstoy objects that this is humiliating, and therefore bad. Levinas would perhaps counter that this is humbling and therefore good. Whereas Tolstoy is embarrassed by the sight of a deposed king, Levinas believes that it is only by deposing ourselves that we are able to escape the horrors of solitary being and achieve true exteriority and subjectivity. According to Levinas, 'I become a responsible or ethical "I" to the extent that I agree to depose or dethrone myself – to abdicate my position of centrality – in favor of the vulnerable other.'[42] Over the course of the drama, Lear appears to move in this direction, as a number of virtue-minded critics have demonstrated. What I hope to have added to this growing body of work is greater appreciation for the myriad ways the Fool and his humour add momentum to that movement. In staking out this argument, I take a stand against those who see the Fool as useless: scholars like Arthur Davis, who alleges that '[t]he fool is of no practical help to the King', and Indira Ghose, who is of the opinion that 'the Fool makes nothing happen'.[43] My position, on the other hand, is that the Fool is instrumental in Shakespeare's virtuous theatre. His humour disrupts Lear's egoistic totality, entices him to consider other points of view, creates a connection across bodies and situations, helps him take a distance from himself in the direction of excendence, offers him a more saturated experience of the other, invites him to approach the 'other under-the-skin' by way of laughter, and shows him how to make of himself an object for the other. Previous scholars have helped us see how Cordelia, Kent and Edgar contribute to Lear's ethical awakening. Yet the Fool and his humour play a part that should not be overlooked.

Not all fools and not all humour tend towards excendence, but my reading of the Fool's role in *King Lear* aims to persuade that stage comedy can model virtuous activity and promote ethical relations. In this larger objective, I find an ally in Julia Lane, a clown and clown scholar, who seeks to harmonise her own performance practices with Levinas's ethics. She begins by showing that clowning organises itself around otherness, as does Levinas's ethics. Clowns, Lane explains, are fundamentally other in that they are perceptibly out of step with the expectations of their societies, cultures and circumstances. Yet they perform their otherness in such a way as to evoke virtuous responses

---

[42] Emmanuel Levinas, 'Dialogue with Emmanuel Levinas', in *Face to Face with Levinas*, ed. Richard A. Cohen (Albany: State University of New York Press, 1986), pp. 13–33 (p. 27).

[43] Arthur G. Davis, *The Royalty of Lear* (New York: St. John's University Press, 1974), p. 85; and Indira Ghose, *Shakespeare and Laughter: A Cultural History* (Manchester and New York: Manchester University Press, 2008), p. 197.

of generosity and benevolence.[44] One of the ways fools and clowns do this is by willingly, sincerely and openly giving themselves over to the audience. In their eagerness to please, clowns do not shy away from exposure, abasement and humiliation. They do not allow their egos to interfere, nor do they hide behind the fourth wall. Indeed, clowns cannot refrain from engaging with their audiences: they transgress theatrical boundaries to be with them, involve them in the action, take their reactions and suggestions to heart, and so forth.[45] Clowns are enduringly and open-endedly oriented towards the other, and by committing to this course, clowns remind audience members of their own responsibilities to the other. As a result, Lane proposes that clown theatre is uniquely ethical, creating the conditions for uplifting intersubjective experiences that are not often facilitated through other forms of art.[46]

Lane's ideas, informed by her own theatrical praxis, can give us a better sense of how clowning might constitute an energetic virtuous activity. The work of Paolo Virno can take us even further, for he persuasively ties clowning and humour, particularly the telling of jokes, to the virtue of *phronesis*, which he defines as 'practical know-how'. Virno argues that jokes succeed only to the extent that they break with established norms of behaviour and offer up abnormal alternatives that turn out to be unexpectedly appropriate to the situation at hand. To make a joke, then, one must skilfully evaluate a contingent, singular and unrepeatable event and formulate a response that is far afield yet still fitting. Moreover, one must do this in a timely fashion. According to Virno, the innovative action of jesting is always urgent, requiring the jokester to judge – under pressure of non-reproducible circumstances – the proper

---

[44] Lane's notion of a genial relationship between clowns and their audiences is not altogether in step with the theatrical scene at the start of Shakespeare's career. Richard Preiss demonstrates that Richard Tarlton, the most famous clown of the 1580s, could be quite aggressive and antagonistic towards audience members. By the time of *King Lear*, however, the situation had shifted. Robert Armin, the clown for Shakespeare's company at the time of *King Lear*, was small in stature and had a beautiful singing voice – qualities which did not lend themselves to combative or contentious relations with the audience. Accordingly, Armin tended to present himself as vulnerable or defenceless, inviting audiences to pity him rather than attack him. In *Lear*, the King displays a tender regard for the Fool ('How dost, my boy? Art cold?') that approximates the more generous and benevolent interactions that Lane imagines between clowns and their audiences. See Richard Preiss, *Clowning and Authorship in Early Modern Theatre* (Cambridge: Cambridge University Press, 2014), esp. pp. 79–80 and 203–6.

[45] In addition to unscripted interactions, which might have been abundant, *Lear*'s Fool speaks directly to the audience in at least two places: at the end of 1.5, where he talks to the maids in the theatre (1.5.44–5); and at the end of 3.2, where he offers his Merlin prophecy to the assembly at large (3.2.80–94).

[46] See Julia Lane, 'A Clown in Search of Ethics', in *Comedy Begins with Our Simplest Gestures*, pp. 163–84.

moment to make their move. Seizing this moment, Virno explains, 'is the condition that renders the humorous utterance effective, or even, simply, sensible', and those who accomplish it 'are always in a state of emergency'.[47]

Lear's Fool knows this all too well. His tragic state of emergency could not be more trying. Coming up with an appropriate response to this particular set of circumstances is virtually impossible. Nevertheless, the Fool will not go to kennel. To the contrary, he dogs Lear for the first three acts of the play. Throughout this time, his words and deeds accord with Kevin Curran's conceptualisation, articulated in this volume's Afterword, of virtue as a dynamic and interactive social practice through which one acts in and upon the world. Indeed, Lear's Fool exemplifies many of the virtues that Curran identifies with 'practical wisdom' and the state of general well-being and social flourishing known as *eudaemonia*. As Lear's Fool evaluates his circumstances and options, he practises prudence. As he balances priorities and outcomes, he practises temperance. As he commits to take action on the basis of his assessments, he practises courage. And as he seeks to restore balance and order, he practises justice. In so doing, he dramatically demonstrates that virtue, as Curran puts it, is not something one *is* but something one *does*.

At the start of this essay, I asserted that *King Lear* is centrally concerned with virtue. I hope to have shown that the Fool's part in this virtue-minded play is not inconsequential. In this tragedy, the ethical efficacy and virtuous potential of clowning, wit and humour are vividly expressed by the actions and example of the Fool, a figure that I believe Shakespeare introduced into the Lear story precisely to perform this role.[48] As Lear's constant companion for the first half of the play, the Fool shepherds him with jokes and jests that continue to push and pull long after the Fool's mysterious disappearance. Whatever amount of enlightenment and virtue Lear manages to achieve at the end comes in no small part through his interactions with his royal jester. Almost as soon as the Fool enters in Act 1 and begins to speak, Kent turns to the King and remarks, 'This is not altogether fool, my lord' (Q 1.4.139 only). On this count, Kent is more than correct. What the Fool says and does is not 'altogether fool'. His humour has virtue.

---

47 Paolo Virno, *Multitude: Between Innovation and Negation*, trans. Isabella Bertoletti, James Cascaito and Andrea Casson (Los Angeles: Semiotext(e), 2008), pp. 73 and 92 respectively. I am grateful to Carolyn Sale for bringing this discussion to my attention.
48 There is no fool character in Shakespeare's source-text, *The True Chronicle History of King Leir* (c. 1594).

Chapter 7

Vita Energetica: Love's Labour's Lost and Shakespeare's Maculate Theatre

Ian Munro

The highest goal of Eutrapelus: to prevail over all men in Art and Virtue; to exceed the keenest men with an indomitable spirit; to surpass the most diligent men in industry and the best men in merit; finally, to outshine the most worthy men in worthiness.[1]

So writes Gabriel Harvey in one of hundreds of ecstatic invocations of Eutrapelus, chief among the dramatis personae or alter egos that strut and fret on the margins of his books – in this case, his double-bound copy of Lodovico Domenichi's *Facetie, motti, et burle di diversi signori et persone private* and Lodovico Guicciardini's *Detti, et fatti piacevoli et gravi*, two Italian collections of jests and apophthegms (see figure opposite). In Harvey's rhapsodic account – which traverses Latin, English and occasionally Italian and Greek, and which is so voluminous that it can only be lightly sampled here – Eutrapelus is 'a peerles Artist: a matchles Professour: & a most excellent man, at euerie proofe of the Worthiest men', possessing '*a unique zeal for words, things, and actions, and a singular abundance of the highest faculties*'; he '*surpasses all in the elegant art* . . . [adding] *grace and dignity to his profession and to every pragmatic ability*'.[2] A '*living mirror of every excellence*', Eutrapelus is 'the onlie surprising Witt, toung, hand, foote, & sowle of the World. . . . *A man for all seasons: a philosopher therefore for all things; a most*

[1] Lodovico Domenichi, *Facetie, motti, et burle di diversi signori et persone private* (Venice: Printed by Andrea Muschio, 1571), p. 378. Throughout this essay I have italicised material from these jestbooks that has been translated (principally from Latin). All transcriptions and translations of Harvey's marginalia are the copyright of the wonderful Archeology of Reading project (www.archeologyofreading.org), which has digitised this volume and other significant volumes from Harvey's library. (Every effort has been made to secure permission for their use here.)

[2] Lodovico Guicciardini, *Detti, et fatti piacevoli et gravi, di diversi principi filosofi, et cortigiani* (Venice: Printed by Domenico and Gio Battista Guerra, 1569), p. 23; Domenichi, *Facetie*, p. 380; Guicciardini, *Detti*, p. 59.

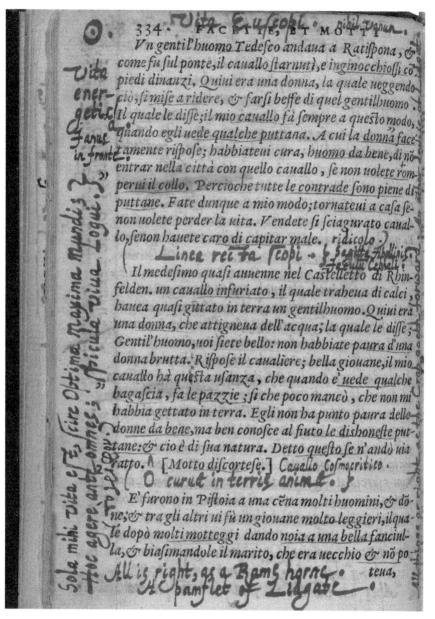

334.   FACETIE, ET MOTTI.

Vn gentil'huomo Tedesco andaua a Ratispona, &
come fu sul ponte, il cauallo starnutì, e inginocchiossi cõ
piedi dinanzi. Quiui era una donna, la quale ueggendo
ciò, si mise a ridere, & farsi beffe di quel gentilhuomo.
Il quale le disse; il mio cauallo fà sempre a questo modo,
quando egli uede qualche puttana. A cui la donna face-
tamente rispose; habbiateui cura, huomo da bene, di nõ
entrar nella città con quello cauallo, se non uolete rom-
perui il collo. Perciochè tutte le contrade sono piene di
puttane. Fate dunque a mio modo; tornateui a casa se
non uolete perder la uita. Vendete si sciagurato cauallo, se non hauete caro di capitar male.   ridicolo.

Il medesimo quasi auuenne nel Castelletto di Rhin-
felden. un cauallo infuriato, il quale traheua di calci,
haueua quasi gittato in terra un gentilhuomo. Quiui era
una donna, che attigneua dell'acqua; la quale le disse;
Gentil'huomo, uoi siete bello: non habbiate paura d'una
donna brutta. Rispose il caualiere; bella giouane, il mio
cauallo hà questa usanza, che quando e' uede qualche
bagascia, fa le pazzie; si che poco mancò, che non mi
habbia gettato in terra. Egli non ha punto paura delle
donne da bene, ma ben conosce al fiuto le dishoneste puttane: & ciò è di sua natura. Detto questo se n'andò uia
ratto. [Motto discortese.]   Cauallo Cosmocritico.

E' furono in Pistoia a una cẽna molti huomini, & dõ-
ne; & tra gli altri ui fù un giouane molto leggieri, il quale dopò molti motteggi dando noia a una bella fanciul-
la, & biasimandole il marito, che era uecchio & nõ po-   teua,

Annotations by Gabriel Harvey in *Facetie, motti, et burle di diversi signori et persone private* and *Detti, et fatti piacevoli et gravi, di diversi principi filosofi, et cortigiani* [manuscript], c. 1580–1608?, fol. 7v (Domenichi, p. 334). Call #: H.a.2. Used by permission of the Folger Shakespeare Library.

capable actor for singular matters: most timely in all things. Ahead in the beginning, last at the end; one worth all the rest.'[3]

This essay explores the relationship between Harvey's virtuous marginalia and Shakespeare's *Love's Labour's Lost*, two unrelated creations that are nevertheless strangely entangled through their mutual engagement with *eutrapelia*, the Aristotelian virtue of conversational wit that forms a central element of Renaissance discourses of civility and courtesy.[4] In making this juxtaposition I am not suggesting that Harvey's marginalia, or Harvey himself, operates as a 'source' for the play (although there is a long, albeit somewhat outdated, critical tradition of reading aspects of *Love's Labour's Lost* as direct references to the Harvey–Nashe quarrel). Rather, I want to highlight some fundamental homologies between how Harvey formulates the relationship between *eutrapelia*, practice and virtue and how *Love's Labour's Lost* orchestrates its witty engagements. *Love's Labour's Lost* is generally considered Shakespeare's most 'witty' play, in the sense that it foregrounds verbal artifice and wordplay to an unusual degree, and certainly its ladies and lords (Berowne above all) display a capacity and predilection for brilliant social performance perhaps worthy of Eutrapelus himself. Still, the play's celebration of the witty world it fashions might be questioned on a number of levels. This is, after all, a play about failure: a theme expressed on the most basic level through the failure of dramatic structure and convention – Jack hath not Jill – but also found on every other level of the play. My goal is to use Harvey as a foil for the play, connecting the latter's comic catastrophes to the former's inability to transform himself into his eutrapelian alter ego in order to help excavate what I see as Shakespeare's critique of the Aristotelian principles that guide Harvey's understanding of wit, virtue and performance. Ultimately, I see *Love's Labour's Lost* as providing a vision of what theatre *is*, and how theatre *works*, profoundly at odds with the philosophical imperatives of Harvey's marginal virtue theatre.

In the *Nicomachean Ethics* Aristotle groups *eutrapelia* with veracity and affability as social virtues that 'are concerned with our sharing in speeches and actions'.[5] The *eutrapelos* occupies the median between the excesses of the rustic *agroikos*, who rigidly refuses to participate in

---

[3] Domenichi, *Facetie*, pp. 352 and 425 respectively.

[4] For more on the conventional virtue of *eutrapelia* vis-à-vis Shakespeare, see Indira Ghose, 'Shakespeare and the Ethics of Laughter', in *Shakespeare and Renaissance Ethics*, ed. Patrick Gray and John Cox (Cambridge: Cambridge University Press, 2014), pp. 56–75.

[5] Aristotle, *Nicomachean Ethics*, trans. Robert C. Bartlett and Susan D. Collins (Chicago: University of Chicago Press, 2011), 2.7; p. 22.

verbal banter, insensible to its pleasures, and the *bōmolochos*, whose responsiveness is overly flexible, constantly seeking the pleasures of wit and jesting without concern for the decorum of the situation. Unlike such boors and buffoons, the *eutrapelos* has a kind of tact or social dexterity (*epidexiotēs*; literally, 'towards the right') that guides his witty performances and establishes the norms of verbal decorum. *Eutrapelia* is also discussed in *On Rhetoric*, where Aristotle describes it as *pepaideumene hubris*, 'cultured insolence', and deems this paradoxical (and witty) fusion the specific province of the young.⁶ This joining of 'culture' and 'insolence' resonates with the concept of *epidexiotēs* in the *Ethics*: the culture and/or education of the speaker frames and insulates the hubris at the heart of the joke; moreover, unlike the buffoon, the witty speaker will keep culture and insolence in balance, not letting the latter dominate. In the *Ethics*, however, *eutrapelia* is broader in terms of content and narrower in terms of context: 'But since rest [or relaxation] too is a part of life, and a part of rest involves passing the time with playful amusement [*diagōgēs meta paidias*], it seems here too there is a certain suitable manner of association.'⁷ Virtuous *eutrapelia* thus encompasses all the pleasures of verbal interaction, but only in the context of leisure, where conversation is friendly and uncompetitive, and serves to refresh the mind for more labour: 'play [*paidia*] resembles relaxation, and because people are incapable of labouring continuously, they need relaxation. Relaxation, then, is not an end [*telos*]: it arises for the sake of activity [*energeias*].'⁸ *Energeia*, the source of the modern word 'energy', is one of Aristotle's richest and most complex terms, playing an important role not only in the *Ethics* but also in the *Rhetoric*, the *Physics*, the *Metaphysics* and *De Anima*. In most of these works, *energeia* (which derives from *ergon* or 'work') designates a making-active of a potentiality, faculty or capacity (*dunamis*): marking a difference between the power of sight and seeing a particular object, for example, or between a block of wood and the statue carved from it. In the context of the *Ethics*, as I will discuss more below, the expected relationship between *energeia* and *dunamis* is paradoxically reversed: with enough and appropriate repetition, virtuous action can create a capacity for virtue.⁹

⁶ Aristotle, *On Rhetoric: A Theory of Civic Discourse*, trans. George Kennedy (Oxford: Oxford University Press, 2007), 2.12; p. 151.
⁷ Aristotle, *Nicomachean Ethics*, 4.8; pp. 86–7.
⁸ Ibid., 10.6; p. 223.
⁹ Exactly how ethical habituation takes place is notoriously vague in the *Nicomachean Ethics*; for a good overview of the issues, see Marta Jimenez, 'Aristotle on Becoming Virtuous by Doing Virtuous Actions', *Phronesis* 61 (2016), 3–32.

Aristotle's divergent treatment of *eutrapelia* in the *Ethics* and the *Rhetoric* speak to tensions inherent to verbal wit, especially in its overlapping functions in eristic and non-eristic speech. In the *Ethics*, Aristotle observes that 'Those who are playful in a suitable manner are called witty [*eutrapeloi*], as in those who are "versatile" [*eutropoi*], since such witticisms seem to be movements of their character [*ēthous*], and characters, like bodies, are judged by their movements.'[10] The key to ethical *eutrapelia* is thus its basis in *tropē* or 'turning', both in the sense of the turning of words and in the sense of the witty person's kinetic ability to turn himself to the social situation at hand, promoting pleasant recreation. And yet Aristotle's observation that witty jests '*seem* to be movements of their character' potentially opens up the possibility that they might not in fact be so. In the *Rhetoric*, Aristotle makes clear the artificial basis of eloquence: 'authors should compose without being noticed and should seem to speak not artificially but naturally. . . . An example is the success of Theodorus' voice when contrasted with that of other actors; for his seems the voice of the actual character, but the others' those of somebody else.'[11] But such deceptions are antithetical to the *Ethics*, which quarantines *eutrapelia* within the province of communal recreation precisely to avoid the topic of its other applications. *Arete* is a term common to both the *Ethics* and the *Rhetoric*,[12] and in both works it denotes a medial virtue positioned between two excesses, but rhetorical virtues are a matter of natural gifts and practical experience, while ethical virtues are categorically not natural gifts, but rather stable dispositions that are 'completed [*teleioumenois*] through habit [*ethous*]'.[13] As Aristotle's use of the word *teleioumenois* makes clear, the conversion of habit into character, *ethos* into *ēthos*, depends not only on doing the right thing but doing it for the right reason, ever attentive to the *telos* of the particular virtue.[14] The challenge of fitting wittiness into this model, given that it is not clear that it has a specific *telos*, is shown by its explicit exclusion from the virtues in the *Eudemian Ethics*, as well as continued disagreement among modern Aristotelians as to just what the activities, goals and appetites of *eutrapelia* are.[15]

---

[10] Aristotle, *Nicomachean Ethics*, 4.8; p. 87.

[11] Aristotle, *Rhetoric*, 3.2; pp. 198–9.

[12] On this distinction, see especially 3.13 of the *Rhetoric*, where Aristotle plays with the idea of virtue in both contexts.

[13] Aristotle, *Nicomachean Ethics*, 2.1; p. 26.

[14] For more on Aristotelian *telos* in this collection, see the chapters by Daniel Juan Gil and Thomas Moretti.

[15] See William Fortenbaugh, 'Aristotle and the Questionable Means-Dispositions', *Transactions and Proceedings of the American Philological Association* 99 (1968), 203–31; David Bostock, *Aristotle's Ethics* (Oxford: Oxford University Press, 2000), esp.

The Aristotelian ideal of the *eutrapelos* figures prominently in Renaissance civility discourses, albeit strongly inflected by the related Roman concept of *urbanitas*, which expands the province of playful conversation from leisure to a broad range of social interactions and provides it with a more concrete *telos*: the maintenance of civil society.[16] Giovanni Pontano's magisterial *Virtues and Vices of Speech* (1509), among the most influential treatises of Italian humanism, begins with the declaration that 'man's life is particularly occupied with actions and with civil assemblies and meetings, of which speech itself is the foremost bond, as it is of all human society, and without which it is by no means possible to attain the highest good'.[17] Following the example of Cicero's discussion of jesting in *De oratore*, Pontano illustrates his discussion of verbal virtue with copious examples of jesting encounters, gathered not only from his urban academy but also from literature (Plautus, especially) and from earlier collections of *facetiae*. In turn, Pontano's jests were subsequently collected into later jestbooks, including that of Domenichi; Harvey praises Pontano in the margins of one such joke as '*born for pleasantries*' and '*wonderfully pleasant*'.[18] In the introduction to his translation of *The Virtues and Vices of Speech*, G. W. Pigman III describes it as 'first and foremost a treatise of Aristotelian moral philosophy', but observes as well that in the Renaissance it was 'most appreciated as a collection of witticisms'.[19] This was certainly the case for Gabriel Harvey, whose marginalia does not typically envision a communal world of recreational pleasantry enlivened by decorous badinage. Instead, the conversational model for both Eutrapelus and his creator is combative and agonistic – mirroring the world of the Italian jestbooks that provide the material platform for Harvey's fantasies, in which every social encounter ends with a deft put-down or a sharp riposte.[20]

---

pp. 47–8; John Lippitt, 'Is a Sense of Humour a Virtue?', *The Monist* 88 (2005), 72–92; Howard Curzer, *Aristotle and the Virtues* (Oxford: Oxford University Press, 2012), esp. pp. 167–87; and Matthew Walker, 'Aristotle on Wittiness', in *Laughter, Humor, and Comedy in Ancient Philosophy*, ed. Pierre Destree and Franco Trivigno (Oxford: Oxford University Press, 2019), pp. 103–21.

[16] For more on the Renaissance virtue of conversational wit, see Kristina Sutherland's chapter.

[17] Giovanni Giovano Pontano, *The Virtues and Vices of Speech*, trans. G. W. Pigman III (Cambridge, MA: Harvard University Press, 2019), p. 5.

[18] Domenichi, *Facetie*, pp. 336–7.

[19] Pontano, *Virtues and Vices of Speech*, p. xiii. As Pigman remarks a little later, 'Aristotle provides the conceptual framework; Cicero provides particulars about different kinds of witticisms' (p. xx).

[20] In a sense, wittiness has a double function in Italian humanism: conviviality in the discourses and combat in the jests, with the former providing something of an ethical cover for the improprieties of the latter.

'Vita Energetica', Harvey writes at the top of one margin, adding '*Janus before*' underneath and appending a double-headed gloss: '*One life belongs to me: to know the greatest best things of the world*' and '*To do this before all; to speak living barbs*' (see figure on p. 149).[21]

Interwoven in the marginal performance space of Eutrapelus and his fellow avatars is what might be described as a programme of study and instruction, as shown both in brief commands to practise levity – '*Not one day without aphorisms, epigrams, and a joke taken from the heart of the Facetie*' – and longer exhortations to intellectual labours:

> *Chief piece of wisdom for the self-instructed and universally pragmatic man. Live sparingly with eating and most sparingly with drinking: moreover, be more sparing with sleep: but even more sparing with Love. However, be lavish alone in study, and in deep skill, and superior behaviour, and in every kind of good. Being so sparing and so lavish, I cast away all trifles: I pursue strictly practical concerns. That which art can do, or virtue, or skilful action, to be extended on one's own, should be multiplied. For this purpose, the mysteries of perfection, and stratagems drawn from on high: more and more intellect: here more beyond works. Eutrapelus heaps over the movement of persuasive head-swaying: and with impressed faith, the wonderful work works.*[22]

At such points Harvey sounds much like an early modern Jay Gatsby (or James Gatz, rather), setting himself to a course of self-improvement: 'Practice elocution, poise and how to attain it. . . . Study needed inventions. . . . Read one improving book or magazine per week.'[23] And yet the goal of Harvey's exercises is not pragmatic but transcendent: '*Always mindful of a lofty way of living, of actualization* [entelechiae], *of multiplying, and of refinement, which most surpasses everything else. Singular matters which are easily the most consummate. Eutrapelus in bloom. Never faltering in any way.*'[24] More precisely, transcendence and pragmatism are essentially entwined, as they are in Aristotle: the *vita energetica* – the life of *energeia* – involves a double movement where practical application produces ethical development: '*Art is the quintessence of its faculty. Virtue is the actualization* [Entelechia] *of its perfection.*'[25] Harvey frequently describes this transcendence with the term *entelecheia*, or actualisation, which Aristotle uses in the *Metaphysics* to describe the final, complete, permanent endpoint of

21 Domenichi, *Facetie*, p. 334.
22 Guicciardini, *Detti*, *6r; Domenichi, *Facetie*, p. 347.
23 F. Scott Fitzgerald, *The Great Gatsby* (New York: Scribner, 2004), p. 173.
24 Domenichi, *Facetie*, p. 401.
25 Guicciardini, *Detti*, p. 149.

energeia.[26] Harvey's understanding of wit is thus explicitly *metaphysical*, in the mode often ascribed to poets such as Donne, Herbert and Crashaw: moving 'beyond ornament, ingenuity, and clever invention', wit 'provides a transcendent vision of life and a means to truth'.[27] '*Eutrapelus is all spirit and pure industry: and yet sport and jest precede actualization* [Enteleche] *itself*', Harvey reminds himself; speaking living barbs is thus understood as a path to perfection.[28]

How is Harvey to achieve *eutrapelia*, to become Eutrapelus? Over and again he insists on the necessity of learning texts *ad unguem*, typically translated as 'by heart'. In a characteristic set of instructions, Harvey advises, 'He shall neuer be good at an extemporall descant, that hath not all Heywood, and Martiall ad unguem: with the pithiest Apothegs of Laertius, and Plutarch. Neither can a discourser at the Table want his Quintessence, and Mensa Philosophica.'[29] Harvey's use of the term 'descant' illustrates his purpose: a 'discourser at the Table' must be prepared to extemporise on any given topic much as a musician improvises pleasing variations on a theme. The model is rhetorical: one must thoroughly digest one's selected store of *copia* (topics, adages, examples, maxims and so on) in order to improvise freely upon any subject. Yet the terms whereby Harvey imagines this process are more typically alchemical, as in his above reference to 'Quintessence', or in addressing favourite books as '*Familiar spirits by heart* [ad unguem]; *O Lord, make it complete*', or in direct references to the hermetic tradition: '*The occult properties of Eutrapelus; Hermes Trismegistus from the machine.*'[30] Harvey's memorised pages are thus the base matter that will create a pure quintessence of wit and a golden mastery of the world: 'Animus est entelechia: ingenium, quinta essentia: ars, aureum magisterium.'[31]

In the *Adages*, Erasmus explains the Horatian origins of the phrase *ad unguem*:

> The metaphor is taken from workers in marble, who draw the nail over the surface to test the joins in the stone. Horace: 'Fonteius, finished to the finger-nail', that is, a really polished person [*Satires* 1.5.32–3]. Again, in the *Art of*

---

[26] See Aristotle, *Metaphysics*, trans. Hugh Lawson-Tancred (New York: Penguin, 1998), pp. 253–77.

[27] Paul Stanwood and Lee Johnson, 'The Structure of Wit', in *The Wit of Seventeenth-Century Poetry*, ed. Claude Summers and Ted-Larry Pebworth (Columbia: University of Missouri Press, 1995), pp. 22–41 (p. 23). See also Bryan Lowrance, 'Marlowe's Wit: Power, Language, and the Literary in *Tamburlaine* and *Doctor Faustus*', *Modern Philology* 111 (2014), 711–32.

[28] Domenichi, *Facetie*, p. 406.

[29] Guicciardini, *Detti*, p. 146.

[30] Domenichi, *Facetie*, p. 427; Guicciardini, *Detti*, p. 89.

[31] Guicciardini, *Detti*, p. 89.

Poetry: 'That poem you should blame, / Where time and tenfold proving has not shaped / The finished work, and smoothed it to the nail'.[32]

As this gloss makes clear, the point *ad unguem* is the perfection of matter through meticulous craft, whether in sculpture or poetry or social performance. The primal source for *ad unguem* for an Elizabethan humanist, though, would have been William Lily's *Grammar*, from its 'Carmen de Moribus', a song of moral instructions that also illustrates various grammatical forms, which contains this instruction: 'And whatever you recite to me must be so well learned that it is at your fingertips [*ad unguem*], and give me every word with the book shut.'[33] *Ad unguem* is thus also a profoundly pedagogical virtue, bound to the scene of instruction, the schoolboy's struggle to master the linguistic and ethical *translationes* of the humanist curriculum.

In effect, Harvey's project is to perform witty virtue *ad unguem*, removing any gap or seam between *ethos* (habit) and *ēthos* (character). This transcendence is implicitly theatrical: unlike the actor Theodorus, who merely seemed to become his character, Harvey will have no screen between the part he plays and him that plays it: absolute Eutrapelus. 'Assume a virtue if you have it not', Hamlet tells Gertrude, 'For use almost can change the stamp of nature' (3.4.158, 166); for Harvey, the virtue of *ad unguem* promises to eliminate that 'almost', erasing all evidence of the labour of performance and the apparatus of theatricality.[34] Of course, Hamlet's instruction is profoundly ironic, coming from a theatrical character who insists on a categorical division between 'actions that a man might play' and 'that within which passes show' (1.2.84, 85), and a play world in which performance is the dram of eale that corrupts all the noble substance of being. And indeed, as Harvey ruefully acknowledges at points, smoothing away the seam between his scripts and his social performance of *eutrapelia* seems to require more of him than he can provide: '*Without daily exercise of the whole, and continual movement of every part, one's vital vigour wanes, and actualization itself, the most potent thing of all things, becomes feeble. Work conquers all, but only heroic work*'; '*Nothing is more visible or welcome, nothing is as excellent or as memorable as the singular deeds of Eutrapelus. But still, the mind in the prison of the body lacks con-*

[32] *The Collected Works of Erasmus*, vol. 31, trans. Margaret Mann Phillips (Toronto: University of Toronto Press, 1982), p. 463.

[33] William Lily, *An introduction of the eyght partes of speche, and the construction of the same . . .* (London: Thomae Bertheleti, 1547), sig. I1r.

[34] *The Arden Shakespeare: Hamlet, Revised Edition*, ed. Ann Thompson and Neil Taylor (London: Bloomsbury, 2016). All citations are to this edition.

tinual reminders and a divine stimulus.'[35] Eutrapelian transcendence beckons, but Harvey lags, unable to commit to sufficient labour, unassisted by his extemporal god. '*Whoever needs books for speaking and acting expertly is not yet a man*', he vigorously chides himself, and yet Eutrapelus remains trapped on the margins of the jestbooks, unable to move into the world and enact his *vita energetica*.[36]

Harvey's sole attempt to become a public Eutrapelus began promisingly, with the publication of his witty correspondence with Edmund Spenser, but rapidly descended into the farcical pamphlet war with Thomas Nashe for which he is best known today. In tract after tract, Harvey attempted to school Nashe on decorum and the appropriate uses of *eutrapelia* while hypocritically sneering at the very witty works he glorifies in his marginalia, and by most accounts ended up thoroughly trounced. The Nashe affair makes only one appearance in the marginalia of these jestbooks, in the context of this jest:

> There was an insolent pedant, of poor manners like most of them, and certain gentlemen of the court made fun of him and his gaucheries, which had become unbearable: trying to be a literary man, he only spat out Cicero and Virgil, boring everyone. So Captain Bartolomeo di Poggio, a gentleman of Lucca . . . said to him, 'Sir, tell me, do you have Virgil memorised [alle mani, 'in hand']?' The pedant replied, 'Have you not noticed my familiarity?' 'In that case', replied the captain, 'please give me a page of it to wipe my ass.'[37]

In the margin Harvey writes, 'I haue wiped mie taile with su[m] peese of thie works to nash'. The deep irony of this gloss, of course, is that Harvey cannot recognise his actual position in the jest, which operates through a precise rebuttal of the ideal of *ad unguem*: the final thrust delaminates the pedant's learning from his social performance, exposing his affectation by emphasising the gross, untranscendent materiality of his memorised script. The diligent efforts of the pedant to cultivate his extemporal wit are destroyed in an instant by an impromptu riposte from a truly witty gentleman. At one point in their battle, sneering at Harvey's attempts to 'counterfeite a good witte', Nashe opines: 'He hath some good words, but he cannot writhe them and tosse them to and fro nimbly, or so bring them about, that hee maye make one streight thrust at his enemies face.'[38] Nashe, like the rest of us, judges character by its witty movements, the facility of its turns and tropes.

---

[35] Domenichi, *Facetie*, p. 410; Guicciardini, *Detti*, p. 72.
[36] Guicciardini, *Detti*, p. 87.
[37] Domenichi, *Facetie*, pp. 292–3.
[38] *The Works of Thomas Nashe*, ed. Ronald McKerrow (London: A H. Bullen, 1904), 1.282.

At the broadest level, I want to argue that Harvey is wrong about wit – and, perhaps, that Aristotle is wrong about virtue. That is, Harvey's investment in the metaphysical *telos* of witty virtue, as a kind of movement towards a perfection of being, represents a foundational mistake that wholly explains his failure to achieve *eutrapelia*. My perspective on these points is informed by Douglas Lanier's meditations on 'Shakespearean rhizomatics' in the context of adaptations of Shakespeare. As Lanier explains, Gilles Deleuze and Félix Guattari 'stress the fundamentally dynamic nature of existence, distinguishing potentiality from actuality, *dynamis* from *entelecheia*. But unlike Aristotle, the dynamic process of "becoming" is . . . not governed by any teleology, end-point or final form'.[39] Instead, existence is flux; what we misperceive as stable identity is in fact a ceaseless, antitelic process of becoming, whereby we are deterritorialised by our encounter with what we consider as other. Rather than framing existence in arborescent or tree-like terms – hierarchical, teleological, binary, linear, articulated, organised – Deleuze and Guattari offer the model of the rhizome: an endlessly spreading, non-hierarchical biological multiplicity, operating on principles of connectivity, where any segment of the multiplicity can connect to any other, or to anything else. Thus what matters is not virtue but *virtuality*: 'what a thing might become through the inexorability of difference and desire'.[40] Harvey seeks witty *entelecheia*, but is trapped inside an arborescent model of change and fulfilment: his tragedy is that he cannot think, or exist, rhizomatically – even when it actually happens to him. That is, in his paper war with Nashe something *happens* to Harvey's wit: it becomes outré, excessive, eccentric and extravagant, noticeably shifting it from the fastidious conceits of his first publications with Spenser. Throughout their battles Harvey mimics Nashe's words in order to mock and correct them, but this imitative interaction changes how he writes and thinks: one might say he undergoes a partial becoming-Nashe, contaminated by his contact with strange matter and manner. Whatever else might be said about it, the quarrel is certainly the most *creative* writing Harvey ever accomplishes. But he recoils from it, cannot come to terms with what Nashe makes him become, constantly retreats into decorum, eventually abandons the conversation, chooses stasis over transformation.

---

[39] Douglas Lanier, 'Shakespearean Rhizomatics: Adaptation, Ethics, Value', in *Shakespeare and the Ethics of Appropriation*, ed. Alexa Huang and Elizabeth Rivlin (New York: Palgrave Macmillan, 2014), p. 27. See also the work of Bryan Reynolds, especially *Performing Transversally: Reimagining Shakespeare and the Critical Future* (New York: Palgrave Macmillan, 2003).
[40] Lanier, 'Shakespearen Rhizomatics', p. 27.

In the space that remains I want to essay some rhizomatic connections between Harvey's failed project of metaphysical wit and what I see as Shakespeare's anti-metaphysical wit (and, at least implicitly, his antitelic modelling of virtual becoming) in *Love's Labour's Lost*. My approach, inevitably, is via another jest involving another pedant:

> COSTARD: Go to, thou hast it *ad dunghill*, at the fingers' ends, as they say.
> HOLOFERNES: O, I smell false Latin, 'dunghill' for *unguem*. (5.1.78–80)

The exchange seems to occupy the same terrain as the riposte out of Harvey's jestbook, with the difference that here the pedant's sniggering affectation triumphs; the jest is a condescending sneer at Costard's imperfect education, associating country clowns with incivility and filth. This is a characteristic mode for Holofernes, of course, who spends the play schooling the verbal pretensions of others while glorying in the achievements of his own wit. From an arborescent perspective, '"dunghill" for *unguem*' is what we now call a malapropism, words that are out of place, not apropos; the foul odour, or perhaps ordure, of Costard's 'false Latin' results not only from its matter but also from its disordered application. In miniature, then, Holofernes's fastidious response recapitulates the play's drive to reinforce hierarchy and orthodoxy through a rejection of the base, bodily and disorderly in favour of the pure, the polite and the virtuous – as shown immediately in Armado's response to Holofernes: 'Arts-man, preambulate. We will be singuled from the barbarous' (5.1.71–2). The arborescent aspect of the play is of course crowned by the inaugural ambitions of King Ferdinand: 'Navarre shall be the wonder of the world, / Our court shall be a little academe, / Still and contemplative in living art' (1.1.12–14).[41] Coupled to this pursuit of knowledge is a rejection of worldly pleasures; the King enjoins his would-be fellow scholars to 'war against your own affections / And the huge army of the world's desires' (1.1.9–10), and all vow to forgoe 'The grosser manner of these world's delights' (29). As sovereign, Ferdinand's personal renunciation of worldly delights is arborescently visited upon his subjects with the force of a decree – '*thy established proclaimed edict and continent canon*', as Armado puts it, in his written complaint against '*that low-spirited swain, that base minnow of thy mirth, . . . that unlettered, small-knowing soul, . . . that shallow vassal, . . . which, as I remember, hight Costard*' (1.1.240–9). The scene that begins with the establishment of Ferdinand's virtuous academy thus concludes with the arraignment and sentencing of Costard on charges of violating its purity.

---

41 All citations of the play are from *The Arden Shakespeare: Love's Labour's Lost*, ed. H. R. Woudhuysen (Walton-on-Thames: Thomas Nelson and Sons, 1998).

The lords' academic plan follows the Aristotelian model of using *eutrapelia* and *paidia* to further the *telos* of virtuous instruction. In response to Berowne's plaintive question, 'But is there no quick recreation granted?' (159), Ferdinand explains that he has retained 'a refined traveller of Spain' to break up their long work of studying with interludes of chivalric tales: 'This child of fancy, that Armado hight, / For interim to our studies shall relate / In high-born words the worth of many a knight / From tawny Spain, lost in the world's debate' (161, 168–71). Yet the pleasure of these recreational intermissions lies not in the stories of knights but in the ridiculous figure of Armado himself, 'A man in all the world's new fashion planted, / That hath a mint of phrases in his brain, / One who the music of his own vain tongue / Doth ravish like enchanting harmony' (162–5). Ferdinand explains, 'I love to hear him lie / And I will use him for my minstrelsy' (173–4). As with Harvey, then, the lords' ambition to know the greatest best things of the world – 'things hid and barred . . . from common sense', in Berowne's formulation (59) – proceeds in tandem with the speaking of living barbs, which will both revive the lords' pedagogical energies and reinforce the distinction between their true wit and the efforts of buffoons like Armado.

The arborescent structure of Ferdinand's academy persists throughout *Love's Labour's Lost*, even as the lords are propelled out of their proposed *vita contemplativa* into an awkward *vita activa* by the arrival of the Princess of France and her ladies, and the play's initial progress narrative refracts through a series of narrative slippages, deferrals and defeats. Abandoning their never-begun studies in favour of impotent infatuation, the lords agonise over their love and lost honour, until they enthusiastically endorse Berowne's rectifying alignment of amorous pursuits with the life academic:

> O, we have made a vow to study, lords,
> And in that vow we have forsworn our books; . . .
> From women's eyes this doctrine I derive:
> They sparkle still the right Promethean fire;
> They are the books, the arts, the academes,
> That show, contain, and nourish all the world
> Else none at all in aught proves excellent. (4.3.292–4, 324–8)

Remade as Neoplatonic pedagogy, love is made to conform with the play's progress narrative, with the lovers' beloveds repositioned from 'the stops that hinder study quite / And train our intellects to vain delight' (1.1.70–1) to the Promethean path to true knowledge. The Neoplatonic tenor of Berowne's speech needs little elaboration as a commonplace of Renaissance thought. Alas, nothing avails the lovers' travails, which undergo a series of dismissals. Receiving their letters, the ladies deem them too long and laborious; after they approach in person, the ladies complain of their 'shallow shows and prologue vilely penned, / And their rough carriage so ridiculous' (5.2.305–6). These failures of writing and performance are explicitly defined in terms of wit: 'Folly, in wisdom hatched, / Hath wisdom's warrant and the help of school / And wit's own grace to grace a learned fool'; 'Are these the breed of wits so wondered at?'; 'O poverty in wit, kingly-poor flout!' (5.2.70–2, 265–6, 269). Despite their strenuous efforts, Berowne concludes, they cannot match the polished artificiality and poise of someone like 'honey-tongued Boyet', who 'pecks up wit as pigeons peas / And utters it again when God doth please', but who knows how to perform his imitative complements: 'we that sell by gross, the Lord doth know, / Hath not the grace to grace it with such show' (5.2.315–20). As elsewhere in the play, 'grace' here has the complexity of Castiglione's *grazia*, its movements between virtue, embellishment and facility limning the outline of the perfect courtier.[42]

In a sense, the failure of the lords' wit is that it is taken as *only* wit. Hearing of the planned Muscovite masque, the Princess declares that 'they do it but in mockery merriment' (5.2.139), a belief apparently based on the unpersuasiveness of their love letters: 'We have received your letters full of love. / ... And in our maiden counsel rated them / At courtship, pleasant jest, and courtesy, / As bombast and as lining to the time' (5.2.771–5). That is, they interpreted them as *diagōgēs meta paidias*, of no further significance than eutrapelian recreation, a mere interludic pastime. In metaphysical terms, the problem with the amorous wit of the lords is that it cannot transcend the gross matter of its good words: the theatrical seam always shows. 'If I were a mistress', Philip Sidney remarks in a related context, '[such writers] would never persuade me they were in love; so coldly they apply fiery speeches, as men that had rather read lovers' writings ... than that in truth they feel those passions, which easily (as I think) may be betrayed by that same forcibleness or *energia* (as the Greeks call it) of the writer.'[43] Like Gabriel Harvey, the lovers of *Love's Labour's Lost* cannot achieve their *vita energetica* because they cannot find the path from performance to actuality; no 'extemporal god of rhyme' appears to guide their way (1.2.175).

What, then, of the virtualities of *ad dunghill*? We might begin by noting that Costard, despite (or perhaps because of) his ignoble entry to

---

[42] See Jennifer Richards, 'Assumed Simplicity and the Critique of Nobility: Or, How Castiglione Read Cicero', *Renaissance Quarterly* 54.2 (2001), 460–86.
[43] Philip Sidney, *An Apology for Poetry (Or The Defence of Poesy)*, ed. R. W. Maslen (Manchester: Manchester University Press, 2002), p. 113.

the play, is perhaps its only victor: in the 'Masque of the Nine Worthies' (a parade of models for virtuous emulation), Holofernes is 'out-faced' and driven from the stage by the mockery of his aristocratic audience, while Costard, as 'Pompey the Great', triumphs in his extemporised battle with Armado, impelling him along the virtuous path towards marriage with Jaquenetta. In a broader vein, we might consider Costard's malapropism as a signal example of the play's habit of 'preposterous reversals', as Patricia Parker labels them, whereby 'the language of the "high" . . . is contaminated or brought low by the "low matter" of the bodily and sexual'.[44] Parker argues that the play's pervasive obscene, scatological and sodometrical elements have been politely ignored by the critical tradition because of 'the later triumph of precisely the decorum (and "singulation" from the "barbarous") that is pilloried in this play', and works to 'situate both the play and this critical myopia within a broader early modern history, a history of the ordering (and "civilizing") of both body and body politic'.[45] To valorise *ad dunghill*, then, is to deterritorialise the arborescent territorializing of the play – a process that begins within the play but extends into its long reception history.

Of course, to call such moments 'preposterous reversals' is to use a language hostile to the unpredictable effects of their virtual becomings, the flux of experience that they inaugurate, a point also made by the shaming inversions Berowne uses to describe the effects of love: 'To see a king transformed to a gnat! / To see great Hercules whipping a gig, / And profound Solomon to tune a jig' (4.3.163–5). In the play's final scene, Berowne blames their failures on their beloveds – 'For your fair sakes have we neglected time, / Played foul play with our oaths. Your beauty, ladies, / Hath much deformed us, fashioning our humours / Even to the opposed end of our intents' (5.2.749–53) – but it would be fairer to say that the lords recoiled from the unexpected *détournements* that love invited, choosing instead to force it into the *telos* they already know. Like Gabriel Harvey in his rhetorical combat with Thomas Nashe, they retreat from the possibilities of the rhizomatic encounter, rewriting transformation as deformation. After Armado declares, 'My love is most immaculate white and red', his page Moth replies, 'Most maculate thoughts, master, are masked under such colours' (1.2.87–8). Katherine Eggert observes, 'Eager to translate his love into the well-worn language of love sonnets, Armado also purifies her alchemically', as red and white are colours associated with the highest stages of the

---

[44] Patricia Parker, 'Preposterous Reversals: *Love's Labour's Lost*', *Modern Language Quarterly* 54.4 (1993), 435–82 (p. 437).
[45] Ibid., p. 475 and p. 478 respectively.

alchemical process; more broadly, 'the play flirts openly with alchemical modes of learning, especially with alchemical modes of converting troublesome women into a purer and more tractable form'.[46] Such rhetorical alchemy lines up neatly with the teleologies of virtuous transcendence, yet Moth's quipping reply, while on one level reinforcing the stereotype of women as impure and intractable, might also be taken to acknowledge, or even endorse, the presence and persistence of the maculate. The reason the labour of the lovers is lost is because they force themselves to frame love as a labour, still waging war against their affections, unable to play freely in their passions. Berowne, love letter in hand, describes his love for Rosaline by declaring, 'I am toiling in a pitch – pitch that defiles. Defile! A foul word' (4.3.2–4). The problem of love in the play, one might say, is that the lovers refuse to truly embrace the maculate, the gross manner of the world's delights – to make material their love in something other than stilted rhyme (as always, with the exception of Costard, who took care of this with Jaquenetta before the play began).[47]

The idea of the immaculate overlaying and/or disguising the maculate resonates at every level of the play, including the pairing of 'ad unguem' and 'ad dunghill'. In a sense, it is as if there is an entirely different play operating underneath the glossy surface of the drama, a maculate, rhizomatic drama that underpins and makes possible the immaculate fantasy of virtuous perfection – in the same way, perhaps, that the idyllic pleasure of the play's Arcadian romances are underpinned by a mercenary dispute surrounding land title and financial payments, resolved by a 'packet' of 'specialities' (2.1.163, 164) whose arrival is elided from the represented action. I want to conclude by suggesting that another name for this maculate substrate is 'wit': not wit as the refined quintessence that the lords (and Gabriel Harvey) imagine will carry them into virtuous perfection, but wit as the very cunning of the scene, a craft or vehicle that carries something into action, an antitelic lexical and dramaturgical *energeia* that makes promiscuous connections, multiplying virtual possibilities. As with Harvey's metaphysical implementation of wit, I think Shakespeare's wit is something more than just verbal ingenuity and lexical intensity. And, like Harvey's ideal, Shakespeare's wit is always practical and energetic, involving a movement from potential to specific actuality – it is hard to imagine a theatrical worker doing otherwise. But I also see it as rhizomatic, and thus persistently deterritorialising the

---

[46] Katherine Eggert, *Disknowledge: Literature, Alchemy, and the End of Humanism in Renaissance England* (Philadelphia: University of Pennsylvania Press, 2015), pp. 199 and 193.
[47] Relevant here are Emily Shortslef's and Kristina Sutherland's discussions in this collection of the asymmetries of masculine and feminine virtue.

arborescent principles of order, sequence and transcendence that under-
gird metaphysical wit.

The rhizomatic virtualities of the clown's *ad dunghill* move and
spread even beyond the perimeters of the play. Dunghills, like malapropisms, may be matter out of place, but they are not without their virtues.
We might consider in this context Erasmus's witty encomium (in the
Adages) to the humble dung-beetle in its unceasing war with the majestic eagle, which among many other virtues points out that 'Alchemists,
obviously godlike men, are not ashamed to use dung in the search for
their "fifth essence."'[48] Or we might consider how paper was often made
from dunghill rags – a point Nashe and Harvey both allude to at points
in their pamphlet war – providing a corporeal slant on the digestion and
processing of *copia*, and the recycled, generative matter of the paper
bullets of the brain. Or we might especially consider Montaigne's scoff-
ing observation that 'man . . . perceiveth and seeth himselfe placed here,
amidst the filth and mire of the world . . . yet dareth imaginarily place
himself above the circle of the Moone, and reduce heaven under his
feete'.[49] This anti-metaphysical opposition between the fantastical trans-
ports of our imagination and the filthy reality of our existential location reverberates in complex ways in Shakespeare's corpus, especially
in its relation to his theatrical medium. Hamlet, despairing of human
transcendence, maps his disgust with our 'quintessence of dust' onto
the space in which he performs, declaring the 'excellent canopy' and
'majestical roof' of the Globe to be 'a foul and pestilent congregation of
vapours' (2.2.308, 299–304). Antony, by contrast, rejects 'the wide arch
/ Of the ranged empire' and claims the fecund materiality of both body
and stage: 'Here is my place! / . . . Our dungy earth alike / Feeds beast
as man' (1.1.34–7).[50]

'Theater', Samuel Weber argues, 'marks the spot where the spot
itself reveals itself to be an ineradicable macula, a stigma or stain that
cannot be cleansed or otherwise rendered transparent, diaphanous.'[51]
What Weber refers to here is the 'irreducible opacity' of the theatrical
apparatus itself, including the bodily labour of the actors – the seams

[48] *The Collected Works of Erasmus*, vol. 35, trans. Denis L. Drysdall (Toronto:
University of Toronto Press, 2005), p. 201.
[49] *The Essays . . . of Michaell de Montaigne*, trans. John Florio (London: Printed for
Edward Blount, 1603), p. 260. On this point, see Katie Adkison's anti-Aristotelian discussion of Montaigne and human voice in the context of *King Lear*.
[50] *The Arden Shakespeare: Antony and Cleopatra*, ed. John Wilders (London:
Bloomsbury, 1995). Cf. Carolyn Sale's fascinating analysis of Shakespeare's theatre as a
'sympoietic' ecology generative of social relations.
[51] Samuel Weber, *Theatricality as Medium* (New York: Fordham University Press,
2004), p. 7.

and spots that cannot be worn away or made invisible by the regimen of *ad unguem* because they are the very matter of theatricality.[52] Hamlet recoils from that reality; Antony fitfully, finally, embraces it. In this regard, we might also think about the contrast between *Love's Labour's Lost* and *The Taming of the Shrew*, another play that begins with the pursuit of Aristotelian virtue, but frames its imagined 'nursery of arts' (1.1.2) with the maculate space of a crossroads beside a country inn, with a company of players eking out a living on the road, a drunken beggar sleeping on the filthy ground, a raving hostess who keeps the till.[53] 'The dunghill is your freehold', Harvey declares to Nashe, without understanding the rhizomatic potency of such a location, and I would suggest the same is true of Shakespeare's theatre – including *Love's Labour's Lost*, despite the brilliance of its glossy surfaces and the refined character of its eutrapelian recreations.[54] Fusing love and edification, the lords imagine their desires as climbing a ladder to virtuous perfection; yet the miscarriage of this masterful image reveals that the true habitation of the play – the animating source of its graceful turns – is that copious, heterogenous, generative place where all the ladders start.

---

[52] Ibid., p. 7.
[53] *The Arden Shakespeare: The Taming of the Shrew*, ed. Barbara Hodgdon (London: Bloomsbury, 2010).
[54] Gabriel Harvey, *The Works of Gabriel Harvey*, ed. Alexander B. Grosart (London: 1884), 2.230.

Part III
Virtue in Transit

Chapter 8

Cymbeline and the Renewal of Constancy

Jesse M. Lander

Virtue is having a moment. This development owes something to the current political climate, which appears to have disproven Rochefoucauld's maxim that hypocrisy is the tribute that vice pays to virtue. But in truth the present sense of urgency has been building over time.[1] I open with a gesture towards history because I am interested in examining the entanglement of virtue ethics with history. While there is much that separates various versions of virtue ethics, these approaches invariably involve a sensitivity to cultural and historical context. In other words, virtue is understood to be a situated practice responsive to the exigencies of a particular shared lifeworld. In what follows, I will provide a description of Shakespearean constancy emerging principally from a reading of *Cymbeline*, but an important preliminary step in my analysis involves a consideration of the Neostoicism of Justus Lipsius, a Flemish humanist whose *De Constantia* (1584) presented a Christianised version of Seneca that proved to be enormously popular.[2] This procedure aims to clarify what Roman or Stoic constancy afforded Shakespeare and what, in turn, Shakespearean constancy affords us.

The recent prominence of virtue in Shakespeare studies has many sources, but the emergence of virtue ethics within moral philosophy deserves careful consideration. Many students of literature will immediately recognise names such as MacIntyre, Nussbaum and Williams, but G. E. M. Anscombe is likely less familiar, and yet when philosophers consider the question of modern virtue ethics, she is invariably

[1] Important developments include the emergence of virtue ethics within moral philosophy, the ethical turn within deconstruction and the later work of Foucault. More recently, an ethical turn in literary studies has been under way since the 1980s. See, for example, Amanda Anderson, *The Way We Argue Now: A Study in the Cultures of Theory* (Princeton, NJ: Princeton University Press, 2006).
[2] Adriana McCrea, *Constant Minds: Political Virtues and the Lipsian Paradigm in England, 1584–1650* (Toronto: University of Toronto Press, 1997).

identified as the starting point.[3] 'Modern Moral Philosophy' was first published in *Philosophy* in 1958, and despite its seemingly innocuous title, Anscombe's essay made a significant splash. At the risk of gross simplification, Anscombe's assessment of modern moral philosophy was sharply negative, and her key claim against its defenders was that they illegitimately resort to a version of moral obligation that presupposes the existence of a lawgiver. Though she does not in the essay make an extended case for virtue ethics, she observes that Aristotle's approach provides an alternative to the law-based versions of morality promulgated by Christianity, which 'derived its ethical notions from the Torah'.[4] Aristotle, in contrast, operates without a term for 'illicit', according to Anscombe, and his account of the virtues is not dependent on the idea of a lawgiver. Whether she intended to present virtue ethics as a viable programme for modern moral philosophy has been questioned, but there is no doubt that many read her essay as making just such a proposal.[5] Moreover, in the later part of the twentieth century and into the early twenty-first century, virtue ethics emerged as a third branch within moral philosophy, a distinct alterative to Kantian deontology (duty-based ethics), on the one hand, and varieties of consequentialism or utilitarianism, on the other.[6]

[3] Alasdair MacIntyre's *After Virtue* (Notre Dame, IN: University of Notre Dame Press, 1981) is probably the best-known single contribution to virtue ethics; Martha C. Nussbaum's *The Fragility of Goodness: Luck and Ethics in Greek Tragedy and Philosophy* (Cambridge: Cambridge University Press, 1986) initiated a wide-ranging body of work on classical virtue that has frequently touched on literary topics; and Bernard Williams, an important influence on Nussbaum, has deployed the resources of classical virtue in a sustained critique of modern moral philosophy, most comprehensively in his *Ethics and the Limits of Philosophy* (Cambridge, MA: Harvard University Press, 1984).

[4] G. E. M. Anscombe, 'Modern Moral Philosophy', *Philosophy* 33:124 (1958), 1–19 (p. 5). A useful introduction is Roger Crisp and Michael Slote, *Virtue Ethics* (Oxford: Oxford University Press, 1997).

[5] The reasons for doubt come down to the place of religion in her argument and her personal life. Her argument seems to take for granted a secular world in which the idea of a divine legislator is no longer credible (and thus versions of moral obligation that ultimately draw on law and presuppose a lawgiver fail), and yet Anscombe's personal commitment to Catholicism led some to suspect that the true import of her argument was to suggest that moral philosophy could only be rescued by recovering its religious sources.

[6] For scepticism about the category of 'virtue ethics', see Martha C. Nussbaum, 'Virtue Ethics: A Misleading Category?', *The Journal of Ethics* 3 (1999), 163–201. Nussbaum makes two central objections. First, virtue is not absent from the work of both utilitarians and deontologists and so cannot count as the distinctive interest of virtue ethics. Second, the extraordinary range of work being done under the banner of virtue ethics suggests that the approach is not unified enough to count as a coherent alternative to either utilitarianism or deontology. Despite these concerns, in the twenty-two years since, virtue ethics seems to have solidified its claim as a third way. See also Daniel C. Russell, *The Cambridge Companion to Virtue Ethics* (Cambridge: Cambridge University Press, 2013);

The rehabilitation of virtue ethics by contemporary moral philosophers has, however, had a limited impact on Shakespeare studies.[7] The reasons for this are several. First, the ethical turn in literary studies has tended to draw on other sources. In particular, scholars of literature have been influenced by writers working in the area once called 'theory', where a foregrounding of ethics emerged both in the writing of particular theorists (for example, Derrida and Foucault) but also as a more general response to the charge that there was something ethically deficient about theory.

Moreover, proponents of virtue ethics frequently adopt a conspicuously anti-theoretical stance. Though the target of their criticism was the arid philosophical systematising of modern moral philosophy, their privileging of situated virtue often sounds antiquarian to those inclined to take the concerns of theory seriously. Second, the notion of a return to virtue was bound to sound superfluous to scholars immersed in a period in which the discourse of virtue is ubiquitous.

Unlike contemporary moral philosophers attempting to persuade their colleagues of the fruitfulness of a turn to classical sources, Shakespearean scholars, working with texts that often seem intransigently antique, must struggle to make an argument about why such seemingly retrograde material has a claim on the attention of the contemporary world. And, from this perspective, the discourse of virtue seems to be an obstacle rather than a resource, for the same reason that many contemporary moral philosophers reject virtue ethics: the language of virtue is too entrenched in an alien world and its values. The root sense of virtue (*arête*) in its Aristotelian conception is excellence, and it seems indelibly tied to an aristocratic view of the world. The values of equality, freedom and universality can appear alien to this framework and as a consequence early modern virtue often appears conservative, traditional and oppressive. Third, and finally, the term *virtue* itself carries a whiff of sanctimony in contemporary English. The recently conspicuous phrase 'virtue signalling' is a perfect example. The

and Lorraine L. Besser-Jones and Michael Slote, *The Routledge Companion to Virtue Ethics* (London: Routledge, 2015).

[7] Two important exceptions are Richard Strier, 'Against Morality: From *Richard III* to *Antony and Cleopatra*', in *The Unrepentant Renaissance: From Petrarch to Shakespeare to Milton* (Chicago: University of Chicago Press, 2011), pp. 98–149; and Sara Coodin, 'What's Virtue Ethics Got to Do With It? Shakespearean Characters as Moral Character', in *Shakespeare and Moral Agency*, ed. Michael D. Bristol (London: Bloomsbury Academic, 2010), pp. 184–99. As his title suggests, Strier draws on Bernard Williams's critique of morality as a 'peculiar institution'. For an opposing view of Shakespeare and virtue, see David N. Beauregard, *Virtue's Own Feature: Shakespeare and the Virtue Ethics Tradition* (Newark: University of Delaware Press, 1995).

phrase not only indicts hypocrisy, but suggests that there is something at once performative and antiquated about virtue itself. Those inclined to call out virtue signalling are not, for the most part, interested in some robust or sincere version of virtue; instead, they are associating the word with a priggish desire to police the behaviour of others. These associations, combined with a well-developed aversion to didacticism in literary studies, are enough to guarantee suspicion, hesitancy, even hostility.

Despite these headwinds, there is a compelling argument for drawing on the work of virtue ethicists in an account of Shakespearean virtue. Such work is clarifying to the extent that it enables us to discriminate more clearly between the various versions of virtue promulgated at distinct historical moments. Though there are significant differences between the various scholars associated with virtue ethics, they all share an awareness that the project involves a sympathetic engagement with the past, that there is something untimely about virtue – untimely in the sense used by Nietzsche when he writes, in the *The Uses and Disadvantages of History for Life*, 'I do not know what meaning classical studies could have for our time if they were not untimely – that is to say, acting counter to our time and thereby acting on our time and, let us hope, for the benefit of a time to come.'[8] At the same time that such work contributes to a more precise delineation of historical difference, it also encourages us to be explicit about the uses we make of the past. While virtue ethicists are primarily interested in drawing on the past in order to articulate a normative ethics for the present, my primary aim is to elucidate constancy as it appears in *Cymbeline*. However, I also intend my engagement with Shakespearean constancy to open a conversation about the ways that reading and watching Shakespeare's plays can clarify our thinking about ethics in the contemporary moment. If virtue per se commands little respect in the broader culture at present, we nonetheless continue to conduct debates about right and wrong, good and bad, using what Bernard Williams has referred to as 'thick ethical concepts' – evaluative terms, such as *cowardice* and *brutality* – and this aspect of the contemporary world suggests that there is a place for the historical investigation not just of virtue but of particular virtues.[9] The persistence of certain virtue terms as well as the obsolescence of others invites critical reflection on the uses to which ethical language is put both in the past and the present.

---

[8] Friedrich Nietzsche, *Untimely Meditations*, ed. Daniel Breazeale, trans. R. J. Hollingdale (Cambridge: Cambridge University Press, 1997), p. 60.
[9] Williams, *Ethics*, pp. 129 and *passim*.

The virtue of constancy is distinctly pre-modern. From a present-day perspective that privileges innovation, change and creativity, the virtue of constancy seems sterile and immobile. In their succinct account of Renaissance constancy, Charles and Michelle Martindale observe, 'For many moderns it requires an effort of the historical imagination to warm to the idea of the static personality.'[10] In addition, our sense of the term is coloured by its troubling association with female sexual fidelity and subordination, exemplified, for instance, in the story of patient Griselda. Indeed, the gendered aspect of constancy is obtrusive in the early modern period: the misogynistic discourse that identifies women as essentially changeable codes constancy as specifically male. When, for example, Cleopatra, initially described as embodying 'infinite variety', declares herself to be 'marble-constant', she is, in one reading, positioning herself in her final moments as an exemplar of a peculiarly Roman and masculine virtue, an ethos that she has actively resisted throughout the play. Similarly, Elizabeth I's adoption of 'semper eadem' as a personal motto, whether a savvy piece of PR or an anxious retort to her detractors, is an attempt to neutralise the commonplace accusation that women are inconstant and thus incapable of rule. This straightforward gendering of constancy becomes more complex when the virtue is considered in connection with classical Rome. In the context of the Roman plays, constancy is understood to be a particularly Roman trait, one displayed by both women and men. Robert Miola, for example, makes the case for constancy as one of the fundamental attributes of *Romanitas* as depicted by Shakespeare, and Geoffrey Miles's *Shakespeare and the Constant Romans* provides a persuasive account of Shakespeare's treatment of two alternative lines of development within Stoicism.[11] Miles distinguishes between Senecan and Ciceronian versions of Stoic constancy; the first is starkly individualistic, emphasising the impervious detachment of the sage, while the second is socially embedded, emphasising the importance of consistently performing one's role. However, Miles, though he expands on Monsarrat's strict definition of Stoicism, is himself unwilling to be too expansive.[12] Observing that 'the *OED* distinguishes three

---

[10] Charles and Michelle Martindale, *Shakespeare and the Uses of Antiquity: An Introductory Essay* (New York: Routledge, 1990), p. 169.

[11] Robert S. Miola, *Shakespeare's Rome* (Cambridge: Cambridge University Press, 1983); Geoffrey Miles, *Shakespeare and the Constant Romans* (Oxford: Clarendon Press, 1996), p. 69.

[12] While themes and traditions entail inevitable vagueness, an insistence on a strictly defined set of Stoic concepts or doctrines is unnecessarily frugal. Gilles D. Monsarrat, *Light from the Porch: Stoicism and English Renaissance Literature* (Paris: Didier-Erudition, 1984), for example, provides an account of Stoicism that is so restrictive that it barely registers on the Tudor-Stuart stage.

senses of the word as a moral term, which may be labelled constancy (steadfastness), constancy (consistency), and constancy (fidelity)', Miles explains that the Stoic tradition combines the first two senses (steadfastness and consistency), and as a consequence his own discussion takes little notice of the third sense: fidelity. 'The originality of Shakespeare's treatment', according to Miles, 'lies in his awareness of the complexity of "constancy", the different senses of the word and the potential conflicts between them.'[13] However, by focusing on steadfastness and consistency, which he aligns with Senecan and Ciceronian Stoicism respectively, Miles gives an account of Shakespearean constancy that leaves out fidelity. Despite this, Miles, by attending to a more flexible Ciceronian version of constancy, significantly enriches the picture presented by Gordon Braden whose important book *Renaissance Tragedy and the Senecan Tradition: Anger's Privilege* identifies Stoicism on the stage with 'autarkic selfhood', a godlike self-sufficiency that typifies both the Senecan revenger and Stoic sage.[14]

Braden's 'autarkic selfhood' is clearly discernible in Sir John Stradling's translation of *Two Bookes of Constancie* by Justus Lipsius. It defines constancy as 'a right and immovable strength of the mind, neither lifted up nor pressed down with external or casual accidents'. Stradling adds: 'By strength, I understand a steadfastness not from opinion, but from judgment and sound reason. For I would in any case exclude obstinacy (or as I may more fitly term it, frowardness) which is a certain hardness of a stubborn mind, proceeding from pride or vainglory.'[15] Stradling here engages in the sort of elaboration that invariably accompanies an attempt to define a specific virtue. The distinction between steadfastness and obstinacy owes a debt to the Aristotelian tradition that situates each virtue as a mean between two extremes, but the substitution of *frowardness* for *obstinacy* is an example of rhetorical redescription.[16] *Obstinacy* is a Latinate word that shares a root with *constancy*, but *froward* descends from Old English and has an entirely different set of meanings. The root sense of departing (*from* + *ward*) gives rise to senses

---

[13] Miles, *Constant Romans*, p. 17.

[14] Gordon Braden, *Renaissance Tragedy and the Senecan Tradition: Anger's Privilege* (New Haven, CT: Yale University Press, 1985). For a perceptive account of Braden's 'autarkic selfhood', see Patrick Gray, 'Shakespeare vs. Seneca: Competing Visions of Human Dignity', in *Brill's Companion to the Reception of Senecan Tragedy: Scholarly, Theatrical and Literary Receptions*, ed. Eric Dodson-Robinson (Boston, MA: Brill, 2016), pp. 203–30, esp. p. 212.

[15] Justus Lipsius, *Two Bookes of Constancie* (London, 1595), p. 9.

[16] Quentin Skinner, 'Rhetorical Redescription and its Uses in Shakespeare', in *From Humanism to Hobbes: Studies in Rhetoric and Politics* (Cambridge: Cambridge University Press, 2018), pp. 89–117.

such as perverse, refractory, ungovernable. *Obstinacy* makes the adjacency of a virtuous and a malign rootedness too palpable; *frowardness* is, in fact, the opposite of stasis. In addition, by making constancy's evil twin the result of pride and vainglory, Stradling seeks to defuse the accusation made against the Stoics from at least Augustine's time that they were guilty of pride in imagining humans to be capable of godlike detachment.[17]

While Shakespeare's Roman plays are not uncritical in their depiction of a specifically Roman version of constancy (for example, Julius Caesar's claim to be 'as constant as the Northern Star'), *Cymbeline*, itself a quasi-Roman play, offers a sustained critique or revision of what Colin Burrow has termed 'one of the key words of the Roman moral vocabulary'.[18] The familiar plot of a woman slandered, illuminated by Kristina Sutherland's 'Masculine *Virtù* and Virtue in *Much Ado about Nothing*' in this volume, is not in itself surprising, but the way that the play forces a consideration of male inconstancy alongside female constancy produces a compelling reworking of the Stoic constancy found in Stradling's translation of Lipsius.[19] The version of constancy presented in *Cymbeline* combines all three of the senses identified by Miles: steadfastness, consistency and fidelity. Imogen's adoption of the alias Fidele is a fairly straightforward indicator of her deep connection to the concept of fidelity. Importantly, her faith is a faith in another person, not an abstract commitment to a set of principles or propositions. The version of constancy exemplified by Imogen is informed by the word's Latin etymology: *con-* + *stare*. This sense, to stand together, to stand with, gives the concept an intersubjective aspect that is absent from strict Stoic claims about autonomy and self-sufficiency.

The argument that breaks out in Rome begins with the recollection of a prior dispute between Posthumus and the Frenchman. As the Frenchman recounts, Posthumus had identified Imogen as 'more fair, virtuous, wise, chaste, constant, qualified, and less attemptable than any the rarest of our ladies in France' (1.4.60–3).[20] It is possible to read this inventory of virtues as mere *copia*, elaborating with variation on a single female virtue: chastity. Alternatively, one might argue that

[17] Christopher Brooke, *Philosophical Pride: Stoicism and Political Thought from Lipsius to Rousseau* (Princeton, NJ: Princeton University Press, 2012).

[18] Colin Burrow, *Shakespeare and Classical Antiquity* (Oxford: Oxford University Press, 2013), p. 222.

[19] In addition to Sutherland, see Helen Cooper, *The English Romance in Time: Transforming Motifs from Geoffrey of Monmouth to the Death of Shakespeare* (Oxford: Oxford University Press, 2004).

[20] William Shakespeare, *Cymbeline*, ed. Valerie Wayne, The Arden Shakespeare, 3rd series (London: Bloomsbury, 2017). All quotations are from this edition.

each element points to a distinctive attribute that overlaps but does not entirely coincide with the adjacent terms. While the list does not prioritise constancy, an exchange that comes soon after does. In response to Posthumus's question, 'What lady would you choose to assail?', Iachimo says: 'Yours, whom in constancy you think stands so safe' (1.4.128–9). The phrase 'in constancy' appears initially to apply to Posthumus's false opinion of Imogen. Iachimo insinuates that Posthumus mistakenly believes she stands in constancy (a phrase that threatens to collapse into 'inconstancy'). At the same time, his accusation may be that Posthumus's own constancy towards Imogen has overrated her virtue. The unsettled aspect of the phrase, which may be attached to either Posthumus or Imogen, suggests the intersubjective quality of their constancy as a joint enterprise.

In the action that follows, Posthumus's own claim to constancy swiftly evaporates. Once duped, the Briton exhibits a striking inconstancy. His repudiation of Imogen is immediate and starkly hyperbolic. In a rant that vies for top billing in terms of its conventional misogyny (Lear, Leontes and Hamlet offering the obvious competition), Posthumus concludes that women are responsible for all faults: 'All faults that name – nay, that hell knows – why, hers / In part or all, but rather all' (2.5.27–8). While Posthumus glances at the loathing over female generativity that Carolyn Sale finds at the heart of Lear's misogyny, his diatribe focuses less on the female body and more on the abstract question of virtue and vice.[21] Having catalogued the many vices that are attributable to 'the woman's part', he concludes, 'for even to vice / They are not constant but are changing still, / One vice but of a minute old for one / Not half so old as that' (2.5.23, 28–31).

Even commitment to a particular vice would have some redeeming quality, according to Posthumus, for whom inconstancy is the ultimate vice. But when Posthumus arrives in England as part of the Roman army, having received news of Imogen's supposed death from Pisanio, he repents his rash demand that she be killed. This change of heart has recently been discussed by Robert Miola, who credits Posthumus with an extraordinary forgiveness.[22] But what interests me is the way that his change of heart results in a change of sides: 'So I'll fight / Against the part I come with' (5.1.24–5). When the British forces prevail against the odds, Posthumus again changes sides: 'I have resumed again / The part

---

[21] The speech's single vivid image of sexual intercourse – 'Like a full-acorn'd boar, a German one, / Cried "O!" and mounted' (2.5.16–17) – refers to Iachimo.

[22] Robert Miola, '"Wrying but a little"? Marriage, Punishment, and Forgiveness in *Cymbeline*', in *Shakespeare and Renaissance Ethics*, ed. Patrick Gray and John D. Cox (Cambridge: Cambridge University Press, 2014), pp. 186–210.

I came in' (5.3.75–6). These vacillations are, however, subordinate to a serious purpose as an increasingly and explicitly suicidal Posthumus actively seeks death.

Being constant for death, Posthumus invites comparison to both Stoic sages and Christian martyrs, and the same points of comparison are relevant for an assessment of Imogen's response to the news that Posthumus has ordered Pisanio to murder her.[23] Imogen's initial reaction is extreme. When she invites Pisanio to use the knife on her, she appears on the verge of becoming a martyr for love. When Pisanio throws down the dagger, she chides him for failing to observe his master's command and declares herself incapable of suicide: 'Against self-slaughter / There is a prohibition so divine / That cravens my weak hand' (3.4.76–8). The echo of Hamlet's 'Or that the everlasting had not fixed his canon 'gainst self-slaughter' is an important reminder that Imogen here asserts that she is not an 'antique Roman' for whom constancy might serve as justification for suicide. At the same time, her readiness to submit recalls Desdemona's abject submission to Othello. The dynamic is similar: an innocent woman responds to an accusation of infidelity by reasserting her commitment to an abusive husband. However, unlike Desdemona, Imogen excoriates Posthumus for failing to stay true to her: 'All good seeming / By thy revolt, O husband, shall be thought / Put on for villainy' (3.4.54–6). At the same time that Imogen insists on what she describes as Posthumus's 'great fail' (64), she also, as Julia Reinhard Lupton has observed, stresses the importance of her own unconstrained choice in electing to marry Posthumus in the first place. 'In this scene', according to Lupton, 'she verbalizes, perhaps for the first time, that her choice of Posthumus as her husband established her ethical freedom.'[24] Despite her emphasis on his failure – what is initially deemed to be a sexual fault is subsequently understood to be a failure of judgement that is only partially ameliorated by the supposition that he has been deceived – Imogen does not repudiate Posthumus. Instead, she takes Pisanio's advice and adopts the disguise of Fidele in order find Posthumus and discover the cause of his errancy (3.4.143–51). Having embarked on this course, Imogen soon finds herself alone, lost, hungry and tired in the Welsh wilderness, where she declares, 'I should be sick / But my resolution helps me' (3.6.3–4). The steadfastness of purpose that Imogen here invokes is presumably her intention to offer her service to Lucius in order to make her way to Rome and discover Posthumus 'As truly

---

[23] The term 'constant martyr' is a common collocation in the post-Reformation discourse of martyrdom.

[24] Julia Reinhard Lupton, 'Birth Places: Shakespeare's Beliefs / Believing in Shakespeare', *Shakespeare Quarterly* 65 (2014), 399–420 (p. 409).

as he moves' (3.4.151). Having been misdirected in her attempt to find Milford Haven, she reflects on the problem of lying, a line of thought that brings her back to Posthumus: 'My dear lord, / Thou art one o' th' false ones. Now I think on thee / My hunger's gone, but even before, I was / At point to sink for food' (14–17). Imogen's 'resolution' is not merely determination in the abstract; it is more specifically a steadfast purpose to resolve her ambivalence regarding Posthumus who is at once 'one o' th' false ones' and the paragon of virtue she chose to marry.

Imogen's discovery of what she takes to be Posthumus's body appears to resolve her ambivalence. Mistakenly concluding that Pisanio has conspired with Cloten to murder an innocent Posthumus, whom she now describes as 'this most bravest vessel of the world' and, more simply, as 'A very valiant Briton, and a good' (4.2.318, 368), Imogen here displays a facet of constancy that comes close to what modern psychologists term 'resilience'. Absorbing the traumatic loss of her husband, she accepts Lucius's invitation: 'Wilt take thy chance with me?' (381). Her ability to adjust after catastrophe, to take her chances with Lucius, distinguishes her from tragic lovers for whom the loss of the beloved is the loss of all. Imogen insists that Posthumus be properly buried and that she be given the opportunity to pray for him, but once this ritual is performed, she is prepared to embrace an uncertain and open-ended future.

The play's final scene is notorious for its head-spinning sequence of revelations. Sarah Beckwith has recently described the play's conclusion as enacting a particular form of post-Reformation confession: 'So language returns as gift through the offerings of truthful speech, speech animated by the realizations, the making real of each to each in remorse.'[25] Her account is compelling, and the observation that the people assembled on the stage 'are unknown to one another in a variety of ways' is an apt description. However, her claim that 'All, in any case, have mistaken or confused views of each other' universalises a condition of misrecognition that appears not to apply to Imogen.[26] It is Imogen who compels a confession from Iachimo. His story staggers Posthumus who, in turn, volunteers his own confession, but Imogen is unsurprised by his account. In a shocking bit of stage action, her attempt to comfort the grief-stricken Posthumus with the news of her survival is met with an angry and violent rebuff. Cast off and momentarily unconscious, Imogen replays her earlier 'death' and recovery. Once up, she embraces

---

[25] Sarah Beckwith, *Shakespeare and the Grammar of Forgiveness* (Ithaca, NY: Cornell University Press, 2011), p. 126.
[26] Ibid., p. 122.

Posthumus and asks, 'Why did you throw your wedded lady from you?' (5.5.260). Posthumus does not, perhaps cannot, answer the question. Instead, he testifies to their inseparability: 'Hang there like fruit, my soul, / Till the tree die!' (262–3).

The sequence of revelations that structure the last scene finally concludes with the Soothsayer's etymological explication of Jupiter's riddling prophecy:

> The piece of tender air, thy virtuous daughter,
> Which we call *mollis aer*, and *mollis aer*
> We term it *mulier*: which *mulier* I divine
> Is this most constant wife, who even now,
> Answering the letter of the oracle,
> [*to Posthumus*] Unknown to you, unsought, were clipped about
> With this most tender air. (5.5.445–51)

The phrase 'constant wife' is so commonplace that it seems beneath comment. However, alongside the Soothsayer's etymological punning, *constant* here activates its root sense of standing with, an apt description of the reunited couple. Importantly, Imogen's version of constancy is significantly intersubjective. The claim that Stoicism addresses itself to a world understood in terms of atomistic individualism is familiar, and Stoic constancy, whether understood as steadfastness or consistency, involves the internal conditions of the individual. Constancy as fidelity, however, involves an attachment to something outside the person. Fidelity to a cause or a principle seems not to have captured Shakespeare's imagination, but fidelity to another person is, in contrast, a constant preoccupation. And Imogen is, in Michael Gadaleto's apt phrase, an 'agent of active fidelity'. The pursuit of attachment, in other words, is not a diminishment but an enlargement of agency.

Perhaps the best Shakespearean illustration of constancy as shared understanding appears in Hippolyta's response to the scepticism of Theseus in *A Midsummer Night's Dream*:

> But all the story of the night told over,
> And all their minds transfigured so together,
> More witnesseth than fancy's images
> And grows to something of great constancy. (5.1.23–6)

Hippolyta's version of constancy is able to accommodate growth and change, and it is significantly intersubjective, uniting the four lovers around a shared understanding of the night's events. Despite the shape-shifting and the changing allegiances that give the play its comic energy, *A Midsummer Night's Dream* ends with an invocation of a capacious sort of constancy that is durable but not static. This expansive version of constancy contrasts favourably with the more restrictive account offered in Sonnet 105:

> Kind is my love today, tomorrow kind,
> Still constant in a wondrous excellence;
> Therefore my verse, to constancy confined,
> One thing expressing, leaves out difference.

The familiar theme of poetic exhaustion is presented here in terms of constancy: the poet's verse, 'to constancy confined', excludes difference, presenting a monotonous sameness. Suggesting that there is a meaningful difference between the version of constancy in Sonnet 105 and that developed in *Midsummer Night's Dream* and *Cymbeline* points to the importance of context in accounts of virtue and particular virtues.

Questions of cultural rather than textual context are central to Bernard Williams's account of thick ethical concepts, a notion developed in order to expose the weakness of thin concepts like right and wrong. Introduced in *Ethics and the Limits of Philosophy*, Williams first elaborates on the term in a discussion of the fact–value distinction where he points to the existence of '"thicker" or more specific ethical notions ... such as *treachery* and *promise* and *brutality* and *courage*': 'The way these notions are applied is determined by what the world is like (for instance, by how someone has behaved), and yet, at the same time, their application usually involves a certain valuation of the situation, of persons or actions.' Elsewhere, Williams claims that 'the application of these concepts is at the same time world-guided and action-guiding'.[27] Readers familiar with New Historicism may hear an echo of Clifford Geertz's 'thick description', and both approaches emphasise the importance of local culture, but Williams's interest in the history of moral thought led him to focus on continuity as well as difference.[28] Thick concepts come laden with history and this historical freight gives them potency but also invites debate about their proper meaning and application.

I have been making the argument that *Cymbeline* is, among other things, an engagement with the virtue of constancy that responds to Neostoic claims by insisting on the value of attachment to others. As a thick ethical concept, constancy has a long history before Shakespeare takes it up, and it goes on to have a long afterlife. As important as this diachronic history is, there is a synchronic aspect that also needs

---

[27] Williams, *Ethics*, pp. 129 and 141 respectively.
[28] Presumably, both Geertz and Williams were influenced by Gilbert Ryle, an analytical philosopher at Oxford, who first developed the notion of 'thick description'.

attention. Virtues tend to come in groups. Indeed, one of the appealing aspects of virtue ethics is that such approaches tend towards value pluralism: the various virtues identified point towards different, specific values that contribute to human flourishing. That said, classical virtue theories regularly take up the question of the unity of the virtues, and virtue theorists invariably want to systematise the messy and proliferating set of terms used to name 'ethically admirable dispositions of character'.[29] Despite the systemic treatments of virtue available in both classical and medieval philosophy, the Renaissance habit of gathering precepts and commonplaces encouraged an opportunistic or occasional approach to the virtues. Furthermore, the tendency to combine precepts from classical sources with prohibitions and imperatives drawn from scripture created a vibrant but volatile culture of virtue in which genuine conflict existed.[30] Shakespeare draws on this ferment to offer dramas about characters facing ethical quandaries, who themselves regularly deploy thick evaluative concepts as they navigate the world of the play and its challenges. But there is very little that is systematic or programmatic about this endeavour. The virtues exhibited by Shakespearean characters seem tightly bound to their dramatic contexts: often what appears as virtue in one play becomes a liability in another. That said, it is possible to imagine a specifically Shakespearean list of virtues, which would include constancy, but would not sort itself into a legible hierarchy or identify a single pre-eminent virtue. In *Cymbeline*, the virtues of honesty and loyalty, which will be discussed below, are prominent, but so also are courage, charity, piety and resourcefulness. These virtues are unevenly distributed among the play's characters, and yet the possession of one virtue is usually complemented by possession of the others. Nonetheless, the constellation of virtues on display in the play do not resolve into a single, pre-eminent virtue.

In contrast, Lipsius in *Of Constancy* does suggest that constancy is the necessary condition for all other virtues. 'A right and immovable

---

[29] Williams, *Ethics*, p. 9. For a helpful account of the unity of virtues in Greek philosophy, see John M. Cooper, 'The Unity of Virtue', in Cooper, *Reason and Emotion: Essays on Ancient Moral Psychology and Ethical Theory* (Princeton, NJ: Princeton University Press, 1999), pp. 76–117. Cooper identifies a 'strong tradition', exemplified in 'the moral thought of Socrates ... and in Stoic ethical theory' that 'insisted that there was only a single unified condition, virtue itself, of which the particular virtues that we normally distinguish from one another are (in one way or another) actually only aspects' (p. 76).

[30] For a succinct account of virtue ethics in a Christian context, see Jean Porter, 'Virtue Ethics in the Medieval Period', *The Cambridge Companion to Virtue Ethics*, pp. 70–91. Porter opens her account by observing that the centrality of virtue in the moral discourse of the Middle Ages should surprise us more than it does: 'In contrast to the categories of law and sin, "virtue" is not a scriptural motif, nor does this concept have obvious theological connotations' (p. 70).

strength of the mind, neither lifted up nor pressed down with external or casual accidents' is, in his presentation, what enables the pursuit of virtue, and, in keeping with the tradition of Stoicism, Lipsius insists that virtue is invulnerable because it has judged correctly that 'external or casual accidents' are irrelevant. However implausibly, the collapse of one's life partner into error and violence would, by this account, not disturb the equilibrium of a constant person. A different argument for the pre-eminence of constancy is made by Alasdair MacIntyre in his account of Jane Austen's novels. In *After Virtue*, MacIntyre presents Austen as 'the last great effective imaginative voice of the tradition of thought about, and practice of, the virtues which I have tried to identify'.[31] In his telling, Austen's two chief virtues are self-knowledge and constancy, which MacIntyre puzzlingly describes as 'relatively new to the catalogue of virtues'. Austenian constancy turns out to be distinctively modern, as MacIntyre makes clear in distinguishing it from patience:

> Constancy is reinforced by and reinforces the Christian virtue of patience, but it is not the same as patience, just as patience which is reinforced by and reinforces the Aristotelian virtue of courage, is not the same as courage. For just as patience necessarily involves a recognition of the character of the world, of a kind which courage does not necessarily require, so constancy requires a recognition of a particular kind of threat to the integrity of the personality in the peculiarly modern social world, a recognition which patience does not necessarily require.[32]

According to MacIntyre, Austen's constancy is like Aristotle's *phronesis*: it is the virtue that makes other virtues possible. At the same time, it is a peculiarly modern response to a modern condition of fragmentation and alienation. MacIntyre's account of virtue insists that it be located within the 'unity of a human life', and constancy serves as the virtue that unifies a life for Austen: 'any specific account of the virtues presupposes an equally specific account of the narrative structure and unity of human life and *vice versa*'.[33] Having begun with the idea that the virtue of constancy is distinctly pre-modern, it is surprising to have arrived at an argument suggesting that is, in fact, peculiarly modern.

However one assesses MacIntyre's claim for Austenian constancy, it is immediately evident that this version of constancy is at some remove from the Shakespearean version available in *Cymbeline*. Though constancy has, as I have argued, a central place in the play, it is not treated as the primary virtue, but is instead placed among an array of other par-

---

[31] MacIntyre, *After Virtue*, p. 240.
[32] Ibid., p. 242.
[33] Ibid., p. 243.

ticular strengths of character. Additionally, constancy is itself revealed to be highly situational. There are challenges that demand constancy, but there are others that require flexibility (or resourcefulness). This points to a basic issue for all virtue-based ethics: virtues are not rules to be applied to particular cases, but are instead durable dispositions. And yet the problem of fit remains: in certain circumstances particular virtues are infelicitous. For many virtue theorists both ancient and modern, this banal observation motivates arguments designed to shore up virtue against the circumstantial and contingent. The most emphatic version of this argument is the Stoic assertion that true virtue is invulnerable to external circumstance and contingency.

The claim that *Cymbeline* is unsystematic in its treatment of the virtues is only to observe that it is, after all, a play and not a treatise on ethics. As a play it offers something more than a convenient scaffold for a constellation of ethical commonplaces. The affordances of character and narrative enable an engagement with the various virtues and vices on display that falls short of theory but amounts to something more than mere agglomeration. An inventory of the conspicuous virtues in *Cymbeline* would include courage, charity, piety, honesty, loyalty and constancy. The vices include irascibility, duplicity, self-regard and ambition. What this suggests is an attention to particular virtues, which often seem to shade into adjacent virtues, and a general neglect of the systematic. Honesty and loyalty, for example, feature prominently in the play as explicit virtues attached to particular characters. Belarius celebrates his life of rustic exile as 'honest freedom' (3.3.71), which he distinguishes from the corruption and slander of court. The two brothers are described by both Belarius and Imogen as ingenuous and transparent; all three of the men are described by Imogen after she wakes from the sleeping draught as 'honest creatures' (4.2.298). At the opening of the final scene when Cymbeline prepares to knight Belarius, Guiderius and Arviragus for their service in the battle, Belarius identifies them as gentlemen from Cambria, adding 'Further to boast were neither true nor modest, / Unless I add we are honest' (5.5.18–19).[34] Though here Belarius associates his honesty with truth-telling, it is evident that the virtue of honesty does not entail consistent truth-telling. After all, Belarius has misled the princes about their birth for the last twenty

---

[34] Aristotle's account of truthfulness in the *Nichomachean Ethics*, trans. Terence Irwin (Indianapolis, IN: Hackett Publishing, 1985), is preoccupied with boastfulness, which is construed as a blameworthy excess of truthfulness, whereas self-deprecation is identified as a deficiency of truthfulness: 'The intermediate person, however, is straightforward, truthful in what he says and does, since he acknowledges the qualities he has without belittling or exaggerating' (1127a25).

years. Moreover, the false accusation against Belarius, that he was con-
federate with the Romans (that is, disloyal and dishonest), leads to his
theft of the princes ('I stole these babes' [3.3.101]) an act that he justifies
as a reprisal for the seizing of his lands. The simple honesty that Belarius
claims turns out to be qualified.

In a similar fashion, the play works variations on the virtue of loyalty.
The central example, of course, is the loyalty of Imogen to Posthumus
and his to her, but the play also treats political and personal loyalty.[35]
The loyal Morgan driven to treason is one example. But perhaps the most
interesting case is Pisanio whose divided loyalties are tested throughout
the play. After the departure of Imogen from court, Cymbeline questions Pisanio about his daughter's whereabouts and threatens him with
torture. Unsurprisingly, Pisanio disclaims any knowledge, and begs,
'Beseech your highness, / Hold me for your loyal servant' (4.3.15–16).
Unexpectedly, he gets support from a nameless Lord, who affirms:
'I dare be bound he is true and shall perform / All parts of his subjection loyally' (4.3.18–19). Of course, this self-defensive bit of dissimu-
lation pales in comparison to the scene at 3.4. where Imogen rebukes
Pisanio for failing to perform Posthumus's order: 'Come, fellow, be
thou honest, / Do thou thy master's bidding' (3.4.65–6). Moments later
she adds: 'Why, I must die, / And if I do not by thy hand, thou art / No
servant of thy master's' (3.4.74–6). When Pisanio declares his incapacity, Imogen understandably demands to know: 'Why hast thou abused
/ So many miles with a pretence?' (3.4.102–3). Disloyal to Posthumus,
Pisanio has also not been honest with Imogen. His explanation reveals
that his own sense of his fundamental honesty has not been diminished
by the need to deceive: denying any intention to kill Imogen, Pisanio
declares that he undertook the trip in the hope of discovering a way out
of the 'bad employment' of his master, believing that 'if I were as wise
as honest, then / My purpose would prove well' (3.4.110, 118–19). In
his disobedience in the face of a bad command, Pisanio bears a marked
similarity to the rebellious servant in *King Lear* and Camillo in *The
Winter's Tale*, figures who both refuse the command of their liege lord
in order to preserve a greater good. At the same time, Pisanio, a remote
descendant of the tricky slave found in Roman comedy, believes that
his good intentions will be vindicated by events and that his resourceful
improvisation will 'prove well'. Pisanio's honesty is subject to explicit,
if ironic, commentary in the following scene when Cloten tries to recruit

---

[35] For an argument identifying a Lipsian version of political constancy in *Richard II*, see
Conal Condren, 'Skepticism and Political Constancy: *Richard II* and the Garden Scene as
a "Model of State"', *The Review of Politics* 78 (2016), 625–43.

him to his service: 'Sirrah, if thou wouldst not be a villain but do me true service, undergo those employments wherein I should have cause to use thee with a serious industry – that is, what villainy soe'er I bid thee do, to perform it directly and truly – I would think thee an honest man' (3.5.108–14). Perverse, paradoxical and funny, Cloten's take on honesty invites the audience to reflect on what makes this virtue virtuous.

Our version of honesty tends to be understood as an expressive virtue, a habit of sincere self-disclosure that we associate with truth-telling, and yet the early modern version of the virtue is clearly more expansive. The word itself derives from Anglo-Norman and its earliest uses have a strong connection to ideas of honour and social status (for example, 'the honesty' used to designate the honorable or respectable people as a group[36]). The generalised sense of displaying exemplary moral behaviour, virtue or rectitude becomes more specialised in the sixteenth century when the word comes to designate 'fair dealing; truth-fulness; integrity. Also: openness, candidness'.[37] The virtue claimed by both Pisanio and Belarius is this more general sense of integrity, a virtue lodged at the level of character and not in any serious way impugned by their occasional resort to misrepresentation and misappropriation.[38]

Constancy in *Cymbeline* is adjacent to both honesty and loyalty, and yet within the world of the play these three virtues are distinguished. Though all three are clearly social virtues, each points to a slightly different area of concern. Loyalty carries strong legal and political associations and prioritises attachment, duty and obligation. Honesty does not involve the same relational aspect, and it puts greater emphasis on the individual, especially when understood as a generalised condition of integrity. Even so, all versions of honesty require a social scene (whether of disclosure or collective approbation) for their realisation. Constancy involves elements of both loyalty (fidelity) and honesty (consistency), but also includes steadfastness, determination and perseverance. What this suggests is that these thick ethical concepts are deeply embedded in *Cymbeline*, but not so deeply embedded as to be invisible. The play foregrounds these virtues as objects of inquiry and reflection as well as habits of behaviour, and it clearly invites its audience to make ethical judgements about the characters on the stage. That said, it is important to acknowledge the distance between Shakespeare's *Cymbeline*, a drama for the public stage, and other literary genres that pursue a more

---

[36] *OED* 'honesty' n. I.1.d.

[37] *OED* 5.a. The development of *honest* displays the same trajectory.

[38] The character-based or agent-centred aspect of virtue ethics has provoked criticism. See, for example, J. B. Schneewind, 'The Misfortunes of Virtue', *Ethics* 101 (1990), 42–63.

programmatic inculcation of virtue. Spenser's famous letter to Raleigh describes the *Faerie Queene* as designed 'to fashion a gentleman or noble person in vertuous and gentle discipline', and while there is disagreement about what Spenser meant by Aristotle's 'twelve private morall vertues', there is broad agreement concerning the centrality of particular virtues to the extant books of the *Faerie Queene*.[39] Shakespearean drama works differently. Though Imogen at times comes close, she never turns into a personification of constancy.[40] What gives Shakespeare's virtues dramatic life is that they are integral to particular characters who argue and act. Conflict and ensuing plot entanglements reveal that virtue is never simple (that is, unmixed), that ethical quandaries are real and that virtue (however defined) is no guarantee against misfortune. This may seem an odd point to make in a discussion of *Cymbeline*, where a sequence of improbable contingencies saves the various virtuous characters from disaster, but the conspicuous role played by an inscrutable fate or providence in bringing things to a happy conclusion also serves as a reminder that it could have been otherwise.

As an example of dramatic romance or tragicomedy, *Cymbeline* foregrounds both contingency (plot twists and turns, sudden surprises, swift shifts in tone and register) and the power of virtue. At the risk of simplification, the genre of romance is virtue-centric. Romance narratives are, of course, capable of depicting ethical complications, but these stories, often focusing on quests or trials, inevitably vindicate the claims of virtue. They typically display, as Helen Cooper writes, 'a concern with ideals, especially secular ideals, and with human perfectibility within a social context'.[41] Indeed, at times, moral virtue assumes a quasi-magical status imbuing particular individuals with an extraordinary power to resist violence and overcome dangers. In the plays usually designated late romances, Shakespeare retains the providential framework that guarantees the ultimate success of virtue, but puts new scrutiny on the relationship between virtue and fortune both good and bad.[42] The

---

[39] *The Faerie Queene* (1609) includes the two Mutability Cantos which are described as 'parcell of some following Booke of the Faerie Queene, under the legend of Constancie' (Hh4r).

[40] Elsewhere in this collection, Michael Gadaleto makes this point emphatically in his argument for Imogen's 'moral development'.

[41] Helen Cooper, *The English Romance in Time: Transforming Motifs from Geoffrey of Monmouth to the Death of Shakespeare* (Oxford: Oxford University Press, 2004), p. 9.

[42] The problem of moral luck – the question of whether the moral status of an act is significantly impacted by factors beyond the agent's control – as a topic in modern moral philosophy can be traced to the publication of a pair of essays by Bernard Williams and Thomas Nagel, 'Moral Luck', *Proceedings of the Aristotelian Society*, supp. vol. 50 (1976), 115–50. Both essays were principally concerned to criticise the Kantian claim that a good will is invulnerable. Williams was a key influence on Nussbaum's *The Fragility*

upheavals and catastrophes that punctuate the action present a world that appears both irrational and illegible, and the response to such a world is often bewilderment. In *Cymbeline*, characters are regularly described as being in a state of perplexity. At the moment when Pisanio sighs and hesitates before revealing the content of Posthumus's letter to her, Imogen remarks, 'One but painted thus / Would be interpreted a thing perplexed / Beyond self-explication' (3.4.6–8). Later, Pisanio, distressed at not having received word from Imogen and ignorant of what has become of Cloten, complains that he remains 'Perplexed in all' (4.3.41). And yet he affirms that 'The heavens still must work' and that 'Fortune brings in some boats that are not steered' (41, 46). Imogen is herself described as 'perplexed' by Lucius when she spies the forfeited ring on Iachimo's finger (5.5.108). However, the best example of this condition is unaccompanied by the word itself. Waking from what he takes to be a visionary dream, Posthumus discovers a tablet containing an enigmatic prophecy, and, unable to interpret its meaning, he concludes: 'Be what it is, / The action of my life is like it, which I'll keep, / If but for sympathy' (5.4.119–21). Bewilderment, then, is a common response among the play's characters, but the fundamental optimism of the romance genre insists that ignorance, uncertainty and error are corrigible faults.

Despite the reassurances provided by genre, *Cymbeline*'s engagement with constancy and other virtues is sustained and subtle. Unlike many classical accounts of virtue, *Cymbeline* never suggests that constancy (or virtue) makes a person invulnerable. Indeed, the prospect of serious misfortune gives Shakespearean constancy its peculiar power. Fidelity to another person invariably involves exposure to a host of calamities, but the alternative, a refusal of such connection, is impoverished. The appeal of this version of Shakespearean constancy, combining steadfastness, consistency and fidelity, is, I hope, recognisable. And, yet, while it is evident that the thick concepts of honesty and loyalty continue to have, despite their various transformations, a purchase on the anglophone world of the twenty-first century, constancy does not. Our contemporary vocabulary of praise and blame includes terms that cover some of what was embraced by Shakespeare's constancy – determination, resourcefulness, reliability, consistency, commitment, faithfulness – but these characteristics are all narrower, and some of them, such as consistency and faithfulness, are not uniformly considered to be virtues.

---

of Goodness, which argues that Aristotle was, like the tragedians, highly sensitive to the problem of moral luck. See also Anthony Kenny, *Aristotle on the Perfect Life* (Oxford: Oxford University Press, 1992), pp. 56–85.

Clearly, this state of affairs reflects a shift from the early modern to the late modern or post-modern, but the obsolescence of some virtues and the untimeliness of virtue in general are no cause for lamentation. Instead, they are a reminder that though virtue and the virtues are not immutable, the language of virtue is durable, and it remains a powerful resource at a moment marked by fundamental ethical disagreement.

Chapter 9

Cymbeline and the 'Swan's Nest' of Britain: Insularity, Chastity and Imogen's Transnational Virtues

Michael Gadaleto

The temple
Of virtue was she; yea, and she herself.
– Posthumus, 5.5.220–1

Prithee, think
There's livers out of Britain.
– Imogen, 3.4.139–40[1]

Shakespeare's plays have long been aligned with a widespread move-ment in Elizabethan and Stuart literature to define, delimit and justify the sovereign English nation that, over the course of the sixteenth century, was fast replacing the older concept of a kingdom or realm. Accompanying this change was an acute anxiety over England's cultural identity, in response to which a generation of writers crafted literary signs of Englishness in order to fashion for their new state a national sense of self. Thus, as scholars such as Richard Helgerson have argued, Shakespeare's plays are invested in writing an emerging nation-state and rethinking the question of its identity – that is, of what constitutes 'This England' in the first place, of the source and authenticity of its supposed roots and origins, of the foundations and legitimacy of its governmental structures, and, indeed, of its very geographical and territorial demarca-tions.[2] Perhaps the most famous Shakespearean and larger Elizabethan

---

[1] *Cymbeline*, ed. Valerie Wayne, The Arden Shakespeare, 3rd series (London: Bloomsbury, 2017). All quotations from *Cymbeline* follow this edition and are cited parenthetically.

[2] See Richard Helgerson, *Forms of Nationhood: The Elizabethan Writing of England* (Chicago: University of Chicago Press, 1994), p. 4. The idea of an early modern 'nationalism' is still debated, as many political theorists have traditionally viewed nationalism as a strictly modern phenomenon, one that emerged in the mid-eighteenth century and depended upon such structural conditions of modernity as democracy, industrialisation and mass participation; see, for example, Ernest Gellner, *Nations*

characterisation of England is that of an 'island nation' – an early conception of national identity so potent that it can still be observed in the Brexit saga of today. Though based on a blatant misrepresentation of geographic reality that appropriated both the contiguous Scotland and Wales and the island of Ireland, this discourse of 'England' as an elect island state, coherent unto itself, was shaped by Protestant isolationism and physical separation from Catholic Europe; catalysed by Henry VIII's break with Rome; and concretised by the miraculous salvation from the Spanish Armada.[3] Noting that nationalism tends to be 'rooted in claims about land', island studies scholar Alex Law identifies early England's version as 'maritime island nationalism', an idea that 'derives its force from an island mentality that conceives Britain or, more usually, England, as an "island race"', a chosen people placed in a paradisal garden 'bounded by clearly defined watery borders'.[4] It is precisely this idea of nation that one finds in such history plays as *King John* (1594–6), where 'that England' is praised as a 'water-wallèd bulwark, still secure / And confident from foreign purposes' (2.1.26–8).[5] The most famous example, of course, is John of Gaunt's utopian encomium in *Richard II* (1595):

and Nationalism (Ithaca, NY: Cornell University Press, 1983), and E. J. Hobsbawm, *Nations and Nationalism since 1780: Programme, Myth, Reality*, 2nd edn (Cambridge: Cambridge University Press, 1992). However, as David Loewenstein and Paul Stevens (eds) argue in *Early Modern Nationalism and Milton's England* (Toronto: University of Toronto Press, 2008), early modern scholarship – influenced by Benedict Anderson's *Imagined Communities: Reflections on the Origin and Spread of Nationalism*, rev. ed. (London: Verso, 2006) – has persuasively 'pushed the roots of English nationalism back earlier, finding important evidence for the nation itself as an artificial and literary construct variously shaped by writers in sixteenth- and seventeenth-century England' (p. 7).

[3] This national self-image was also partly indebted to and legitimised by Virgil's famous image in *Eclogues* 1 of Britain as a far-off land, 'wholly sundered from the world' (*et penitus toto divisos orbe Britannos*).

[4] Alex Law, 'Of Navies and Navels: Britain as a Mental Island', in 'Islands: Objects of Representation', special issue, *Geografiska Annaler. Series B, Human Geography* 87.4 (2005), 267–77, esp. pp. 267 and 270. See also Liah Greenfeld, 'God's Firstborn: England', in Greenfeld, *Nationalism: Five Roads to Modernity* (Cambridge, MA: Harvard University Press, 1992), pp. 27–87; and Jonathan Scott, *When the Waves Ruled Britannia: Geography and Political Identities, 1500–1800* (Cambridge: Cambridge University Press, 2011), pp. 6–7.

[5] *The Norton Shakespeare*, gen. ed. Stephen Greenblatt, 3rd ed. (New York: W. W. Norton, 2016). Quotations from all Shakespeare plays other than *Cymbeline* follow this edition, with line numbers cited parenthetically. For more on Shakespeare's early formulation – and nascent critique – of island nationhood in *King John*, see Michael Gadaleto, 'Shakespeare's Bastard Nation: Skepticism and the English Isle in *King John*', *Shakespeare Quarterly* 69.1 (2018), 3–34.

This royal throne of kings, this sceptered isle,
This earth of majesty, this seat of Mars,
This other Eden, demi-paradise,
This fortress built by Nature for herself
Against infection and the hand of war,
This happy breed of men, this little world,
This precious stone set in the silver sea,
Which serves it in the office of a wall
Or as a moat defensive to a house
Against the envy of less happier lands –
This blessèd plot, this earth, this realm, this England . . . (2.1.40–50)

Gaunt's paean perfectly captures the essence of island nationhood, with its emphasis on a self-contained and 'defensive' sovereignty; on a natural, providential separation from a lesser outside realm; and on the Edenic nature of the 'little world' and its 'happy breed' of blessed inhabitants.

It is at this point that the concept of virtue and individual character can begin to be seen as crucial to any theory of nationhood, especially Shakespeare's. For alongside its confirmation of the English race's natural superiority and religious/moral exceptionalism, what the isolationist island model appears to have offered on an even more fundamental level (as it still offers many today) was a promise of identity and self-coherence that might perhaps be called 'comfortable' (or conformable). This model, and its complementary view of the wider world, assured the belonging national subject, first, of a sense of security from those supposedly ever-dangerous, 'less happier lands' beyond, from which the English need be kept 'secure / And confident from foreign purposes' (*King John* 2.1.27–8); and, second, of a deeper validation of the unique *rightness* and utter *sufficiency* of one's own 'little world' – and, hence, of oneself. From such a perspective, what one already knows (or thinks one knows) cannot be but best; and that which one does not know or has never experienced cannot be but worse and dangerous. The shoreline 'wall[s]' of the island 'fortress' thus both proffer protection from an inferior yet oddly dreaded 'outside' world and, perhaps more importantly, serve as the imagined bounds and internal structure of the island subject himself. In a very real way, to remain within the island is supposedly to be assured of who one is.

In Shakespeare's plays, 'virtue' is not an attribute explicitly attributed to England or any other nation, but rather a term (one used hundreds of times) to describe moral individuals or general moral qualities. Yet Shakespeare's model of exceptionalist, insular nationhood coheres to a striking degree with certain key notions of virtue in his work. First – and as will be discussed below – the idea of an isolated and specially protected geographic body aligns not only with the political cult of the Virgin Queen but also with the larger Elizabethan social construction of 'virtue' as that all-important ethic of female chastity and purity. Even more, however, the very concept of national uniqueness and self-coherence – qualities that then supposedly translate to the elect subjects belonging to that body politic – draws on the idea of 'virtue' in Shakespeare as more a kind of *power* and a source of defining, positive identity (as in, say, the virtue of a potent medicine or of an individual's distinctive character). Thought in this way, the elect island nation becomes a kind of virtuous subject writ large – a positively unique entity whose 'virtue' and defining potency lies in its separation from others and whose same virtue serves as a kind of providential protection from outside threats. Indeed, in this sense, Shakespeare's conception of the virtuous island nation anticipates Milton's term 'virtue-proof', which the epic poet would use to describe the seemingly invulnerable Eve, protected in her own prelapsarian island garden: 'no veil / She needed, virtue-proof, no thought infirm / Altered her cheek' – a term denoting that which 'is impervious to sin or some other harm as a result of being virtuous'.[6]

Yet what of the later Shakespeare? One of the playwright's most complex and significant representations of nationhood occurs some fifteen years after the well-known instances just cited – namely, in the fascinating but oft-neglected romance *Cymbeline* (1609–10), a play whose tragicomic depiction of Anglo-Roman history reflects, I believe, a fundamental departure from the earlier dramatisations of nationhood of the 1590s. For one thing, *Cymbeline*'s depiction of the nation is no less hybridic than the play's markedly mixed genre. 'Britain', not England, is the explicit subject of this strange work (the word itself is used twenty-eight times, appearing only thrice in all the other plays), an emphasis that aligns both with *Cymbeline*'s setting in the heterogeneous world of the first century CE as well as the larger archipelagic identity theoretically established by James I's Union of the Crowns.[7] Furthermore, as in

---

[6] John Milton, *Paradise Lost*, ed. Alastair Fowler, 2nd edn (London: Longman, 2007), 5.383–5. *OED* 'virtue' C2.

[7] The other three uses of 'Britain' all appear in that other 'ancient' British play, *King Lear*. See Emrys Jones, 'Stuart *Cymbeline*', *Essays in Criticism* 11 (1961), 84–99; Mary Floyd-Wilson, 'Delving to the Root: *Cymbeline*, Scotland, and the English Race', in *British Identities and English Renaissance Literature*, ed. David J. Baker and Willy Maley (Cambridge: Cambridge University Press, 2002), pp. 101–15; Maurice Hunt, 'Dismemberment, Corporal Reconstitution, and the Body Politic in *Cymbeline*', *Studies in Philology* 99.4 (2002), 404–31; Willy Maley, *Nation, State and Empire in English Renaissance Literature: Shakespeare to Milton* (New York: Palgrave, 2003), pp. 31–44; Ros King, *'Cymbeline': Constructions of Britain* (Burlington, VT: Ashgate,

plays like *King John* and *Henry V*, 'this ~~England~~ Britain' is bound in a complex relationship with a Continental polity, as King Cymbeline's island kingdom is here a tributary of the great Roman Empire of Augustus; and the conflict and interrelationship between Britain and Rome serve as the backdrop for the more intimate drama between the play's romantic heroes, Imogen and Posthumus.

Indeed, *Cymbeline* effectively stages two parallel foreign attempts to corrupt British virtue: first, the Italian Iacomo's plot to seduce and descriptively rape/disgrace Imogen, Britain's princess and heir presumptive; and second, the Roman Empire's attempt to invade and conquer the isle of Britain, thereby supposedly threatening not merely Cymbeline's rule but, more fundamentally, the nation's very identity and sense of self. The present essay considers how Shakespeare links the virtues of his great heroine, Imogen, with the virtues of the British nation; and how both individual and national virtue change over the course of the play, evolving from a traditional (misogynist) emphasis on purity, chastity and enclosed protectiveness into a more vulnerable but bold emphasis on hybridity and engagement with the other. The word 'virtue' and its derivatives appear some thirteen times in *Cymbeline*, the majority in the first three acts and most often in relation to Imogen's virginity and wifely chastity,[8] that central crux powering the plot which seemingly must be preserved from outside corruption at all costs. By the play's end, however, Imogen's virtue comes to signify something more than this insular and primarily negative definition, transforming into a far more dynamic ethic of courage, active fidelity and openness to the larger world. Crucially, then, *Cymbeline*'s rethinking of just what constitutes moral virtue – and female virtue in particular – guides and echoes the play's reconceptualisation of the 'true' British national character, a question given especial urgency in the context of a disorienting imperial environment where Romans so often look like Britons and Britons so often resemble Romans. What exactly is the defining 'virtue' of the nation, this play asks – what is it that really makes Britain Britain, and what makes this political entity special? In answer, I argue, *Cymbeline* ultimately rejects the comfortable identity of the island-nation model, instead conjuring a thornier but more compelling world in which a distinct 'British' identity yet exists, not in spite of but precisely because of its transnational character and ties.

2005); and Elizabeth Jane Bellamy, *Dire Straits: The Perils of Writing the Early Modern English Coastline from Leland to Milton* (Toronto: University of Toronto Press, 2013), pp. 106–13.
[8] *OED* 2c.

Transnational *Cymbeline*

Within *Cymbeline*, then, lies a critical tension – both ethical and political – between the supposed power of purity and that of hybridity.[9] As suggested above, the play reveals a different side of Shakespeare's 'writing of the nation' – namely, a transnational one, an approach to national identity based less on enclosure and purity than on England's multiple hybridic connections to other states and peoples.[10] As Barbara Fuchs and others have argued, at a time when the very concept of 'the nation' was still highly fluid, Shakespeare's plays show acute sensitivity to the dialectical formation of early nations and of newly nationalised subjectivities.[11] Far from merely endorsing the Elizabethan idea of an enclosed and water-walled 'island garden', *Cymbeline*'s exploration of early nationhood portrays what the transnational theorist Laura Doyle has described as 'the implicitly Other-oriented interactions between and among early nations, making them mutually shaping and mutually contingent phenomena'.[12] The unique Britain that Shakespeare envisions in *Cymbeline* ultimately exists, in other words, not because of its providential separation from other nations but thanks to its inescapable bonds with them.

Let us begin, then, by considering the ways in which *Cymbeline* reflects this more transnational view. With its self-consciously overstuffed plot, the play has often been read as a retrospective assortment of characters, conceits and devices from Shakespeare's earlier works, and the scene (3.1) in which Cymbeline defies the Roman demand for tribute certainly

[9] See Jean Feerick, 'The Imperial Graft: Horticulture, Hybridity, and the Art of Mingling Races in *Henry V* and *Cymbeline*', in *The Oxford Handbook of Shakespeare and Embodiment: Gender, Sexuality, and Race*, ed. Valerie Traub (Oxford: Oxford University Press, 2016), pp. 211–27, and Feerick, '*Cymbeline* and Virginia's British Climate', in *Strangers in Blood: Relocating Race in the Renaissance* (Toronto: University of Toronto Press, 2010), pp. 78–112.

[10] On the theory of early English island nationhood on the one hand versus a nascent transnationalism on the other, see Lynn Staley, *The Island Garden: England's Language of Nation from Gildas to Marvell* (Notre Dame, IN: University of Notre Dame Press, 2012).

[11] See Fuchs, 'Another Turn for Transnationalism: Empire, Nation, and Imperium in Early Modern Studies', *PMLA* 130.2 (2015), 412–18, and 'No Field Is an Island: Postcolonial and Transnational Approaches to Early Modern Drama', *Renaissance Drama* 40 (2012), 125–33. See also Carole Levin and John Watkins, *Shakespeare's Foreign Worlds: National and Transnational Identities in the Elizabethan Age* (Ithaca, NY: Cornell University Press, 2009).

[12] Laura Doyle, 'Towards a Philosophy of Transnationalism', *Journal of Transnational American Studies* 1.1 (2009), 1–29, esp. p. 1.

fits this pattern.[13] Here, the patriotic language of island nationhood so familiar from plays like *Richard II* is explicitly revived – only now not by a Shakespearean hero but by *Cymbeline*'s villains. While the British king addresses the Roman ambassador with amicable politeness, the reliably ridiculous Cloten announces that 'Britain's a world / By itself, and we will nothing pay / For wearing our own noses' (3.1.12–14). The evil (and nameless) Queen then follows up her son's oafish remark with an ode to the island nation worthy of John of Gaunt:

> Remember sir, my liege,
> The kings your ancestors, together with
> The natural bravery of your isle, which stands
> As Neptune's park, ribbed and paled in
> With oaks unscalable and roaring waters,
> With sands that will not bear your enemies' boats,
> But suck them up to th'topmast. (3.16–22)

Persuaded by such talk of Britain's self-containment within its providential 'salt-water girdle' (3.79–80), Cymbeline asserts his nation's independence and refuses to pay tribute, thereby initiating war with Rome.

Yet throughout the play one senses that this familiar rhetoric of insular separateness no longer suits with the later Shakespeare's vision of Britain. Upon learning of the plot against her life by the deluded Posthumus, Imogen confers with Pisanio about where to flee for safety:

> PISANIO: If not at court,
>   Then not in Britain must you bide.
> IMOGEN: Where then?
>   Hath Britain all the sun that shines? Day, night,
>   Are they not but in Britain? I'th' world's volume
>   Our Britain seems as of it but not in't,
>   In a great pool a swan's nest. Prithee, think
>   There's livers out of Britain. (3.4.134–40)

As if in refutation of Cloten's earlier image of Britain as 'a world / By itself', Imogen paints a lovelier and far more nuanced picture that sets Britain in a larger, meaningful world of which it forms a special but no longer exceptionalist part. Indeed, for her, the nation's vaunted isolation may be more a detriment than a benefit: comparing the world to a book, she suggests that Britain is like a page of that greater 'volume', but one not properly bound up with the rest – a piece of text perplexedly divorced from its true, more extensive context. Simultaneously, these same lines echo that most important of all early modern books, the

---

[13] See Wayne's introduction to the Arden edition, pp. 28–30.

Bible – specifically John 17:16, where, in one of several biblical passages responsible for the well-known commonplace that Christians should be 'in' the world but not 'of' it, Jesus defines his faithful followers as being 'not of the world, even as I am not of the world'. Imogen inverts this commonplace, however, suggesting that insular Britain is in fact too much 'of' the world – defined, that is, by its inhabitants' all-too-worldly shortcomings, sins and brutishness – while yet somehow failing to be properly 'in' it, to engage with and *be part of* the so-called 'outside' world.

Her figuration of the nation then evocatively shifts from the textual to the ecological, as the torn page is quietly transformed into the inspired image of a 'swan's nest' set in 'a great pool'. Shakespeare was almost certainly familiar with the nesting habits of swans, since the so-called Mute Swan had long been, as it thankfully remains today, a famous occupant of the river Avon, as well as the Thames. As Shakespeare thus likely knew, a pair of such swans – a male (cob) and female (pen), paired for life – would cooperatively construct a large, floating nest from an assemblage of nearby vegetation; and this make-shift island would, as Imogen's metaphor suggests, typically be constructed atop or just beside a body of slow-moving water – close, that is, but still somewhat separate from the earthen shore. In a single line, then, Imogen's image articulates a profound revision of Shakespeare's earlier idea of the island nation, converting it from Cloten and Gaunt's providentially isolated fortress-utopia into something rich and strange: a beautiful but temporary site of participatory companionship, protection and birth; a vulnerable but vital ecological space, apart from yet part of the nearby shore and all-encompassing 'great pool'; a pastoral home, distinct but connected, where new life is created, fostered and readied for the inevitable move *outward* towards neighbouring shores beyond.[14]

---

[14] I am indebted for my newly acquired knowledge of Britain's swans and their nesting habits to Michael A., Ciaranca et al., at the Cornell Lab of Ornithology (https://www.allaboutbirds.org/guide/Mute_Swan/lifehistory); the Royal Society for the Protection of Birds (https://www.rspb.org.uk/birds-and-wildlife/wildlife-guides/bird-a-z/mute-swan/nesting-and-breeding-habits/); Emily Cleaver's article of 31 July 2017 in *Smithsonian Magazine* (https://www.smithsonianmag.com/history/fascinating-history-british-thrones-swans-180964249/); Catherine Thompson's article of 8 April 2017 in *Stratford Observer* (https://stratfordobserver.co.uk/news/swan-population-a-welcome-sight/); and J. A. Hardman and D. R. Cooper's 'Mute Swans on the Warwickshire Avon – A Study of a Decline', *Wildfowl Journal* 31 (1980), 29–36. See also James Edmund Harting's *The Birds of Shakespeare* (London, 1871), pp. 201–8; Sir Archibald Geikie's *The Birds of Shakespeare* (Glasgow, 1916), pp. 85–7; and Peter Goodfellow's *Shakespeare's Birds*, complete with beautiful illustrations by Peter Hayman (Woodstock, NY: Overlook, 1985), pp. 10–12.

Imogen is not alone in *Cymbeline* in conveying and even personifying a more transnational orientation, for a similar if differently focused dynamic can be seen in the characterisation of her husband. In this highly British-centric work, Shakespeare nevertheless makes the 'outside' world concrete in a famously anachronistic scene in Rome where Posthumus, who spends the majority of the play in exile on the Continent, dines with a decidedly contemporary European coterie made up of his Italian rival, Iacomo, '*a Frenchman, a Dutchman and a Spaniard*' (1.4 s.d.). Much like the enigmatic Bastard Faulconbridge in *King John*, Posthumus seems to be *Cymbeline*'s strongest embodiment of hybrid Britishness. For, much like the nation itself, his origins are hazy and ambiguous: as one courtier puts it, 'I cannot delve him to the root' (1.1.28). What is known is that Posthumus derives from a great soldier named Sicilius – a name perhaps intentionally evocative of the Latin for Sicily, 'Sicilia' – who fought against Julius Caesar after 'join[ing] his honour' with Cassibelan, and who earned his titles along with the surname 'Leonatus' (lion-born) from Tenantius, Cassibelan's successor and the father of Cymbeline (1.1.28–33). Despite this honourable British war record, Sicilius is never actually identified as being British himself – and, indeed, it *is* stated that he was comrades with Filario, Posthumus's unquestionably Italian host in Rome: 'His father and I were soldiers together, to whom I have been often bound for no less than my life' (1.4.25–7). The possibility that Posthumus's father was in fact non-British tantalisingly hangs over this play, which throughout emphasises the strong ties of obligation, honour and wealth binding the Roman and British worlds together, as when Cymbeline proudly declares that Augustus himself 'knighted me; my youth I spent / Much under him; of him I gathered honour' (3.1.69–70).[15] Thus, when war at last reaches Britain in Act 5, it is telling that Posthumus arrives with it – dressed not as a Briton but as an Italian gentleman serving in the Roman army. Like his father before him, he soon dons the garb of 'a Briton peasant' (5.1.24) and 'join[s] his honour' to the British side, heroically aiding in the rescue of Cymbeline and securing the British victory (5.2) before resuming his Roman identity and being captured just prior to the final revelation scene (5.5).

Despite the British victory, however, *Cymbeline* ends not with an invocation of proud, self-reliant insularity but with an unexpected (and seemingly unnecessary) submission to the Roman Empire, as the king lays the blame for his earlier revolt and isolationist policy squarely on the shoulders of his now deceased Queen and stepson:

[15] See Peter Parolin, 'Anachronistic Italy: Cultural Alliances and National Identity in *Cymbeline*', *Shakespeare Studies* 30 (2002), 188–215.

> My peace we will begin. And Caius Lucius,
> Although the victor, we submit to Caesar,
> And to the Roman empire, promising
> To pay our wonted tribute, from the which
> We were dissuaded by our wicked Queen . . . (5.6.458–62)

Cymbeline thus concludes with an official affirmation of the transnational bond between Britain and its Continental Other, demonstrating that – in comparison with earlier works – Shakespeare's initial instinct towards hybridity and cross-cultural likeness had won substantial ground over the competing instinct towards containment and exclusion. Undoubtedly, a certain exceptionalist conception of British identity is still projected here: the Britons defeat the renowned Romans in battle; the geographic emphasis on Wales and Milford Haven (the site of Henry Tudor's landing before his victory over Richard III in 1485) allows Shakespeare to align national identity with a territory traditionally associated with ancient British-ness; and the protean Posthumus ultimately aligns himself with the British world rather than the European mainland. Yet *Cymbeline* clearly desires to have its Continental cake, even if it chooses to eat it back in Britain. The play revives Shakespeare's old language of insular separatism only to firmly reject it, ending not with a defensive separation between island and Continent but with an assured, symbolic union between them that *yet* allows Shakespeare's Britain to maintain a distinctive sense of national selfhood.[16]

Imogen's Virtue

As indicated above, however, in order to fully appreciate the significance of this more outward-looking orientation at *Cymbeline*'s end, we must consider the character of Imogen and the question of virtue. 'Your daughter's chastity – there it begins', states Iacomo in his closing confession (5.5.179). Interestingly, the very first appearance of the term 'virtue' in the play associatively connects Imogen's worth with Posthumus's, as a courtier declares that 'his virtue / By her election may be truly read'

---

[16] Patricia Parker and others have argued that *Cymbeline*'s positive representation of British-Roman relations indicates a kind of *translatio imperii*, a symbolic passing of Roman imperial greatness to Shakespeare's Britain; see Parker, 'Romance and Empire: Anachronistic *Cymbeline*', in *Unfolded Tales: Essays on Renaissance Romance*, ed. George M. Logan and Gordon Teskey (Ithaca, NY: Cornell University Press, 1989), pp. 189–207. See also Lisa Hopkins, '*Cymbeline*, the *Translatio Imperii*, and the Matter of Britain', in *Shakespeare and Wales: From the Marches to the Assembly*, ed. Willy Maley and Philip Schwyzer (Burlington, VT: Ashgate, 2010), pp. 143–55.

(1.1.52–3); thus, it is ultimately Imogen's virtue that signifies and confirms her husband's. Imogen's honour and fidelity become more explicitly central to the play thereafter, of course, when in 1.4 Posthumus instigates a sexist competition with his new Continental acquaintances over whose 'country mistresses' are 'more fair, virtuous, wise, chaste' and so on (1.4.58–9, 61). Provokingly challenged by the dangerous Iacomo, Posthumus insists of his wife that 'She holds her virtue still, and I my mind' (66); but when falsely persuaded of her infidelity, he quickly reverses this position in a misogynist soliloquy, exclaiming that 'The vows of women / Of no more bondage be to where they are made / Than they are to their virtues, which is nothing' (2.4.110–12). In this lewd linking of female (non)virtue with the 'no-thing' of the vagina (cf. *Hamlet* 3.2.105–8), Posthumus highlights one of the recurrent tensions in *Cymbeline* and in many of Shakespeare's plays: that between pleasing exteriors and foul, unseen interiors.[17] Iacomo, a cynical denigrator of women, nevertheless expresses this pervasive anxiety in positive terms upon first seeing Imogen: 'All of her that is out of door, most rich. / If she be furnished with a mind so rare, / She is alone th'Arabian bird' (1.6.15–17). The irony is that, while Imogen *is* effectively that 'rare' phoenix whose inner quality matches her external form, this singular virtue does not end up preventing her from being violated and slandered by Iacomo.[18]

This matters, in part, because Imogen represents *Cymbeline*'s most potent and complex symbol for Britain itself, an identification made explicit more than once – for instance, when the princess herself declares, self-referentially, 'My Lord, I fear, / Has forgot Britain' (1.6.111–12). Named after the wife of Brutus, the mythical founder of the British race, and recognised as the sole heir of Cymbeline, Imogen bears the weight of a purer and nobler British ancestry than her ambiguous husband. Thus, when the foreign Iacomo commits his trunk trick to overcome her defences (2.2), his sly but successful violation of Imogen's 'virtue' – understood in its original sense – signifies not only a threat to British identity but to the very model of virtue upon which that identity has been based: female chastity and, deeper than that, the idea of purity itself. For, in a way, the virtuous British heir's seclusion within the carefully described walls of her bedchamber (2.4.66ff.) symbolises the isolationist island-nation model itself: supposedly protected from external foes and situated in a site of elect virtue and providential safety,

[17] Eve Rachelle Sanders, 'Interiority and the Letter in *Cymbeline*', *Critical Survey* 12.2 (2000), 49–70.
[18] Robert Y. Turner, 'Slander in *Cymbeline* and Other Jacobean Tragicomedies', *ELR* 13.2 (1983), 182–202.

the nation/princess is meant to rest secure from external harm.[19] But this model and its attendant promise of security no longer serve: such 'rare' defences, *Cymbeline* suggests, still remain vulnerable to potentially fatal incursion. It is important to note here that, in contrast to many contemporaries, Shakespeare displays a striking scepticism towards the notion of any kind of historically 'pure' English or British genealogy, of a select race somehow 'unmixed with baser matter' (*Hamlet* 1.5.104).[20] This scepticism is ubiquitous, from his treatment of Anglo-French history in *King John*, to the archipelagic configurations of national community highlighted in *Henry V*, down to the British-Roman hybridity of *Cymbeline*. Throughout his career, it seems, the problem was thus how to balance this scepticism against his own (or his London audience's) apparent proclivity for tales of British exceptionalism. By the time of *Cymbeline*, Shakespeare's initial instinct towards hybridity and cross-cultural likeness appears to have won out, so that the distinctive virtue of the nation lies less in any supposed insular purity than in the very transnational and hybridic links that earlier seemed the greatest threat.

The evolution of Imogen's character, and of her virtues, over the course of the play has long been a controversial issue. More than one critic has argued that, despite her popularity as a seemingly strong female character, Imogen ultimately suffers a kind of diminution by the play's end that signals a larger rejection in *Cymbeline* of female agency.[21] After the turning point of Iacomo's violation, Imogen undergoes a series of transformations that could be read as subsuming her into a more masculine framework that ultimately excludes her from authority. Indeed, after disguising herself as the male 'Fidele' and unknowingly reuniting with her long-lost brothers in the Welsh wilds, Imogen supposedly expires from consuming a poison-turned-sleeping potion, prompting her brothers to hold a hasty funeral service (4.2.230–7). In their symbolic obsequies, one can read an image of the death of one Britain and the birth – or rebirth – of another, particularly in a play set during

[19] On the features of this bedroom and the key role of objects in *Cymbeline*, see Julia Reinhard Lupton, 'Nativity and Natality in *Cymbeline*', in Lupton, *Shakespeare Dwelling: Designs for the Theater of Life* (Chicago: University of Chicago Press, 2018), pp. 153–94. See also Valerie Wayne, 'The Woman's Parts of *Cymbeline*', in *Staged Properties in Early Modern English Drama*, ed. Jonathan Gil Harris and Natasha Korda (Cambridge: Cambridge University Press, 2002), pp. 288–315.

[20] Andrew Escobedo, 'From Britannia to England: *Cymbeline* and the Beginning of Nations', *Shakespeare Quarterly* 59.1 (2008), 60–87.

[21] On the gender dynamics in *Cymbeline*, see Jodi Mikalachki, '*Cymbeline* and the Masculine Romance of Roman Britain', in Mikalachki, *The Legacy of Boadicea: Gender and Nation in Early Modern England* (London: Routledge, 1998), pp. 96–114; and Coppélia Kahn, 'Postscript: *Cymbeline*: Paying Tribute to Rome', in Kahn, *Roman Shakespeare: Warriors, Wounds, and Women* (London: Routledge, 1997), pp. 160–70.

the age of Christ. Upon waking and mistaking Cloten's dismembered body for that of her husband, Imogen – almost as if in anticipation of Posthumus's forthcoming martial deeds – smears her face with blood and, still dressed as a man, joins the Roman army. In the final scene, then (thanks to the offstage death of the Queen), the stage is populated entirely by men, with one sole woman disguised as a man. Thus, the British world of the play, no matter how transnationally open it may be, has struck some as a definitively masculine one, a national construction privileging the Roman ethic of martial *virtus*, the re-establishment of patriarchy, and the complete marginalisation of women. (For more on Shakespearean explorations of and tensions between masculine *virtù* and feminine virtue, see Kristina Sutherland's essay on *Much Ado about Nothing* earlier in this volume.) Tellingly, when Guiderius and Arviragus – fresh from their manly slaughter of Romans – are reunited with their royal father, the first order of business is to restore the long-lost male heirs to the succession: 'O Imogen', Cymbeline notes in passing, 'Thou hast lost by this a kingdom' (5.5.371–2). And, indeed, Imogen's resumption of her female identity in the final scene is also accompanied by a punning reduction of her status from 'heir' to 'air', as her new role in the brave new British order is codified in the official interpretation of Jupiter's prophecy about 'a lion's whelp [Posthumus Leonatus] ... be[ing] embraced by a piece of tender air [Imogen]' (5.5.434–6). As the Soothsayer explains, 'The piece of tender air [is] thy virtuous daughter, / Which we call *mollis aer*, and *mollis aer* / We term it *mulier*' (445–7). In the fading of that 'virtuous daughter' from heir to air, from aspirant monarch to humble wife, would appear to lie, too, a transformation of the idea of nation in *Cymbeline*, an idea based less on an ethic of feminine virtue than masculine martial *virtus*.

Yet such a view overlooks, or fails to appreciate, the true dynamism of Imogen's character and moral development – a 'development' not in the sense of improvement but rather in terms of the *kinds* of virtue she represents. For whereas Imogen's virtue is chiefly defined early on – and almost exclusively by male characters – in terms of her faultless adherence to a prohibitive code of female chastity, this situation changes by the play's end. Doubtless, Imogen shows herself to be 'true', proving time and again her loving faithfulness to Posthumus and thereby living up to the high standard of fidelity represented by her assumed name, Fidele. But the very meaning of her 'fidelity' changes over the course of *Cymbeline*, and this change relates to the play's rethinking of nationhood. (On the key role of constancy throughout *Cymbeline* and Shakespeare's exploration of interpersonal virtue more generally, see Jesse M. Lander's essay in this volume.) In the first half of the play,

Imogen's virtue is largely defensive and contained. All Shakespeare's romance heroes must learn patience, but Imogen is particularly tested – her husband's unjust banishment, her father's wrath, her stepmother's schemes, and daily onslaughts from the insufferable Cloten are more than most could bear. But when that same husband makes his selfish wager, a new plague arrives from across the Channel to torment the princess: Iachimo, who only after failing to seduce Imogen with lies sneaks into her bedroom to steal her virtue as she sleeps – the only time, seemingly, that the vigilant Imogen can be bested.

As has already been suggested, then, the success of Iachimo's incursion into Imogen's private space and his symbolic theft of her virtue signifies, first, a critique of a defensive and limited conception of the ideal of chastity; and, second, a parallel critique of a defensive and bounded conception of nationhood. Neither Imogen nor Britain, Shakespeare suggests, can afford to define themselves in terms of the enclosed island language explicitly supported by the Queen, Cloten and Cymbeline (and implicitly supported by others like the humorously reclusive Belarius). Instead, a more expansive and courageously engaged sense of virtue and national selfhood is necessary. Thus, Act 3 finds Imogen at last leaving the insular space of the court and its false protection, risking both life and virtue by venturing into the Welsh wilds. The choice of Wales is significant insofar as this traditional border area at once challenged old geographies and mythologies of pure 'Englishness' while at the same time representing a kind of heart of Britannic identity, thanks to its historic associations with the ancient Britons and Arthurian legend.[22] In daring to travel to Wales, the British princess inadvertently lays claim to and rediscovers a crucial part of her own and her nation's identity: it is here that she reunites with her royal brothers, inspiring them to abandon their own form of misguided isolation, and where she begins to heal her broken family's past. Perhaps more importantly, it is in Wales that both Imogen *and* Posthumus symbolically die. Imogen's funeral in Act 4 and subsequent awakening next to the headless body of a man dressed in her beloved's clothes is one of the strangest and most sublime moments in all of Shakespeare. Just who has died – Imogen? Fidele?

---

[22] On the significance of Milford Haven and the Welsh setting in *Cymbeline*, see Ronald J. Boling, 'Anglo-Welsh Relations in *Cymbeline*', *Shakespeare Quarterly* 51.1 (2000), 33–66; Philip Schwyzer, *Literature, Nationalism and Memory in Early Modern England and Wales* (Cambridge: Cambridge University Press, 2004), pp. 169–74; John Kerrigan, *Archipelagic English: Literature, History, and Politics (1603–1707)* (Oxford: Oxford University Press, 2008), pp. 115–40; and Marisa R. Cull, 'Contextualizing 1610: *Cymbeline, The Valiant Welshman*, and The Princes of Wales', in *Shakespeare and Wales*, ed. Willy Maley and Philip Schwyzer (London: Routledge, 2010), pp. 127–42.

Cloten? Posthumus? 'Richard du Champ'? – is purposely unclear to almost everyone. Yet, in a key sense, for just a moment both Imogen and Posthumus, the one in Wales and the other in Rome, lie symbolically side by side in death – just beside, as it happens, the grave of Belarius's wife, Euriphile: 'lover of Europe'.

What symbolically dies in the Welsh forest is a bygone notion of nationhood, and what emerges in the joint resurrection and eventual reunion of Imogen and Posthumus is a new one. Far from being diminished by the demise of 'Fidele', Imogen mourns Posthumus but immediately sets to work fulfilling her plan of relocating to Rome, persuading Caius Lucius to adopt her into his service. Ironically, then, when Imogen and Posthumus at last reunite on stage in the closing scene, both are dressed in Roman attire. The return to court of the king's sons does remove Imogen from the succession and solidify, so to speak, her transformation from heir to air. But to overemphasise this is to miss Shakespeare's real reconception of political community. Not Guiderius nor Arviragus, but Imogen and Posthumus represent the play's ideal of Britain; and that ideal, far from being static, patriarchal and militant, is decidedly hybridic, intersubjective and based on a set of virtues now associated with Imogen and *her* journey through the thorny wilds of the play – active fidelity, courage, openness to the unknown, patience and forgiveness. Like Cymbeline's pacific and amicable reunion with Rome, Imogen's reunion with the hybridic British-Roman Posthumus – a man who, like the nation itself, cannot be 'delved to the root' and whose very name signifies rebirth after death – represents a new understanding of the nation a thousand miles removed from that of the 'water-walled' island of Shakespeare's earlier plays.

In a way, then, the character of Imogen and her distinctive virtues represent a fragile balance that Shakespeare attempts to strike, with varying levels of success and emphasis, throughout his career. On the one hand, he recognises even in his earliest histories the artificial and arbitrary constructedness of all national identities, and the perverse, absurd uses to which rulers and subjects alike tend to put those national narratives – almost always in the service of selfish and ignoble ends. From such a perspective, 'nation' appears little more than a farce, and a destructive, decidedly non-virtuous one at that. On the other hand, committed as he is to the myriad forms that human community might take, Shakespeare cannot ignore the appeal, the meaning or the sheer reality of early national identity – the bonds it claims, the complex histories it engenders and the virtuous or vicious individuals it shapes. How, then, his plays ask, can one be 'true' or faithful to a nation without becoming the slave to an idea? How can a nation be true to itself without devolving into exclusionary, paranoiac, self-obsessive idolatry? In short, how can one be *true* and *open* at the same time – both an engaged part of the wider world ('in' it, as it were, and not merely 'of' it) and, at the same time, distinctly 'British'?

More than perhaps any other Shakespearean character, Imogen embodies the achievement of this elusive balance. For having forgone the constraint of mere defensive chastity, she ventures out into the world as an agent of *active fidelity*, donning various guises and names while never abandoning her core selfhood. At the very end of her key aforementioned speech, Imogen concludes with an intriguingly peculiar line: 'Prithee, think / There's livers out of Britain' (3.4.139–40). This is, of course, the challenge to all isolationist thinking: to imagine and truly feel that life meaningfully exists outside the bounds of one's own circumscribed (and supposedly superior) *natio*. By that awkward word 'liver', Imogen ostensibly means one who lives or is alive;[23] but present, too, is the more common sense of the bodily organ thought in the early modern period to be the seat of the passions and perhaps the most important for the maintenance of life.[24] The unavoidable, fleshly materiality of the pun here may be precisely the point: for the entirety of Imogen's speech aims at manifesting, both for herself and her audience, that there is in fact a larger world outside of Britain, one in which the sun still shines, consequential events occur, and in which other flesh-and-blood beings – real, physical 'livers' – feel, think and act. Equipped with this unusual awareness that there are 'livers' outside Britain, and perfectly willing to become one herself, Imogen is at the same time a committed Briton – indeed, a royal 'piece of tender air'. Especially in her union with the mysteriously Britannic-Roman Posthumus, Imogen thus represents the later Shakespeare's ideal of British identity: faithful, courageous, always already hybridic and radically more open to the world. Her virtue represents the new transnational orientation that Shakespeare most fully embraces in *Cymbeline*, and serves as a critique of the island-nation thinking more familiar from earlier plays. Ultimately, Imogen's virtue, much like the very concept of 'Britain' itself, is at one and the same time as material, indisputable and localised as a liver, as ethereal and ubiquitous as air – the unique specificity, and the marvellous potentiality, of a swan's nest.

---

[23] *OED* n.2.

[24] *OED* n.1. In the closing reconciliation scene, for instance, Cymbeline honours Belarius, Guiderius and Arviragus as the saviours of his kingdom by naming them 'the liver, heart, and brain of Britain, / By whom, I grant, she lives' (5.5.14–15) – note the order of precedence. See, too, Belarius's lines at 3.3.8–9, where he uses the term in the same sense as Imogen: 'Hail, thou fair heaven! / We house i'th' rock, yet use thee not so hardly / As prouder livers do'.

Chapter 10

Sufi Theoeroticism, the Sophianic Feminine and Desdemona's Tragic Heroism

Unhae Park Langis

Destiny is recognizing the radiance of the soul that,
even when faced with human impossibility, loves all of life.
– Marion Woodman, *Bone: A Journal of Wisdom,*
Strength and Healing, p. xvi

This little point [*point vierge*] of nothingness and of absolute poverty
is the pure glory of God in us.
– Thomas Merton, 'A Member of the Human
Race', *A Thomas Merton Reader*, pp. 346–7

Sixteenth-century Venice, the setting of *Othello*, was an archetypal city-state where Beauty and Love interacted towards ends of transcendence and pleasure. Promoting its reputation as an international trade centre and a cosmopolitan city-state, Venice curated itself 'as a city founded on principles of equality, magnanimity, domestic harmony, and justice for all of its citizens'.[1] The most visible and ubiquitous icon of its civic aspirations combines both the divine and pagan emblems, the Virgin Mary and Venus Anadyomene, into a single female figure of Justice: Venetia, beautifully depicted in Paolo Veronese's ceiling allegory, *The Apotheosis of Venice* (1579). Aspiring to social and political concord, Venice, overseen and protected by this conflation of Venus and Virgin, was equally known for the unparalleled beauty of its courtesans and

[1] Margaret Rosenthal, *The Honest Courtesan: Veronica Franco, Citizen and Writer in Sixteenth-Century Venice* (Chicago: University of Chicago Press, 2012), p. 3. This essay is dedicated to my mother, Nancy Hyunsup Park, who passed during its writing. She was the one who combed into me the spiritual striving that kindled this essay decades before its realisation. It's been a great comfort that my thoughts on Desdemona as the Bride-Soul, as the 'excellent wretch', have supplied me with the language to honour and celebrate my mother, who, buried on her 64th wedding anniversary, joined her heavenly lord like her fictional exemplar. Many thanks to Jane Mikkelson and Marguerite Tassi for feedback, friendship and spiritual camaraderie; Katie Adkison, Robert Pierce and our discerning editors for their comments and encouragement, without which this essay would not have evolved into its present shape.

the unruly licentiousness to which Iago discreetly refers as 'our country disposition' (3.3.197).[2] According to English traveller Thomas Coryat, their 'allurements' were 'so infinite' that their fame 'hath drawn many to Venice from some of the remotest parts of Christendome, to contemplate their beauties, and enjoy their pleasing dalliances'.[3]

Against this backdrop of Venice's paradoxes, *Othello* intriguingly dramatises the theoeroticism surrounding the double-sided Venus whose divinity is misconstrued as lust in the sensible world. The play's embodiment of Venus is the great-souled Desdemona, who binds herself – 'soul and fortunes' (1.3.348) – to Othello, noble Moor of Venice. Triggered by the efforts of his perfidious ensign Iago who exploits the duality of Venus towards destructive self-serving ends, Othello detaches from his theoerotic partner and their conjoined aspirations to virtuous piety, signalling a further narrowing of the circumscribed sphere of female action. Against all adversity Desdemona still manages to present herself as a female archetype of virtue. A champion of bold humility, Desdemona trumpets an unexamined tragic heroism grounded in Sufi-Christian spirituality channelling Neoplatonism, the Hellenistic philosophy exhibiting elements common to the mystical expressions of Islam, Judaism and Christianity.

Theoeroticism as explored here is more often understood metaphorically in the Sufi sense of a path of intimate companionship with God, akin to the Christian sense of joining with the mystical body of Christ. Nonetheless, the sexual union of pious couples inspired by and aspiring towards divine love, the paradigm operative for Othello and Desdemona, is supported by worldly models of conjugal piety offered both in Qur'anic and Christian teachings of marital love.[4] In this physical manifestation, theoeroticism is 'intimacy with Spirit literally realized through union with a human lover, private encounters where sexual love reveals the face of God'.[5] Whether metaphorical or physical, love for the divine must be pure, untainted by lust: 'Blessed are the pure in heart,

---

[2] All citations from Shakespeare are from *The New Oxford Shakespeare: Modern Critical Edition Online*, ed. Gary Taylor, John Jowett, Terri Bourus, and Gabriel Egan (Oxford: Oxford University Press, 2016). Arabic names and references are cited here without diacritical accents.

[3] Thomas Coryat, *Coryat's Crudities* (London: 1611); qtd. in Rosenthal, *The Honest Courtesan*, p. 12.

[4] *Surah al-Baqarah* 2:187; qtd. in Camille Helminski, *Women of Sufism: A Hidden Treasure* (Denver, CO: Shambhala Publications, 2003), p. 39; Ephesians 5:22–8; and Herman von Wied, *The Glasse of Godly Love, A brief and a plain declaration of the duty of married folks*, trans. Haunce Dekin (London: J. Charlewood, 1588).

[5] Jenny Wade, 'Meeting God in the Flesh-Spirituality in Sexual Intimacy', *ReVision* 21.2 (1998), 35–41.

for they shall see God'.[6] Those pure of heart, or 'spiritualized mind', are in the world but not of it.[7] By contrast, those who are enmeshed in the world have the heart 'at the service of the personal, psychological self'.[8] Such denizens of the sensible world more readily see ecstasy in disparaging sexual terms culturally inscribed into the female body.[9] The *seeming* paradoxes and ambivalences in the theoerotic traditions surrounding female wisdom and beauty obtain in the dualistic, contingent world from men's fears of the female body as a threat to male spirit, intellect and rationality and from their incomprehension of female embodied knowledge as interlinked with sexuality, creativity and nurturance coiled in sacred being.[10] Revising the misogyny undergirding these patriarchal structures and narratives, I suggest here that the feminised soul, embracing 'both that which is lowest in man and that which is most sublime in God', is the archetypal *human* soul, embodying the truth of the human experience rather than the illusory pre-modern construct of man as the 'finished, completed' human.[11] This essay explores the gender, racial and religious differences – unfortunate nodes of conflict in the world as we know it – through the Sufi lens of a non-dual imaginal realm.[12] This ethically evolved order of reality is characterised by 'moral coherence', 'fine-tuned compassion' and a *discordia concors* of the sensible and the divine, perceived and wrought by those who walk the Path, guided by a sapient eye, or heart-mind.[13]

---

[6] Matthew 5:8.

[7] Kabir Helminski, *Living Presence: The Sufi Path to Mindfulness and the Essential Self* (New York: Penguin, 2017), p. 206; John 2:15, 15:1–19.

[8] Cynthia Bourgeault, *The Wisdom Way of Knowing: Reclaiming an Ancient Tradition to Awaken the Heart* (Hoboken, NJ: John Wiley & Sons, 2003), p. 34.

[9] On Mary Magdalene as a paradigmatic example of a devout virgin or 'good wife' misogynistically regarded as a harlot, notably by Pope Gregory I – a narrative which stuck in ecclesiastical and popular culture – see Bart D. Ehrman, *Peter, Paul and Mary Magdalene: The Followers of Jesus in History and Legend* (Oxford: Oxford University Press, 2006), pp. 189–90.

[10] Coppélia Kahn, *Man's Estate: Masculine Identity in Shakespeare* (Berkeley: University of California Press, 1981); Mark Breitenberg, *Anxious Masculinity in Early Modern England* (Cambridge: Cambridge University Press, 1996).

[11] Maria Massi Dakake, '"Walking upon the Path of God like Men": Women and the Feminine in the Islamic Mystical Tradition', in *Sufism: Love and Wisdom*, ed. Jean-Louis Michon and Roger Gaetani (World Wisdom, 2006), pp. 131–51 (p. 135); Mikhail Bakhtin, *Rabelais and His World* (Indianapolis: Indiana University Press, 1984) pp. 26–7 (p. 320); qtd. in Peter Stallybrass, 'Patriarchal Territories: The Body Enclosed', in *Rewriting the Renaissance: The Discourses of Sexual Difference in Early Modern Europe*, ed. Margaret Ferguson and Maureen Quilligan (Chicago: University of Chicago Press, 1986), pp. 123–42 (p. 124).

[12] Kabir Helminski, *Living Presence: A Sufi Way to Mindfulness and the Essential Self* (New York: Jeremy Tarcher/Putnam, 1992), p. 157.

[13] Sa'diyya Shaikh, *Sufi Narratives of Intimacy: Ibn 'Arabi, Gender and Sexuality*

Shakespeare astutely situates this theoerotic drama at the Venetian outpost of Cyprus, where the ontological values of love, beauty and devotion as well as the social issues of religion, race and gender come together in an unparalleled fashion. First of all, Cyprus is the home of Venus's votaries since the goddess, according to Hesiod's *Theogony*, is known to have risen from the sea near billowy Cyprus from the severed genitals of Uranus (Aphrodite means 'risen from foam' in Greek).[14] As such, Cyprus channels antithetically both the divine Venus, inspiring her beholder with love, desire for the Good, or in Berowne's words, 'the true Promethean fire' (*Love's Labour's Lost*, Quarto [1598], 4.3.285.D9), as well as the 'mortal Venus' (*Troilus and Cressida*, 3.1.29–30) and the threat of male castration or cuckoldry she poses.[15] Upstart Iago exploits the latter misogynistic trope to usurp his superior, re-enacting the mythical archetype of the *senex–puer* contest, which results in Cronos *agonistes* supplanting his father.[16] Secondly, Cyprus's fifty-mile proximity to the Turkish coast evokes the threat of Ottoman invasion (as realised in 1573, and, more recently, in the 1974 Turkish occupation of northern Cyprus) and the anti-Muslim sentiment that Iago easily wields to turn Othello from his better self and his quest for 'perfect soul' (1.2.30). Following his mythic counterpart Cronos, Iago acts, allegorically speaking, to separate Heaven and Earth, by opposing Desdemona, the play's theoerotic votary whose role, in this Neoplatonic-Sufi reading, is to wed the sensible and the divine realms of life.

Neoplatonism, arising from Hellenistic syncretism in Egypt, enjoyed influence on both sides of the Mediterranean. It appealed not only to Augustine of Hippo (Berber turned Christian, 354–430 CE) and Aquinas (1225–74 CE) but also to al-Farabi (872–950 CE) and Avicenna/Ibn Sina (980–1037 CCE) through its doctrine of the One, which signified both a single living organism and the first principle of reality. From the One derives the underlying and active *Nous*, that is, Mind, or absolute consciousness, whose self-reflection generates the world of Platonic Forms

(Chapel Hill, NC: University of North Carolina Press, 2012), pp. 98 and 112; Cynthia Bourgeault, 'Buddha at the Gas Pump' podcast, ep. 420 (3 October 2017), available at https://batgap.com/cynthia-bourgeault/.

[14] Hesiod, *Theogony*, trans. H. G. Evelyn-White, p. 176, available at https://www.theoi .com/Text/HesiodTheogony.html.

[15] Plato, *Symposium*, in *Complete Works*, ed. John M. Cooper and D. S. Hutchinson (Indianapolis, IN: Hackett Publishing, 1997), 180d–185c. The integration of noble and sensual love, as discussed in Marsilio Ficino's *Commentary on Plato's Symposium on Love*, trans. and commentary by Sears Reynolds Jayne (Columbia: University of Missouri Press, 1944), ch. 7, is revitalised variously in the Italian Renaissance through the works of Petrarch, Dante and Ficino, which in turn inspired Neoplatonically infused paintings such as Botticelli's *The Birth of Venus* and Titian's *Sacred and Profane Love*.

[16] Hesiod, *Theogony*, p. 176.

and the Cosmic Soul, which animates and organises disparate matter.[17] By the extensive force of the Good, our fundamental movement as human beings involves descent to the sensible world and, through a life of purification, ascent back to the intelligible world of the One. In Annemarie Schimmel's words, 'Everything that is separate from God, that has been cast out of the primal union and into a world of time and space by the very act of creation, yearns for the lost whole.'[18]

Aligned with Neoplatonism, Sufism is generally understood as 'an interiorization of Islam, a personal experience of the central mystery of Islam', which posits that 'God is One', that 'God is the only Reality'.[19] Broadly defined as the 'belief in the possibility of union with or absorption into God by means of contemplation and self surrender',[20] mysticism was a common element in the religious traditions arising from Mesopotamia and Egypt including Neoplatonism, Hermeticism, Gnosticism, Judaism, Christianity and Islam.[21] Sufism was the religion of the heart, par excellence, through its selfless, burning love (Arabic *ishq*) for God, which resonates in the Platonic tradition with the 'irresistible passion [*erôs*] for that which is "more divine" [*daimoniôteron*] than us'.[22] Love within the world can have many objects – people, wealth, fame – but *ishq* involves an enduring sort, which links back to the Divine One as the word *religion* ('link back') suggests, and which resembles Platonic-Peripatetic objects of contemplation – unchanging, eternal and noble.[23]

Shakespeare's *Othello* invites a Sufi-infused interpretation of Desdemona, the play's Venetian votary in Ottoman-adjacent Cyprus, especially in relation to its apparent dramatisation of the Neoplatonic interplay of Beauty and Love. Sufism was a strong influence in the

[17] Plotinus, *Enneads*, IV.8.3, 1–2; Christian Wildberg, 'Neoplatonism', *The Stanford Encyclopedia of Philosophy*, ed. Edward N. Zalta (Summer 2019 Edition), available at https://plato.stanford.edu/archives/sum2019/entries/neoplatonism/.

[18] Annemarie Schimmel, *My Soul Is a Woman: The Feminine in Islam* (London: Bloomsbury, 2003), p. 111.

[19] Annemarie Schimmel, *Mystical Dimensions of Islam* (Chapel Hill, NC: University of North Carolina Press, 1975), p. 17.

[20] *OED* 'mysticism' n., 2.

[21] Frithjof Schuon, *The Essential Writings of Frithjof Schuon*, ed. Seyyed Hossein Nasr (Amity, NY: Amity House, 1986), pp. 149–50.

[22] Stephen Halliwell, *Between Ecstasy and Truth: Interpretations of Greek Poetics from Homer to Longinus* (Oxford: Oxford University Press, 2012), p. 366; Plato, *Symposium*, 203c.

[23] *OED* 'religion' n. Aristotle, *Nicomachean Ethics*, trans. W. D. Ross, in *Introduction to Aristotle*, ed. Richard McKeon (New York: Random House, 1947), VI.6.1139a6–8; Amelia Oksenberg Rorty, 'The Place of Contemplation in Aristotle's *Nicomachean Ethics*', *Mind* 87.347 (July 1978), 343–58 (p. 344).

early modern Islamic world, and more particularly in North Africa, Othello's place of origin, a once 'thriving world of devotion and pious foundations'.[24] This Sufi reading of Desdemona's theoerotic 'turn' to the Moor presents an integrative alternative to critical views of the play fixing on the fear of 'turning Turk'.[25] Rejecting views that turn on an anti-Muslim, pro-Christian dualism, this reading focuses rather on how *Othello* participates in the broadly shared human aspiration to selfless love and the Good that rises above doctrinal difference. This concordant view of conversion is a refreshing alternative to the more common negative view featuring Othello turning into a barbaric 'Turk' (code for Muslim), with Desdemona 'as the victim of Islamic erotic tyranny'.[26]

My argument rests, instead, on a more general premise of a shared ethical thoughtworld throughout the multicultural Mediterranean. Sprung from 'a soil in which ancient oriental, Neoplatonic, and Christian influences were strong', the Islamic tradition of seeking wisdom (*hikma*) was enriched by encounters with Greek philosophy, notably, Aristotelianism and Neoplatonism.[27] The Shakespearean canon, in its own way, richly displays evidence in *Othello* as well as other plays of an imaginative engagement with multicultural traditions throughout the Mediterranean and beyond. The syncretism of ethnic and religious images in Othello's final soliloquy – 'base Indian', or 'Judean' in the Folio version, 'Arabian trees', 'turbaned Turk' (5.2.345, 348, 351) – suggests that Othello and Desdemona's marriage itself instantiates a wedding of wisdom traditions.[28] The experience of the historical couple Robert Sherley (1581–1621), the 'famous English *Persian*',[29] and his Persianate wife, Lady Teresa Sampsonia Sherley (1589–1668), conveys such a possibility. The cosmopolitan Teresa Sampsonia hailed from a Northwest Causcasian region straddling three religious traditions

---

[24] Nabil Matar, *Europe through Arab Eyes, 1578–1727* (New York: Columbia University Press, 2008), p. 79.

[25] Daniel Vitkus, *Turning Turk: English Theater and the Multicultural Mediterranean* (New York: Springer, 2016), p. 90.

[26] Vitkus, *Turning Turk*, p. 99.

[27] Schimmel, *Mystical Dimensions*, p. 10.

[28] For the complicated historical interaction of Islam and Hinduism, see S. M. Ikram, *Muslim Civilization in India*, ed. Ainslie T. Embree (New York: Columbia University Press, 1964), available online at http://www.columbia.edu/itc/mealac/pritchett/00islamlinks/ikram/part1_09.html.

[29] Thomas Middleton, 'Sir Robert Shirley his Entertainment in Cracovia', in *Thomas Middleton: The Collected Works*, ed. Gary Taylor and John Lavagnino (Oxford: Oxford University Press, 2007), p. 677, line 360. See also Anthony Nixon's pamphlet, *The Three Brothers* (London, 1607), and John Day, William Rowley and George Wilkins' play *The Travels of the Three English Brothers* (London: Printed by Iohn Wright, 1607) adapted from it.

– Muslim, Christian and pagan – and ultimately sought refuge in Carmelite spirituality, which 'resonate[d] with the Sufi-infused spirituality of the Safavids and the shamanistic heritage of the Circassians' – diverse religious traditions that, Bernadette Andrea suggests, converge through mysticism.[30] In this inclusive sense that Schimmel also defines it, mysticism is that consciousness of One Reality, call it 'Wisdom, Light, Love or Nothing'.[31]

In Sufi theoeroticism, yearning for this Reality sets one on the mystical path (*tariqa*), whereby the lover is a chalice, opening herself to Divine Love – her single virtuous aim, to keep from falling out of the path of Love. The tropic braiding of love and pilgrimage in the Shakespearean canon, I suggest, is poignantly dramatised in *Othello*, where the concept of 'pilgrimage', as the Moor calls his life's traverse, is evident in both Islam and Christianity, especially through their shared Neoplatonic heritage. The spiritual Path is the Lover seeking Beauty, and one thus purified by the Beloved is called a Sufi.[32] Sufi thought is conveyed most effectively and beautifully through its lyric poetry, which attempts to capture 'the constant interplay between unchanging beauty (God, the cupbearer, the rose) and the ever-longing lover (the human being, the winebibber, the nightingale)'.[33] Shakespeare's dramatic poetry presents itself in ways similar to and different from Sufi lyric. As elements of a cross-cultural language of virtue poised between divine and profane love, the Sufi-Christian motifs in *Othello* are robe/sheet, mirror and willow/reed, among others. Shakespeare taps thus into a deeply historied and ensouled lyric of shared tropes employed for centuries within a cross-fertilised wisdom tradition. Linking past to the present, directors of modern-day productions might explore through this Sufi-infused reading further ideas towards presenting the play as a concordant human experience uniting a diverse audience above creed, color and gender. To this end, Shakespeare's *Othello* offers an interreligious exploration of the spiritual journey as Othello wavers between divine and profane love while Desdemona exemplifies the Sufi-Christian Bride-Soul, who in attaining supreme virtue via the pain of death, ascends to the Sophianic Feminine prefigured in the divinity (*daemon/daimon*)

[30] Bernadette Andrea, *The Lives of Girls and Women from the Islamic World in Early Modern British Literature and Culture* (Toronto: University of Toronto Press, 2017), p. 36.

[31] Schimmel, *Mystical Dimensions*, p. 4.

[32] 'Ali ibn Uthman al-Hujwiri. *The 'Kashf al-Mahjub', the Oldest Persian Treatise on Sufism by al-Hujwiri*, ed. V. A. Zukovskij (Leningrad, 1926, reprint; Tehran, 1336 sh./ ig57.34), 34; qtd. in Schimmel, *Mystical Dimensions*, p. 16.

[33] Annemarie Schimmel, *A Two-Colored Brocade: The Imagery of Persian Poetry* (Chapel Hill, NC: University of North Carolina Press, 1992), p. 38.

inscribed in her name.[34] Against the backdrop of a pluralist, Islamic-and-Byzantine-infused Venice, Desdemona's quest for 'perfect soul' (1.2.30) harmonises Sufi and Christian endeavours of spiritual devotion by attentive, whole-body striving towards the Good.

Divine Courtship

Othello's storytelling at Brabantio's home offers not only a rousing narrative of 'hair-breadth scapes' but also, within a medieval tradition of allegorical drama, an account of a 'pilgrimage', an understated but clearly spiritual quest for 'perfect soul' (1.3.135, 152; 1.2.30). In this latter account, Desdemona and Othello's theoerotic courtship offers two votaries of virtue the opportunity to hearten their practice in a conjoined quest for spiritual purity. Desdemona's theoeroticism literalises what Romeo and Juliet say and do in their secular wooing, invoking the 'saint[ly]' language of palmers to join 'palm to palm' in physical intimacy (*Romeo and Juliet*, 1.5.97). Indeed, Desdemona, actively responding to Othello's tales (a gender reversal of Scheherazade's *Arabian Tales*), plays 'half the wooer' in a sacred courtship, informed by the ideas of the sublime in both Hellenistic and Islamic philosophies. Longinus's first-century treatise *Peri Hypsous* (*On the Sublime*, 1554) theorises a concept of 'heroic spirituality' centred on sublimity, a transformative ecstasy fusing thought and emotion and anchored in a vision of metaphysical truth.[35] On the Islamic side, medieval Persian philosopher-theologian Al-Ghazālī (1058–1111 CE), in his influential *Alchemy of Happiness*, reflects on beauty and love and their relationship to virtue. As Domenico Ingenito explains, Al-Ghazālī 'hints at the intimate bonds that place lyric poetry within the scope of the experience of sexuality and desire'.[36] In doing so, he paved the way for Sufi poets to compose sacred lyric about the theoerotic experience using the language of awareness and sublimity. The two seemingly disparate philosophies hark back to the Platonic notion of *erôs*, which Longinus describes as 'an unconquerable passion for whatever is great and more divine than ourselves',[37] in other words, *ishq*, the theoerotic core of Sufism.

---

[34] *OED*, 'demon', etymology: Greek *daimonion*, meaning 'divinity, lesser deity'.

[35] Kelly Lehtonen, *The Sublime and the Remaking of Renaissance Epic* (Toronto: University of Toronto Press, forthcoming 2023); and Halliwell, *Between Ecstasy and Truth*, pp. 350 and 365.

[36] Domenico Ingenito, *Beholding Beauty: Sa'di of Shiraz and the Aesthetics of Desire in Medieval Persian Poetry* (Leiden: Brill, 2020), p. 165.

[37] Longinus, *On the Sublime*, trans. W. H. Fyfe, rev. Donald A. Russell, in *Aristotle*:

Both philosophies, in different ways, help to illuminate Othello and Desdemona's courtship as a sublime experience. Longinian theory offers not only an ontology of the sublime but also rhetoric advice to extend the transcendent experience to others. The account of Othello and Desdemona's courtship cannily profits from this Longinian interweaving of philosophy and rhetoric. Othello, through skilful, moving expression, makes Desdemona experience 'something a little like clambering hazardously, even vertiginously, over precipitous crags': 'the orator "dragging" or "pulling" his audience along with him on the journey, filling them with "fear" that the sentence might collapse, "compelling" them to "share in the danger" with the speaker, and eventually being "stunned" ... by the way he finally delivers them to their destination'.[38] For Desdemona, this sublime experience is indeed, as Longinus describes, like the sudden impact of a thunderbolt, a *coup de foudre*, which 'reveals the concentrated power of the speaker instantaneously'.[39] Othello's powerful narration sparks a 'storm' of emotions between them and, a hundred lines later, 'downright violence and storm of [fused] fortunes' (1.3.243) for the theoerotic couple – what Longinus would call 'rough sublimity'. Unlike the Longinian model, the Islamic one focuses overtly on union with the Divine, regarding 'all aesthetic experiences as techniques ... capable of catalyzing the beholder's spiritual appreciation of the invisible through sensory exposure to perceptible forms of beauty'.[40] Al-Ghazālī metaphorically refers to 'the heart as an iron which, if struck by a stone, delivers a mysterious spark signifying a spiritual commotion before the visual or aural contemplation of beauty'. Both models in somewhat different ways employ metaphors of light, stone and stunning to articulate the experience of sublimity.

When Desdemona 'Devour[s] up [his] discourse' 'with a greedy ear' and makes 'a prayer of earnest heart / That [he] would all [his] pilgrimage dilate' (1.3.148–52), these actions could be taken as stirrings of profane love.[41] In this theoerotic reading, I suggest the added possibility that Desdemona, devouring his exotic adventures as signs of his spiritual

The Poetics. Longinus: On the Sublime. Demetrius: On Style (Cambridge, MA: Harvard University Press, 1995), 35.2.

[38] Ibid., 22.3–4; Halliwell, *Between Ecstasy and Truth*, p. 334.

[39] Longinus, *On the Sublime*, 1.4; Halliwell, *Between Ecstasy and Truth*, p. 352; Lehtonen, *The Sublime and the Remaking of Renaissance Epic*, pp. 39 and 66 respectively.

[40] Ingenito, *Beholding Beauty*, p. 474.

[41] For a more conventional reading on Desdemona's desire for travel, see Stephanie Chamberlain 'Eroticizing Women's Travel: Desdemona and the Desire for Adventure in Othello', in *Travel and Travail: Early Modern Women, English Drama, and the Wider World*, ed. Patricia Akhimie and Bernadette Andrea (Omaha: University of Nebraska Press, 2020), pp. 199–214.

yearning, experiences also 'a powerfully charged arousal' upon seeing in Othello a Lover who has undergone tests of virtue along the spiritual Path.[42] In Longinian terms, Desdemona is 'receptive to and aware of an act of [sublime] communication', in which 'one mind's conception of something great can be felt to "echo" in the minds of others ... exposed to it', ideally in a Platonic union of 'like likes' (*All's Well That Ends Well*, 1.1.193).[43] Her aspiration to the Sophianic Feminine necessitates the bold humility of a receptive woman-soul, which manifests itself in both female and male bodies. As the Moorish Sufi master Ibn 'Arabi (1165–1240) explains, a woman-soul contemplates God completely from the perspectives of both *agens* and *patiens*, allowing for 'a more perfect witnessing of God': the true adept must simultaneously be *agens* with 'complete sway over [one's] soul' (*nafs*) and *patiens* in being 'submissive and devoted' to God.[44] As long as Othello presents himself in affinity to the ultimate Other, Desdemona, for a brief time, is able to harmonise divine sovereignty of the metaphysical realm and male sovereignty of the social realm within a rarified window of theoerotic sublimity.

Understood in the terms of Islamic theo-aesthetics, the sublime *harmonia* made possible by Othello's moving travel account operates as the sympathetic reflection of divine presence in the world, particularly in figures of human beauty and virtue, founded on the 'correspondence between the proportions of the visible world and the balanced architecture of the supernal realm'.[45] In such a theoerotic experience, Desdemona weds compassion with desire, fusing the Passion of Christian theology – the appropriation of human sin and suffering – with sensual passion in her exchange of 'kisses' for Othello's 'pains' (1.3.158). In so doing, Othello and Desdemona inhabit what Sufis call the imaginal realm of the awakened heart, or what Christ calls 'the Kingdom of Heaven ... within you'.[46] Desdemona's declaration that she finds these 'pains' 'wondrous pitiful' (1.3.160) suggests a Sufi-Christian-Longinian 'process of emotional "participation" or "communion" ... of minds in which truth (contact with the real) and ecstasy (moments of transformative consciousness) meet'.[47] '[S]w[earing], in faith', in wondrous bewilderment,

---

[42] Halliwell, *Between Ecstasy and Truth*, p. 340.

[43] Ibid., pp. 333–4.

[44] Sa'diyya Shaikh, *Sufi Narratives of Intimacy*, p. 179; Ibn 'Arabi, MC 1: 155–56; qtd. in Schimmel, *My Soul Is a Woman*, p. 103.

[45] Ingenito, *Beholding Beauty*, p. 473.

[46] Bourgeault, *Wisdom Way of Knowing*, pp. 48–9; Luke: 17:21.

[47] Halliwell, *Between Ecstasy and Truth*, p. 363. See p. 340 for an account of the sublime as 'birthing' and as 'exaltation and expansion'. See also Longinus, *On the Sublime*, 7.3; and Plato, *Symposium*, 206b–c.

''twas strange, 'twas passing strange' (1.3.159), Desdemona taps into a numinous experience that converts Othello from the strange Moor into a visible emblem of God as Stranger. A well-known *hadith* underscores a core idea of both Islamic and Christian mystical traditions, 'Be in this world as if you were a stranger or a traveler',[48] a precept that would have guided Othello in his traverses and travails within this theoerotic dispensation.

Even as Othello mirrors the Stranger vertically along the divine plane, Desdemona endeavours to mirror her virtuous (soul)mate horizontally across the temporal plane, in their conjoined pursuit of this Divine Beauty. She publicly 'trumpet[s]' before the Senators her 'downright violence and storm of fortunes' (1.3.243–4), boldly proclaiming her status as spiritual traveller alongside Othello. Matching him 'Even' in 'heart', virtuous 'quality' and 'soul', she avows: 'I saw Othello's visage in his mind, / And to his honour and his valiant parts / Did I my soul and fortunes consecrate' (1.3.245–8). The invisible Beloved is comprehended through the visible beloved. Linking 'mind' to the divine *Nous* of Neoplatonic dispensation, she sees him numinously as the emblem of God/Good. The convergence of the visible and the invisible manifests itself in the human being, who by her primordial 'antinomy' has the potential to inhabit both the sensible and sacred spheres. Neoplatonism, Eastern Christian Patristics and Arab-Islamic philosophy – all 'took the true purpose of Man to consist in knowing these two worlds while ascending to God'.[49] From Othello's self-account of bravery, endurance, physical prowess, and practical wisdom materialises the ideal man that Desdemona wished 'God had made her' (1.3.162), a man of 'solid virtue' (4.1.248), who, reflexively, embodies heaven. This unusual wooing results in a mythic-theoerotic joining of Mars and Venus, of male and female energies (also occurring in *Antony and Cleopatra*), to facilitate their finest aspirations to virtue. Together, Desdemona and Othello earnestly 'consecrate' 'soul and fortunes' (1.3.248) to the theoerotic aim of harmonising divine and profane love in the contingent world they inhabit. Such transcendent union, according to early Christian Gnostic Valentinus (d.160 CE, Cyprus), occurred only between *pneumatics*, 'men and women who were able to experience [intercourse] as a mystery and a sacrament'.[50] In pursuing this rarified theoerotic love, so easily tainted in temporal light,

[48] *Sahih al-Bukhari* 6416, trans. Dr M. Muhsin Kahn, see https://sunnah.com/bukhari:6416.

[49] Nur Kirabaev and Olga Chistyakova. 'Knowing God in Eastern Christianity and Islamic Tradition: A Comparative Study', *Religions* 11.675 (2020).

[50] Gilles Quispel, *Gnostica, Judaica, Catholica. Collected Essays of Gilles Quispel*, ed. Johannes Van Oort (Leiden: Brill, 2008), p. 167.

Othello and Desdemona engage the risk that the Longinian pursuit of sublime heroism involves – an endeavour further imperiled by their gendered, racialised, Christian-Muslim environs.[51]

Double-sided Venus

As the play's Venus figure attempting to wed profane and divine love in the sensible world, Desdemona instead becomes an object of misperception, planting the seed for tragedy. Like its Venetian double-sided counterpart, the Sufi Bride-Soul, as yearning woman-soul, symbolises both the human soul (*nafs*), sometimes incited to evil, and the divine essence (*al-Dhat*) that resides in us all. In Sufi thought, the created world is compared to a mirror, echoing the Neoplatonic idea of 'the world's reflecting the downward stream of divine light' so that the soul might return again into the heights.[52] To this end, 'the human heart, defiled by worldly thoughts and deeds, has to be polished of its rust, of the verdigris of secular relations': 'by constantly thinking of God', the Lover prepares 'to take in [His] Light'.[53] The mirror – polished and clear versus defiled and obscure – emblematically illustrates Desdemona's and Othello's divergent progress in their ability to reflect the Divine, resulting in their secular tragedy. Insofar as Desdemona becomes spiritually ascendant through the play, the mirror, 'that womanly utensil', operates as the ubiquitous trope by which the spiritually receptive woman-soul is able to 'reflect the image of the beloved' perfectly, 'without adding anything of its own to that reflection'.[54]

Othello, however, regresses spiritually. In reuniting with Desdemona at Cyprus in 2.1, Othello gazes at her with 'wonder great' (2.1.174). He, too, poignantly experiences the numinous through the contemplation of earthly beauty – as the visual mirroring of Desdemona's theophanic experience in hearing his stories. This sublime moment is, in hindsight, his spiritual apex, from which everything goes south. Othello proves unable to arm himself with an 'enchiridion' – an ethical handbook, figuratively an Erasmian hand 'dagger'[55] – to cut through his delusions about profane love, namely, the thick lies by which Iago turns Desdemona's 'virtue into pitch' (2.3.322). The Judaic-Islamic-Sufi wisdom tradition

---

[51] Lehtonen, *The Sublime and the Remaking of Renaissance Epic*, p. 99.
[52] Schimmel, *My Soul*, p. 112.
[53] Ibid., pp. 111–12.
[54] Ibid.
[55] See Erasmus, *The Manual of a Christian Knight* (London: Methuen, 1905), p. 35, on 'sword of the spirit'.

reveals an example of an ethical tool in which the figurative turns quasi-literal: 'the *nafs* was said to take the form of a snake; but this serpent can be turned into a useful rod, just as Moses transformed serpents into rods'.[56] This Islamic-Sufi teaching highlights the twist within the internal *jihad*: the ethical tool must be applied upon the enemy that resides within oneself. Othello's fatal failure to turn his internal serpent, as external-ised in Iago, into a rod to kill the *nafs* in himself, reveals, instead, that his 'clear spirit' has been 'puddled' by 'some unhatched practice' (3.4.132), thereby leaving him a defiled mirror by which to perceive the truth of things. When Othello misreads Desdemona's magnanimity in mediating between her husband and his estranged lieutenant Cassio as a sign of her infidelity, he signals his own 'infidel' turn to ego/Iago – away from God and His Bride-Soul Desdemona, who successfully mirrors the Good.[57]

Othello's inability to sustain an integrative theoerotic view of Desdemona may also be explored through the social lens of courtly etiquette delineated in Castiglione's *The Book of the Courtier*, even as it conflicted with Muslim mores regarding aristocratic women. Such a pos-sibility suggests that audience members then and now, regardless of their knowledge of Sufism, will very likely grasp this theoerotic dimension embedded in the play. Subject to the contradictory demands of courtesy, the court lady, according to this Neoplatonic treatise and manual on virtuous conduct, 'must observe a certain difficult mean' of being 'no less chaste, prudent and benign than she is pleasing, witty and discreet'.[58] As such, female courtesy is as challenging for Desdemona as it is per-plexing for Othello. In the Islamic tradition, aristocratic women, veiled as emblems of the sacred as well as for protection, resided in their own quarters, or *haram*, sacred spaces that invoked the kind of deference and prohibition (*haraam*) commanded by holy places. Nabil Matar's studies of early modern Arab travel writing reveal that 'socially interactive' European women often had disturbing effects on Moorish envoys visit-ing and living in Christian lands, who in *Dar al-Islam* 'hardly ever got to see a well-guarded woman outside [their] own immediate famil[ies]'.[59] Othello the Moor, inexperienced in the moral intricacies of the Venetian world, has trouble reading the social and ethical conduct of a lady who mingles freely in Cypriot high society as well as in a military setting. Venetian courtiers apparently have no trouble discerning Desdemona's virtue. The otherwise foolish Rodrigo rightly calls Desdemona 'blessed'

[56] Schimmel, *Mystical Dimensions*, p. 13.
[57] Schimmel, *My Soul*, pp. 113–14.
[58] Baldesar Castiglione, *The Book of the Courtier*, trans. George Bull (London: Penguin, 1976), pp. 291–2.
[59] Matar, *Europe through Arab Eyes*, p. 107; Schimmel, *My Soul*, p. 100.

(2.1.232) in his so-called Annunciation speech. Lodovico, knowing her for a virtuous, 'obedient lady' (4.1.230), protests Othello's most untoward act of slapping her face. The once judicious Moor, however, becomes the perfect dupe for Iago's stratagem on account of his inexperience with European mores and the schemer's special targeting of his 'stranger' status. Tapping the numinous in beholding Desdemona's face in 2.1, Othello might have modelled Pietro Bembo's older, wiser lover focused on beauty 'in its own . . . purity' more than sensual experience.[60] But Desdemona's assurances of their 'marriage of true minds' (Sonnet 116, 1), banked on 'perfect soul' and 'solid virtue' (1.2.30, 4.1.248), are suddenly swept aside by Venetian racist and anti-Muslim ideologies, which deform his rationality and diminish his exercise of virtue. The externals and 'accidents' of his skin colour and his Muslim affiliation – steeped as he is in the sensible world – derail him from the North Star of Divine Love into the derangement of cuckoldry, the ultimate sexual affront to egoic love.[61]

'[E]xcellent courtesy' (2.1.169), at the intersection of conflicting Moorish-Venetian mores regarding women, is what Iago exploits to ruin Desdemona. His toxic meddling in 150 lines is what abruptly crystallises Othello's affectionate, bewildering love for his 'excellent wretch' into a declaration of retaliation: 'I am abused, and my relief / Must be to loathe her' (3.3.89–91, 261–2). These oxymorons highlight the paradox underlying the courtly feminine ideal: dual association to divine and sensual love, evoking various figures of the Sophianic Feminine – Venus, the Sufi Bride-Soul and Woman Wisdom of the Proverbs. Woman Wisdom in Proverbs 8, as Christine Roy Yoder describes her, is a force of life, serving as prophet and teacher, sheer delight, beloved companion, mother, reflection of God, fashioner of all things and more.[62] Against the 'blessed' Force of Life after which Desdemona is modelled, Proverbs presents a more negative feminine figure of the sexualised Strange Woman:[63] the loud, seductive harlot in the streets, whose mingling with men is seen as commingling with them. Thus, Proverbs 7:11–12 exhibits what Michael Slater identifies as 'the deeply entrenched connections between a woman's speech, a woman's travel outside the home,

---

[60] Castiglione, *The Book of the Courtier*, p. 471.

[61] 'Accidents' are distinguished from 'substance' in Castiglione, *The Book of the Courtier*, p. 300.

[62] Christine Roy Yoder, 'Personified Wisdom and Feminist Theologies', in *The Oxford Handbook of Wisdom and the Bible*, ed. Will Kynes (Oxford: Oxford University Press, 2021), pp. 273–4.

[63] Julia Reinhard Lupton, 'Cleopatra and Hebrew Wisdom Literature in Transit', work in progress.

and her sexual promiscuity': 'She is loud and stubborn; her feet abide not in her house: Now is she without, now in the streets, and lieth in wait at every corner.'[64] Early modern moral writers such as Barnabe Rich alluded to Proverbs to confine women to housework as part of the feminine domestic ideal.[65] Iago's ascription of Desdemona as 'the super-subtle Venetian' (1.3.338) alerts us to her imminent declension from divine Other to feminine other. Hegel's observation, 'Evil is also the gaze which sees evil everywhere around it', reminds us, however, that the epithet serves equally well to critique Iago's 'super-subtlety' in observing Desdemona.[66] Iago's invention of vice in the virtuous and Othello's complicit insistence on 'ocular proof' (3.3.354) estrange both lead characters 'from the spirit of the Bible and its perceived relevance to human experience', resulting in their divergence from wisdom.[67] Iago's defiling of Desdemona's magnanimity as egoic lechery is impiously mirrored in Othello's downshift from divine to self-focused love, from a mindset of sacred *haraam* to that of the bewhoring harem. The dangers of courtliness prove fatal for Desdemona, a declension also traceable in the etymological matrix of cognates: 'courtesy', through misdirection and misperception, can take the colour of 'courtship' (2.1.169, 165), signifying 'both courtly behavior and romantic flirtation',[68] as well as courtly love and its association with adultery.

Failing to balance sacred and profane love in his conjugal relationship with Desdemona, Othello expectedly turns to the polar opposite response of female repression common in both Islamic and Christian cultures, as reinforced by Aristotle in particular. In Act 1, Desdemona, by proclaiming her love for noble Othello, 'trumpet[ed]' her alliance with virtue. She raised her excellent voice like Woman Wisdom in Proverbs 1:20–33, calling out to people in the streets to seek wisdom, which will make them 'dwell safely, . . . quiet from fear of evil'. By Act 4, when

---

[64] Michael Slater, 'Desdemona's Divided Duty: Gender and Courtesy in *Othello*', in *Travel and Travail: Early Modern Women, English Drama, and the Wider World*, ed. Patricia Akhimie and Bernadette Andrea (Lincoln: University of Nebraksa Press, 2019), pp. 215–35, 218; Proverbs 7:11–12.

[65] Barnabe Rich, *My Ladies Looking Glasse* (London: 1616), pp. 43–44; qtd. in Slater, 'Desdemona's Divided Duty', pp. 218–19.

[66] Georg Hegel, qtd. in Slavoj Žižek, 'Hegel on the Future, Hegel in the Future', *Philosophy Now*, available at https://philosophynow.org/issues/140/Hegel_On_The_Fu ture_Hegel_In_The_Future (accessed 23 January 2023).

[67] See Folly's critique of medieval scholastics' 'subtle refinement of subtleties' in Desiderius Erasmus, *Praise of Folly and Letter to Martin Dorp*, trans. Betty Radice (Harmondsworth: Penguin, [1509 and 1515] 1971), p. 156; qtd. in Andy Mousley, *Re-Humanising Shakespeare: Literary Humanism, Wisdom and Modernity* (Edinburgh: Edinburgh University Press, 2007), p. 20.

[68] Slater, 'Desdemona's Divided Duty', p. 230.

Desdemona's speech seemingly challenges his male authority in public, Othello sibilantly turns Desdemona's 'trumpet[ing]' of virtue into the cries of a 'strumpet' (1.3.244, 4.2.78). In 4.1, some 100 lines after Othello's denunciation of Desdemona as a 'strumpet' (4.1.93), trumpets are sounded – their heraldic blazon heightening alarm in Othello, who misreads Desdemona's assertive magnanimity as impudent adultery, publicly slaps her, and sardonically commands her to 'turn ... turn again' like a 'well painted' (4.1.235, 239) whore. Plotinus's Neoplatonic trope of turning and turning as an integrative strategy of navigating adeptly between the sensible and intelligible worlds is thus effectively dichotomised and demonised as lust, the base counterpart to divine love.[69]

The Willow Song

Two musical instruments – one brass and the other wind – signal Desdemona's change of fortune and correlated disposition from bold assertion to subdued melancholy. The brassy trumpets give way, in my mind, to mellow recorder, with its association with funerary and heavenly music.[70] I imagine Desdemona singing the Willow Song accompanied by the dulcet strain of a reed flute. Desdemona's mournful song is invariably interpreted as one about earthly love, specifically about a lovelorn maid named Barbary – subliminally associated with the 'saint-oriented' Barbary Coast.[71] Calling it 'one of the most dramatically compelling scenes in Shakespeare', Eamon Grennan notes the 'quotidian familiarity' and 'unhurried simplicity' of the 'willow scene', which 'composes both a "theatrical" and a "dramatic" interlude suggesting peace and freedom, within the clamorous procession of violent acts and urgent voices'.[72] Grennan rightly appreciates the 'pivotal position' the female voice 'occupies ... in the play's moral world'. Extending from his affective focus, I argue that the entire theatrical space – animated by dialogue, movement, song and musical instrument – becomes a vessel for a

---

[69] Plotinus, *Enneads IV.8: On the Descent of the Soul into Bodies*, trans. and commentary by Barrie Fleet (Las Vegas: Parmenides Publishing, 2012), p. 61.
[70] Alan C. Dessen and Leslie Thomson, *A Dictionary of Stage Directions in English Drama, 1580–1642* (Cambridge: Cambridge University Press, 1999), pp. 177–8; glossed in Ross W. Duffin, 'Music and the Stage in the Time of Shakespeare' in *The Oxford Handbook of the Age of Shakespeare*, ed. R. Malcolm Smuts (Oxford: Oxford University Press, 2016), pp. 748–63 (p. 755).
[71] Matar, *Europe through Arab Eyes*, p. 57.
[72] Eamon Grennan, 'The Women's Voices in *Othello*: Speech, Song, Silence', *Shakespeare Quarterly* 38 (1987), 275–92, esp. pp. 276–7.

quietly powerful dramatisation of Desdemona as a spiritual ascendant, most effectively adumbrated by Sufi theoerotic understandings.

Even while mourning the loss of Othello's love, the Willow Song, I suggest, pivots Desdemona's eyes upward as she begins to assume the Sophianic Feminine. In his *Kimiya*, Al-Ghazālī outlines 'a theory of aesthetic enjoyment that correlates his phenomenology of the spiritual vision with the effects of artistic beauty on the human heart/soul'.[73] He speaks in terms of degrees. Drawing on Al-Ghazālīan theo-aesthetics, Desdemona's Willow Song can be regarded, in the first degree, in a mundane sense as 'an entrancing aesthetic experience . . . detached from any spiritual connotation'.[74] The second degree, as Domenico Ingenito explains, describes the experience from the perspective of 'spiritual aesthetics' as 'cognitive awareness' (*fahm*) that leads to inner spiritual knowledge (*ma'rifa*): the insight that the Divine is the sole Reality, as opposed to 'the ephemeral nature of all created things, which partake in the ontological absolute as its pale reflections'.[75] This spiritual knowledge 'convert[s] the passion triggered within the heart . . . into a form of controlled rapture', a subdued expression of the Sufi sublime (*zawq*).[76] While principally experienced by the audience as profane music, the Willow Song, within a theoerotic dimension, may perform a sacred function of ratifying Desdemona's desire for and knowledge of the Divine as her mortal pining turns into 'immortal longings' (*Antony and Cleopatra*, 5.2.270): her 'heart [becomes] subdued / to the very quality of [her heavenly] lord' (1.3.244–5). This spiritual wisdom, experienced during her earlier sublime encounter with Othello, is now dissociated from her infidel partner as the Willow Song signals her ascension to the Sophianic Feminine and reorients her to the true Beloved.

The Willow Song, replete with religious significance stemming from ancient Mediterranean wisdom traditions, hints at this spiritual passage in its reference to

> The poor soul [who] sat sighing by a sycamore tree,
> Sing all a green willow.
> Her hand on her bosom, her head on her knee,
> Sing willow, willow, willow. (4.3.37–40)

The resilient, water-loving willow tree is prominent in wisdom and lay traditions around the Mediterranean and beyond. Symbolising vitality and birth as well as grief and death, the willow is closely tied to Osiris,

---

[73] Ingenito, *Beholding Beauty*, p. 474.
[74] Ibid., p. 477.
[75] Ibid., pp. 477–8.
[76] Ibid., p. 494.

Artemis, Persephone and Orpheus – figures of Egyptian and Greek mythology.[77] The sycamore tree also brims with divine significance. Before its biblical reference in Luke 19:1–4, the sycamore was already known as the ancient Egyptian Tree of Life, associated with the goddesses Nut, Isis and Hathor, the tree-goddess of Memphis, also known as the 'Lady of the Sycamore'.[78] More broadly, Hathor is the mother goddess from Old Kingdom Egypt with a host of roles: consort to the falcon god Horus, who represents the sky and the sun; the sun god Ra's violent and protective agent; and the goddess of sexuality, love and beauty, motherhood and queenship, and resurrection and the passage from life to death. These functions roughly correspond to the multiple roles and themes that Desdemona depicts in *Othello* as Venus *armata* and the Bride-Soul. During the Macedonian Ptolemaic dynasty (305–30 BCE), the Ptolemies linked their queens with Isis, Hathor and Aphrodite, often referring to Hathor as Aphrodite in a syncretic practice of *interpretatio graeca*.[79] Plutarch, familiar to Shakespeare and his contemporaries, likewise, syncretises 'Athyri' or Hathor with Isis, further amplifying her significance as a mother god, sky god and 'Methyer', which 'is compounded of Full and the cause: for Matter is full of the world, as being maried and keeping companie with the first principle, which is good, pure, and beautifully adorned'.[80] Here, Plutarch draws severally on the syncretic conception of Woman Wisdom as consort, mother and creator; as well as her material role both in the manifold manifestation in the world of the Platonic One and the wedding of Aristotelian form and matter.

A Middle Kingdom temple to Hathor-Nebethetepet stands at Heliopolis, northeast of Memphis, suggesting Hathor's role as a sky and sun goddess vital in the processes of birth and death. Intriguing for our purposes, hieroglyphic inscriptions at its chapels indicate, furthermore, the existence in two different courtyards of a willow tree and a sycamore tree, respectively, linked with the worship of Hathor.[81] Like the willow tree, the *Ficus sycomorus* of Africa and the southern Mediterranean,

---

[77] Fred Hageneder, *The Living Wisdom of Trees: A Guide to the Natural History, Symbolism and Healing Power of Trees* (London: Watkins Media Limited, 2020), p. 347.
[78] Donald B. Redford (ed.), *The Oxford Essential Guide to Egyptian Mythology* (New York: Berkley Books, 2003), pp. 157–61; Alison Roberts, *Hathor Rising: The Power of the Goddess in Ancient Egypt* (Rochester, VT: Inner Traditions, 1995), pp. 26–7.
[79] R. H. Wilkinson, *The Complete Gods and Goddesses of Ancient Egypt* (London: Thames & Hudson, 2003), p. 141.
[80] Plutarch, *Moralia*, trans. Philemon Holland (London: Arnold Hatfield, 1603), 1310.20.
[81] Stephen Quirke, *The Cult of Ra: Sun Worship in Ancient Egypt* (London: Thames & Hudson, 2001), pp. 102–5.

distinguished from the sycamore of northern climates, grows near water, offering solace and refreshment in life, and divine union, rejuvenation and spatial release in the afterlife.[82] Along with Nut and Isis, Hathor, as nurse and nurturant, 'manifests herself as a sycamore, the tree of life, who dispenses eternal nourishment to the deceased', or 'divine dew', as one deceased explains in the *Book of the Dead*.[83] Depicted in Egyptian funerary texts as being sometimes of this world and sometimes of the next world, the sycamore, with its sacramental properties associated with Hathor, is key to the passage from life into death and the afterlife.

Desdemona, singing of Barbary under the shade of the sacred Egyptian sycamore, symbolically standing at the threshold between life and death, encourages a dual account of the scene as mourning and abandoning profane love while anticipating death, transformation and rebirth. To wit, the tree symbolism of ancient Egyptian mythology sets the stage for the Willow Song's striking resonance with Sufi master Rumi's (1207–73) *Nay-nameh*, 'Song of the Reed [Flute]'.[84] Both the droopy willow tree and the thin-stalked reed, growing near water, have accrued synaesthetic connotations of melancholy, possibly through the associations of water with tears and of sorrow with the lyre (Psalm 137) and the reed flute. In the Celtic tradition of making harps with a sound-body of willow, the willow becomes 'the resonating feminine vessel that receives the vibration of the string and gives birth to music'.[85] Similarly, the reed flute in the Sufi tradition becomes the perfect instrument of the yearning woman-soul. Further cementing the connection between the two species, willows, 'to help purify and recycle water naturally', are planted as a 'reed bed',[86] which becomes an emotive image in Rumi's song.

Prefacing his famous *Masnavi*, Rumi's *Nay-nameh* presents in its beginning couplets the analogy of a homesick soul to a reed flute, followed by a tale of a lovesick slave-girl much like Barbary[87]:

Listen to this reed as it is grieving;
it tells the story of our separations.
'Since I was severed from the bed of reeds,
in my cry men and women have lamented.

[82] Jan Assmann, *Death and Salvation in Ancient Egypt* (Ithaca, NY: Cornell University Press, 2011), p. 361.

[83] Ibid., p. 171 and *Book of the Dead*, qtd. in Assmann, *Death and Salvation*, p. 130.

[84] Amir H. Zekrgoo, 'Metaphors of Music & Dance in Rumi's *Mathnawi*', *KATHA: The Official Journal of the Centre for Civilisational Dialogue* 8.1 (2012), 1–14 (p. 1).

[85] Hageneder, *Living Wisdom of Trees*, p. 348.

[86] Ibid., p. 344.

[87] Cyrus Ali Zargar, *Polished Mirror: Storytelling and the Pursuit of Virtue in Islamic Philosophy and Sufism* (New York: Simon & Schuster, 2017), p. 304.

I need the breast that's torn to shreds by parting
to give expression to the pain of heartache'.[88]

As Amir Zekrgoo explains, the flute or reed symbolises the pure human being who 'being hollow of ego and worldly desires, feels empty and sad' in her 'longing for the Beloved who is absent'.[89]

In hearing Desdemona sing, accompanied by the hauntingly hollow sound of the reed flute, we, as audience, might imagine her literally and figuratively inspired with and by the divine *pneuma* of Oneness, prefiguring her own expiration into the Beloved. In Shakespeare's tragedy, Desdemona, exhibiting the 'transpersonal mode of experience' as opposed to Othello's 'egoic perception',[90] superbly exemplifies 'the breast that's torn to shreds by parting', the spiritually aching 'men and women [who] have lamented' the 'sever[ance] from the bed of reeds'. We, as audience members, may become attuned to the Neoplatonic-Sufi extension of love through the theatrical representation of Desdemona, who feels acutely 'the pain of heartache' in the severings of friendship and love across the human plane – her own as well as others' (for instance, Cassio's) – all manifestations of the primordial separation from the Divine Beloved.

The Willow Song's strains of theoerotic longing continue into Desdemona's exchanges with Emilia and with Othello. Even while singing, Desdemona has Emilia lay out her bridal sheets – but these are not for earthly consummation, for she knows better not to look to men, who 'are not gods, / . . . for such observances / As fit the bridal' (3.4.140). Indeed, the tragedy for Desdemona, as Lover par excellence, is less the worldly separation from her husband than the moral consequence that with Othello's divergence from God/Good, they may not proceed together towards the One. With every word and action, Desdemona assumes the Bride-Soul in preparation for this otherworldly union. Not only does the Willow Song augur death in one of the missing lines to the song (she is 'to die for [his] love'),[91] but Desdemona specifically asks Emilia that if she dies before her she will 'prithee, shroud' (4.3.22) her in her bridal sheets. We, as audience, imagine how Desdemona, thus

---

[88] Jalāloddin Rumi, *Spiritual Verses: The First Book of the Masnavi-ye Ma'navi*, trans. Alan Williams (New York: Penguin, 2006), I.1–3, p. 46.

[89] Zekrgoo, 'Metaphors of Music & Dance', p. 1.

[90] Jenny Wade, 'Meeting God in the Flesh: Spirituality in Sexual Intimacy', *ReVision* 21.2 (1998), 35–41.

[91] 'A Lovers complaint being forsaken of his Love', c. 1615, English Broadside Ballad Archive, https://ebba.english.ucsb.edu/, presenting the Willow Song from the perspective of a lovelorn male includes a specific mention of death: 'Let no body blame me, her scornes I do prove, / O *Willow, etc.* / She was borne to be faire, and I die for her love.'

achieving the sublime Bride-Soul, 'dwell[s] safely', with wisdom, 'quiet from fear of evil',[92] fear of death. Like her spiritual sister Cordelia (*King Lear*, 5.3.6), Desdemona exhibits *amor fati*, bravely and openly accepting *dusdaimonia*, as inscribed in her name. In the broadest terms of human experience, this Greek word meaning 'misfortune, unhappiness', points etymologically to death as the common 'destined' or 'apportioned journey' for us all.[93] As boldly receptive woman-souls, Desdemona and Cordelia rehearse for us the equanimity and courage we must show at the threshold of our ultimate *dusdaimonia*.

Desdemona's display of boundless love and forgiveness lends further evidence for her ascension to divine wisdom. When her premonition becomes true, Desdemona's effort to dissuade Othello from killing her is as much about preserving his soul as preserving her life: she tries to prevent him from committing a heinous deed that he will self-immolatingly regret. Falling short of her aim, Desdemona, nevertheless, like Barbary in the Willow Song ('Let nobody blame him; his scorn I approve' [4.3.47]), does not blame Othello for uxoricide:

DESDEMONA: A guiltless death I die.
EMILIA: O, who hath done this deed?
DESDEMONA: Nobody; I myself. Farewell
  Commend me to my kind lord. O, farewell. (5.2.123–5)

At this point in the scene, Desdemona's theoerotic longing exhibits itself in what Sufis might call divine bewilderment, marked by cognitive contradictions. To wit, she asserts a blameless death in which 'Nobody' kills her but herself. Insofar as Desdemona recalls Mary, the Christian figure of the Sophianic Feminine,[94] Desdemona's 'guiltless death' is the eschatological complement to Mary's virgin birth. While some might interpret her words as an instance of weak submissiveness, what the play may be asking us to imagine is a character whose reflections on the *imago Dei* occasion a magnanimous act of forgiveness: her compassion arises from the wisdom that no one is entirely free of accountability in the interdependence of moral actions and that Othello, once enlightened, will be tortured enough by his stupefying ignorance of the truth.

In Sufi theoerotic understandings, this magnanimity would have a sacred dimension, that of Desdemona's eventual fusion with the Divine.

[92] Proverbs 17:33.
[93] Halliwell, *Between Ecstasy and Truth*, p. 355; 'daimon', in Henry Liddell and Robert Scott, *A Greek–English Lexicon* (Oxford: Oxford University Press, 1996).
[94] For an insightful elaboration, see David Hillman, 'Ave Desdemona', in *Shakespeare and Hospitality: Ethics, Politics, and Exchange*, ed. David B. Goldstein and Julia Reinhard Lupton (London: Routledge, 2016), pp. 139–62.

As if hearing Sufi poet Sa'di Shīrāzī's (1210–c. 1292) pious advice, she 'clear[s] the Tablet [*lawḥ*] of [her] heart of all images that are not of [H]im' and loses cognition of all other things so that 'nothing [else] will remain but the remembrance [*zikr*] of God Almighty'.[95] In Al-Ghazālī's words, the 'meaning of unity' is thus: she 'does not see anything but God, and will say "all things are Him, and I am not"'. It is perhaps in this theoerotic sense that 'Nobody' kills Desdemona but herself as she momentously accepts spiritual annihilation (*fanā*). 'So come[s her] soul to bliss' (5.2.247), despite her inability to save Othello. Desdemona goes to 'receiv[e] the kisses' not of Othello but 'of the Spouse Himself, that is, the Word of God, and will receive them not through reading and pondering on scriptures, but through the embracing of tragic experience by which she achieves the Sophianic Feminine'.[96] It is Desdemona, not Othello, who earns this Solomonic kiss invoked in the Song of Songs, which the Neoplatonic proponent Pietro Bembo also recalls in Castiglione's *The Book of the Courtier*: her soul is 'transported by divine love to the contemplation of celestial beauty and by its intimate union with this beauty might forsake the body'.[97] By this divine light, her last words, 'Commend me to my kind lord', serve as a herald to signal her ascension to God, rather than an earthbound farewell to Othello.[98]

In the worldly plane, Othello smothers her, literalising her position as *feme covert*,[99] as legal and sexual nothing. In the spiritual plane, however, the white bridal gown and sheets that cover her symbolise, Murshid Samuel Lewis suggests, the spiritual body: 'man's condition after he has received the life and light and love and the Grace of God pouring them upon him'.[100] In other words, the white coverings represent both her 'hard-won esoteric knowledge (*gnōsis*)' and *eudaemonia*, 'the happiness of [her] true and luminous self in this alien universe',[101] even as she experiences her worldly misfortune. As this Sufi reading eminently unveils, the scene of 'unpinning' and dressing Desdemona

---

[95] Sa'di Shirāzi, *Ghazalhā-ye Sa'di*, ed. Gholām-Hoseyn Yusofi (Tehran: Sokhan, 1385/2006), p. 59; qtd. in Ingenito, *Beholding Beauty*, p. 494. Al-Ghazālī, *Kimiya*, 1: p. 491; qtd. in Ingenito, *Beholding Beauty*, p. 494.

[96] Origen, qtd. in Seyyed Hossein Nasr, *Knowledge and the Sacred* (New York: State University of New York Press, 1989), pp. 18–19.

[97] Castiglione, *The Book of the Courtier*, p. 469.

[98] Luke 23:46.

[99] Frances E. Dolan. 'Home-Rebels and House-Traitors: Murderous Wives in Early Modern England', *Yale Journal of Law and the Humanities* 4.2 (1992), 1–32 (p. 5).

[100] Samuel L. Lewis, 'The Perfection of the Heart. An Original Sangatha', p. 9, available at https://www.ruhaniat.org/index.php/major-papers/sufi-practices-ryazat/2247-the-per fection-of-the-heart--an-original-sangatha (accessed 23 January 2023).

[101] J. R. Russell, 'Hymn of the Pearl', *Encyclopædia Iranica*, 2012, available at https://ira nicaonline.org/articles/hymn-of-the-pearl (accessed 23 January 2023).

into her bridal robe is indispensable in dramatising her quietly powerful assumption of the Bride – code for 'Meaning' in Persian Sufi poetry.[102]

Desdemona, Bride-Soul, extinguished in a tragic matrix of love and beauty, achingly dramatises the Sufi-Christian narrative of the 'excellent wretch' (3.3.89) as sublime hero. To be fully human is to be Desdemona, woman-soul – regardless of gender – mindfully longing for the reed-bed and acting with magnanimous care in accordance with that spiritual wisdom. *Othello* effectively transforms the theatrical space into a spiritual space, where we may see movingly dramatised an immersive and devotional practice of acting for others and thereby being truly a part of the Whole. To be fully human is to be Rumi's reed emerging from the mud – fragile, hollow, reaching for the sky, seeking purpose, connection, and all that is fine amidst the inanities of the world. Desdemona's Willow Song resonates in varied strains all over the globe – in our attained and aborted achievements and our aching desires for virtue and happiness, redemption and safe return, and the healing and recovery of self, community and earth.

---

[102] Schimmel, *A Two-Colored Brocade*, p. 41.

Part IV
Sustaining Virtue

Chapter 11

Enduring the Eventual: A Virtuous Way of Reading Shakespeare

Thomas J. Moretti

How can the act of reading *Othello* or *Macbeth* become virtuous? I ask this question as a Shakespearean at a liberal arts institution whose mission is to prepare students to lead an ethical life (not because my university's namesake is the island where Macbeth is buried).[1] When it comes to Shakespeare in higher education, though, Iona University is not an outlier. Students might read one Shakespeare play, many English majors and some Education majors must take one Shakespeare course, and some elect to take two. Because most students encounter Shakespeare for small spans as undergraduates, my pedagogical goals are less informed by long-standing historical, archival or theoretical queries than they are by the very real possibility that many students are offered what might prove 'the be-all and end-all' of their Shakespeare experience, their last chance to dwell among a community of burgeoning Shakespeare readers who must struggle with the distinctiveness of Shakespeare's art – the poetics, the contexts, the performances and the implications.

Among my goals is to encourage students to experience Shakespeare's major works as 'proper stuff' for honing their emotional and mental faculties against any 'perilous stuff / that weighs upon the heart' in their future (*Macbeth* 3.4.61, 5.3.44–5). I hope that some students will absorb, resonate with and even internalise the discoveries that close reading Shakespeare affords them. Perhaps some will then peruse Shakespeare after graduation, when they will sadly but most likely encounter much of what Shakespeare makes profound through poesis and eventual performance, if they have not already – the often isolating human struggles and travails, the accompanying ambivalence, doubt, guilt, shame, anger,

---

[1] 'Colmeskill, / The sacred storehouse' noted by Macduff is the Isle of Iona (2.4.33–4). Unless otherwise noted, all Shakespeare quotes are from *The Norton Shakespeare*, ed. Stephen Greenblatt et al., 3rd edn (New York: W. W. Norton, 2016).

frustration, desperation and grief that may remain afterwards, perhaps during sleepless nights when thoughts haunt and sting like scorpions, in a world beset with social ills and ecological turmoil.

My standard scholarly approaches to Shakespeare seem ill suited for the task. Reading Shakespeare's *Macbeth* through a combination of textual analysis and contextualisation – that is, within its early Jacobean milieu – might not counter attempts to nudge students towards a more virtuous life, but it typically does not support those efforts either. Overviews of the Gunpowder Plot, fears over casuistry and the history of English Jesuits from Edmund Campion to Robert Southwell to Henry Garnet have never rattled readers to rethink who they are and how they ought to be in relation to others. Nor do the associations between *Macbeth* and its mystery and morality play antecedents evidently pique student interests beyond the moment they learn about those linkages in class. Of course I could attribute the disconnect to my own limitations as a teacher-scholar, but even a formidable master of the craft would have to admit that students whose medium-term goals are non-literary would more likely treat resemblances between Macbeth and Cambyses or the porter and Titivillus as just as trivial as the fact that Iona is Colmekille – not as the material for performing and habituating the virtues required to participate ethically in the relationships, communities and society to which one might belong now or in the future.

This is not to say that tracing the historical trajectory of Catholic recusancy from the Babington Plot to the Gunpowder Plot, previewing the conditions of early modern marriage or investigating the problems of Christian kingship, scanning early modern cultural attitudes towards witchcraft and the occult, investigating a Shakespeare play through performative analysis or introducing different theoretical approaches to reading Shakespeare are extraneous to an undergraduate Shakespeare class. However, reliance upon these approaches to catalyse a long-term affinity for Shakespeare's works, let alone to help undergraduates practise living virtuously for the sake of the well-being of others, may very well trivialise Shakespeare for students demurred by all the secondary considerations that choke the art and its ethical potential for them.

Perhaps there is more intrinsic value in treatments of Shakespeare's dramas as refractions of contemporary moral conditions and situations. Still, the type of parallel readings that especially were in vogue in the United States during and after the 2016 presidential election do not smack of virtue or the self-cultivating investigations which virtue ethics requires. The extent to which the 45th US President was a parodic mixture of Shakespeare's villains and tragic heroes is a question that turns the act of reading Shakespeare into a test of Shakespeare's cultural currency. Perhaps reading *Macbeth* can offer students a lesson on the inner workings of an autocrat, definitely more poetically than, say, the 2021 Netflix documentary series 'How to Become a Tyrant', a set of six shows narrated by Peter Dinklage that offers scant historical information on the most atrocious tyrants of the twentieth century to trace the tactics that despots typically deploy to gain and to maintain dominance. If a dictator (or an elected official with authoritarian predilections) is comparable to Shakespeare's Coriolanus, Julius Caesar or Richard III, then engaged citizens could perceive the analogies well enough to recognise tyranny before it arrives.[2] At least they could learn about tyranny by studying Shakespeare.[3] Such comparisons could also grant proponents of representative democracy, freedom of expression and jurisprudence enough cultural capital to advocate for a freer and more just society, to denigrate Manchurian candidates and political opportunists and to join and strengthen communities that seek to do both. As Stanley Cavell asks about *Macbeth*, 'might you learn how not to become the victim of a tyrant' by 'learning [that] what has happened is exemplified by the learning of what is happening now?'[4]

However, if students conclude that all Shakespeare offers is an enriching poetic playbook to help expose the authoritarian roots of some of our own era's horrors and injustices, then I worry that too many students will tend towards content that they deem less obfuscating and intimidating, more accessible and accommodating to provide such an exposition. The result, I fear, would be a false sense of assurance that viewers know enough to recognise and avoid the narcissism, greed, resentment and hubris on display in a documentary. Shakespeare should offer my students an early modern lens for current inequities and power dynamics, but is that enough if the project of reading Shakespeare ought to disclose to readers how they themselves might lead a more virtuous

---

[2] For Coriolanus, see James Shapiro, 'The Shakespeare Play That Presaged the Trump Administration's Response to the Coronavirus Pandemic', *New Yorker*, 8 April 20, available at https://www.newyorker.com/culture/culture-desk/the-shakespeare-play-that-presaged-the-trump-administrations-response-to-the-coronavirus-pandemic. For Julius Caesar, see reviews of the 2017 Shakespeare in the Park Production of *Julius Caesar*, including the following: Nicholas Moschovakis, 'Review of the Public Theater's Julius Caesar', for *Shakespeare Quarterly*, available at https://shakespearequarterly.folger.edu/web_exclusive/public-theater-julius-caesar/; for Richard III, see Stephen Greenblatt, 'Shakespeare Explains the 2016 Election', *New York Times*, 8 October 2016, available at https://www.nytimes.com/2016/10/09/opinion/sunday/shakespeare-explains-the-2016-election.html.

[3] Stephen Greenblatt, *Tyrant: Shakespeare on Politics* (New York: W. W. Norton, 2018).

[4] Stanley Cavell, *Disowning Knowledge in Seven Plays of Shakespeare* (Cambridge: Cambridge University Press, 2003), p. 250.

life for the betterment of their society, or how they might otherwise be implicated in or directly contribute to future personal, cultural, political and social injustice?

An Ethical Way of Reading Shakespeare

An appropriate place to start sketching out a self-oriented ethical approach to reading Shakespeare is to consider the emphasis placed on virtue by those who wrote in defence of plays in early modern London. Thomas Heywood envisaged a stage 'fill[ed]' with actors for God's amusement and judgement: from the 'starre-galleries of hye ascent', God could 'applaud the best' and 'doom the rest'.[5] There is virtue in the fall of a doomed hero, because, according to John Taylor, theatre is '[w]here man m[a]y see his virtue or his crime / Layd open, either to their vices shame, / Or to their vertues memorable fame'. 'A Play's a true transparent Christall mirror, / To shew good minds their mirth, the bad their terror', he insists, as if plays can supplant *A Mirror for Magistrates*, if not *Imitatio Christi*.[6] For Taylor, theatre serves as a corrective or a reassurance not simply to those who have committed acts of violence or benevolence, but also to those who have thoughts of doing either. Perhaps no spectator in the audience is a murderer, but perhaps several have dreamed up and gravitated towards the 'horrible imaginings' of becoming one, or could at least empathise with the physiological sensations (the 'heart knock' against 'the ribs') of succumbing to what 'is but fantastical' (*Macbeth* 1.3.137–41).

The notion that good plays, like good poems, serve as a mirror to previous, current or potential thoughts, impulses, sensations and actions of readers and spectators was a common protheatrical trope by the time Heywood wrote.[7] When Shakespeare's Richard II breaks the mirror in

---

[5] Thomas Heywood, *An Apology for Actors* (London: Printed by Nicholas Okes, 1612), sigs. A8r–A8v. For more on protheatricality in early modern England, see Jeffrey Knapp, *Shakespeare's Tribe: Church, Nation, and Theatre in Renaissance England*. (Chicago: University of Chicago Press, 2002), esp. pp. 14–15 and 27–38.

[6] Heywood, *An Apology*, sig. a3v.

[7] See George Puttenham, *The Art of English Poesy*, ed. Frank Whigham and Wayne A. Rebhorn. (Ithaca, NY: Cornell University Press, 2007), p. 124. See also Philip Sidney, *Defense of Poesy* (London, 1595), available at http://www.luminarium.org/renasce nce-editions/defence.html (accessed 23 January 2023). According to Sidney, tragedy 'openeth the greatest wounds, and showeth forth the ulcers that are covered with tissue; that maketh kings fear to be tyrants, and tyrants to manifest their tyrannical humours; that with stirring the effects of admiration and commiseration, teacheth the uncertainty of this world, and upon how weak foundations gilded roofs are builded; that maketh us know, "qui sceptra sævus duro imperio regit, timet timentes, metus in authorem redit"

his deposition scene, he not only recognises his shattered status as king and, by extension, the jagged state of 'this sceptered isle'; he also tragically dramatises what for Heywood was a central purpose of theatre – for spectators to find themselves in the 'shadows' on the stage, and adjust their future behaviour if necessary to lead a more virtuous life (*Richard II* 2.1.40, 4.1.292–302). Puttenham limits the virtue ethics of spectating to monarchs and aristocrats, but Heywood generalises the effect of theatre on the masses: 'If we present a Tragedy, we include the fatall and abortive ends of such as commit notorious murders, which is aggravated and acted with all the Art that may be, to terrifie men from the like abhoored practices.'[8] Theatre is not a source of moral contagion, but rather its preventative, and it was the place to catch the conscience of not merely the king.

Nevertheless, stark problems persist with the mirror analogy. To find one's thoughts, behaviours or situations mirrored in a play does not automate a self-oriented critical response. Also, inherited and imbricated superstructures and belief systems, along with social, cognitive, neurological, psychological and physiological conditions, impact how we perceive and are perceived; to try to find oneself reflected in a Shakespeare character or in that character's narrative arc could very well reinforce long-standing prejudices and biases, including those that some unfortunately hold against themselves. Virtuous reading demands more than attention to the mimetic function of a tragic hero in Shakespeare's work or to its associations to people in our world. Forced parallels between Shakespeare characters and historical or political figures offer less than the potential resemblances between the ethical quandaries of early modern Londoners and those that students might eventually face. Accounting for and scrutinising these resemblances holds more promise for virtue cultivation and the social good.

I find historical phenomenology particularly instructive here, with pieces of its approach manageable enough to distil and put into a practice that my students could habituate. As a critical apparatus, historical phenomenology helps scholars to hypothesise 'the embodied experiences' of those who attended the plays in early modern London.[9] This

---

["An evil ruler's heavy sceptre makes him afraid of those who fear him, and the fear returns to its author", Seneca, *Oedipus*]'. Sidney was responding to Stephen Gosson's *A School of Abuses*. Cf. Thomas Lodge, *A Reply to Stephen Gosson's Schoole of Abuse in Defence of Poetry, Musick, and Stage Plays* (London, 1580), available at http://www.luminarium.org/renascence-editions/lodge.html (accessed 23 January 2023), where Lodge defends tragedies in particular based on his understanding of their original purpose: 'to giue thankes and prayses to G O D'.

8 Heywood, *An Apology*, sig. F3v.

9 See Jonathan Gil Harris, *Untimely Matter in the Time of Shakespeare* (Philadelphia:

approach to literary and cultural studies can also give texts like *Othello* or *Macbeth* especial resonance when they approximate, even anticipate our current ethical concerns. The march of Birnam Wood and other signs of impending doom in *Macbeth*, when set alongside current acts of deforestation for short-sighted economic, political or territorial advantage, are not as far apart as New Historicist approaches might suggest. But opportunities for intersubjectivity need not be limited to prevalent and long-standing cultural inequities, social problems or ecological strain in the abstract or in general terms. To serve the purpose of virtue ethics, intersubjective readings ought to stoke the 'fantastical horrors' in a reader's imagination (or the shared imagination of a community of readers). If you hosted a person whose death or misery could benefit you, or if you realised that the only person to love, trust and confide in – spouse, partner, friend or daughter – had criminal intent, or if you suddenly witnessed domestic violence in public, not just what would or should you do, but what must you do to prepare for the sudden impulse, dilemma, opportunity or shock? Attending to and interrogating the ways ethical situations in a given Shakespeare tragedy might resemble our own ought to tie the reader critically and personally to the ethical situations that Shakespeare represents.

Of course, attention to such ethical resemblances can construct or reinforce material means for dangerous ends (interpretation and identification with situations in plays like *Coriolanus* and *Merchant of Venice* became fodder for Nazi propaganda, after all). But that is due to unquestioned self-referential reading, a type of reader response that inhibits deep inquiry.[10] 'If I/we were in that situation' should not lead a reader to one answer. With regard to self-oriented critical reading, there is 'much virtue in If' only when the reader follows up one possibility ('If/

University of Pennsylvania Press, 2009), p. 121. For a more detailed account of historical phenomenology, see Bruce Smith, *Phenomenal Shakespeare* (Oxford: Wiley-Blackwell, 2010). Taking part in the 'affective turn' in the social sciences and performance studies, Smith claims that 'intersubjectivity' between contemporary readers and early moderns is not only possible, but advantageous, given the blind spots of other literary approaches and theories to 'sensations, feelings, emotions, aesthetic pleasure' (p. 7).

[10] See Ayanna Thompson and Laura Turchi, *Teaching Shakespeare with Purpose: A Student-Centred Approach* (London and New York: Bloomsbury, 2016), pp. 11–17, for their insightful list of 'tyrannies', or constraints on teaching Shakespeare well. These include 'structural' and the 'more insidious' 'self-imposed tyrannies'. Basic reader response is among the latter because, when used as the only lens for interpretation, it hinders investigations into (and more 'sophisticated' discussions and debates over) 'the meaning and significance of a text'. Overall, this teaching resource offers practical insights on what to expect when you are intending to teach Shakespeare, and what lessons tend to be more successful to create and maintain a constructive, critical and inclusive classroom for a diverse group of students.

then') with others ('but if/then'). To slightly adapt Banquo's call after Duncan's murder, 'let us meet / And question this most bloody piece of work / To know it further', and let 'Fears and scruples shake us', but not necessarily with 'our naked frailties hid' (*Macbeth* 2.3.124–7a).

This way of reading Shakespeare and of appreciating his penchant for ambiguity is based upon the premise that Shakespeare's plays are particularly suitable for the practice of virtue. Surely plenty of literary texts could offer students similar opportunities to grapple with their own capacity for virtue, especially texts that focus on the actions of characters under duress – after all, 'the telling of stories has a key part in educating us into the virtues'.[11] Nevertheless, tragic stories are notably apt for ethical work because of their concentrated appeal to reason, emotion, imagination and instinct as interdependent human faculties. I would venture to argue that the art of a Shakespeare tragedy, when studied closely, prevents the reader from the artifice of a strictly cerebral, abstract, conceptual and consequently distant ethics precisely because close readers must attend to their own physiological, emotional and creative reactions to tragedy, with all its concomitant stresses and anxieties.[12]

Shakespeare's tragedies further demonstrate their unique suitability to the cultivation of virtue with their tacit demand that readers slow down to peruse, to deliberate over, to question and to reconsider. I cannot emphasise enough how the challenge of reading Shakespeare today has as much to do with its stumbling pace as it has to do with the complexities of Shakespeare's language. More than reading a Shakespeare play, cultivating virtue through praxis is hard, slow and even humbling work. Studying how tragic heroes like Macbeth and Othello fail at this work (even when they persist in their efforts), and doing so at the slow pace that self-cultivation also necessitates, allows for an acknowledgement of the ethical quandaries we may face, the enormity of the demands that virtue ethics places on the individual, and the support system necessary to engage in the work anyway for the betterment of ourselves and others.

And so, to read Shakespeare virtuously is to understand characters within their ethical contexts, to consider their actions in those contexts

---

[11] Alasdair MacIntyre, *After Virtue: A Study in Moral Theory* (Notre Dame, IN: University of Notre Dame Press, 1981), p. 201.

[12] For the unique opportunities that tragedies avail the ethicist, see Martha Nussbaum, *The Fragility of Goodness: Luck and Ethics in Greek Tragedy and Philosophy* (New York: Cambridge University Press, 1986), pp. 12–16. Nussbaum's decision to study ancient Greek tragedies resonates with me precisely because Shakespeare's tragedies, like their ancient Greek counterparts, are rich in the ambiguities of human trials and tribulations. Shakespeare's tragic drama 'lays open to view the complexity, the indeterminacy, the sheer difficulty of actual human deliberation' (p. 14).

and to sketch out how those situations could (no matter how loosely) lay over those in which we might find ourselves.[13] This self-oriented method of critical analysis is designed not simply to focus on the deontological implications of the situation (what is the right thing to do), but to have readers recognise what skills and habits they lack and what remains latent, to test their capacity for goodness in a low-stakes form of inter-pretation that treats art as a medium for virtue ethics. Ironically, setting up Shakespeare tragedies as low-stakes material for ethical work can reveal the high moral stakes for students who do (or do not) make per-sonal the ethical questions that Shakespeare's plays raise. This method appreciates Shakespeare's drama by attending to ethically framed even-tualities that Shakespeare poeticises and dramatises, and it prepares readers for similar ethical encounters even as it has them possibly reflect on past experiences.[14]

Rash impulse and myopia are what hurl Othello and Macbeth to their tragic ends and away from the two virtues at the centre of my investi-gations below: prudence and courage. It takes courage and prudence to face some of the obstacles set in Shakespeare's tragedies – duplicity, rage, inebriation, misogyny and racism. To cultivate prudence and courage, readers of Shakespeare must contend with ethically charged eventualities, moments when they may have to think and act, perhaps simultaneously, to prevent or redress a wrong.

I cannot survey the long-standing philosophical discussions of these virtues here, but for the purposes of this essay, I consider 'courage' to be the will and nerve to confront and persist against a contrary force in the face of danger and harm.[15] 'Prudence', a term often made interchange-able with 'practical wisdom', is the combination of awareness, foresight and knowledge necessary to choose what is good. When set together, as they are in both *Othello* and *Macbeth*, prudent courage, or coura-geous prudence, is the will to confront and persist against what one rightly deems a threat to what is truly good for oneself and for others,

---

[13] In fundamental ways I am indebted to Michael Bristol's call to aim for 'deep conge-niality' with literature and to view context as 'a craft practice' that appreciates 'the par-ticular excellence of Shakespeare's achievement', that accommodates 'the creativity of the reader' in what he calls 'vernacular criticism', and emphasises 'the formal organization of the work'. See 'Macbeth the Philosopher: Rethinking Context', *New Literary History* 42.4 (2011), 641–62 (p. 649).

[14] I have in mind Michael Witmore, 'Eventuality', *Early Modern Theatricality*, ed. Henry S. Turner (Oxford: Oxford University Press, 2013), pp. 386–401. His essay ponders the eventualities of performance in theatre, but it has helped me to consider the moral implications of foresight.

[15] See MacIntyre, *After Virtue*, p. 179, where MacIntyre also links this virtue with 'care and concern'.

and the wherewithal to face that threat in the most proper way possible.[16] Of course, not all threats are controllable or defensible. Prudence and courage also work together to help one determine the right course of action in the face of threats that are avoidable, and threats that are inevitable. As Epictetus remarks, 'we must be at once cautious and courageous: courageous in what doth not depend upon choice, and cautious [or deliberative] in what doth'.[17] With these virtues in mind, what follows are investigations into starkly distinct ethical situations: Lodovico's discovery of domestic abuse in *Othello*, Macbeth's murderous fixation on one self-serving *telos*, and the mishandling of Macbeth's inner turmoil.

The Problem with Lodovico

Lodovico first enters Cyprus (and *Othello*) in 4.1 to proffer a letter on behalf of the Senate that instructs Othello to return home to Venice. The former lieutenant, Cassio, will take military command at Cyprus upon Othello's departure. The letter says nothing of Desdemona, but her attendance upon her 'lord' must be the expectation (1.3.189). If anything, the letter reinforces the patriarchal underpinnings of early modern marriage that have troubled Othello and Desdemona for a few scenes now: Othello's wife is his responsibility, and even the Senate has no jurisdiction over their relationship: 'Be it as you shall privately determine, / Either for her stay or going', the Duke of Venice declares to Othello (1.3.272–3a).

With Lodovico's invitation for Othello (and Desdemona) to return home from Cyprus, the play should begin to end here – in triumph, with the newlyweds returning to a grand celebration through the Venetian canals, to the Senate halls and to their bedchamber. Lodovico ought to expect as much, until Othello's ireful musings burst into the public ear. Lodovico witnesses Othello strike Desdemona, bully her with misogynistic epithets and interject private haranguing with public courtesies:

> . . . Proceed you in your tears. –
> Concerning this, sir – O well-painted passion! –

---

[16] Aristotle also seemed to pair these virtues when observing that 'what we do deliberate about are the things that depend on us and are doable', that 'decision is a desire informed by deliberation', and that prudence has to do with action. *Nicomachean Ethics*, ed. Sarah Broadie and Christopher Rowe (Oxford: Oxford University Press, 2002), pp. 127, 177 and 180 respectively. See also MacIntyre, *After Virtue*, p. 151.

[17] *Moral Discourses of Epictetus*, trans. Elizabeth Carter, ed. W. H. D. Rouse (London: J. M. Dent & Sons, 1910, 1950), p. 69.

> I am commanded home. – Get you away.
> I'll send for you anon. – Sir, I obey the mandate
> And will return to Venice. – Hence, avaunt!
> Cassio shall have my place. And sir, tonight
> I do entreat that we may sup together.
> You are welcome, sir, to Cyprus. – Goats and monkeys! *Exit.* (4.1.243–50)

Lodovico does not know about Othello's urges to 'Hang her', to 'chop her into messes' or to suffocate her, but he learns enough (4.1.184, 196). After Othello strikes, Lodovico interposes himself. 'My lord, this would not be believed in Venice / Though I should swear I saw't. / 'Tis very much; Make her amends, she weeps' (4.1.241–3). And after, to Iago, he questions. 'What, strike his wife! [. . .] Are his wits safe? Is he not light of brain?' When Iago suggests that Othello may do worse – 'yet would I knew / That stroke would prove the worst' – Lodovico laments, 'I am sorry that I am deceived in him' (4.1.256–69).

Lodovico's show of courage is temporary and ultimately misguided. He tries to enforce public civility, but he does not quite advocate marital respect, and never suggests mutuality. Lodovico is more shocked by Othello's inability to be civil than he is over the ongoing private abuse that any bystander would suspect has tormented Desdemona. Lodovico cherishes Desdemona, but only with 'Truly obedient, lady', because she follows her rankled husband's command, 'Out of my sight!' Lodovico even urges Othello to 'call her back' (4.1.234–5).[18] That Lodovico requests an abuser to 'call [. . .] back' the abused signals a desire not to protect the victim but to publicise reconciliation and to return Othello to his 'nature / Whom passion could not shake [. . .] whose solid virtue / The shot of accident nor dart of chance / Could neither graze nor pierce' (4.1.252–4). The scene of abuse horrifies Lodovico for what it suggests about the character of the abuser. And so we have a script that furthers the same premise underlying the rejection of wife beating in 'An Homilie on the State of Matrimony', 'for that is the greatest shame that can be, not so much to her that is beaten, as to him that does the deed'.[19] The trauma of the victim is secondary to both the abuser and the rationale for that abuse ('It is the cause, it is the cause, my soul' [5.2.1]). Othello

---

[18] Lodovico's line could also read 'Truly, an obedient lady'. See *Othello: A Revised Edition*, ed. E. A. J. Honigmann, intro. Ayanna Thompson (London and New York: Bloomsbury Arden, 1997, 2016), 4.1.246.

[19] Cited in Sara Munson Deats, '"Truly, an obedient lady": Desdemona, Emilia, and the Doctrine of Obedience in *Othello*', in *Othello: New Critical Essays*, ed. Philip C. Kolin (New York and London: Routledge, 2002), pp. 233–54 (p. 237). Also see Renaissance Electronic Texts 1.1, ed. Ian Lancashire, University of Toronto, available at http://www.anglicanlibrary.org/homilies/bk2hom18.htm (accessed 23 January 2023).

becomes the focus; Lodovico diplomatically pushes for a return to an untenable status quo.

Otherwise, why does Lodovico have no regard for the violent outburst later in 4.3, when Othello walks with him before the murder scene? 'I do beseech you, sir, trouble yourself no further', Lodovico tells Othello. Over what? Have they spoken off-stage about the previous incident? Othello takes it as a polite cue to leave Lodovico's company, but Othello refuses: 'O, pardon me; 'twill do me good to walk'. Lodovico's lines and his role are minor, and the tragedy is afoot, so his quick departure before the 'Willow' scene makes dramaturgical sense. Still, Lodovico walks with Othello off stage, as if past is not prologue, but prohibited, suppressed and made a secret in the open. Lodovico was 'deceived' of Othello's virtues, but all seems right again within the span of a day. Othello was mad, but apparently a 'good' 'walk' is all he needed. Lodovico the 'proper man' easily turns to civil discourse – 'Madam, good night. I humbly thank your ladyship' – and offers no response to Othello's curt command to his wife to go straight to bed and 'dismiss' Emilia (4.3.1–14). Nor does he come to the aid of Desdemona, the past and eventual victim of Othello's domestic tyranny. Theatregoers and readers know what Othello plans, but Lodovico ignores or dismisses the earlier warning signs. He next appears in the play with an armed retinue to ask, 'Where is this rash and most unfortunate man?', as if the murder was an unpredictable misfortune for the husband (5.2.276). In his presumption of command at play's end, Lodovico mentions nothing of Desdemona or Emilia, victims of uxoricide, because men are Lodovico's only lasting concern.

We might see Lodovico, then, as a character lacking courage and prudence. To make do with historical phenomenology, we might even parallel his half-hearted response to spousal abuse alongside troubling signs that wife beating was socially tolerable at the time.[20] Or, we could shape loose associations between Lodovico's situation and a contemporary

---

[20] On 11 July 1608, William Gager defended in Comitia at Oxford the proposition that it is lawful for men to beat their wives to enforce domestic obedience and patriarchal order. For more on Gager's work, see *William Gager: The Complete Works*, ed. Dana F. Sutton, 4 vols (New York and London: Garland, 1994). For domestic abuse in early modern England, see Frances Dolan, *Dangerous Familiars: Representations of Domestic Crime in England, 1550–1700* (Ithaca, NY: Cornell University Press, 1994), pp. 12–19, 20–58 and 89–120; and Susan Dwyer Amussen, 'Punishment, Discipline, and Power: The Social Meanings of Violence in Early Modern England', *Journal of British Studies* 34.1 (1995), 1–34. According to Dolan and Amussen's extensive research on violence in early modern England, archives tend to note only egregious acts of violence against women. Also, Dolan and Amussen have noted that incidents of sexual assault were less likely to lead to charges than murder.

instance of ineffective or more harmful witnessing. Lodovico's intervention was temporary, but how does it compare to looking the other way from the start or even raising a public outcry *in defence* of a man credibly accused of violence against a woman? Close to two years before the first performance of *Othello*, and perhaps less than a year after Shakespeare first composed the play, Margaret White went before the Court of Bridewell on 27 October 1602, to answer charges of 'having a child in whoredom'.[21] In written notes from the proceedings, White claimed that a Henry Moore was the father, but she then accused Christopher Beeston of rape. This player began his career as a boy actor for the Lord Chamberlain's Men and transferred to the Lord Worcester's Men by 1602 (plausibly the year that *Othello* was written).[22] The accusation came only a few weeks after Beeston had married.[23] In her testimony, she accused Beeston of raping her 'at one winters house in Star alley without Bishopsgate'. During the alleged assault, he bragged that he had 'lyen with a hundred wenches'.[24]

Margaret White's allegations were deemed credible. Christopher Beeston was called to respond to them, twice: on 5 and 13 November. During his second appearance, he brought a group of his friends, 'his confederats plaiers'. The document offers no names, but with Beeston's reputation on the line, it is hard to imagine a better way to defend himself than vehemently to deny the charges in the presence of his fellow actors: Will Kemp, Robert Armin, Richard Burbage, John Lowin, Thomas Heywood, John Duke, Henry Condell, John Heminges, William Sly, Alexander Cooke and William Shakespeare. Whoever it may have been, they with Beeston 'did verie vehementlie demeane them selves to certen governors and much abused the place'.[25] They did nothing to assuage the court, though, which 'greatelie suspected' that Beeston had 'committed the facte'. The court eventually did nothing. Beeston was never convicted, and it seems, based on the extant records, that the 13 November hearing was the last on the matter.[26]

---

[21] For the following account, see Duncan Salkeld, 'Literary Traces in Bridewell and Bethlem, 1602–1624', *The Review of English Studies* 56, 225 (2005), 379–85 (381–2); and Salkeld, *Shakespeare and London* (Oxford: Oxford University Press, 2018), pp. 84–6.

[22] For *Othello*'s possible year of composition, see Clare McManus, 'Textual Introduction', *Norton Shakespeare*, p. 2081.

[23] Stanley Wells, *Shakespeare and Co.* (London: Vintage, 2008), p. 82.

[24] Salkeld, 'Literary Traces', p. 381.

[25] 'Demean' could simply mean 'conduct oneself' and need not have a negative connotation (*OED* 'demean' v. 1–2).

[26] For more on Beeston's successful career as a theatre and playing company owner after this accusation and his departure from the Lord Chamberlain's Men, see Andrew Gurr, 'Beeston [Hutchinson], Christopher', in *Oxford Dictionary of National Biography* (Oxford: Oxford University Press, 2004).

Such anecdotal contexts might enable the 'intersubjectivity' esteemed by proponents of historical phenomenology, and perhaps readers could then notice associative patterns in the public sphere today, but contexts must be stretched towards critical self-referentiality to hold any practical ethical bearing for the reader. Here is a question to pose to make this reading self-cultivating: are our semblances of virtue blemished in moments when we are passive bystanders (or worse, active saboteurs of fair adjudication) to such domestic atrocities? We might learn mantras like 'see something, say something', but if we fail to act precisely because we see ourselves as minor characters in someone else's tragic arc, especially someone whom we highly regard, befriend or love, to what extent have we failed to act with courage and prudence? The challenge that Lodovico ought to pose readers is not simply whether he or men of his time should have acted differently, but whether readers would or should act differently, and to what extent bystanders commit a wrong through inaction and passivity, even if only the bystander knows of the inaction, even when no one else questions or considers the inaction of the bystander.

To examine a play that focuses so heavily on reputation, I would contend that readers ought to assess the situations that test the virtues of its characters, central or ancillary, and not simply in terms of how others view those characters. Lodovico's prudence, courage and capacity for discernment prove suspect precisely because he avoids meddling in the domestic affairs of an increasingly violent and unhinged husband who also happens to have a reputation as a stoic general. Readers ought to implement that ethically charged critical reading of Lodovico for the purpose of self-directed application: what would they do in an analogous situation, what should they do, what virtues must they practise and perform to do what they ought, and how should they habituate those virtues?

Through such critical self-oriented investigations, readers can then consider the best ways to handle such situations. According to the formidable resource for bystanders of violence, the organisation Right to Be, direct intervention can often exacerbate tension and create conditions for violence against both victim and bystander (cue Emilia).[27] This organisation also notes how avoidance or passive tolerance can treat patterns of abuse as hardly remarkable until the abuser, in their

---

[27] This organisation (formerly called Hollaback!) offers bystander-intervention training. It emphasises five tactics that, when used judiciously, could defuse harassment and abuse: Distract, Delegate (call for help), Document, Delay (offer help to the victim after the incident) and Direct (or directly respond to the perpetrator): see https://righttobe.org /guides/bystander-intervention-training/.

minds, 'loved not wisely, but too well' (*Othello* 5.2.337). Required is the prudence and courage necessary to adequately, if not expertly, intercede. Scene adaptation and performance could help readers begin to practise developing those virtues. Employing bystander intervention training methods, readers could redraft Lodovico's responses to Othello and act out their versions of a more 'proper man', one with a reputation for civic engagement and social awareness, perhaps with guidance from guest crisis management experts.

Treating Lodovico's poor handling of Desdemona's ongoing trauma as an analogous situation directs students to link the study of Shakespeare to a method of individual empowerment and virtue cultivation in preparation for that situation to recur. Critical appreciation of Shakespeare's art now becomes an evidently practical means towards living a more engaged and actively virtuous daily life. That the play offers other opportunities for such an approach – Othello's poetic treatment of Desdemona as a wild hawk or as 'monumental alabaster', or Othello's self-demeaning expressions of melancholy, or Iago's expressions of racism and misogyny, sometimes with the intention of abhorrently comic effect – bears witness to the play's rich potential for situational contextualisation and self-oriented critical analysis during encounters with Shakespeare's art (*Othello* 3.3.301, 5.2.5).

Treating Macbeth's Infirmity of Purpose

Macbeth can be ethically exigent for readers as well, in part because of Macbeth's struggle to espouse courage amid cynicism in the play's final act. Macbeth is nothing virtuous, and yet he persists despite the horrors of his end – 'Yet I will try the last' (5.7.62) – in an attempt to epitomise the same militant masculinity that some of Shakespeare's other tragic militant heroes try to claim for themselves, with varying degrees of failure (Othello, Coriolanus and Antony). Macbeth fails because he cannot discern the future and tries to overcompensate with a form of bloody persistence that perverts the courage he was reputed to exhibit at the start of the play. He cannot 'look into the seeds of time and say which grain will grow and which will not', and he fears prophecies of his doom and erasure, perhaps because he has privileged one goal at the expense of others – an error hardly possible for a more flexibly attuned mind (1.3.59–60). He also fixates on one method to achieve that goal and accelerates his narrative self towards that goal without accounting for the consequences of that method. His lack of prudence and his misguided attempts at courage have determined his fate. Macbeth's inadequate anticipation of the future, and his attempts to rush into the future, suggest how easily a goal – in this case, coronation and perpetual rule – can turn vile through the gross act of murder, a horrific conclusion to the accelerated pace and the obsession with which Macbeth charges towards that goal. He proves unaware of the temporal limitations and ethical implications of an act designed to achieve his self-serving goals, and he lacks the tolerance, courage and discernment necessary to adapt to changing conditions and outcomes. 'Infirm of purpose', indeed (2.2.55).

As a 'rarer monster' (from the Latin *monere*, 'to warn'), Macbeth horrifically sabotages his capacity to endure by way of a narrow-minded and vicious commitment to one selfish goal (5.7.55). He confines his *telos*, and thereby corrupts his capacity to live a virtuous and flourishing life. He attempts to ignore the past through sheer will and to endure present panic over future doom – a recipe for villainy, cynicism and despair. Macbeth portends that a person's capacity to live in accordance with virtue can suffer through a preoccupation with some concocted future – 'a false creation', 'a dagger of the mind' (2.1.38–9) – and through a lack of prudence evidenced by untimely acts:

> MACBETH: I'll fight till my bones my flesh be hacked.
>   Give me my armor.
> SEYTON: 'Tis not needed yet. (5.3.32–3)

Macbeth is a tyrannical cynic who confuses desperation with courage, grandiosity with honour, haste with strength and obsession with commitment.

Perhaps, in far different contexts, readers lack adaptive foresight into eventualities based on current conditions. Perhaps searching for resemblances with Macbeth's ethical failings risks oversimplification, but we ought to consider how such a wiser orientation to one's temporal condition – a flexible presence in the face of potential calamities – might potentialise a virtuous practice, even if we know that the alternative would not be that we murder our guests. In other words, readers could imagine failing to achieve some future goal, to collaboratively process that possibility, and to invent or discover strategies to avoid the despair and cynicism that Macbeth exhibits, let alone the perverted sense of courage that such despair and cynicism might fuel. Again, Macbeth's bloody, tyrannical deeds (I hope) would hardly resonate with most readers (including my students). The intensity of obsession and fixation on a particular future for oneself seems more apt for readers to analogise (especially my students). What goals do they have, what goals do others have for them, and how should they prepare themselves *now* for the possibility that they might not reach those goals, or that they have misread what might be required to achieve those goals, or that they misjudged what their goals ought to be (perhaps too lofty, perhaps encompassing)? In other words, ethical investigations into Macbeth's obsessions, haste and misplaced determination can help readers at least recognise the utility of flexible anticipation and its ties to virtues like prudence and courage, as well as temperance and even hope.[28]

Macbeth's fall also arises from his inability to discern truth from the signs he witnesses. When he sees a dagger, just as when he hears the omen about Birnam Wood or the man not of woman born, Macbeth's interpretation is first literalistic, then simplistic and consequently damning. He fails to see the moral and religious significance of another dagger of the mind, what Erasmus calls an '*enchiridion*, a certayne lyttlel dagger, whome never lay but of thy hand, no not whan thou arte at meate or in thy chaumbre' because 'the lyfe of mortall men is nothinge but a certayne perpetuall exercise of warre' against vice.[29] If only Macbeth had interpreted the dagger anagogically, not as a beckoning to kill, but as a warning to arm himself against his regicidal and fratricidal desires.

Whereas Macbeth obsesses over imagined threats around him, Erasmus cautions his readers to recognise and distinguish those especially perilous vices 'which counterfeit vertue', and to 'discerne things to be refused, fro[m] things to be accept[ed]', especially when we are alone with our thoughts or goaded to pursue them by a loved one.[30] While a common call to remain vigilant, Erasmus's also brings to mind what we might call interoception, the process of focusing attention on one's physical and emotive reactions (scorpions of Macbeth's mind, for instance [3.2.35]) so that one may properly name and interpret the meaning of those reactions.[31] With unfixed hair and knocking heart, Macbeth's

---

[28] For the potential that hope could persist in spite of personal, communal, social and even cultural disaster, see Jonathan Lear, *Radical Hope: Ethics in the Face of Cultural Devastation* (Cambridge, MA: Harvard University Press, 2006).

[29] Erasmus, *Enchiridion Militis Christiani, which may be called in English, the han[d]some weapon of a Christian Knight* (London, 1576), sig. Gii v–Gii r and sig. Di v.

[30] Erasmus, *Enchiridion*, sig. Niiii r and sig. Ivii v. For Shakespeare's poetic and theatrical investigation of psychomachia and Erasmus's Christian ethics, see my essay, 'Misthinking the King: The Theatrics of Christian Rule in *Henry VI, Part 3*', *Renascence: Essays on Values in Literature* 60.4 (2008), 275–94.

[31] See Annie Murphy Paul, *The Extended Mind: The Power of Thinking Outside the Brain* (Boston, MA: Houghton Mifflin Harcourt, 2021), pp. 22–4, 58 and 61–4. She synthesises scientific research that has mapped out cognitive connections between what lies outside the brain – self-referential movements (like hand gestures), our physiological sensations, our environment, and the people in our company – and high-level cognitive processes like deliberation and memory retention. Awareness of those connections can lead to more informed choices about who we interact with and how we interact with them,

inner struggle against his desire to murder is set in starkly physiological terms from the start (1.3.136–9). He construes those sensations as an urge to commit a crime, rather than as a warning against crime, just as he understands the witches' prophecy as an invitation, not a warning.

Macbeth seems quite aware of the consequences of his cruelty, but whenever there is the chance for introspection, reconsideration and remorse (if not repentance), Macbeth redirects his focus towards external threats or shifts the cause for his own inner turmoil to external forces. Fundamentally, Macbeth is not equipped for the inner struggle that Erasmus envisages. The knocking at the door after Macbeth muses about his inability to say 'Amen' comes to mind, as do Banquo's prophecy, Fleance's survival and the witches' equivocations. His woeful reactions and their tragic outcome suggest a warning that psychomachia is not to be a private, self-absorbed affair, because it may become self-consuming as a result.

Macbeth's last act, to fight Macduff to the death, might seem more courageous than his acquiescence to his 'black and deep desires' (1.4.58), but there remains a more radical version of courage. Macbeth could surrender rather than duel, relent rather than rage. Perhaps that might signal cowardice within his warrior culture, but a seeming lack of courage in the face of what seems fated could lead to an ethical reckoning that a prudent person would face if it effected a more peaceful transfer of power and a memorable critique of the evils embedded in one's culture. Perhaps Macbeth's former subjects (and readers) would have a different speech about 'tomorrow' to heed – not nihilistic, but reparative. Perhaps relenting in the face of death would have proven bold enough to jostle others to reconsider the ties between war, physical prowess, masculinity and rule in medieval Scotland, in early modern England and in many countries today.

Readers could also deliberate over enigmatic questions about the cultural and social forces that might inhibit a virtuous life. When Macbeth faces defeat, his cynicism and subsequent persistence coalesce into an approximation of courage that seems more like an avoidance of shame – shame over his bloody hands, over his failure to anticipate and to endure various eventualities, and over his inability to restore his mind from its homicidal impulses.[32] His musing that his 'way of life / Is fall'n

---

what setting we work in, and what choices we make when facing an urgent dilemma or an ambiguous, indeterminate set of options that conscious processing and problem-solving could never resolve or sort out. Recent studies in cognition reveal that people often make good choices when, in Paul's words, 'the heart, and not the head, leads the way'.

[32] For the avoidance of shame (in *King Lear*), see Cavell, *Disowning Knowledge*, pp. 48–9.

into the sere, the yellow leaf, / And that which should accompany old age, / As honor, love, obedience, troops of friends, / I must not look to have' intones regret over a lost, alternative future that could have provided community, camaraderie and belonging (5.3.22–6). And yet, he rules over a realm that tragically reverberates his selfishness and self-reliance. Even the doctor cannot fathom helping another who suffers in the spirit:

> MACBETH: Canst thou not minister to a mind diseased,
>   Pluck from the memory a rooted sorrow,
>   Raze out the written troubles of the brain,
>   And with some sweet oblivious antidote
>   Cleanse the stuffed bosom of that perilous stuff
>   Which weighs upon the heart?
> DOCTOR: Therein the patient
>   Must minister to himself. (5.3.40–6)

Without directions or instructions, readers are left with the possibility that those tormented in the mind and heart are on their own. Perhaps that condition is a fitting consequence for the Macbeths, but if Harry Berger is right that a 'subtler evil' 'obscures the Scottish air' because of 'problematic structural tendencies' in the play's quintessential Hobbesian cultural backdrop – 'the war of every man against every man' – then the play offers Macbeth the bloody tyrant as a hellhound scapegoat for a vicious, individualistic society whose members exploit Macbeth's villainy to avoid ethical introspection and the shame that might result.[33]

During Lady Macbeth's disturbing somnambulism the doctor had already been given one opportunity to intervene, if only for the sake of the oppressed realm. His responses – 'this disease is beyond my practice' and 'more needs she the divine [as in a priest] than the physician' – are true as far as they go for a practitioner of medieval and early modern medicine, but should the doctor limit his response to his professional practice? The same question should hover over his reaction to Macbeth's sudden desire to cure a diseased mind (his own, his wife's). Perhaps Macbeth's murderous tyranny justifies his despair over the lack of a cure, but that is not the doctor's concern. The doctor's point is that what ails them is beyond his practice and therefore up to them to remedy on their own or up to someone else to show them how – virtually impossible in a culture hell-bent on individual prowess and self-achievement rather than support, charity and hospitality.

---

[33] Harry Berger, Jr, *Making Trifles of Terrors: Redistributing Complicities in Shakespeare* (Stanford, CA: Stanford University Press, 1997), pp. 72 and 93.

There is also nothing in this play to suggest that mutuality is possible in Scotland's culture, so long as that culture is entrenched in war and individualism; the doctor says the wrong thing precisely because it is the thing one is expected to say in this play. The endless line of kings from Fleance to the end should horrify because it brings with it no hope for a cultural reckoning that does away with the bloody roots of tyranny. Moreover, there seems no desire in the play for any kind of political transformation beyond the alteration of state that Malcolm celebrates at play's end – one that has removed a tyrant and replaced thanes with earls, but has done little else to prevent future tyranny or to deracinate the cultural preconditions of tyranny. No wonder the doctor exclaims 'God, God forgive us all' once Lady Macbeth goes to bed (5.1.79).

How does one resist harmful urges that a culture might feed, or even instigate? How could one work against the self-serving habits that a culture might instil and encourage? How might one envision a future beyond the cultural parameters in which one finds oneself? Perhaps the play suggests that radical political alteration and cultural amelioration can only start at a site of vulnerability, like the one where the doctor finds himself in Act 5, with a tyrant in search of a remedy for the torment and sorrow that he and his spouse have inflicted upon themselves. And perhaps the doctor could have talked of some remedy beyond his practice, beyond the norms of a warrior culture, and beyond Macbeth's ability to perform on his own – the act of repentance, perhaps not to serve any salvific function for the bloody monster of the play, but rather to try to catalyse a cultural reckoning.

Macbeth would have likely refused such a religiously intoned prescription in Act 5 ('bear-like, I must fight the course' [5.7.2]). Nonetheless, his struggle with his own thoughts in Act 1, coupled with his inability to say 'Amen' when he was in most need of it in Act 2, suggests that, for early modern London audiences, what is lacking in this play is, first, any guidance through the processes of introspection and interoception, and, second, any ritual of repentance that early modern Londoners would have certainly recognised – the chance to repent in public, even with just a moment left on the scaffold, and to end that repentance with an 'Amen'. Perhaps that form of repentance could have signalled a shift away from Scotland's warrior culture. If that possibility proves unfathomable, at least readers could find in the play a lesson that the psychomachia in which Macbeth and Lady Macbeth engage throughout most of the play should not be, must not be, a strictly private and isolating struggle, but rather a struggle to share with others beyond the walls of the mind and the home. Even if we are to take it as a given that the struggle with one's urges, fears, regrets and sorrows is intensely personal, it must also be a communal, mutually supported one, whatever our professions might be, if it is to lead to a more hopeful future.[34]

In general, I advocate for encounters with Shakespeare's plays that habituate virtue for active, critical readers in a safe and imagined space before they might confront real situations that test their capacity for goodness (or, so that they might come to terms with experiences during which that capacity has already been tested). They could prepare for eventual struggles and crises perhaps too dreadful to imagine, or a moment of realisation that a past act has led to a trammelling consequence. I do not wish to claim that the mere act of reading Shakespeare, or any literature, builds virtue and leads to a good life, or that a Shakespeare course could completely prepare one for a murky hell. Rather, I propose that readers avail themselves of the ambiguities that enrich Shakespeare's art to make a virtuous way of life more possible.

Once readers at least acknowledge the virtues required to avoid hasty acts of desperation, to process the possibilities of personal failure, social deprivation, isolation and cultural determinism, and to prepare to say the right thing during moments of exposure and vulnerability, perhaps there might be desires to inquire further into the play's social and political milieu (the self-reliant masculine culture that Macbeth epitomises), the temporal and material conditions of the early modern theatre (the smell of gunpowder and its polychronic associations), or the wisdom traditions that to one extent or another may have allowed early modern Londoners to bear the worrisome signs of things to come (whether a disappearing star, a failed terrorist plot, a plague, a benighted day or rumours of cannibalistic horses).[35] Readers might also better internalise the rejoinder to Macbeth's contemptuous view of 'tomorrow' that many in Shakespeare's time would have recalled: 'Care not then for the morowe: for the morowe shal care for itself: the day hath ynough with his owne grief.'[36] Arguably, these other aspects of Shakespeare's work would prove more intriguing to readers if they were to investigate a Shakespeare play's ethical situations through textual analysis and moral

---

[34] See MacIntyre, *After Virtue*, pp. 204–5, for the intrinsic social features of our moral selves.

[35] For polychronicity in *Macbeth*, see Jonathan Gil Harris, 'The Smell of *Macbeth*', *Shakespeare Quarterly* 58.4 (2007), 465–86. For disasters, omens and catastrophising in early modern England, see Gerard Passannante, *Catastrophizing: Materialism and the Making of Disaster* (Chicago: University of Chicago Press, 2019).

[36] Matthew 6:34, *The Geneva Bible: A Facsimile of the 1560 Edition* (Peabody, MA: Hendrickson, 2007).

self-inquiry. Fluid investigations into the wondrous aesthetic expressions of tragic happenstance could prepare readers to last, even flourish, through an ethically exigent present and future, for themselves and for others.

Chapter 12

Sustaining Courage in the Humanities: The Example of *Hamlet*

Daniel Juan Gil

In a discussion of the persistence of 'heroic culture' at the cusp of the European Middle Ages, Alasdair MacIntyre affirms the continuing importance of what he terms 'the heroic table of the virtues' in the medieval Aristotelian-infused virtue ethics tradition whose rise and fall he tracks in *After Virtue*:

> [T]he moral standpoint of heroic society [was] a necessary starting-point for moral reflection within the tradition with which we are concerned. So the medieval order cannot reject the heroic table of the virtues. Loyalty to family and to friends, the courage required to sustain the household or a military expedition and a piety which accepts the moral limits and impositions of the cosmic order are central virtues, partially defined in terms of institutions such as the code of revenge in the sagas.[1]

Hamlet looks back to the historical moment MacIntyre evokes, as the play is built from source material and a worldview drawn from premodern sagas (not least in its concern with 'the code of revenge') but also marks the transformation of this source material and worldview into the ethical universe of medieval Aristotelianism adverted to in the play by engagement with schools and schooling, including the kind of schooling that is accomplished at the University of Wittenberg, and by engagement with a discourse of the virtues and vices. And yet at the same time the play also looks back on all this from much later, during the seventeenth century when the neo-Aristotelian ethical project that MacIntyre celebrates is already marked as everywhere in full disintegration. *Hamlet* therefore occupies a unique ethical space – analogous to the position MacIntyre himself occupies – at the intersection of three ethical world-systems: the heroic age, the scholastic Middle Ages and the world of humanism.

[1] Alasdair MacIntyre, *After Virtue: A Study in Moral Theory* (Notre Dame, IN: University of Notre Dame Press, 1984), p. 166.

In the midst of this ethical intersection, MacIntyre singles out the importance of '[l]oyalty to family and to friends, the courage required to sustain the household or a military expedition' as a holdover from the heroic age and yet also as a cornerstone of the whole edifice of virtue ethics he describes in *After Virtue*. The kind of courage to which MacIntyre points here is not the courage of the classical Stoics – 'valor' or 'fortitude', the individual's ability to face danger or even defeat.[2] Rather, MacIntyre refers to a species of courage that is oriented 'to sustain' something – and as examples of things that need such courage to be sustained he cites the household and the military expedition. And here it is important that households and military expeditions are complex, institutionalised webs of connections between people. This fact accounts for the admixture of loyalty – loyalty to others or to a whole way of life – in MacIntyre's 'courage'.

I will term this kind of courage 'sustaining courage'. By 'sustaining courage' I do not mean individual courage in the face of setbacks, nor do I mean individualised courage that is sustained for a long period of time. Rather the virtue of 'sustaining courage' amounts to the ability to maintain or keep going the collective endeavour exemplified by a household or a military expedition. The household and the military expedition – and questions about what can go wrong with them and how they can be sustained – play a central role in *Hamlet*. But if the play invites reflection on the role of sustaining courage in the household and the military expedition then the play also invites reflection on the role of sustaining courage in the life of the school or the university that is so prominent a subtext in the play. And in posing the question of the role of sustaining courage in the life of the school or the university, *Hamlet* poses a question to us as we think about the future of our discipline: how might the virtue of sustaining courage apply to the problem of sustaining an academic discipline (like English) or a subdiscipline (like Shakespeare studies)?

Hamlet is a relentless diagnosis of the kinds of failures and breakdowns that both households and military expeditions are subject to. The household is a focus in the play precisely insofar as it appears to have become corrupted or hollow as the result of Hamlet Sr's death and Gertrude's marriage to Claudius. Despite Claudius and Gertrude's rhetoric of happy domestic and household life, within which they eagerly seek to incorporate Hamlet, Hamlet himself sees their relationship with

---

[2] Drawing on this Stoic tradition, for example, Hannah Arendt identifies courage as what is needed 'to leave the household'. Hannah Arendt, *The Human Condition*, intro. Margaret Canovan, foreword by Danielle Allen (Chicago: University of Chicago Press, 2018), p. 36.

each other and his own relationship with them as the simulacrum of a household and not as its reality. Hamlet responds to this situation with nothing but nihilistic (and misogynistic) destructiveness. He tells Ophelia:

> I have heard of your paintings well enough. God hath given you one face, and you make yourselves another. You jig and amble, and you lisp; you nick-name God's creatures and make your wantonness your ignorance. Go to, I'll no more on't; it hath made me mad. I say we will have no more marriage. Those that are married already – all but one – shall live. The rest shall keep as they are. To a nunnery, go. (3.1.142–9)

The misogynistic attack on the falseness of women – emblematised, as ever in early modern culture, by the use of cosmetics – is, for Hamlet, an emblem of the falseness of all households as Hamlet now sees them.

The household's hollowness is shadowed (doubled, we might almost say) by a hollowness in military life. The play begins with Denmark in military mobilisation, but without a widely shared understanding of the purpose of this military activity. Marcellus, a grunt in the Danish war machine, asks why everyone in Denmark is being kept so busy with military preparations:

> Why such impress of shipwrights, whose sore task
> Does not divide the Sunday from the week.
> What might be toward that this sweaty haste
> Doth make the night joint laborer with the day?
> Who is't that can inform me? (1.1.71–9)[3]

Horatio gives an answer: 'to recover of us by strong hand / And terms compulsatory those foresaid lands / So by his [that is, Fortinbras's] father lost; and this, I take it, / Is the main motive of our preparations' (1.1.102–5). But this answer rings hollow. It rings hollow because of Horatio's hint of not finding this answer fully convincing ('I take it', he says, as though it were just his best guess) and it only gets more hollow with the back and forth of Fortinbras's motives and plans as he shifts from preparing to attack Denmark to merely wanting to march through Denmark on the way to attacking a plot of land in Poland, an under-taking that we later learn is utterly without strategic purpose or signifi-cance, as the Captain tells Hamlet:

> Truly to speak, and with no addition,
> We go to gain a little patch of ground

---

[3] All quotations from *Hamlet* are taken from *The Complete Pelican Shakespeare*, ed. Stephen Orgel and A. R. Braunmuller (NY: Penguin Classics, 2002). Citations are given internally.

That hath in it no profit but the name.
To pay five ducats, five, I would not farm it,
Nor will it yield to Norway or the Pole
A ranker rate, should it be sold in fee. (4.4.17–22)

In the military expedition and in the household, the play points to a process of hollowing out in which the outward appearance of a household or a military body is maintained but the essence is somehow gone.[4] If something is rotten in the state of Denmark, then this rottenness takes the form of something rotten in the household and the military expedition, the key institutions around which the play is structured.

But the play also evokes a creeping sense of hollowness or simulacra in academic institutions including the life that takes place at the University of Wittenberg from which Claudius bars Hamlet. His first speech to Hamlet closes with 'For your intent / In going back to school in Wittenberg, / It is most retrograde to our desire' (1.2.112–14). On the one hand, the idea of the university seems to stand apart from Denmark (home of corrupt households and military expeditions) as some kind of refuge – at least that is how Hamlet appears to see things. And yet if Hamlet's 'two schoolfellows' (3.4.202), Guildenstern and Rosencrantz, are any guide, the life of the school is also suffering from a creeping hollowness. Moreover, the whole point of Denmark as a theatrical space is to prove to Horatio – that exemplary creature of the university – that 'there are more things in heaven and earth, Horatio, / Than are dreamt of in your philosophy' (1.5.169–70). Throughout the play, the characteristic postures and stances of intellectuals are on display, and again and again they seem empty or inadequate to the moment.

In all three cases – the household, the military expedition and the school – the play invites reflection on how institutions or forms of life become corrupted and on what the appropriate response might be. And in all three cases the play points to the absence of an appropriate remedy or response. Hamlet himself diagnoses what is missing as his own lack of willpower or decisiveness. But what MacIntyre might suggest is that what is missing is the specific virtue of sustaining courage. In that sense, the play can be understood as an object lesson in what a world without sustaining courage is like.

To see what exactly sustaining courage would amount to in the world of the play, or in our world, will require some philosophical analysis

---

[4] In twentieth-century performances of the play, the existentially ungrounded wilfulness of Fortinbras has opened him to being played as a military strong man. For a review of major twentieth-century performance interpretations of the character, see Gregg Dion, 'Fortinbras, Our Contemporary', *Theater Studies* 38 (1993), 17–27.

of the logical structure of households and military expeditions. What do households and military expeditions have in common such that MacIntyre can imagine a single species of courage to sustain both of them? And in what way might an academic discipline or subdiscipline be *like* a household or a military expedition such that the particular kind of courage required to sustain those practices might also be the particular kind of virtue required to sustain those institutions?

Let us take the military expedition first. A military expedition, quite obviously, is not an end in itself; it is a means to an end. Military manoeuvres in general are oriented towards an objective, and MacIntyre highlights this with the slightly old-fashioned-sounding word 'expedition' which suggests the idea of going somewhere, being on the move towards some goal. In the context of military life, even if the expedition is subordinated to some ultimate goal, the daily life of a military expedition takes on a life of its own. Day in and day out, the life of the army – its discipline, its routines – is the framework through which the members of the army manage their lives, and indeed the ultimate goal or purpose of the expedition may not be uppermost in the average enlisted person's mind. But it is there in some ultimate way nonetheless and makes the daily routine meaningful. In short, an army is a 'form of life', one that is only possible against the backdrop of an ultimate goal that is quite separate from the day in and day out routine, but which ultimately makes that routine life legible and meaningful.[5]

In the case of the military expedition, the ultimate ends for which it exists are embedded in the daily practices, providing their rationale. And when this rationale is no longer legible, it must be rearticulated, as Marcellus asks Horatio to do. To put it another way, a military expedition, or military life more generally, is what MacIntyre terms a 'practice' because in it a set of routines and daily practices have a purpose or goal

---

[5] The discussion of courage and meaningfulness intersects with Paul Tillich's account of courage as the willingness to affirm meaning in the face of anxiety around ultimate ends. His account is, however, still quite individualistic, whereas I (following MacIntyre) emphasise the role of the collective practices or forms of life as the mediators of meaningfulness, with courage being applied first and foremost to the maintenance of practices or forms of life. See Paul Tillich, *The Courage to Be*, 3rd edn (New Haven, CT: Yale University Press, 2014). The forms of life connected to armies are often quite destructive. Jairus Victor Grove argues that we are the inheritors of the 'martial ecologies' of the Eurocene, and a kind of retrograde militarism is, indeed, one of the problems afflicting Hamlet's Denmark. See Jairus Victor Grove, *Savage Ecology: War and Geopolitics at the End of the World* (Durham, NC: Duke University Press, 2019). But, at the same time, military structures also mobilise people and can create a certain experience of meaningful collectivity, a view of military life that is emphasised, for example, by Fredric Jameson's discussion of war as adumbrating an experience of 'general will' or 'multitude'. See Fredric Jameson, 'War and Representation', *PMLA* 124.5 (2009), 1532–47 (p. 1547).

woven into their very core.[6] Moving closer to the goal is the essential purpose for which the practice exists; the practice *is* the process of moving towards the goal, and if members of the expedition ever lose track of that goal, then the connection between the military expedition or military life more generally and its ultimate goals can be made explicit anew, thus breathing new life and coherence into the military expedition.

The life of the household seems different in that people do not normally imagine that the household has an ultimate goal or purpose. The household would seem to be an end in itself. But at the same time, people do found households because of a commitment to some goods that transcend the household; people found households because they wish a certain kind of life, a life in conjunction with cherished others to whom they are bound through time. To some extent, the household exists for the purpose of creating relationships that are capable of encountering the future, come what may. Claudius articulates this when he says to Hamlet:

> We pray you throw to earth
> This unprevailing woe, and think of us
> As of a father, for let the world take note
> You are the most immediate to our throne,
> And with no less nobility of love
> Than that which dearest father bears his son
> Do I impart toward you. (1.2.106–12)

The impulse to use the household to establish relationships that transcend time is even more apparent if the household includes children. Obviously, if children are part of the household, then the household points forward in time because the household is the scene of transmission between parents and children. But the household also points backward because the household is understood as an inheritance and perhaps a repetition or continuation of the earlier households founded by parents and grandparents or other exemplary models. The household is therefore understood as a practice that sustains certain kinds of relationships between people across time. In that sense, as is the case with the expeditionary force, the household is not an end in itself but a means to an ultimate end or ends. But as with the military expedition, these ultimate ends do not exist separate from the practices of the household but rather they are woven into them so that practising the life of the household *just*

---

[6] The notion of a 'practice' plays a vital role throughout *After Virtue*. Not everything humans do is a practice; rather, practices are specifically defined by the fact that they have ultimate goals woven into them. As such, this essay's argument amounts to the claim that academic disciplines and subdisciplines ought to be understood and defended precisely as 'practices'.

is moving towards the goals for which the household exists. Thus, as with the expeditionary force, the ultimate goals for which the practice exists become concrete in a form of life, a daily routine, that may be much more prominently and centrally the focus of the members of the household than any ultimate purpose may be. But, as with the military expedition, when members of the household lose track of the connection between the household's daily routines and the ultimate purposes for which the household exists, then that connection can be articulated and made explicit anew, thus breathing new life into the life of the household.

We can therefore say that the military expedition and the household are both forms of life that are ultimately made possible by an orientation towards something outside of themselves, a horizon of some kind. In both cases, the routines of the military expedition and the household are not conceived as merely instrumental means to get to the goal. Rather, the goal is implicit in, rendered concrete through, and woven into the daily life and routines of the military expedition and the household, so that even the most mundane and routine elements of those forms of life are at least potentially suffused with a sense of meaningfulness. Practising daily life within a household or a military expedition *just is* advancing towards the ultimate goals for which those institutions exist, and vice versa.

Now, under what circumstances might a specific kind of courage be required to maintain social practices structured in the way that the expedition and the household are? To answer that, we must understand what sorts of challenges or breakdowns the military expedition and the household might face, and here *Hamlet* proves useful since it amounts to a detailed examination of how households or military expeditions can become hollowed out. I can imagine three sorts of challenges:

1. Challenges having to do with breakdowns in the daily out routine or functioning of the expedition or the household.
2. Challenges having to do with breakdowns in the desirability or rightness of the ultimate goals towards which these forms of life are oriented.
3. Challenges having to do with the connection or the link or the integration between the daily routine of a form of life and the ultimate goals for which that form of life ultimately exists.

I claim that the specific virtue that is 'sustaining courage' applies particularly to type 3 challenges.[7] Type 1 challenges are garden-variety break-

---

[7] For a somewhat countervailing discussion of the potential costs of 'endurance' in organising life, including the life of a discipline such as English, see Thomas Moretti's essay in this collection.

downs between people, and they might require revisiting the rules and procedures, the organisation, the fairness, the forms of communication of the quotidian routines and disciplines of the military expedition or the household. Type 2 problems, breakdowns or changes in ultimate goals, might include a change in the situation such that the particular goal of the practice is no longer relevant or desirable. It is easy to imagine this in the case of the military expedition: the sovereign might send an expeditionary force out in pursuit of a strategic goal and then decide the goal is not important after all and countermand the army – as happens when Norway countermands Fortinbras's planned invasion of Denmark. It is harder to imagine this in the case of a household, though it might take the form of questions about whether the particular structure of family life inherited from grandparents or parents or others is, in fact, worthy of being reproduced, or whether the specific relationships that the household makes possible and projects into the future are ultimately worthy of being so sustained and so projected. Questions about ultimate ends are either very practical questions (we wanted to sack this city but then we decided that doing so would not be strategically useful) or they can be ultimate questions that require a full accounting of the purpose of one's life. In none of these cases does the specific virtue of sustaining courage seem to apply.

But it is type 3 challenges that are the particular domain of the virtue of sustaining courage. A breakdown of the links between – the integration of – ultimate ends and a particular form of life is a very specific type of breakdown and sustaining courage is the specific virtue that can reaffirm and reassert the link between an ultimate purpose that passes beyond the present moment and the daily, routinised practices and disciplines of a concrete form of life through which that ultimate purpose is expressed. And if we glance back to *Hamlet* we can say that this is precisely the kind of breakdown in which the play is most interested. It is not the practical routines of the military or the household *in themselves* that *Hamlet* questions, nor the ultimate goodness of family life or military honour – if anything, Hamlet is too invested in these ultimate ends, having an overly romantic or idealised view of family life and also of military values, including the unhinged sense of honour that pushes him to his fatal duel with Laertes at the end of the play. The point of the play is that Hamlet sees no way to concretely operationalise his ultimate commitments in the practical day in, day out routines within the institutionalised practices that his world offers him. This is obviously true of the household, but it is also true in Hamlet's relationship to military life. The drumbeat of empty military activity only punctuates the fact that Hamlet cannot fuse it with any sense of ultimate purpose. Throughout the play there is a hint that Hamlet has the potential to lead a military expedition that would rid Denmark of Claudius, something that Claudius himself seems to fear when he says that he is sending Hamlet to England because 'He's loved of the distracted multitude' (4.3.4). One critic has identified the underlying structure of Hamlet's predicament as being a 'conscript in a war' that he cannot take responsibility for, his bursts of guerrilla ruthlessness (as when he sends Guildenstern and Rosencrantz to their deaths) notwithstanding.[8] As if to punctuate the idea of Hamlet as a kind of failed or thwarted (or self-thwarted) military leader who fails because he could not motivate decisive military action in the name of correcting what is rotten in the state of Denmark, Fortinbras wraps up the play with 'Bear Hamlet like a soldier to the stage' (5.2.379).

What both Hamlet and *Hamlet* lack is a vision of sustaining courage that might knit the daily life of the household and the military expedition back to some sense of ultimate purpose. In short, the play confronts the very specific problem of a dissolution of the link, the integration, between what people do, day in and day out, and some sense of an ultimate transcendent good that is incorporated into that daily practice. This specific type of breakdown in a way of life is what calls forth the virtue of sustaining courage, which is precisely what is absent in the play.

In the passage with which I began, MacIntyre posits sustaining courage as a kind of leftover from the heroic age, but at the same time he says that this leftover virtue is a 'necessary starting-point for moral reflection within the tradition with which we are concerned'. In what way might the 'sustaining courage' that knits a particular way of life back into a background of some transcendent overall goal be a starting point for the picture of the virtues that MacIntyre develops in *After Virtue*?

As against some of the ways his work has been appropriated, MacIntyre does not think of virtues as simply voluntaristic, freely chosen out of sentimentality or as an end in themselves or out of personal preference. MacIntyre takes for granted that virtues (and an ethic of virtues) only make sense in a community organised – at the highest level – around a shared understanding of a purpose or goal for human beings. For Aristotle, this is imagined as a *telos* that is both universally human and also shaped at the level of the polis or socially constituted

---

[8] Patrick Cruttwell, 'The Morality of Hamlet: "Sweet Prince" or "Arrant Knave"?' in *Hamlet: A Casebook*, ed. John Davies Jump (New York: Aurora Publishers, 1970), pp. 174–95 (p. 194). The essay was originally published in 1963.

community. The notion that human beings have a shared purpose or goal is, of course, much easier to imagine in the small-scale, homogeneous political and social world of the Greek polis.[9] In the kind of world that Aristotle imagines, virtues are habits and practices that help to move the person in the direction of the ultimate goal or purpose or form of perfection of human beings in general. It becomes much harder to imagine a universal human perfection in large, heterogeneous social universes defined by massive de facto variation in how to be human and how to live a good human life. Nevertheless, as against a deontological, reason-based Kantian understanding of morality and as against emotivism in which people justify moral judgements by appeal to their own subjective feelings of right and wrong, the virtues as MacIntyre understands them are practices designed to help a person advance towards a shared understanding of human perfection within some specifiable community.

Even if a large-scale understanding of human perfection in general is difficult to achieve under conditions of modernity, MacIntyre's version of virtue will be possible precisely in communities that are oriented towards a goal in the way I have suggested both the military expedition and the household are. Both the expedition and the household are forms of community that are structured around a goal that transcends but also suffuses the community and gives it a rationale. It is only within such institutions that genuine virtues are possible, for MacIntyre views the virtues neither as abstract duties nor as kindly impulses but as habits and dispositions that *just are* the person advancing towards the goal that he and his community share. And if, under conditions of modernity, we cannot specify a large-scale shared understanding of human nature itself as having a specific goal or purpose built into it, it is nevertheless possible to do so within specific institutions (such as a household and the military expedition) precisely insofar as they have ultimate goals woven into them. And insofar as the virtue of sustaining courage is designed precisely to *knit together* daily practices and ultimate goals, it does indeed function as a cardinal or keystone virtue that makes all the other virtues possible. The virtues will apply precisely because perfecting the daily routines of life with others within the institution just is advancing towards the goal for which the institution exists and which is woven into those day in, day out practices.

---

[9] Aristotle's notion of a seemingly universal human *telos* is obviously built upon invidious exclusions of whole classes of persons from what Aristotle would understand as a fully human life. For one of many examples of an effort to universalise an Aristotelian approach to basic human capabilities, see Martha C. Nussbaum, *Creating Capabilities: The Human Development Approach* (Cambridge, MA: Harvard University Press, 2013).

Insofar as the household and the military expedition are defined by being oriented towards a goal that is woven into the daily practice of those institutions, they stand in contrast to merely voluntaristic communities that are defined by a completely contingent or external relationship to the goals pursued, such as a jogging club that satisfies the individual interest of each of its members to improve their physical conditioning. Such voluntaristic communities are defined by the shared voluntary interest of their members rather than a transcendental horizon, an ultimate purpose woven into the practice, and no matter how well the jogging club functions, it is not moving towards some greater end beyond providing an opportunity for each individual jogger to jog. Voluntaristic communities exist for the convenience and pleasure of their individual members, and when members cease to share the shared interest they drop out, and if everyone drops out the voluntaristic community simply ceases to exist. The military expedition and the family are different in that they exist for a transcendent purpose that is woven into their practice and thus their collapse is problematic in a way that the dissolution of a jogging club never can be. The collapse of an expedition or a household suggests a crisis in which a form of life has become unravelled or disconnected from the ultimate goal or purpose for which these forms of life ever existed. In such cases, the ultimate goal for which the military expedition or the household was initially conceived may still be in place and may still have value, but the connection between it – and its integration with – the practices through which that ultimate goal might have been achieved has come unravelled. It is precisely to remedy or, better yet, to forestall such a situation that the expedition or household can call for the specific virtue of 'sustaining courage' that might reattach or reintegrate the daily routines back with the ultimate reason for which they exist. And the characteristic work of sustaining courage – affirming a link between a form of life or a practice and an ultimate purpose or goal or *telos* that is essentially woven into that form of life or practice – is the precondition for any of the other virtues as MacIntyre understands them. Only once that connection has been reaffirmed can the military expedition or the household again become scenes for the practice of the other virtues – such as prudence, self-sacrifice, persistence or loyalty. Insofar as sustaining courage is a virtue that reaffirms the imbrication of some ultimate goal or *telos* within a specifiable community, sustaining courage is a kind of cardinal virtue that makes all the other virtues possible.[10]

---

[10] For a cognate discussion of the way that the virtue of 'constancy' makes other virtues possible, see Jesse M. Lander's essay in this collection.

We are now in a position to look at the discipline of English and the subdiscipline of Shakespeare studies to ask whether they are the kinds of communities that are structured by a transcendental goal – like the military expedition and the household – or whether they are merely voluntaristic; and if the former, whether or how the virtue of 'sustaining courage' might play a role in their survival. Obviously, many scholars believe that Shakespeare studies is not just the Shakespeare equivalent of a jogging club, a community that exists only to allow us to exercise our individual, hobbyistic appreciation of Shakespeare. We believe that, in fact, Shakespeare studies is more like a household or a military expedition in the sense that it exists for the sake of something, some ultimate goal that transcends the immanent pleasure in reading Shakespeare's plays but that is nevertheless woven into that practice. But we suffer from a problem where we cannot easily articulate to ourselves and to others how the routine daily activities we perform as Shakespeare scholars are connected to or advance those ultimate purposes. The institutions and practices of life in the discipline or subdiscipline are threatened with the same hollowness or taint of simulacra that afflicts the household and the military expedition in *Hamlet*.

Seen in this light, the crisis of the humanities in general is a crisis in the connection between the normal practices and forms of life (the norms, the institutions, the relationships) of being a humanities scholar and the transcendent horizon for the sake of which those forms of life exist and which makes them meaningful. In the terms I proposed earlier, the crisis of the humanities is a type 3 institutional crisis. And as a response to this type 3 crisis, sustaining courage would have to rearticulate and reconnect a sense of ultimate goal or purpose to the daily routine of the academic humanities, including English studies or Shakespeare studies. Absent such an integration, we may still engage in the routines of scholarly or academic life, but those routines will have a creeping emptiness or purposelessness to them. Moreover, the pursuit of English or Shakespeare studies will become the scene not for genuine virtues – oriented to advancing towards some ultimate goal – but pseudo-virtues only. Thus, the genuine virtue of persistence may become mere quantitative productivity; the genuine virtue of humility may become successful self-ingratiation in the context of professional networking. Sustaining courage would reknit the daily practices of life as a member of an English department or of a scholarly guild such as Shakespeare studies to an ultimate goal and thereby make the other virtues genuinely possible once again within that discipline or subdiscipline. In this context, sustaining courage would be the courage to articulate the ultimate purpose of the discipline or the subdiscipline and to reconnect it with the daily practices and routines of scholarly life.

To the question of the ultimate purpose of English as a discipline, scholars have explicitly or implicitly offered a number of answers. One answer that is popular, because it appears to answer to market 'rationality', is that the ultimate aim of English as a discipline is to cultivate the portable critical-thinking, problem-solving and writing skills that are socially valued, for example in the great corporations of the land. In a thoughtful discussion, Sharon O'Dair describes the legitimation crisis in the humanities and proposes that we confine ourselves to training undergraduates in 'the skills of close reading and elegant . . . writing' because these are 'valuable in the marketplace'.[11] But since any number of disciplinary pursuits might serve to teach these skills, the goal of cultivating portable critical-thinking, problem-solving and writing skills is only contingently related to the daily life of English as a discipline. It would be as though we said that in the case of the military expedition, its ultimate purpose is to provide an opportunity for its members to travel and see the world. It may have that effect, but that cannot be why it exists.

Another rationale – that may seem more tempting to readers of the present volume – is that English as a discipline inculcates virtues or that it helps to advance political agendas. It is true that one of the distinctive moves of the 'virtue ethics' approach is to define virtues as skills, learnable dispositions and practices that can be taught, and that can perhaps therefore be taught by means of literature, including Shakespeare's plays.[12] This argument in fact picks up a hope that was very much at the core of Renaissance humanism which did imagine that the teaching of the classics was also an ethical education. Several essays in this volume consider the possibility that studying Shakespeare's plays offers training in virtue, though several essays also consider that Shakespeare's plays would be precisely a miseducation in the virtues. It is not, in fact, obvious what specific ethics inhere in a particular literary text or literary texts in general, which opens an extra-disciplinary regress to determine what virtues we (as English or Shakespeare scholars) should be teaching.

A similar problem afflicts claims that the ultimate aims of English as a discipline are political. Politics is not in any ultimate sense about liter-

---

[11] Sharon O'Dair, 'Who Did Kill Shakespeare?', in *Shakespeare and the 99%: Literary Studies, the Profession, and the Production of Inequity*, ed. Sharon O'Dair and Timothy Francisco (Cham: Palgrave Macmillan, 2019), pp. 225–46, 242 and 241 respectively. Several of the essays in the volume offer interesting and sometimes symptomatic discussions of the question of what the ultimate purpose of Shakespeare studies might be.

[12] For discussion of the potential ethical benefit of English as a discipline, see Thomas Moretti's essay in this collection.

ary or cultural or historical scholarship at all, and if literary scholarship is subordinated to political agendas, then once the literary or cultural or historical scholarship has achieved whatever political usefulness it is deemed to possess, the literary or cultural or historical scholarship can be jettisoned, like the first stage of a rocket. The same might be said of claims about the goal of effecting a generalised stance of 'critique'. Ultimately, the discipline of English and the subdiscipline of Shakespeare studies are at best instrumentally useful to any political goals.[13]

A potentially more helpful path lies in affirming that the ultimate aim of English as a discipline and Shakespeare studies as a subdiscipline is to produce and maintain a certain kind of knowledge that is built up (or corrected) through the daily routines of studying, reading, writing, critiquing, discussing, attending conferences and teaching. What sort of knowledge would the discipline or subdiscipline be aimed at producing and maintaining? This is a non-trivial question. Several scholars have recently called for a return to disciplinarity, to an understanding of the particular kinds of knowledge that are specific to particular disciplines, and therefore, in our corner of the humanities, a return to the particular kind of knowledge that is specific to English as a discipline or to Shakespeare studies as a subdiscipline. In a discussion of the dangers of disciplinary breakdown, Michael Clune writes that

> we have seen enough to know that the eradication of disciplinary norms doesn't create powerful new forms of knowledge by destroying old forms of oppression. Literary studies' anti-disciplinary thought led to an empty, despised professional discourse while covering an entirely unprofessional intellectual and personal tyranny over a dwindling body of students.[14]

This perspective suggests that the specific kind of knowledge that might sustain English or Shakespeare studies would need to be oriented towards the specific objects of study and inquiry that define the discipline. The knowledge that we produce through our daily routines and practices as scholars would therefore need to be situated in relation to the specific objects that we study and that no other disciplines study. In other words, the specific and particular kind of knowledge which might ground our daily routines and form of life as scholars will be a

---

[13] Some may point to scholarly projects that trace the (indubitably) political uses to which Shakespeare has been put: for example, being used to build, affirm and police the borders of English national culture or being used to define a socially differentiating form of high literacy. But studying phenomena such as these is still not the same as engaging in politics; to anticipate my discussion somewhat, I see such projects as productions of disciplinary knowledge – namely, about *how* Shakespeare has been used in political projects.
[14] Michael Clune, 'The Bizarro World of Literary Studies', *Chronicle of Higher Education*, 26 October 2018.

knowledge that is adequate to the objects that we study. In trying to help us return to some sense of disciplinarity, Jonathan Kramnick defines a discipline as 'a body of skills, methods, and norms able to sustain internal discussions and do explanatory work'.[15] Moreover, Kramnick notes that 'the humanities, like other fields of study, tell us important truths about some parts of the world. Disciplinary diversity is grounded in a pluralistic vision of things'.[16] Kramnick's vision of a discipline, in other words, is inherently part of a pluralistic vision since a discipline is by definition one among many, an institutionalised perspective that produces a specific class of knowledge that is understood not to be total but merely one part of understanding a proliferating and endlessly pluralistic world. From this perspective, attacks on disciplinary knowledge turn out to be attacks on an essentially pluralistic view of the world and the kinds of knowing that humans are capable of, including the kinds of knowing that English as a discipline is capable of.

Obviously, one of the distinctive powers of literature is to draw on and represent many extra-literary realities and discourses. To respond fully to a literary text therefore often requires at least junior varsity competence in something else – perhaps the history and theology of the Reformation or the history of the Scientific Revolution or the ins and outs of Elizabethan lawyerly jargon, or perhaps the political theory of the nation-state and its claims to territorial sovereignty. Indeed, there are important strands of aesthetic theory that highlight the value of literature precisely as a seismograph of cultural change, seeing literary production as capable of picking up social and even technological changes before they become evident from other disciplinary perspectives. But the cheerleading for interdisciplinarity that we often see goes beyond the recognition that literary scholars require broad tool chests as they pursue the one kind of knowledge that makes them literary scholars. In fact, this interdisciplinary cheerleading may often be a symptom of precisely the type 3 crisis I have been describing. Absent a stronger understanding of the purpose of the discipline, the junior varsity competencies we bring to bear upon literary and cultural objects may appear to be the whole of what we bring as opposed to merely the incidental tools to open the disciplinarily specific claims we (*qua* literary scholars) make.

To hazard a proposal of what disciplinarily specific knowledge might look like, we might say that the kind of knowledge aimed for by us *qua*

---

[15] Jonathan Kramnick, *Paper Minds: Literature and the Ecology of Consciousness* (Chicago: University of Chicago Press, 2018), p. 18.

[16] Jonathan Kramnick, 'The Interdisciplinary Delusion: Saving Disciplines is the Only Way to Save Ourselves', *Chronicle of Higher Education*, 2 November 2018.

Shakespeare scholars is a kind of knowledge that combines historical consciousness with some attention to the power of verbal art and of the particular and distinctive kinds of thinking that verbal art makes possible (the way verbal art is a kind of critical theory, a tool that enables certain kinds of thinking). Reknitting the daily routines of life as a humanities scholar with the ultimate aim of producing and maintaining such a disciplinarily specific kind of knowledge would require precisely the virtue of sustaining courage. It would mean rejecting the compensatory emphasis on portable skills that may be (at best) a by-product of the sort of work we do. Certainly it would require setting aside the excitement about the supposed ethical or political effectiveness of scholarship. It would mean declining the reflexive stance of critique that Rita Felski, among others, has warned about.[17] Finally, it would also mean declining exogenous criteria in evaluating scholarship and scholars, like the cheerleading we often see for the importation of the methods of other disciplines into English. As against these, sustaining courage would seek to reaffirm the ultimate value of a particular kind of disciplinary knowledge – I have hazarded that it is knowledge that combines historical consciousness with attention to the distinctive kind of thinking that verbal art makes possible – and of how this form of knowledge structures and legitimates the routinised life of English as a discipline or of Shakespeare studies as a subdiscipline.

In the case of *Hamlet*, the play offers itself as a test case of the degree to which the subdiscipline of Shakespeare studies demonstrates an orientation towards such a form of knowledge, and at the same time the play is a warning for the discipline of the consequences of a failure to marshal sustaining courage in the face of a type 3 crisis. As I have noted, in Hamlet's eyes the household and military life have both lost their ultimate purposes but no one in the play – and famously not Hamlet himself – is able to respond with the sustaining courage that would knit the daily practices of these forms of life back together with some understanding of the ultimate purpose for which they exist and which ought to sustain them. With respect to both the household and the military expedition, the failure to articulate the connection between a particular set of practices and routines and an ultimate purpose is the main problem that afflicts the character of Hamlet, and the play of *Hamlet* is a sustained warning about the consequences of that failure.

But the place where the consequences of the absence of sustaining courage should be most disturbing to us as Shakespeare scholars is in the play's subtle but profound engagement with the university as the scene

---

[17] See Rita Felski, *The Limits of Critique* (Chicago: University of Chicago Press, 2015).

of a kind of life that combines daily practices (including an engagement with art, such as the verbal art of plays) with a sense of ultimate purpose. Elizabeth Hanson has argued that *Hamlet* captures a complex moment of sociological transition in which the traditional status of the hereditary aristocracy begins to need the supplement of the new cultural capital of humanist education delivered and sealed by universities.[18] From this perspective, the rot that afflicts Wittenberg is the rot of Bourdieuvian symbolic economy in which culture mediates class and status. The play models an intense but unstable friendship between Hamlet – a prince, after all – and Horatio – a 'scholar' whose being 'poor' is an emblem at once of his acknowledged lower social status ('I am', he says in his first line to Hamlet, 'your poor servant ever' [1.2.162]) and of the superiority (and innocence) of his learning, his 'philosophy' (1.5.170). Hanson notes that it is precisely Prince Hamlet's ambiguous openness to this 'poor scholar' friend that has made the play a persistent object of identification for intellectuals who allow themselves to feel flattered by the dream of being acknowledged by actual power. Hansen refers to an article by Patrick Cruttwell in which he notes that the key to the reception of the text by literature scholars has been the equation 'Hamlet = Me', writing that 'the kind of genius which intellectuals attribute to Hamlet is precisely the kind appropriate to intellectuals'.[19]

But if, for the modern Shakespeare scholar, 'Hamlet = Me', then the implied picture of life in the discipline of English and the subdiscipline of Shakespeare studies is far from comforting. Here we can turn to Rhodri Lewis's *Hamlet and the Vision of Darkness*.[20] Lewis writes that the character 'exposes not only the limitations of humanist philosophy, but the inadequacy of most attempts to supplant it at the cusp of the seventeenth century'.[21] Of course, in making this claim, Lewis operates within a historicist framework, and he situates this account of Hamlet in the specific early modern world of a fractured and debased humanist culture that coexists with the fragments of an older scholastic culture that is displaced but still visible in the brittle dialectical structure of 'To be or not to be', among other logical hair-splitting moments in the play. This points us back to where we began, with *Hamlet* (and MacIntyre) looking back from the seventeenth century (or the twentieth) to the earlier moment in which heroic culture encountered Aristotle and the

---

[18] Elizabeth Hanson, 'Fellow Students: Hamlet, Horatio, and the Early Modern University', *Shakespeare Quarterly* 62:2 (2011), 205–29.
[19] Cruttwell, 'The Morality of Hamlet', pp. 174–5.
[20] Rhodri Lewis, *Hamlet and the Vision of Darkness* (Princeton, NJ: Princeton University Press, 2020).
[21] Lewis, *Hamlet and the Vision of Darkness*, p. 239.

scholastic revolution. But must we not also acknowledge in Lewis's account an allegory of the practice of English and of Shakespeare studies that has come unmoored from any ultimate sense of purpose? For Lewis, Hamlet's

> philosophizing is bound to superficiality, to seeming, and to the twin demands of his emotions and self-image. He relies on the language and assumptions of early modern philosophy, but he is not even a philosopher as the early moderns understood the category, let alone an embodiment of philosophical transcendence.[22]

Lewis describes Hamlet is a 'thinker of unrelenting superficiality, confusion, and pious self-deceit' whose thoughts are 'the ill-arranged and ill-digested harvest of his bookish education'.[23]

If, for many scholars, Hamlet = Me, then Hamlet is like an academic who has ceased to be able to articulate the ultimate horizon that would make the daily routines of academic life meaningful. Heading off this allegorical way of reading his book, Lewis pre-emptively distinguishes himself from Hamlet precisely insofar as Lewis (unlike Hamlet) has a disciplinary structure sustained by the institutional reality of a functioning university.[24] Lewis acknowledges that, 'in Oxford, it is my good fortune to belong to a college and a faculty that take seriously their responsibility to sustain the slow burn of reading, thinking, and writing'.[25] It may be so at Oxford, but it is nevertheless worth wondering whether Lewis is protesting too much in his pre-emptive effort to separate himself and the discipline as a whole from the taint of the Hamlet he gives us.

---

[22] Ibid., p. 306.

[23] Ibid., pp. 238 and 277 respectively.

[24] The role of universities in sustaining such practices as English or Shakespeare studies is important, and it is one that MacIntyre is attuned to. MacIntyre appears to have the university in the back of his mind in writing of institutions in general: 'Institutions are characteristically and necessarily concerned with what I have called external goods. They are involved in acquiring money and other material goods; they are structured in terms of power and status, and they distribute money, power and status as rewards. Nor could they do otherwise if they are to sustain not only themselves, but also the practices of which they are the bearers. For no practices can survive for any length of time unsustained by institutions. Indeed so intimate is the relationship of practices to institutions – and consequently of the goods external to the goods internal to the practices in question – that institutions and practices characteristically form a single causal order in which the ideals and creativity of the practice are always vulnerable to the acquisitiveness of the institution, in which the cooperative care for common goods of the practice is always vulnerable to the competitiveness of the institution. In this context the essential function of the virtues is clear. Without them, without justice, courage and truthfulness, practices could not resist the corrupting power of institutions' (MacIntyre, *After Virtue*, p. 226).

[25] Lewis, *Hamlet and the Vision of Darkness*, p. xiv.

The possibility that for many Shakespeare scholars today 'Hamlet = Me', *precisely* because of the unravelling of the daily routines of scholarly life from a sense of ultimate purpose or transcendent horizon, is especially evident in Hamlet's use (or misuse) of the chief object of inquiry in our subdiscipline, namely plays. This takes two forms: his willingness to convert plays into cultural capital and his willingness to treat plays instrumentally as a forensic and political tool. In addressing the players, Hamlet remembers watching a play that 'pleased not the million; 'twas caviar to the general, but it was (as I received it, and others, whose judgments in such matters cried in the top of mine) an excellent play, well digested in the scenes, set down with as much modesty as cunning' (2.2.376–81). Here he converts the occasion of watching the play into an instrumental appropriation of cultural capital that affirms his own superior taste. Equally instrumental is his use of 'The Mousetrap' as an extra-aesthetic forensic trap and political intervention into the life of the court. Both are instrumental uses of the art form rather than the kind of response that would seek Lewis's 'philosophical transcendence' or my own 'body of knowledge that combines historical consciousness with attention to the power of verbal art and of the particular and distinctive kinds of thinking that verbal art makes possible'. But in the play, instrumental uses of the art form are all that are available. The absence of a sense of ultimate purpose in viewing, reading and studying plays forecloses the possibility of any genuinely aesthetic experience.

Hamlet's situation seems to be ours. Too often, we fail to have the courage to affirm any connection between the routine daily practice of scholarship and teaching and the disciplinary knowledge for which that practice exists. Examples could easily be multiplied, but I will merely advert to Melissa E. Sanchez, who concludes her excellent overview, *Shakespeare and Queer Theory*, with a disavowal of the very disciplinary knowledge that her book has itself made visible. She writes that 'methodologically, a queer approach to Shakespeare requires relinquishing a humanist ideal of education and scholarship as the pursuit of mastery and instead lingering with a more tentative, occasional, even amateurish use of his plays and poems'.[26] The almost reflexive disavowal of disciplinary knowledge and expertise is noteworthy, and in that regard Sanchez's book refutes itself, for it points to the massive and innovative structures of disciplinary knowledge that queer approaches within Shakespeare studies have produced over the past twenty years.[27]

---

[26] Melissa E. Sanchez, *Shakespeare and Queer Theory* (New York: The Arden Shakespeare, 2020), p. 177.

[27] See also Sanchez's further reflections on the nature of investment in disciplinarity in

In place of such disavowals we ought to have the courage to lay claim to the knowledge we produce – not *as* political practice or *as* critical thinking skills or *as* anything other than *as* disciplinary knowledge.

The goal of this chapter has been to suggest that *Hamlet* serves as a warning to us of what the discipline of English or the subdiscipline of Shakespeare studies might become absent sustaining courage. In the face of the type 3 breakdowns that are characteristic of the crisis of the humanities in general, we must reaffirm the connection between the 'slow burn' of reading, writing, evaluating scholarship, sifting through archives and teaching *with* the ultimate aim or purpose for which these activities exist – namely, producing and maintaining a unique and distinctive kind of disciplinary knowledge. I have argued that the unique and distinctive form of knowledge that defines and sustains the discipline and the subdiscipline combines historical consciousness with attention to the distinctive kind of thinking that verbal art makes possible, as *Hamlet* has made possible the thinking I have attempted to do here.

'The Pressure to Commit: Professionalism, Periodization, Affect', which is the coda to her *Queer Faith: Reading Promiscuity and Race in the Secular Love Tradition* (New York: New York University Press, 2019).

Chapter 13

On the Virtue of Grief

Michael Bristol

The Voice of Grief

To speak of the virtue of grief seems a doubtful undertaking; at the very least it would ask for reimagining what it would mean to live a virtuous life. In what follows I will propose that Shakespeare's characters conduct such a far-reaching reconsideration of the ethical world, in which virtue as traditionally understood has its say, but where the voice of grief will not be silenced. Grief is one of the 'extremes of passion' mentioned by Edgar, along with joy (*King Lear*, 5.3.197).[1] But in most classical and early modern accounts, virtue is understood to be the governance of the passions by reason. Emotional distress brought on by the exigencies of fortune is a disorder of the mind for which virtue is the remedy. In *Tusculan Disputations* Cicero contends that the wise man does not succumb to grief when faced with misfortune. Reason will be sufficient to overcome every perturbation of the mind: '*At nemo sapiens nisi fortis; non cadet ergo in sapientem aegritudo*'.[2] A wise man is of great soul – *magni animi* – and therefore '*invictus*' – unconquerable. The classical ideal of rational self-sufficiency reflects the interests of men who belong to a privileged military caste. Kristina Sutherland reminds us that virtue is derived from Latin *virtus*, a masculine concept of personal excellence that assigns high value to active dispositions such as courage, fortitude and independence. This understanding of virtue has had enduring currency, persisting in early modern society, and even into our own time.

---

[1] Quotations are from *The Norton Shakespeare*, ed. Stephen Greenblatt et al., 3rd edn (New York: W. W. Norton, 2016).
[2] Cicero, *Tusculan Disputations*, trans. J. E. King, Loeb Classical Library (Cambridge, MA: Harvard University Press, 1927), pp. 240–3.

Michel de Montaigne characterises grief as harmful, noting that 'the stoics forbid this emotion to their sages as being base and cowardly'.[3] He sees himself 'among those who are the most free' from grief, because 'my sense of feeling has a hard skin, which I daily toughen and thicken by arguments'.[4] In a later essay, however, he qualifies this assertion, maintaining that 'we should indeed make some concessions to the simple authority of the common law of Nature but not allow ourselves to be swept tyrannously away by her: reason alone must govern our inclinations'.[5] Montaigne recognises one such concession in his consideration for Seigneur de Monluc, a neighbour of Montaigne who was mourning the death of his son. Monluc 'emphasized the grief and heartbreak he felt at never having revealed . . . the immense love he felt for him'.[6] Montaigne finds Monluc's regret for adopting the 'tyrannous mask' of emotional austerity to be reasonable and appropriate, because the bereaved father denied himself both the joy of expressing his love and the consolation of knowing that he had communicated these feelings to his son before he died. The idea of fighting the tyranny of natural misfortune with the tyranny of virtue ends up costing too much in remorse. This suggests a more responsive conception of what is reasonable that respects the experience of living in a world conditioned by chance, by the fragility of our shared social systems and by our obligation to honour the lifelong attachments we form with others.

Writing in the aftermath of the World Trade Center bombings in 2001, Judith Butler sees the expression of grief as the acknowledgement of our vulnerability in a precarious world:

> What grief displays . . . is the thrall in which our relations with others hold us, in ways that challenge the very notion of ourselves as autonomous and in control . . . Let's face it. We're undone by each other. And if we're not, we're missing something.[7]

The experience of grief marks the loss of something external to the self but essential to its flourishing. Grief, then, is not an emotional allowance granted under exceptional circumstances. The relationships we form – with other people but also with things like our homes or the language we speak – are obscure in many ways and rich in contradictions. And when

---

[3] Michel de Montaigne, 'On Sadness', *Complete Essays*, trans. M. A. Screech (London and New York: Penguin, 2003), p. 7.
[4] Ibid., p. 10.
[5] Montaigne, 'On the Affections of Fathers for Their Children', *Complete Essays*, p. 434.
[6] Ibid., p. 444.
[7] Judith Butler, *Precarious Life: The Powers of Mourning and Justice* (London: Verso. 2004), p. 23.

those relationships are wrecked or broken we are 'at a loss' to repair the damage. The issue raised here is not just that we fail to understand the intelligence of the emotions, although that is an enduring difficulty.[8] Butler's deeper concern is the way defeat in any form is viewed as an intolerable injury to personal and collective *amour propre*.

When grief speaks in a Shakespeare play, reason invokes commonplaces of patience and fortitude drawn from what I would call vernacular stoicism to silence it. In her essay 'Shakespeare and the Virtue in Complaining', Emily Shortslef argues that when a woman protests or raises objections in a Shakespeare play, someone, usually a man, will try to silence her by counselling patience or explaining the value of accepting one's station in life. When it is a man doing the complaining, the example of the Ciceronian 'wise man' is invoked, along with an appeal to virtuous action, taking up arms against a sea of troubles, and by opposing, ending them. Women persist, however, in making virtue answerable to grief by calling into question the masculine goals of rational self-sufficiency, and typically they are ignored, often with fatal consequences to the rationally self-sufficient man. Grief has its own voice in the plays, however, and it speaks with all the eloquence of Shakespeare's rhetorical art in *Richard II*. Shakespeare's imagery is often preposterous and far-fetched in this play, where the figures turn and stretch and take us to unexpected places as it explores the contradictions of grieving. James Siemon has shown that the playfulness of Shakespeare's wordplay is answerable to our own usage and our own concerns.[9] Frequently repeated words such as 'grief' are invested with conflicted evaluations, activated and also misunderstood in face-to-face encounters on stage.

It is reasonable to assume that when Montaigne articulates his feelings about Seigneur Monluc, this is what Montaigne actually believes. Things don't work quite this way with a Shakespeare play, where the script animates and an actor temporarily embodies fictional characters, engaged in dialogue with each other.[10] This means that our response to the text will be conditioned by how the text is realised in performance, which can in turn determine how our sympathies will be distributed. In a pivotal essay in this volume, Carolyn Sale shows that as characters

---

[8] Martha Nussbaum, *Upheavals of Thought* (Cambridge: Cambridge University Press, 2001).

[9] James Siemon, *Word Against Word: Shakespearean Utterance* (Amherst and Boston, MA: University of Massachusetts Press, 2002*)*.

[10] Matthew James Smith and Julia Reinhard Lupton (eds), *Face to Face in Shakespeare in Shakespearean Drama: Ethics, Performance Philosophy* (Edinburgh: Edinburgh University Press, 2019).

like Kent, Gloucester and the Fool in *King Lear* evolve, they reveal deep contradictions in their fictional personalities and that our emotional response will shift along with their development. Her central argument is that Shakespeare's dramatic art guides us away from an ideal of *virtus* based on hierarchy, subordination and radical self-sufficiency in favour of 'the virtue of a shared capacity that is comprehensive in its inclusion'. This is a profound insight into the ethical universe created in the plays, but Shakespeare's art often moves us towards this realisation in ways that are far from straightforward and edifying.

Richard II tells the story of the downfall of a sovereign ruler, supposedly on grounds of his unfitness to rule. I say 'supposedly' because this is how his suffering and death are justified by the characters who depose him. Questions about Richard's fitness to rule or whether Bolingbroke will be any better are difficult to ignore.[11] But the dramatic action of political intrigue is not a good fit with the woeful pageant articulated in the poetic language. A contrasting narrative is woven into the text through a lexical network that branches out from grief to sorrow, weeping, tears, mourning, lament, expanding further to take in notions of weight and pressure along with the social conventions of departure and farewell.[12] Grief is a complex word. It can express notions of injury, hardship and regret, along with the anguish caused by a significant loss. The word also has the derivative sense of grievance, *ressentiment* and a disposition to seek revenge. This is a productive equivocation, and Shakespeare takes full advantage of its expressive mobility.

In the first scene of *Richard II* the King declares, 'We were not born to sue but to command' (1.1.196). This line is a basic premise of the story. In the world of the play Richard is the only character who can truthfully say these words. Since there can be no question of his legitimacy, his fitness to rule is not open for discussion.[13] Richard exists in a condition of regal solitude, '*fière, aristocratique, géniale*' (charismatic, aristocratic, magnificent).[14] The actor's task is to convince us of the beauty

[11] James Boyd White, *Acts of Hope: Creating Authority in Literature Law, and Politics* (Chicago: University of Chicago Press, 1994), p. 48.
[12] Word frequency is based on Eric Johnson, 'Shakespeare's Plays Listed by Genre', Open Source Shakespeare, George Mason University, 2003, www.opensourceshakespe are.org. This resource is most effective when items are cross-referenced to entries in the *OED*. See also Dolores Burton, *Shakespeare's Grammatical Style: A Computer-assisted Analysis of Richard II and Antony and Cleopatra* (Austin: University of Texas Press, 1973).
[13] Mustapha Fahmi, *La Leçon de Rosalinde* (Chicoutimi: Éditions La Peuplade, 2018), p. 123.
[14] Emmanuel Levinas, *Le temps et l'autre* (Paris: Presses Universitaires Français, 1983), p. 35.

of the King, by matching the eloquence of his language with the way he is physically present for us on stage. Otherwise Richard's sermons on vulnerability and death lose their force and the agony of his defeat its power to affect us. The story of dynastic triumphalism in Bolingbroke's ascent is immersed in the grief that flows from Richard's humiliation and death. The larger narrative arc is echoed in the fate of the other characters, from Mowbray to Sir Pierce of Exton, organising the play in a branching, fractal network, where even the smallest detail exhibits the same level of complexity as the whole scene in which it appears. In what follows I will not have much to say about Richard or the coalition of regional barons who oppose him. This essay will focus primarily on a number of minor characters who collectively perform the witnessing function of the chorus in classical drama.

Woodstock's Blood

Although he is not listed in the dramatis personae, there is a ghost that disturbs this play in the unexplained murder of the Duke of Gloucester, the youngest son of Edward III. 'Gloucester's death' is a leitmotif in *Richard II*, a phrase repeated seven times over the course of the play. The audience first hears of this when Bolingbroke accuses Mowbray of committing the murder:

> . . . he did plot the Duke of Gloucester's death, . . .
> Sluiced out his innocent soul through streams of blood:
> Which blood, like sacrificing Abel's, cries,
> Even from the tongueless caverns of the earth,
> To me for justice and rough chastisement. (1.1.100–6)

The death of Gloucester reiterates the ancient crime of fratricide. Cain 'was wroth' when God did not show favour for his sacrifice, and as a result of this grievance he 'rose up against Abel his brother, and slew him' (Gen. 4:6–8). In this re-enactment of the originary crime, Mowbray is assigned the role of Cain, Abel's murderer. Given the terms of the reference in Genesis, however, the killing of Abel is an odd rhetorical choice, since the force of Bolingbroke's denunciation points in a different direction. Abel was killed by his older brother; Gloucester's older brother would be John of Gaunt.

Obviously Bolingbroke cannot intend to implicate his own father in the assassination. However, when Gloucester's widow urges John of Gaunt to take action against her husband's killers, the language of his response is strangely equivocal:

Alas, the part I had in Woodstock's blood
Doth more solicit me than your exclaims,
To stir against the butchers of his life! (1.2.1–3)

For years I was confused by this line, taking 'the part I had in Woodstock's blood' to refer in some way to Gaunt's complicity in the assassination. But of course the reference to 'Woodstock's blood' has the primary intention of signifying Gaunt's kinship with Gloucester, both sons of Edward III, with its attendant duty of avenging his brother's death. We reveal ourselves in our denials. Gaunt can't be suggesting that he is obliged to take action against himself and it's clear he has no intention of taking action against the King. However, Gaunt's language here resonates with Bolingbroke's misprision of Abel's murder by Cain, and the 'sluicing out' of Gloucester's 'innocent blood'. And so my initial 'misreading' of Gaunt's speech captures dialogical possibilities in the language that he might have preferred to suppress. Blood is everywhere in this play, the most extreme condensation of the lexical network of grief. Blood is consanguinity, the bonds of kinship Carolyn Sale identifies as fundamental to organised social life. Blood is also exsanguination, the bloodletting demanded by exacerbated grievance.

In Genesis, God expressly forbids 'rough chastisement'. Cain's punishment for killing Abel was lifelong exile. 'Behold, thou hast driven me out this day from the face of the earth; and from thy face shall I be hid; and I shall be a fugitive and a vagabond in the earth' (Gen. 4:14). Bolingbroke's misprision of Genesis introduces a theme of larger importance, since *Richard II* is a play of restless vagrancy, exile and homelessness. When the King banishes him, Bolingbroke has, in effect, been assigned the role of Cain. And here we come to a puzzling intersection in the lexical web of grieving:

BOLINGBROKE: Must I not serve a long apprenticehood
    To foreign passages, and in the end,
    Having my freedom, boast of nothing else
    But that I was a journeyman to grief? (1.3.271–5)

What does Bolingbroke intend by 'a journeyman to grief?' Emotional distress at being separated from things he loves is certainly part of what he wants to say. A journeyman is an artisan who receives a daily wage – *journée* – working for an established master. In English 'journeyman' has the secondary sense of an itinerant worker. For Bolingbroke the idea of a journeyman is also an affront to his self-esteem as a nobleman of high status. His sense of grief is a grievance he holds against King Richard for the injuries he has suffered, and for a desire for revenge – rough justice – although this is the exemplary case mentioned by

Montaigne of a destructive inclination that ought to be governed by reason.

Although we never find out who is responsible for Gloucester's death, there is no uncertainty about the existential costs of his absence and who ends up paying them. For the Duchess, 'My Gloucester's death' is the murder of her husband; her loss is personal and intimate, and she complains to Gaunt that if he takes no action he will be 'teaching stern murder to butcher thee' (1.2.32). Gaunt can only reply that 'God's is the quarrel', a variant on the usual reply to a complaint, advising patience. Gaunt's refusal to take retaliatory action leads her to display her private grief. Paradoxically, her husband's absence from her life and the consequent emptying out of the richness of her life is experienced as a weight or a burden: 'grief boundeth where it falls, / Not with the empty hollowness, but weight' (1.2.58–61). Grief is derived from old French *grever*, to bear a burden, and farther back from Latin *gravis*, heavy, which gives us both grave and gravity. The concrete sensuous reality of grief is the paradoxical weight of emptiness it compels someone to bear. The image of grief 'bounding' or rebounding, suggests that she can never be free of its burden. And in a sense this is how 'Gloucester's death' will operate throughout the text, not as a question to be answered, but as the heavy weight of an ancient murder bouncing back to conscious awareness at unexpected moments.

The paradoxical burden of grief is associated with loneliness and the collapse of social life:

> DUCHESS: . . . empty lodgings and unfurnish'd walls,
> Unpeopled offices, untrodden stones?
> And what hear there for welcome but my groans?
> Therefore, commend me; let him not come there,
> To seek out sorrow that dwells everywhere.
> Desolate, desolate, will I hence and die:
> The last leave of thee takes my weeping eye. (1.2.68–75)

Losing Gloucester is the equivalent of losing a home, and even though the Duchess will return to her ancestral residence at Pleshy, she will find nobody there. Her bereavement is reflected in the depopulation of a household. It's easy to grasp the sense of empty lodgings and unfurnished walls – the house is abandoned, everybody has moved out and they have even taken away the tapestries. But the real force of what has happened to her as a result of Gloucester's death lies in the powerful condensation of 'unpeopled offices'. We may think first of vacant rooms in a castle that was once full of busy people. But the word, taken from classical Latin *officium*, also speaks to what the busy people were doing. It has the sense of a duty that comes with one's social position or even a general sense of moral obligation. Related to this would be kindness to a stranger or an offer of friendship: 'We are come to you to do a good office, Master Parson' (*Merry Wives*, 3.1.42). Holy office is divine service or worship, often used in relation to the performance of last rites. And we should not overlook the implications of public office, positions of temporary power, in which the responsibilities of office-holders might or might not be faithfully executed.

The emotional force of the imagery represents what it is to be 'at a loss' when a loved one has died. It's not simply that somebody dies and everything else stays the same. Unpeopled offices are the obverse of banishment as servants, guests, friends and even kin desert the widowed person. It's easy to overlook the larger importance of what happens to the Duchess of Gloucester, since she appears only in this one quiet scene between episodes of *sturm und drang* as two men prepare themselves for mortal combat. I would suggest, however, that her story is a condensation of the larger narrative of loss, exile and death that has already been anticipated, for example, in the forcible démarche of Mowbray and the grievous loss of his native language.

'Rue, even for ruth'

The figure of Queen Isabella is the emotional heart of *Richard II*. She is herself an émigré, 'fetched from France' by Thomas Mowbray to marry the King, living as a stranger in a strange land. With Richard absent on his mission to Ireland, the Queen is beside herself, at a loss with anticipatory grief, visible in her demeanour, and she is admonished for this in the same way Gertrude urges Hamlet to 'cast thy nightly color off'.

> BUSHY: Madam, your majesty is too much sad.
>   You promised when you parted from the King
>   To lay aside life harming heaviness.
>   And entertain a cheerful disposition. (2.2.1–4)

Bushy describes the Queen's sadness as heaviness, the weight or burden of grief. What he is asking for is the performance of a 'cheerful disposition', as if you can talk somebody out of sadness just by telling them to cheer up. But she has an answer to this form of reproach and it brings out the ethical centrality of these scenes. The deep rationality of grief finds its sources not in an abstract doctrine of self-mastery but in the lived experience of incompleteness and the loss of a loved one:

> QUEEN: . . . I know no cause
>   Why I should welcome such a guest as grief,

> Save bidding farewell to so sweet a guest
> As my sweet Richard: yet again, methinks,
> Some unborn sorrow, ripe in fortune's womb,
> Is coming towards me, and my inward soul
> With nothing trembles: at something it grieves,
> More than with parting from my lord the king. (2.2.5–13)

'My sweet Richard' echoes the Duchess's reference to 'my Gloucester', identifying the grounds for her experience of 'bidding farewell' to a man who is her lover as well as her husband. Grief can be understood as accounting for a loss, not so much as explaining it as in recording an absence and evaluating its extent. The idea of grief as substitution for what has been lost recalls Constance's 'Grief fills up the room of my absent child' (*King John*, 3.4.134). This suggests a deeper fear, expressed in the language of pregnancy and childbirth. Unborn sorrow, ripe in fortune's womb, is a diffuse terror of the unforeseen brought on by her husband's absence and the alarming news that he is in danger. It also refers more specifically to the child Bolingbroke cannot afford to let her bear, because that child once born would become the legitimate heir to the throne. The Queen has a better grasp not only of what can happen, but more urgently of what is about to happen, than the courtiers who are trying to silence her. Her grief accounts for what is at stake in the precarious situation created by the King's absence.

Whether he fails to understand what the Queen fears, or whether he knows all too well what shape the future holds, Bushy nevertheless insists that the Queen's sorrow is just her morbid imagination. ''Tis nothing but conceit, my gracious lady' (2.2.33). This is a common form of what we now call gaslighting, and not only in early modern society, where a person's fears are not acknowledged, but dismissed as madness. But the Queen has an answer for this:

> . . . conceit is still derived
> From some forefather grief; mine is not so,
> For nothing had begot my something grief;
> Or something hath the nothing that I grieve:
> 'Tis in reversion that I do possess. (2.2.34–8)

Something real has begotten the grief even if it has not yet become apparent. And here Isabella introduces a second metaphor that amplifies the rationality of grief. To possess something in reversion is to have rights of succession, usually for lands or moveable property. It can also have the sense of something returned to its rightful owner, which would suggest that Richard is hers, to have and to hold. But the darker sense here is that she will come into full possession of her grief only when Richard dies.

The Queen's worst fears are confirmed when Green appears to announce that 'the banished Bolingbroke repeals himself / And with uplifted arms is safe arrived / At Ravenspur' (2.2.59–61). The Queen replies:

> So, Green, thou art the midwife to my woe,
> And Bolingbroke my sorrow's dismal heir
> Now hath my soul brought forth her prodigy
> And I, a gasping new-delivered mother
> Have woe to woe, sorrow to sorrow joined. (2.2.62–5)

The Queen's unborn sorrow is now brought forth in the conceit of misshapen birth (prodigy). Richard and Isabella will never have a son to carry on the royal lineage; Bolingbroke is a deformity, a changeling who will become heir to the power of the crown by violent means. The connection between violence and the power to rule is summarised by the Gardener when he reflects on Richard's failures to 'Cut off the heads of too-fast-growing sprays / That grow too lofty in our commonwealth' (3.4.34–5). The idea that a King's fitness to rule requires a willingness to separate a man's head from his body reflects in a most literal way what Carolyn Sale has called a 'culture of division that severs "nature's" bonds'. This will be realised in the reports in 5.6 of the nobility beheaded to secure Bolingbroke's claim to be King Henry IV: Salisbury, Spencer, Blunt, Kent, Brocas, Sir Bennet Seely.

When the Queen overhears the Gardener tell his servant that Richard will be deposed, her sorrow grows more passionate: 'O I am pressed to death through want of speaking' (3.4.73). The image of being crushed by unbearable pressure develops the comparison of grief to heaviness, but the conceit may have a more specific frame of reference. In William Harrison's *The Description of England* there is a gruesome reference to pressing to death as a judicial sanction for refusal to testify in a lawsuit:

> Such felons as stand mute and speak not at the arraignment are pressed to death by huge weights laid upon a board that lieth over their breast and a sharp stone under their backs, and these commonly hold their peace, thereby to save their goods [money and possessions] unto their wives and children, which if they were condemned should be confiscated [seized] to the prince.[15]

There is unimaginable cruelty in the idea of forcing a person to testify by crushing their ribcage, which would make it impossible for them to utter a word. Isabella's reaction to the news is to pronounce a malediction upon the Gardener for being the one who provides the intelligences:

---

[15] William Harrison, *The Description of England* (1587), ed. George Edelen (New York: Dover Publications, 1994), p. 191.

'Pray God the plants thou graft'st may never grow' (3.4.100). This is no doubt vindictive, but grief is always to some degree self-interested, since the grieving person has suffered a significant loss, often tending towards a desire for some form of compensatory justice.

The Gardener's reaction to the Queen's malediction is a powerfully dramatic moment, often overlooked in favour of his notions of realpolitik. He has listened to what the Queen has been saying and his outlook has been changed by her words:

> Poor Queen! so that thy state might be no worse,
> I would my skill were subject to thy curse.
> Here did she fall a tear; here in this place
> I'll set a bank of rue, sour herb of grace:
> Rue, even for ruth, here shortly shall be seen,
> In the remembrance of a weeping Queen. (3.4.102–7)

Rue is an equivocation. The botanical usage refers to a small shrub, *Ruta graveolens*, that has medicinal value as the sour-tasting antidote for 'the poison of wolfesbane, birdlime, mushrooms, or toadestooles, the biting of serpents'.[16] But the word has the etymologically distinct sense of repentance, the bitter antidote for grievance and the desire for revenge. The Gardener is careful to bring out the sacramental valences of rue as ruth, an obsolete usage with the sense of contrition of the heart. We have lost this usage in contemporary speech, but we retain the derivative 'ruthless'. In a play governed by the actions of ruthless men the Gardener is a witness to the destruction they cause and to compassion for everyone who suffers harm as the result of their actions. He has nothing to gain by planting a bank of rue and it offers no benefit to the Queen. The Gardener speaks for the audience here, quietly suggesting that the complexity of the Queen's grief is something we share in common with every character in the play. This is something a little different from disinterested love or the specifically Christian virtue of *agape*. The Gardener's skill lies in his understanding of the 'curse' as an unpaid debt, a collective and transgenerational inability to mourn for suffering caused by the misdeeds of our own ancestors.[17] For what it's

---

[16] John Gerard, *The Herball or, general historie of plants* (London: John Norton, 1597), p. 1075.

[17] Björn Quiring, 'Curse', in *Entertaining the Idea: Shakespeare, Philosophy, and Performance*, ed. Lowell Gallagher, James Kearney and Julia Reinhard Lupton (Toronto: University of Toronto Press, 2021), pp. 86–101. See also W. G. Sebald, 'Constructs of Mourning', *Campo Santo*, trans. Anthea Bell (London: Hamish Hamilton, 2005), pp. 102–30; Jean-Pierre Vernant and Pierre Vidal-Naquet, *Myth and Tragedy in Ancient Greece*, trans. Janet Lloyd (New York: Zone Books, 1990); Bernard Williams, *Shame and Necessity* (Berkeley: University of California Press, 1993); and Alexander Mitscherlich

worth, the sense of a bank as a financial institution in which wealth – the benefits of grace and remembrance, let's say – can be saved against a future need had currency in Shakespeare's time, as it does today, and this sense carries over from ideas of reversion, where the value of a charitable impulse can be held in trust until it is needed for another purpose. What the Gardener is banking on is our ability to accept the burden of a fictional character's sorrow that binds us to everybody else.

The test of that ability comes in the final appearance of Queen Isabella. She is waiting on a street in London to watch Richard pass by on his way to the Tower:

> QUEEN: But soft, but see, or rather do not see,
>   My fair rose wither: yet look up, behold,
>   That you in pity may dissolve to dew,
>   And wash him fresh again with true-love tears. (5.1.7–11)

The actor-in-character is speaking directly to the members of the audience, drawing attention to the beauty, even in his defeat, of a man she continues to love. Is a spectator intended to feel some kind of vindictive satisfaction in witnessing Richard's degradation because of his supposed misrule? Or would it be better to see beyond the judgements of the ruthless men that have brought him to this condition? The Queen is bearing witness here to the ruin and the humiliation of a person that goes well beyond the requirements of any political strategy. If the performance has been staged the way I think it should be, the depth of the Queen's sorrow will be amplified by our own occasions for grief. And when we experience that response at a theatrical performance, we mourn with the assembled gathering.

Grief and Necessity

In their final scene together King and Queen meet in a love duet, in which they undo their marriage vows. They are interrupted by Northumberland who announces that the King will not be taken to the Tower, but to Pomfret Castle instead. When she pleads with him to banish them to France together his answer is, 'That were some love, but little policy' (5.1.84). In the practice of strategic rationality, no consideration can be given for the human figures who stand in the way of achieving a goal. The logic of the situation leaves Northumberland with

and Margarete Mitscherlich, *The Inability to Mourn: Principles of Collective Behavior*, trans. Beverley R. Placzek (New York: Grove Press, 1984).

no other choice. 'Policy' requires him to enforce the permanent separation of the Queen to guarantee that she will never bear a child. Richard is taken away to Pomfret Castle where he will be murdered by Sir Pierce of Exton, 'As full of valor as of royal blood' (5.6.113). For this service Henry IV will banish Exton as Cain to 'wander through the shades of night / And never show thy head by day or light' (5.6.43–4).

The new King has his own burden of grief to assume, and in his final words he mourns for the man he wanted dead:

> Lords, I protest, my soul is full of woe,
> That blood should sprinkle me to make me grow:
> Come, mourn with me for that I do lament,
> And put on sullen black incontinent:
> I'll make a voyage to the Holy Land,
> To wash this blood off from my guilty hand. (5.6.45–52)

As belated readers of this play, we already know that the curse has not been expiated; this is just one more iteration of the primordial crime of Abel's murder by his own brother. Bolingbroke is always and already cast out, the pilgrimage will never be accomplished and his guilty hand will not be cleansed of blood. Northumberland will rebel against the newly anointed King just as Richard predicted, and eventually, after many years of civil strife, another Henry will step in after another Richard has been killed.

In the closing lines of the 1623 Folio *King Lear*, Edgar delivers an enigmatic conclusion to the events we have just witnessed in that play:

> The weight of this sad time we must obey,
> Speak what we feel, not what we ought to say.
> The oldest have borne most; we that are young
> Shall never see so much, nor live so long. (5.3.98–102)

It should be clear by now that this is roughly equivalent to saying that we in the audience are among those who are bound to carry the burden of grief for the fictional events we have just witnessed. Naomi Conn Liebler has managed to clarify the otherwise baffling discrimination between the burden carried by the old, and of the young to 'speak what we feel', suggesting that grief is a transgenerational practice, rather than an individual passion.[18] To 'obey' has the obsolete sense of paying homage (*obéisance*) to its sovereignty in a way that 'honors the elderly dead' and acknowledges the inherited trauma of war and genocide. So

---

[18] Naomi Conn Liebler, '"The oldest hath borne most": The Burdens of Aging and the Morality of Uselessness in *King Lear*', in *Shakespeare and Moral Agency*, ed. Michael D. Bristol (London: Continuum, 2010), pp. 111–26.

the burden of grief is larger than the personal feeling of bereavement and loss. To carry this weight is a duty – *officium* – that asks us to undertake the task of mending the torn fabric of our social life.

There is one thing I would add to this account. The actor-in-character speaks with a double intention.[19] In this scene the actor speaks in the present to the general condition of the audience, but he also speaks as a character in the fiction of *King Lear*. The Folio text makes dramatic sense at this point, because it connects this broader sense of the weight of this sad time we're living in the actual world with the specific burden that Edgar has to bear for himself, the death of his father, whose heart 'burst smilingly' ''twixt the extremes of passion, grief and joy'. Edgar also bears the weight of killing his brother Edmund, yet another re-enactment of the sad story of Cain and Abel. His burden is complex and contradictory, mourning the death of a father who cast him out, and killing the brother who betrayed him, circumstances that make it impossible to arrive at any conclusive judgement on his actions. Grief is never simply a 'perturbation' of the mind of an individual person who ought to know better. 'If my fate is not originally or finally separable from yours, the "we" is traversed by a relationality that we cannot easily argue against.'[20]

In the world imagined by Shakespeare, the dramatis personae are incomplete, deficient in self-knowledge and in some sense broken. Individual virtue, conceived as a fixed disposition like courage or generosity, is at best fallible. Shylock's thrift is overcome by his passion for revenge, Isabella's chastity is preserved by the dodgy strategy of the bed trick, the valour of Coriolanus is transformed into self-destructive rage. Using the example of Kent's loyalty, Carolyn Sale has shown that a narrowly conceived virtue can serve the interests of domination. There is a strong sense in Shakespearean drama that grief is the only 'rational' response to the laws of nature, the precariousness of human lives and also to the way people suffer harm through the exigencies of policy. '*Nous ne sommes jamais chez nous; nous sommes toujours au-delà*' (We are never at home; we are always somewhere else).[21] The phrase *au-delà* is usually translated as 'beyond' but in Montaigne's usage here it is the opposite of 'at home' (*chez nous*) or in other words 'somewhere

---

[19] Gary Saul Morson and Caryl Emerson, *Mikhail Bakhtin: Creation of a Prosaics* (Stanford, CA: Stanford University Press, 1990), pp. 161–70.
[20] Butler, *Precarious* Life, p. 22. See also Avishai Margalit, *The Ethics of Memory* (Cambridge, MA: Harvard University Press, 2004); and Paul Connerton, *How Societies Remember* (Cambridge: Cambridge University Press, 2010).
[21] Montaigne, 'Nos affections s'emportent au-delà de nous', in *Les Essais*, ed. Claude Pinganaud (Paris: Arlea, 1992), p. 9.

else' or 'carried away'. Montaigne thinks we're always 'somewhere else', cast out from ourselves because our desire and our fear, our hope for the settling of accounts and the redress for our grievances, orient us towards the future. Living in this way, he argues, we lose our feeling for what is here for us now.

In *Richard II* all the characters are to a greater or lesser degree *au-delà*, 'carried away' by their need to seek retribution for the loss they have suffered. Only the Gardener is present to the moment. His quality of attention recognises the extent of the world's suffering condensed into a single tear, fallen 'here in this place' where he will plant a bank of rue 'even for ruth'. In addition to its significance as contrition, this phrase is a far-fetched but unmistakable reference to the biblical figure of Ruth, another 'journeyman to grief' like so many of the characters in this play. The scriptural reference to the Book of Ruth is echoed in the Queen's final plea to Northumberland, 'Then whither he goes, thither let me go' (5.1.85), before she is deported, breaking forever the bonds of nature between her and Richard. Like Edgar in *King Lear*, the Gardener speaks prophetically in the moment of performance. His geste bears witness to the extent of suffering of the world, while the work of achieving a just balance remains incomplete, 'beyond the reach' – *au-delà* – of any one person's actions. 'This wide and universal theatre / Presents more woeful pageants than the scene / Wherein we play' (*As You Like It* 2.7.136–9). Grief is not a task to be completed; it's the weight everybody carries for everything that's been lost, for sins of omissions, missed chances and roads not taken. In that way grief is responsive awareness of the accumulated weight of the sorrow endured by others, and helps us understand the ethical ties we have to the stranger as well as to our own loved ones. If virtue is essential to living the best possible life with others, no matter how conflicted our relationships may be, then maybe we are answerable to the voice of grief Shakespeare has created for us to hear.

Everyday Dramaturgy: Virtue and the Craft of Living

Kevin Curran

In the preceding pages, readers have encountered a wide variety of ways in which Shakespearean theatre articulates virtue. By way of drawing this volume to a close, I would like to broaden the discussion and reflect on the idea of virtue as 'everyday dramaturgy', the applied craft of living among others. I hope this will leave readers with two take-aways: first, that virtue is fundamentally theatrical; and second, that theatre – actual theatre – has an important role to play in the cultivation of virtue at a social scale.

To get to these ideas, though, we first have to step back and take up (once again) the most basic question of all: what exactly is virtue? Of all our inheritances from the ancient world, virtue surely must be one of the most elusive. To the general public, the term will have vaguely Christian, or at least moral, overtones. Some will make a particular association with female chastity. Others might picture a knight 'pricking' across a plain (as Edmund Spenser would put it), definitely *doing the right thing* at every opportunity. But this doesn't help us much with the status of virtue in contemporary culture. Is virtue a concept we still understand, a practice we still engage in? The authors in this volume have different answers to this question, some viewing virtue as undergoing a revival of sorts, others feeling it's rather fallen off the rails of modern life.

There is truth in both appraisals, I think. Leaving aside academic trends like the interest in 'virtue ethics', some components of virtue seem to sit well within an increasingly meme-ish self-help industry. Emily Shortslef, for instance, mentions the staggeringly successful Instagram feed of Daily Stoic, which purveys bite-sized morsels of classical wisdom in a you-got-this mode, often having to do with fortitude, courage or other vaguely virtuous attributes. On the other hand, there's something about virtue which can come across as distinctly old-fashioned, something better suited to that chaste maid and that knight than to modern professionals living in a world where success and sanctity have little to do with each other. As Jesse M. Lander points out, virtue 'seems indelibly tied to an aristocratic view of the world'; it 'carries a whiff of sanctimony'. Indeed. Like judgement, another out-of-fashion human capacity, virtue makes an awkward bedfellow with the culture of late capitalism, the logic of which says that all forms of value (moral, social, even aesthetic) should be dictated by the supposedly egalitarian forces of the market. If it's lucrative, it's right. If it has more than 2,000 likes, it's good. Let the consumers decide!

All of this, both the positive and the negative, is premised on a narrow understanding of what virtue is and what it's for. The underlying assumption across the board is that virtue offers scripts for the development of inner qualities. It's about being the best *you* you can be. If this sounds sarcastic, it's unintentional. I can hardly blame anyone for understanding virtue in this manner given the way the concept has come down to us. It does, however, grow out of only one strand of virtue's complex intellectual history, albeit a strand that has been enormously influential. As the *Oxford English Dictionary* records, around the late thirteenth century we begin to see the term 'virtue' being used to describe particular moral qualities possessed by discrete individuals (*OED* 'virtue' n. 2a, 8b). This results largely from the Christian reception and transformation of virtue. The work of Parisian scholastics like Thomas Aquinas and Bonaventure, in particular, integrated the four 'cardinal virtues' (a fourth-century coinage by Ambrose of Milan) with Aristotelian ethics. The result was a version of virtue that was highly internalised, broadly moral in orientation, and keyed to the spiritual hygiene of individual souls. It is not surprising that this account of virtue has had such staying power in our own time. Stripped of its overtly religious trappings, it resides comfortably within democratic, capitalist, libertarian and liberal worldviews; indeed, within any worldview in which the basic ideas of selfhood and autonomy are foundational.

At base, however, what virtue is supposed to do is create well-being for society as a whole, not provide self-care regimens, spiritual or psychological, for individuals. Aristotle called this form of general well-being *eudaemonia*, a state of social flourishing brought about by the practice of virtue. 'Practice' is the operative term here. Virtue is something you do, not something you are. As an example, let's consider the virtue of prudence. Prudence, or *phronesis* in Greek, is typically described in English as 'practical wisdom'. It has to do first and foremost with making and doing, not thinking (1140a–b).[1] Aristotle insists on

---

[1] References are from Aristotle, *The Nicomachean Ethics*, ed. Roger Crisp (Cambridge: Cambridge University Press, 2000).

the fact that the *phronimos* – the prudent person – cannot live in isolation because prudence is a functional virtue (1142a). It does not simply exist as an inner quality. Rather, it takes shape in social, material and transactional environments. It requires not only the judiciousness of the *phronimos*, but also a larger collective of stakeholders who acknowledge that judiciousness and partake in the new conditions it creates.[2] Prudence – like courage, justice or temperance – are ways of acting in and upon the world. As I have written elsewhere, 'virtues are a social logic or dynamic, rather than personality traits or individual moral attributes'. They provide 'a linked set of frameworks for physical, emotional, and ethical participation in the world'.[3]

One doesn't have to seek as far as the ancient world to find more social and active understandings of virtue. One of the reasons Shakespeare's theatre is such a rich repository of ideas about virtue is because the early modern period was heir to multiple ways of thinking about the topic. If Christian virtue was alive and well, so too were Greek and Roman strains of the virtue tradition, thanks primarily to vernacular editions of Cicero's *De Officiis* in 1534 and Aristotle's *Nicomachean Ethics* in 1547, both of which went through numerous reprintings in the sixteenth and seventeenth centuries.[4] Returning to the *Oxford English Dictionary* for a moment, we find that in the century following the emergence of virtue as a moral quality, a few other versions of virtue enter regular usage and persist through the early modern period. This includes virtue as 'physical strength, force, or energy' (*OED* 'virtue' n. 5a), a sense of the term that bears out conceptually the etymological link between virtue and virility. It also links up with the Latin word *virtus*, which in the late Middle Ages could denote an actual assembly of troops, 'an armed force' (*OED* 'virtue' n. 5b).

The latter may seem extreme, especially when compared to the passive virtue of the scholastic tradition, or related to it, that chaste maid whose virtue is neither seen nor felt, but which adheres instead precisely in what she does not do. However, the core idea underpinning the virtue–*virtus* link is simply that virtue *makes things happen*. It's material and

---

[2] Lois S. Self, 'Rhetoric and Phronesis: The Aristotelian Ideal', *Philosophy & Rhetoric* 12 (1979), 130–45.

[3] Kevin Curran, 'The Four Cardinal Virtues: Caesar's Mantle and Practical Wisdom', in *Shakespeare and Virtue: A Handbook*, ed. Julia Reinhard Lupton and Donovan Sherman (Cambridge: Cambridge University Press, 2023), p. 114.

[4] See further, Charles B. Schmitt, *John Case and Aristotelianism in Renaissance England* (Montreal: McGill-Queen's University Press, 1983); Neal Wood, 'Cicero and the Political Thought of the Early English Renaissance', *Modern Language Quarterly* (1990), 185–207; and Christopher Crosbie, *Revenge Tragedy and Classical Philosophy on the Early Modern Stage* (Edinburgh: Edinburgh University Press, 2019), esp. pp. 92–4.

it's transformative. This is a notion that belongs to the Aristotelian tradition, according to which virtue is a social practice through which you act upon, and intervene in, the environment around you. This can work on a variety of scales. A group of armed fighters ousting a tyrannical government certainly counts as 'physical strength, force, or energy' being used to transform one's circumstances to create the conditions for social flourishing. But so too does housework, carpentry, pharmacy and engineering. All involve a certain 'practical wisdom', in the broadest sense: a capacity for applied evaluative thought (prudence), a balancing of priorities and outcomes (temperance), a willingness to materially *do* something based on these assessments (courage) and a leveraging of all this towards a kind of proportional orderliness that benefits a larger collective (justice).

We can trace these various scales of active virtue in the other usages that entered common parlance in the early modern period. For example, 'superiority or excellence in a particular sphere' or 'a social or domestic accomplishment' (*OED* 'virtue' n. 6a, 6c). These definitions remind us that virtue is an assemblage of skills and abilities; it describes forms of expertise that can be developed and transmitted. Closely connected to this, there are versions of virtue that emerge in the early modern period that look like what might be called 'affordances' within design theory. An affordance is the possibility for action or effect that inheres in a given object: a fountain affords bathing or drinking; a hammer affords hitting.[5] In Shakespeare's *Macbeth*, a dagger affords murder. In Christopher Marlowe's *Doctor Faustus*, a book affords conjuring. From the fourteenth century onwards, we find 'virtue' connoting 'a particular quality or power associated with a thing' (*OED* 'virtue' n. 9). This can be taken generally to refer to any object or being's 'capacity for producing a certain effect' (*OED* 'virtue' n. 10a), or more narrowly as 'The beneficial properties of a plant, liquid, or other substance' (*OED* 'virtue' n. 9a). What these strands of the virtue tradition – both the skill-based one and the affordance-based one – have in common is that they describe virtue in terms of the power material things (human or non-human) have to effect material transformation in the world we all share.

The moment one unlocks this dimension of virtue, a sense of urgent relevance begins to hang about it. Over the last ten years, we have seen a series of adamant collective demands for social transformation: stop police violence (Black Lives Matter, Antifa), stop male abuses of power (#MeToo), fight ecological disaster (School Strike for Climate,

---

[5] See Julia Reinhard Lupton, *Shakespeare Dwelling: Designs for the Theater of Life* (Chicago: University of Chicago Press, 2018), esp. pp. 31–84.

Extinction Rebellion). If our cultural moment is as serious about remaking our world as it purports to be, it had better be as serious about virtue too. This is not about morality per se. It has to do with the fact that virtue provides powerful behavioural and cognitive blueprints for setting-things-right. At a functional level, virtue involves coordinating thought, decision and action in such a way that balance – a certain right-ordering – is established among the various components of a collectivity, including human (and human/non-human) collectivities at any number of scales: interpersonal, familial, civic, national, eco-systemic. This idea is borne out in a variety of ways in this volume with contributors consistently locating virtue in sites of transaction, contact and exchange: Thomas Moretti's classroom; Emily Shortslef's complaint; Michael Bristol's grief; Katie Adkison's voice, poised on the frontier of speaking and feeling, inner and outer; Karen Raber's cross-species kinship; and Carolyn Sale's ecological vision of elemental interdependence – to name just a few.

Viewed in these terms, virtue as everyday dramaturgy begins to make sense. Think of it as the collaborative *mise en scène* of social, sexual, emotional and political experience. I choose these terms, 'dramaturgy' and '*mise en scène*', carefully. They are not meant as metaphors, but rather as literal descriptions of the dynamic, interactive and experiential quality of virtue that is so easy to miss out on. The link between virtue and theatre is formal more than conceptual. They share the same basic conditions (collectivity), rely on the same raw materials (bodies and objects arranged in time and space), make meaning through the same methods (the invocation of common deliberation) and aim at the same general outcome (the production of knowledge, wisdom or insight experienced as feeling, language and movement). Theatre, we might say, is virtue-in-action. Grasping the theatricality of virtue is crucial if we are to understand what virtue was in the pre-modern world and what it is, or can be, now. Virtue is phenomenological, not ontological. It *happens*. It inheres in what you do, what you make, and what we experience *together*.

If we can accept this – that virtue, in a formal and phenomenological sense, is theatrical – then the reverse statement should make sense too: theatre is virtuous. This assertion may be the harder pill to swallow. While many will at this point be happy enough to accept that virtue is theatrical (active, participatory, collective), the reverse – yet no less logical – premise that theatre is virtuous may have a slightly cringe-inducing effect. Especially for literary scholars, it will evoke the old idea that *Shakespeare is good for you*; that good people who see good plays or read good literature will become even better people, morally, intellectually and spiritually; an idea that almost fifty years of historical and political criticism has tried to overturn by showing all the ways in which 'good art' has been complicit in bad things (patriarchy, colonialism, racism and institutionalised intolerance of all sorts).

I hope it will be apparent that this is not what I mean when I say, 'theatre is virtuous'. It is not that good plays incarnate good personal attributes which are then transmitted to audience members who internalise them and put them into practice in their own lives. I'm not even particularly concerned with specific plays when I make this assertion. Rather, I wish to suggest that theatre – as an event that fosters feeling, thinking and judgement through the curation of material and social environments – is phenomenologically coterminous with the practice of virtue. Going to the theatre might not make you a better person, but it affords an opportunity to cultivate your capacity for virtue in the active and social sense. The mere fact of gathering with others to bear witness, to evaluate and to collaborate in the process of generating meaning constitutes a training ground for world-making. Consider Prospero's appeal to the audience's sense of prudence, temperance and justice at the end of *The Tempest*:

> Release me from my bands
> With the help of your good hands
> [. . .]
> As you from crimes would pardon'd be,
> Let your indulgence set me free. (5.1.329–30, 37–8)[6]

According to the terms set by Prospero, clapping is both evaluative and generative. It is a verdict on the past (prudence and temperance), a concrete intervention that shapes the future (courage), and a means through which, in the fictional world of the play, balance and order are restored (justice). As fellow makers, rather than just consumers, the audience's collective sense of the good, of what is right and what is wrong, establishes the ethical contours of a world beyond the physical and imaginative thresholds of the stage.

The audience need not actually intervene in a play to be involved in the dynamics of virtue. The mere act of bearing witness – the most basic and politically powerful component of theatrical experience – implicates the audience on both an ethical and phenomenological level. The contemporary Swiss director Milo Rau has been more invested in this idea than any other practising theatre professional. Since taking up the directorship of Belgium's National Theatre Ghent in 2018, Rau has

---

[6] *The Tempest*, ed. Stephen Orgel (Oxford: Oxford University Press, 1987).

committed himself to mounting one production a year in a global conflict zone. Drawing on local populations to perform in his creations, and opening the events to the public, Rau's theatre creates spaces for shared acts of testimony, witnessing and acknowledgement that the courts and political systems have failed to provide. His *Congo Tribunal* (2015), for example, brought together victims and perpetrators of the Congo War in the city of Bukavu, Eastern Congo, to perform a mock trial based on their experiences. The event was open to all members of the public and though it had no actual legal standing, it led to some real reparations for the people of Bukavu. Kate Connolly of the *Guardian* called it 'the most ambitious political theatre ever staged'.[7]

Congo Tribunal is a radical and particularly topical example of the dynamics of theatrical virtue. But the basic process of world-making-through-witnessing obtains in lower-stakes ways whenever a theatre audience is asked to feel, think, question and decide. Any comic denouement, for instance, formally requires this kind of audience investment. Comprised always of a series of revelations and judgements, the denouement depends on the sensory participation of the audience in order for it to work at a theatrical level: only when collectively seen does a revelation have the power to effect social change; only when collectively heard does a judgement become a public event. At the end of *Measure for Measure*, for example, the audience transforms into an extension of the Viennese citizenry, bearing witness to a series of public determinations: Mariana is owed something, Lucio owes something to others, Claudio is innocent, Angelo is guilty. These judgements are not issued simply to end things (the story, the characters' disputes), but also to start things anew, to plot a future course for Vienna; to craft a world which, as with *The Tempest*, must finally take shape beyond the fictional parameters of the play itself. Though juridical in character, the judgements of *Measure for Measure* are also expressions of those virtues which make social life possible: prudence, temperance, responsibility, accountability and justice. The close of *Measure for Measure* requires audiences to experience how collective assessment generates the shared standards that form the scaffolding of community.

Virtue inhabits Shakespearean theatre not because Shakespearean theatre is 'good', but rather because virtue operates according to a theatrical logic. It requires presence and acknowledgement, the coexistence

---

[7] Kate Connolly, 'The Most Ambitious Political Theatre Ever Staged? 14 Hours at the *Congo Tribunal*', *The Guardian* online, 1 July 2015, available at https://www.theguardian.com/world/2015/jul/01/congo-tribunal-berlin-milo-rau-political-theatre (accessed 24 January 2023). See also http://www.the-congo-tribunal.com (accessed 24 January 2023).

of two or more bodies in space. Otherwise, it's unintelligible, and, thus, meaningless. Virtue requires action. Don't be fooled by their noun form: prudence, courage, temperance and justice are things you do – just like grief, speech, complaint and constancy, all forms of virtue recovered in this volume. One undertakes the *labour* of grief, prudence, constancy and courage. It's part of the work of living, *bios* rather than *zoē*. This is what I mean when I say virtue is everyday dramaturgy. Virtue is, quite simply, the applied craft of making a world (big or small), an experience (long or short) that's liveable and sharable. We partake of virtue in our family kitchens, in the city streets and places of public congregation, and in the classrooms where we teach and learn. We experience it in particularly heightened form in the theatre, where people come together by choice, through no external compulsion, to feel, judge, witness, and thereby to *create* a world which they've decided matters.

Looking out around us in the third decade of the twenty-first century, it is tempting to say that now, more than ever, we need virtue. If this is so, we also most certainly need theatre.

Contributors

Katie Adkison is Assistant Professor of English at Bates College in Lewiston, Maine. She is currently working on her first monograph, tentatively titled 'The Sense of Speech: Voice and Sovereignty in Early Modern Tragedy'. This project explores how discourses of the embodied voice bled into political debates about tyranny, justice and representation, arguing that early modern dramatic tragedy leveraged these intersecting discourses of voice to articulate and critique paradoxes of sovereign power.

Michael Bristol is Greenshields Professor Emeritus of English at McGill University. He received his PhD at Princeton in 1966, specialising in Renaissance non-dramatic literature. His professional engagement with Shakespeare's plays began a few years later, directing productions of *Hamlet*, *Twelfth Night* and *Troilus and Cressida*, along with *The Jew of Malta* and Brecht's adaptation of *Coriolanus*. Major publications include *Carnival and Theatre* (1985, reissue 2015), *Shakespeare's America / America's Shakespeare* (1990, reissue 2015) and *Big Time Shakespeare* (1996). He has published extensively on Shakespeare and moral agency. Edited collections include *Shakespeare and Modern Theatre* (2001) with Kathleen McLuskie and Christopher Holmes, and *Shakespeare and Moral Agency* (2010), as well as a 'forum' for *Shakespeare Studies*, with the same title.

Kevin Curran is Professor of Early Modern Literature at the University of Lausanne in Switzerland and general editor of the book series 'Edinburgh Critical Studies in Shakespeare and Philosophy'. He is the author of *Shakespeare's Legal Ecologies* (2017) and *Marriage, Performance, and Politics at the Jacobean Court* (2009), and editor of *Renaissance Personhood* (Edinburgh University Press, 2020), *Shakespeare and Judgment* (Edinburgh University Press, 2016) and (with James Kearney) a special issue of *Criticism* on 'Shakespeare and Phenomenology' (2012). In 2017, Curran was named Distinguished International Visiting Fellow at the Center for the History of Emotions in Australia. He is also the founder and president of the Lausanne Shakespeare Festival.

Michael Gadaleto is an Assistant Teaching Professor of English at the University of North Carolina at Chapel Hill. His research has appeared in such publications as *Shakespeare Quarterly*, *Studies in Philology* and *Sidney Journal*; and he is currently at work on his first monograph, *The Island Nation and Its Discontents: Transnationalism in English Renaissance Literature*. Focusing on Shakespeare's France and British archipelago, Spenser's Ireland, Greville's Low Countries and Milton's Italy, this project reassesses the significance of certain key early modern internationalisms – humanist, Protestant, republican and poetic – in the literary construction of England by exploring how English authors challenged the archetype of the 'elect island nation' through their literary imaginings of more transnational models of community.

Daniel Juan Gil is Professor of English at Texas Christian University. He is the author of three monographs: *Fate of the Flesh: Secularization and Resurrection in the Seventeenth Century* (2021), *Shakespeare's Anti-Politics: Sovereign Power and the Life of the Flesh* (2013) and *Before Intimacy: Asocial Sexuality in Early Modern England* (2006). His scholarship theorises the body, the flesh and sexuality in the context of secularisation and the rise of the sovereign nation-state.

Jesse M. Lander is Associate Professor of English at the University of Notre Dame and a proud graduate of a 'liberal, disgraceful institution'. His interests include the history of books, editorial and textual theory, the history of historiography, intellectual history, and early modern literature. He edited *Macbeth* (2007) and edited the text of *1 Henry IV* for the third edition of *The Norton Shakespeare* (2016). His first monograph, *Inventing Polemic: Religion, Print, and Literary Culture in Early Modern England* was published in 2006. He is currently working on a second monograph, titled 'Special Affects: Staging the Supernatural in Shakespeare's England'.

Unhae Park Langis is a research fellow at the New Swan Shakespeare Center, University of California, Irvine. A former teacher of twenty years, she is the author of *Passion, Prudence, and Virtue in Shakespearean Drama* (2011) and numerous essays in ethical criticism in collections and journals including *Shakespeare Studies*, *EMLS*, *Upstart Crow* and

Literature Compass. Her primary interest in Shakespeare and virtue has recently shifted to his participation with wisdom traditions, especially those of Buddhism, Sufism and Stoicism. Accordingly, she is currently co-editing *Shakespeare and Wisdom: Ecumenical, Ecological and Ethical Horizons* (Edinburgh University Press, forthcoming) with Julia Reinhard Lupton.

Kent Lehnhof is Professor of English at Chapman University. He is author of some two dozen articles on early modern literature and culture and is co-editor (with Moshe Gold and Sandor Goodhart) of the essay collection *Of Levinas and Shakespeare: 'To See Another Thus'* (2018). His articles have appeared in such journals as *Shakespeare Quarterly, Renaissance Drama, English Literary Renaissance, ELH, SEL, Modern Philology* and *Criticism*. He is currently working on a book-length study of vocality and ethics in Shakespeare's late plays.

Julia Reinhard Lupton is Distinguished Professor of English at the University of California (UC), Irvine. She is the author or co-author of five books on Shakespeare, including *Shakespeare Dwelling: Designs for the Theater of Life* (2018), *Thinking with Shakespeare: Essays on Politics and Life* (2013) and *Citizen-Saints: Shakespeare and Political Theology* (2006). She has a strong record of editing and co-editing volumes, including *Entertaining the Idea: Shakespeare, Philosophy and Performance* (2020), with Lowell Gallagher and James Kearney; *Face to Face in Shakespearean Drama* (2019), with Matthew J. Smith; *Shakespeare and Hospitality: Ethics, Politics, Exchange* (2016), with David Goldstein; *Romeo and Juliet: A Critical Reader* (2016); and *Political Theology and Early Modernity* (2012), with Graham Hammill. She is a former Guggenheim Fellow, ACLS Fellow, Shakespeare Association of America Trustee, and *Shakespeare Quarterly* editor with broad connections in the field. She is the co-director of the New Swan Shakespeare Center at UC, Irvine and a contributor to a campus-wide curricular project on the Intellectual Virtues.

Thomas J. Moretti is Associate Professor of English at Iona University and editor of *The Shakespeare Newsletter*. He has published essays on religion, politics and gender in early modern English dramas and on temporal experiences in Shakespeare's plays. His essay on *Henry VI, Part 3* received the Joseph M. Schwartz Memorial Essay Prize from the journal *Renascence*. His pursuit to make the reading of Shakespeare a virtuous act is part of a larger project to foreground the personal value, social purpose and ethical potential of literary study.

Ian Munro is Associate Professor of Drama at the University of California, Irvine. He is the author of *The Figure of the Crowd in Early Modern London: The City and Its Double* (2005) and *A Woman's Answer is Never to Seek: Early Modern Jestbooks, 1526–1635* (2007; part of the 'Early Modern Englishwoman' facsimile series), as well as articles and book chapters on a range of early modern authors, texts and contexts. His current book project, 'Shakespeare and the Matter of Wit', explores the transformations of wit in the early modern period, principally through the plays of Shakespeare.

Karen Raber is Distinguished Professor of English at the University of Mississippi. She is the author of *Shakespeare and Posthumanist Theory* (2018) and *Animal Bodies, Renaissance Culture* (2013), and co-author with Karen Edwards of *Shakespeare and Animals: A Dictionary* (2022). Among her recent published collections is *The Routledge Handbook of Shakespeare and Animals* (2020) co-edited with Holly Dugan, and *Performing Animals: History, Agency, Theater* (2017), co-edited with Monica Mattfeld; she is also the author of over forty articles and book chapters on early modern animals, ecostudies, posthumanist theory and related topics, and is general editor of the series 'Perspectives on the Non-Human in Literature and Culture'.

Carolyn Sale is Associate Professor of English at the University of Alberta. Her work has appeared in journals including *ELH*, *Renaissance Drama*, and *Shakespeare Quarterly*, as well as various essay collections including *The Law in Shakespeare* (2007), *The History of British Women's Writing, vol. 1: 1500–1610* (2010), *Shakespeare and Judgment* (2016), *The Oxford Handbook of English Law and Literature, 1500–1700* (2017), and *The Oxford Handbook of Shakespearean Comedy* (2018). She is completing the book manuscript 'The Literary Commons: The Common Law and the Writer in Early Modern England, 1528–1628'.

Emily Shortslef is Assistant Professor of English at the University of Kentucky. Her work has appeared in the *Journal for Early Modern Cultural Studies*, *Exemplaria* and *ELH*. Her first monograph, provisionally titled 'The Drama of Complaint: Ethical Provocations in Shakespeare's Tragedy', is under contract.

Kristina Sutherland is a recent doctoral graduate from the Department of Comparative Literature at the University of Georgia. Her dissertation, 'Conduct and Carnival: Domestic Soft Power in Early Modern Comedies', delineates the use of carnivalesque comedies to disseminate concepts of courtly conduct to the local gentry and upper classes through the close reading of works by Giovanni Battista Della Porta, John Lyly and Pedro Calderón de la Barca. Her research interests include early modern conduct manuals, dramatic theory, the carnivalesque, and the representation of virtues in comedies.

Bibliography

Abrams, Richard. 'The Double Casting of Cordelia and Lear's Fool: A Theatrical View'. *Texas Studies in Literature and Language* 27 (1985), 354–68.

Aers, David. 'Calvinist Versions of God: A Revolution in Medieval Traditions'. *Journal of Medieval and Early Modern Studies* 52.3 (2022), 445–82.

Ahmed, Sara. *Complaint!* Durham, NC: Duke University Press, 2021.

Airaksinen, Timo. 'Against All the Odds: Machiavelli on Fortune in Politics'. In *Niccolò Machiavelli: History, Power, and Virtue*, ed. Leonidas Donskis. Amsterdam: Rodopi, 2011, pp. 3–14.

Akhimie, Patricia. *Shakespeare and the Cultivation of Difference: Race and Conduct in the Early Modern World*. New York: Routledge, 2018.

'A Lovers complaint being forsaken of his Love', c. 1615. English Broadside Ballad Archive, https://ebba.english.ucsb.edu/.

Allen, John A. 'Dogberry'. *Shakespeare Quarterly* 24.1 (1973), 35–53.

Amussen, Susan Dwyer. 'Punishment, Discipline, and Power: The Social Meanings of Violence in Early Modern England'. *Journal of British Studies* 34.1 (1995), 1–34.

Anderson, Amanda. *The Way We Argue Now: A Study in the Cultures of Theory*. Princeton, NJ: Princeton University Press, 2006.

Anderson, Benedict. *Imagined Communities: Reflections on the Origin and Spread of Nationalism*, rev. edn. London: Verso, 2006)

Andrea, Bernadette. *The Lives of Girls and Women from the Islamic World in Early Modern British Literature and Culture*. Toronto: University of Toronto Press, 2017.

Annas, Julia. *Intelligent Virtue*. Oxford: Oxford University Press, 2011.

Anscombe, G. E. M. 'Modern Moral Philosophy'. *Philosophy* 33.124 (1958), 1–19.

Arendt, Hannah. *The Human Condition*. Chicago: University of Chicago Press, 1957.

Arendt, Hannah. *The Human Condition*, intro. Margaret Canovan, foreword by Danielle Allen. Chicago: University of Chicago Press, 2018.

Ariosto, Ludovico. *Orlando Furioso*, trans. David R. Slavitt. Cambridge, MA: The Belknap Press, 2009.

Aristotle. *Metaphysics*, trans. Hugh Lawson-Tancred. New York: Penguin, 1998.

Aristotle. *Nicomachean Ethics*, ed. Sarah Broadie and Christopher Rowe. Oxford: Oxford University Press, 2002.

Aristotle. *The Nicomachean Ethics*, ed. Roger Crisp. Cambridge: Cambridge University Press, 2000.

Aristotle. *Nicomachean Ethics*, trans. Robert C. Bartlett and Susan D. Collins. Chicago: University of Chicago Press, 2011.

Aristotle. *Nicomachean Ethics*, trans. Terence Irwin. Indianapolis, IN: Hackett Publishing, 1985.

Aristotle. *Nicomachean Ethics*, trans. Terence Irwin. 3rd edn. Indianapolis: Hackett Publishing, 2019.

Aristotle. *Nicomachean Ethics*, trans. W. D. Ross. In *Introduction to Aristotle*, ed. Richard McKeon. New York: Random House, 1947.

Aristotle. *On Rhetoric: A Theory of Civic Discourse*, trans. George Kennedy. Oxford: Oxford University Press, 2007.

Aristotle. *Politics*, trans. C. D. C. Reeve. Indianapolis and Cambridge: Hackett Publishing, 1998.

Aristotle. *Writings from the Complete Works*, ed. Jonathan Barnes. Princeton, NJ: Princeton University Press, 2016.

Ascham, Roger. *The Scholemaster*. London: Printed by Iohn Daye, 1570.

Assmann, Jan. *Death and Salvation in Ancient Egypt*. Ithaca, NY: Cornell University Press, 2011.

Astell, Ann. 'Girard and Levinas as Readers of *King Lear*'. In *Of Levinas and Shakespeare: 'To See Another Thus'*, ed. Moshe Gold and Sandor Goodhart with Kent Lehnhof. West Lafayette, IN: Purdue University Press, 2018, pp. 85–105.

Bailey, Amanda. 'Speak What We Feel: Sympathy and Statecraft'. In *Affect Theory and Early Modern Texts*, ed. Amanda Bailey and Mario DiGangi. New York: Palgrave Macmillan, 2017, pp. 27–46.

Bakhtin, Mikhail. *Rabelais and His World*. Indianapolis: Indiana University Press, 1984.

Basaran, Yasin. 'Islamic Virtues: Ethics in the Premodern Ottoman Empire'. In *Shakespeare and Virtue: A Handbook*, ed. Julia Reinhard Lupton and Donovan Sherman. Cambridge: Cambridge University Press, 2023, pp. 291–8.

Bate, Jonathan. 'Shakespeare's Foolosophy'. In *Shakespeare Performed: Essays in Honor of R. A. Foakes*, ed. Grace Ioppolo. Newark: University of Delaware Press, 2000, pp. 17–32.

Beauregard, David. *Virtue's Own Feature: Shakespeare and the Virtue Ethics Tradition*. Newark: University of Delaware Press, 1995.

Beckwith, Sarah. *Shakespeare and the Grammar of Forgiveness*. Ithaca, NY: Cornell University Press, 2013.

Beckwith, Sarah. 'The Three Theological Virtues'. In *Shakespeare and Virtue: A Handbook*, ed. Julia Reinhard Lupton and Donovan Sherman. Cambridge: Cambridge University Press, 2023, pp. 125–36.

Bellamy, Elizabeth Jane. *Dire Straits: The Perils of Writing the Early Modern English Coastline from Leland to Milton*. Toronto: University of Toronto Press, 2013.

Benjamin, Jessica. *Beyond Doer and Done To: Recognition Theory, Subjectivity, and the Third*. New York: Routledge, 2017.

Berge, Mark. '"My Poor Fool is Hanged": Cordelia, the Fool, Silence and Irresolution in *King Lear*'. In *Reclamations of Shakespeare*, ed. A. J. Hoenselaars. Amsterdam: Rodopi, 1994, pp. 211–22.

Bergen-Aurand, Brian, ed. *Comedy Begins with Our Simplest Gestures: Levinas, Ethics, and Humor*. Pittsburgh, PA: Duquesne University Press, 2017.

Bergen-Aurand, Brian. 'Knock, Knock / Who's There? / Here I Am, Exposed . . .'. In *Comedy Begins with Our Simplest Gestures: Levinas, Ethics, and Humor*, ed. Brian Bergen-Aurand. Pittsburgh, PA: Duquesne University Press, 2017, pp. 83–97.

Berger, Harry, Jr. 'Against the Sink-A-Pace: Sexual and Family Politics in *Much Ado About Nothing*'. *Shakespeare Quarterly* 33.3 (1982), 302–13.

Berger, Harry, Jr. *Making Trifles of Terrors: Redistributing Complicities in Shakespeare*. Stanford, CA: Stanford University Press, 1997.

Bernasconi, Robert. 'You've Got to Laugh'. In *Comedy Begins with Our Simplest Gestures: Levinas, Ethics, and Humor*, ed. Brian Bergen-Aurand. Pittsburgh, PA: Duquesne University Press, 2017, pp. 21–32.

Berry, Edward. 'Laughing at "Others"'. In *The Cambridge Companion to Shakespearean Comedy*, ed. Alexander Leggatt. Cambridge: Cambridge University Press, 2002, pp. 123–38.

Berry, Edward. *Shakespeare and the Hunt: A Cultural and Social Study*. Cambridge: Cambridge University Press, 2001.

Besser-Jones, Lorraine L. and Michael Slate, eds. *The Routledge Companion to Virtue Ethics*. New York: Routledge, 2015.

Bidgoli, Mehrdad. 'Ethical Comicality and the Fool'. *Comedy Studies* 11 (2020), 208–22.

Blank, Paula. *Shakespeare and the Mismeasure of Renaissance Man*. Ithaca, NY: Cornell University Press, 2006.

Bloom, Gina. *Voice in Motion: Staging Gender, Shaping Sound in Early Modern England*. Philadelphia: University of Pennsylvania Press, 2007.

Boehrer, Bruce. *Animal Characters: Nonhuman Beings in Early Modern Literature*. Philadelphia: University of Pennsylvania Press, 2010.

Boling, Ronald J. 'Anglo-Welsh Relations in *Cymbeline*'. *Shakespeare Quarterly* 51.1 (2000), 33–66.

Bostock, David. *Aristotle's Ethics*. Oxford: Oxford University Press, 2000.

Bourgeault, Cynthia. Buddha at the Gas Pump [podcast]. Ep. 420, 3 October 2017, https://batgap.com/cynthia-bourgeault/.

Bourgeault, Cynthia. *The Wisdom Way of Knowing: Reclaiming an Ancient Tradition to Awaken the Heart*. Hoboken, NJ: John Wiley & Sons, 2003.

Boyd White, James. *Acts of Hope: Creating Authority in Literature, Law, and Politics*. Chicago: University of Chicago Press, 1994.

Braden, Gordon. *Renaissance Tragedy and the Senecan Tradition: Anger's Privilege*. New Haven, CT: Yale University Press, 1985.

Breitenberg, Mark. *Anxious Masculinity in Early Modern England*. Cambridge: Cambridge University Press, 1996.

Bristol, Michael. 'Macbeth the Philosopher: Rethinking Context'. *New Literary History* 42.4 (2011), 641–62.

Bristol, Michael. Review of *Shakespeare and Renaissance Ethics*, ed. Patrick Gray and John D. Cox (Cambridge: Cambridge University Press, 2014). *Shakespeare Quarterly* 68.3 (2017), 301.

Bristol, Michael, ed. *Shakespeare and Moral Agency*. New York: Bloomsbury Academic, 2010.

Britton, Dennis. 'From the *Knight's Tale* to *The Two Noble Kinsmen*: Rethinking

Race, Class and Whiteness in Romance'. *Postmedieval: A Journal of Medieval Cultural Studies* 6.1 (2015), 64–78.

Brooke, Christopher. *Philosophical Pride: Stoicism and Political Thought from Lipsius to Rousseau*. Princeton, NJ: Princeton University Press, 2012.

Burrow, Colin. *Shakespeare and Classical Antiquity*. Oxford: Oxford University Press, 2013.

Burton, Dolores. *Shakespeare's Grammatical Style: A Computer-assisted Analysis of* Richard II *and* Antony and Cleopatra. Austin: University of Texas Press, 1973.

Butler, Judith. *Giving an Account of Oneself*. New York: Fordham University Press, 2005.

Butler, Judith. *Precarious Life*: *The Powers of Mourning and Violence*. London and New York: Verso, 2004.

Butterworth, Philip. *Theatre of Fire*. The Society for Theatre Research, 1998.

Calvin, John. *Sermons of Maister John Calvin, Upon the Booke of Job*, trans. Arthur Golding. London, 1584.

Campion, Thomas. *Observations in the art of English Poesie*. London: Printed by Richard Field, 1602

Castiglione, Baldassare. *Il libro del Cortegiano*, ed. Ettore Bonora and Paolo Zoccola, 2nd edn. Milan: Mursia, 1976.

Castiglione, Baldassare. *The Book of the Courtier*, trans. George Bull, rev. edn. London: Penguin, 1976.

Cavarero, Adriana. *For More than One Voice: Toward a Philosophy of Vocal Expression*, trans. Paul Kottman. Stanford, CA: Stanford University Press, 2005.

Cavell, Stanley. *Disowning Knowledge in Seven Plays of Shakespeare*. Cambridge: Cambridge University Press, 2003.

Cavell, Stanley. *Must We Mean What We Say?*, updated edn. Cambridge: Cambridge University Press, 2002.

Chalier, Catherine. 'The Philosophy of Emmanuel Levinas and the Hebraic Tradition'. In *Ethics as First Philosophy: The Significance of Emmanuel Levinas for Philosophy, Literature and Religion*, ed. Adriaan T. Peperzak. New York and London: Routledge, 1995, pp. 3–12.

Chamberlain, Stephanie. 'Eroticizing Women's Travel: Desdemona and the Desire for Adventure in Othello'. In *Travel and Travail: Early Modern Women, English Drama, and the Wider World*, ed. Patricia Akhimie and Bernadette Andrea. Omaha: University of Nebraska Press, 2020, pp. 199–214.

Ciaranca, Michael A. et. al. 'Mute Swan Life History'. Cornell Lab of Ornithology, available at https://www.allaboutbirds.org/guide/Mute_Swan/lifehistory (accessed 24 January 2023).

Cicero. *Tusculan Disputations*, trans. J. E. King. Loeb Classical Library. Cambridge, MA: Harvard University Press, 1927.

Cleaver, Emily. 'The Fascinating, Regal History Behind Britain's Swans'. *Smithsonian Magazine*, 31 July 2017, available at https://www.smithsonianmag.com/history/fascinating-history-british-thrones-swans-180964249/ (accessed 24 January 2023).

Clody, Michael. 'The Mirror and the Feather: Tragedy and Animal Voice in *King Lear*'. *English Literary History* 80 (2013), 661–80.

Clune, Michael. 'The Bizarro World of Literary Studies'. *Chronicle of Higher Education*, 26 October 2018.

Coetzee, J. M. *The Lives of Animals*. Princeton, NJ: Princeton University Press, 1999.

Condren, Conal. 'Skepticism and Political Constancy: *Richard II* and the Garden Scene as a "Model of State"'. *The Review of Politics* 78 (2016), 625–43.

Conn Liebler, Naomi. '"The oldest hath borne most": The Burdens of Aging and the Morality of Uselessness in *King Lear*'. In *Shakespeare and Moral Agency*, ed. Michael D. Bristol. London: Continuum, 2010, pp. 111–26.

Connerton, Paul. *How Societies Remember*. Cambridge: Cambridge University Press, 2010.

Connolly, Kate. 'The Most Ambitious Political Theatre Ever Staged? 14 Hours at the *Congo Tribunal*'. *The Guardian* online, 1 July 2015, available at https://www.theguardian.com/world/2015/jul/01/congo-tribunal-berlin-milo -rau-political-theatre (accessed 24 January 2023).

Coodin, Sara. 'What's Virtue Ethics Got to Do With It? Shakespearean Characters as Moral Character'. In *Shakespeare and Moral Agency*, ed. Michael D. Bristol. London: Bloomsbury Academic, 2010, pp. 184–99.

Cook, Carol. '"The sign and semblance of her honor": Reading Gender Differences in *Much Ado About Nothing*'. *PMLA* 101.2 (1986), 186–202.

Cooper, Helen. *The English Romance in Time: Transforming Motifs from Geoffrey of Monmouth to the Death of Shakespeare*. Oxford: Oxford University Press, 2004.

Cooper, John M. 'The Unity of Virtue'. In John M. Cooper, *Reason and Emotion: Essays on Ancient Moral Psychology and Ethical Theory*. Princeton, NJ: Princeton University Press, 1999, pp. 76–117.

Côrte-Real, Eduardo and Susana Oliveira. 'From Alberti's *virtù* to the *virtuoso* Michelangelo'. *Rivista di estetica* 47 (2011), 83–93.

Coryat, Thomas. *Coryat's Crudities*. London, 1611.

Crane, Mary Thomas. *Losing Touch with Nature: Literature & the New Science in 16th-Century England*. Baltimore, MD: Johns Hopkins University Press, 2014.

Crawford, Jason. 'Shakespeare's Liturgy of Assumption'. *Journal of Medieval and Early Modern Studies* 49.1 (2019), 57–84.

Crisp, Roger and Michael Slote. *Virtue Ethics*. Oxford: Oxford University Press, 1997.

Critchley, Simon. *On Humour*. London and New York: Routledge, 2002.

Crocker, Holly. *The Matter of Virtue: Women's Ethical Action from Chaucer to Shakespeare*. Philadelphia: University of Pennsylvania Press, 2019.

Crosbie, Christopher. *Revenge Tragedy and Classical Philosophy on the Early Modern Stage*. Edinburgh: Edinburgh University Press, 2019.

Cruttwell, Patrick. 'The Morality of Hamlet: "Sweet Prince" or "Arrant Knave"?'. In *Hamlet: A Casebook*, ed. John Davies Jump. New York: Aurora Publishers, 1970, pp. 174–95.

Cull, Marisa R. 'Contextualizing 1610: *Cymbeline, The Valiant Welshman*, and The Princes of Wales'. In *Shakespeare and Wales*, ed. Willy Maley and Philip Schwyzer. London: Routledge, 2010, pp. 127–42.

Curran, Kevin. 'The Four Cardinal Virtues: Caesar's Mantle and Practical Wisdom'. In *Shakespeare and Virtue: A Handbook*, ed. Julia Reinhard Lupton and Donovan Sherman. Cambridge: Cambridge University Press, 2023, pp. 113–23.

Curzer, Howard. *Aristotle and the Virtues*. Oxford: Oxford University Press, 2012.

Daily Stoic. [Quotation from Marcus Aurelius] Instagram, 27 July 2021, available at https://www.instagram.com/p/CR1OA54sUVO/ (accessed 30 July 2021).

Davis, Arthur G. *The Royalty of Lear*. New York: St. John's University Press, 1974.

Day, John, William Rowley and George Wilkins. *The Travels of the Three English Brothers*. London: Printed by Iohn Wright, 1607.

Della Porta, Giovan Battista. *Gli duoi fratelli rivali: The Two Rival Brothers*, ed. and trans. Louise George Clubb. Berkeley: University of California Press, 1980.

Dennis, Carl. 'Wit and Wisdom in *Much Ado About Nothing*'. *Studies in English Literature, 1500–1900* 13.2 (1973), 223–37.

Derrida, Jacques. *The Animal That Therefore I Am*, ed. Marie-Louis Mallet, trans. David Wills. New York: Fordham University Press, 2008.

Derrida, Jacques. *Voice and Phenomenon*, trans. Leonard Lawlor. Evanston, IL: Northwestern University Press, 2011.

Despret, Vinciane. 'Sheep Do Have Opinions'. In *Making Things Public: Atmospheres of Democracy*, ed. Bruno Latour and Peter Weibel. Cambridge, MA: MIT Press, 2006, pp. 360–70.

Despret, Vinciane. 'The Body We Care For: Figures of Anthropo-zoo-genesis'. *Body & Society* 10.2–3 (2004), 111–34.

Despret, Vinciane. *What Would Animals Say if We Asked the Right Questions?*, trans. Brett Buchanan. Minneapolis: University of Minnesota Press, 2016.

Dessen, Alan C. and Leslie Thomson. *A Dictionary of Stage Directions in English Drama 1580–1642*. Cambridge: Cambridge University Press 1999.

Dion, Gregg. 'Fortinbras, Our Contemporary'. *Theater Studies* 38 (1993), 17–27.

Dionne, Craig. *Posthuman Lear: Reading Shakespeare in the Anthropocene*. Santa Barbara, CA: Punctum Books, 2019.

Dolan, Frances. *Dangerous Familiars: Representations of Domestic Crime in England, 1550–1700*. Ithaca, NY: Cornell University Press, 1994.

Dolan, Frances. 'Home-Rebels and House-Traitors: Murderous Wives in Early Modern England'. *Yale Journal of Law and the Humanities* 4.2 (1992), 1–32.

Domenichi, Lodovico. *Facetie, motti, et burle di diversi signori et persone private*. Venice: Printed by Andrea Muschio, 1571.

Downame, John. *Spiritual physicke to cure the diseases of the soule, arising from superfluitie of choller, prescribed out of Gods word*. London, 1600.

Doyle, Laura. 'Towards a Philosophy of Transnationalism'. *Journal of Transnational American Studies* 1.1 (2009), 1–29.

Duffin, Ross W. 'Music and the Stage in the Time of Shakespeare'. In *The Oxford Handbook of the Age of Shakespeare*, ed. R. Malcolm Smuts. Oxford: Oxford University Press, 2016, pp. 748–63.

Eagleton, Terry. *Reason, Faith, and Revolution: Reflections on the God Debate*. New Haven, CT: Yale University Press, 2009.

Eggert, Katherine. *Disknowledge: Literature, Alchemy, and the End of Humanism in Renaissance England*. Philadelphia: University of Pennsylvania Press, 2015.

Ehrman, Bart D. *Peter, Paul and Mary Magdalene: The Followers of Jesus in History and Legend*. Oxford: Oxford University Press, 2006.

Eklund, Hillary and Wendy Beth Hyman, eds. *Teaching Social Justice Through Shakespeare: Why Renaissance Literature Matters Now.* Edinburgh: Edinburgh University Press, 2019.

Empson, William. 'Fool in *Lear*'. *Sewanee Review* 57 (1949), 177–214.

Epictetus. *Moral Discourses of Epictetus*, ed. W. H. D. Rouse, trans. Elizabeth Carter. London: J. M. Dent & Sons, 1910, 1950.

Erasmus, Desiderius. 'Complaint of Peace'. In *The Erasmus Reader*, ed. Erika Rummel. Toronto: University of Toronto Press, 1990.

Erasmus, Desiderius. *Enchiridion Militis Christiani, which may be called in English, the han[d]some weapon of a Christian Knight.* London: 1576.

Erasmus, Desiderius. *Praise of Folly and Letter to Martin Dorp*, trans. Betty Radice. Harmondsworth: Penguin, 1971.

Erasmus, Desiderius. *The Collected Works of Erasmus.* Toronto: University of Toronto Press, 1982.

Erasmus, Desiderius. *The Collected Works of Erasmus*, vol. 35, trans. Denis L. Drysdall. Toronto: University of Toronto Press, 2005.

Erasmus, Desiderius. *The Manual of a Christian Knight.* London: Methuen, 1905.

Erickson, Peter B. 'Sexual Politics and the Social Structure in *As You like It*'. *The Massachusetts Review* 23.1 (1982), pp. 65–83.

Escobedo, Andrew. 'From Britannia to England: *Cymbeline* and the Beginning of Nations'. *Shakespeare Quarterly* 59.1 (2008), 60–87.

Fahmi, Mustapha. *La Leçon de Rosalinde.* Chicoutimi: Éditions La Peuplade, 2018.

Feerick, Jean. '*Cymbeline* and Virginia's British Climate'. In Jean Feerick, *Strangers in Blood: Relocating Race in the Renaissance.* Toronto: University of Toronto Press, 2010, pp. 78–112.

Feerick, Jean. 'The Imperial Graft: Horticulture, Hybridity, and the Art of Mingling Races in *Henry V* and *Cymbeline*'. In *The Oxford Handbook of Shakespeare and Embodiment: Gender, Sexuality, and Race*, ed. Valerie Traub. Oxford: Oxford University Press, 2016, pp. 211–27.

Felski, Rita. *The Limits of Critique.* Chicago: University of Chicago Press, 2015.

Ficino, Marsilio. *Commentary on Plato's Symposium on Love*, trans. and commentary by Sears Reynolds Jayne. Columbia: University of Missouri Press, 1944.

Fitzgerald, F. Scott. *The Great Gatsby.* New York: Scribner, 2004.

Fleetwood, William. *A Treatise vpon the Charters Liberties Lawes and Customes of all Forrestes Parkes Chases and Free Warrens.* Harvard Law School, 1581.

Floyd-Wilson, Mary. 'Delving to the Root: *Cymbeline*, Scotland, and the English Race'. In *British Identities and English Renaissance Literature*, ed. David J. Baker and Willy Maley. Cambridge: Cambridge University Press, 2002, pp. 101–15.

Fortenbaugh, William. 'Aristotle and the Questionable Means-Dispositions'. *Transactions and Proceedings of the American Philological Association* 99 (1968), 203–31.

Fuchs, Barbara. 'Another Turn for Transnationalism: Empire, Nation, and Imperium in Early Modern Studies'. *PMLA* 130.2 (2015), 412–18.

Fuchs, Barbara. 'No Field Is an Island: Postcolonial and Transnational Approaches to Early Modern Drama'. *Renaissance Drama* 40 (2012), 125–33.

Fudge, Erica. '"Forgiveness, Horse!": The Barbaric World of *Richard II*'. In *The Routledge Handbook of Shakespeare and Animals*, ed. Karen Raber and Holly Dugan. New York: Routledge, 2020, pp. 292–306.

Gadaleto, Michael. 'Shakespeare's Bastard Nation: Skepticism and the English Isle in *King John*'. *Shakespeare Quarterly* 69.1 (2018), 3–34.

Gager, William. *William Gager: The Complete Works*, ed. Dana F. Sutton. New York and London: Garland, 1994.

Geikie, Sir Archibald. *The Birds of Shakespeare*. Glasgow: J. Maclehose and Sons, 1916.

Gellner, Ernest. *Nations and Nationalism*. Ithaca, NY: Cornell University Press, 1983.

Geneva Bible, The. A Facsimile of the 1560 Edition. Peabody, MA: Hendrickson, 2007.

Gerard, John. *The Herball or, general historie of plants*. London: John Norton, 1597.

Ghose, Indira. 'Shakespeare and the Ethics of Laughter'. In *Shakespeare and Renaissance Ethics*, ed. Patrick Gray and John D. Cox. Cambridge: Cambridge University Press, 2014, pp. 56–75.

Ghose, Indira. *Shakespeare and Laughter: A Cultural History*. Manchester and New York: Manchester University Press, 2008.

Gil Harris, Jonathan. 'The Smell of *Macbeth*'. *Shakespeare Quarterly* 58.4 (2007), 465–86.

Gil Harris, Jonathan. *Untimely Matter in the Time of Shakespeare*. Philadelphia: University of Pennsylvania Press, 2009.

Gioviano Pontano, Giovanni. *The Virtues and Vices of Speech*, trans. G. W. Pigman III. Cambridge, MA: Harvard University Press, 2019.

Goldberg, Jonathan. 'Dover Cliff and the Conditions of Representation: *King Lear* 4.6 in Perspective'. *Poetics Today* 5.3 (1984), 537–47.

Goodfellow, Peter. *Shakespeare's Birds*. Woodstock, NY: Overlook, 1985.

Grady, Hugh. *Shakespeare's Dialectic of Hope: From the Political to the Utopian*. Cambridge: Cambridge University Press, 2022.

Gray, Patrick. 'Shakespeare vs. Seneca: Competing Visions of Human Dignity'. In *Brill's Companion to the Reception of Senecan Tragedy: Scholarly, Theatrical and Literary Receptions*, ed. Eric Dodson-Robinson. Boston, MA: Brill, 2016, pp. 203–30.

Gray, Patrick and John D. Cox, eds. *Shakespeare and Renaissance Ethics*. Cambridge: Cambridge University Press, 2014.

de Grazia, Margreta. 'The Fool's Promised Exit'. In *Shakespeare Up Close: Reading Early Modern Texts*, ed. Russ McDonald, Nicholas D. Nace and Travis D. Williams. London: Arden Shakespeare, 2012, pp. 177–80.

Green, Lawrence D. '"Where's My Fool?": Some Consequences of the Omission of the Fool in Tate's *Lear*'. *SEL* 12 (1972), 259–74.

Greenblatt, Stephen. 'Shakespeare Explains the 2016 Election'. *New York Times*, 8 October 2016, available at https://www.nytimes.com/2016/10/09/opinion/sunday/shakespeare-explains-the-2016-election.html (accessed 25 January 2023).

Greenblatt, Stephen. *Tyrant: Shakespeare on Politics*. New York: W. W. Norton, 2018.

Greenfeld, Liah. 'God's Firstborn: England'. In Liah Greenfeld, *Nationalism:*

Five Roads to Modernity. Cambridge, MA: Harvard University Press, 1992, pp. 27–87.

Grennan, Eamon. 'The Women's Voices in *Othello*: Speech, Song, Silence'. *Shakespeare Quarterly* 38 (1987), 275–92.

Grove, Jairus Victor. *Savage Ecology: War and Geopolitics at the End of the World*. Durham, NC: Duke University Press, 2019.

Guicciardini, Lodovico. *Detti, et fatti piacevoli et gravi, di diversi principi filosofi, et cortigiani*. Venice: Printed by Domenico and Gio Battista Guerra, 1569.

Gurr, Andrew. 'Beeston [Hutchinson], Christopher'. In *Oxford Dictionary of National Biography*. Oxford: Oxford University Press, 2004.

Hæc-Vir: Or The Womanish-Man: Being an Answere to a late Booke intituled Hic-Mulier. London, 1620.

Hageneder, Fred. *The Living Wisdom of Trees: A Guide to the Natural History, Symbolism and Healing Power of Trees*. London: Watkins Media, 2020.

Halliwell, Stephen. *Between Ecstasy and Truth: Interpretations of Greek Poetics from Homer to Longinus*. Oxford: Oxford University Press, 2012.

Hanson, Elizabeth. 'Fellow Students: Hamlet, Horatio, and the Early Modern University'. *Shakespeare Quarterly* 62.2 (2011), 205–29.

Haraway, Donna. *Staying with the Trouble: Making Kin in the Chthulucene*. Durham, NC: Duke University Press, 2016.

Haraway, Donna. *When Species Meet*. Minneapolis: University of Minnesota Press, 2008.

Hardman, J. A. and D. R. Cooper. 'Mute Swans on the Warwickshire Avon – A Study of a Decline'. *Wildfowl Journal* 31 (1980), 29–36.

Harrison, Peter. 'The Virtues of Animals in Seventeenth-Century Thought'. *Journal of the History of Ideas* 59.3 (1998), 463–84.

Harrison, William. *The Description of England* (1587), ed. George Edelen. New York: Dover Publications, 1994.

Harting, James Edmund. *The Birds of Shakespeare*. London: John van Voorst, 1871.

Harvey, Gabriel. *The Works of Gabriel Harvey*, ed. Alexander B. Grosart. London: 1884.

Helgerson, Richard. *Forms of Nationhood: The Elizabethan Writing of England*. Chicago: University of Chicago Press, 1994.

Helminski, Camille. *Women of Sufism: A Hidden Treasure*. Denver, CO: Shambhala Publications, 2003.

Helminski, Kabir. *Living Presence: A Sufi Way to Mindfulness and the Essential Self*. New York: Jeremy Tarcher/Putnam, 1992.

Helminski, Kabir. *Living Presence: The Sufi Path to Mindfulness and the Essential Self*. New York: Penguin, 2017.

Herdt, Jennifer. *Putting on Virtue: The Legacy of the Splendid Vices*. Chicago: University of Chicago Press, 2008.

Hershinow, David. 'Diogenes the Cynic and Shakespeare's Bitter Fool: The Politics and Aesthetics of Free Speech'. *Criticism* 56 (2014), 807–35.

Hesiod. *Theogony*, trans. H. G. Evelyn-White. Available at https://www.theoi.com/Text/HesiodTheogony.html (accessed 25 January 2023).

Heywood, Thomas. *An Apology for Actors*. London: Printed by Nicholas Okes, 1612.

Hic Mulier: Or, The Man-Woman: Being a Medicine to cure the Coltish Disease of the Staggers in the Masculine-Feminines, of our Times. London, 1620.

Hillman, David. 'Ave Desdemona'. In *Shakespeare and Hospitality: Ethics, Politics, and Exchange*, ed. David B. Goldstein and Julia Reinhard Lupton. London: Routledge, 2016, pp. 139–62.

Hobsbawm, E. J. *Nations and Nationalism since 1780: Programme, Myth, Reality*, 2nd edn. Cambridge: Cambridge University Press, 1992.

Honig, Bonnie. *Antigone, Interrupted*. Cambridge: Cambridge University Press, 2013.

Hopkins, Lisa. '*Cymbeline*, the *Translatio Imperii*, and the Matter of Britain'. In *Shakespeare and Wales: From the Marches to the Assembly*, ed. Willy Maley and Philip Schwyzer. Burlington, VT: Ashgate, 2010, pp. 143–55.

Hornback, Robert D. 'The Fool in Quarto and Folio *King Lear*'. *English Literary Renaissance* 34 (2004), 306–38.

Hunt, Maurice. 'Dismemberment, Corporal Reconstitution, and the Body Politic in *Cymbeline*'. *Studies in Philology* 99.4 (2002), 404–31.

Ikram, S. M. *Muslim Civilization in India*, ed. Ainslie T. Embree. New York: Columbia University Press, 1964, available at https://www.columbia.edu/itc/mealac/pritchett/00islamlinks/ikram/part1_09.html.

Ingenito, Domenico. *Beholding Beauty: Sa'di of Shiraz and the Aesthetics of Desire in Medieval Persian Poetry*. Leiden: Brill, 2020.

Jameson, Fredric. *The Political Unconscious: Narrative as a Socially Symbolic Act*. Ithaca, NY: Cornell University Press, 1981.

Jameson, Fredric. 'War and Representation'. *PMLA* 124.5 (2009), 1532–47.

Jimenez, Marta. 'Aristotle on Becoming Virtuous by Doing Virtuous Actions'. *Phronesis* 61 (2016), 3–32.

Johnson, Eric. 'Shakespeare's Plays Listed by Genre'. Open Source Shakespeare, George Mason University, 2003, available at https://www.opensourceshakespeare.org.

Johnson, Samuel. *The Yale Edition of the Works of Samuel Johnson*, ed. Arthur Sherbo. New Haven, CT and London: Yale University Press, 1968.

Jones, Emrys. 'Stuart *Cymbeline*'. *Essays in Criticism* 11 (1961), 84–99.

Jones, Gwilim. '"This much show of fire": Storm and Spectacle in the Opening of the Globe'. In *The Spectacular in and Around Shakespeare*, ed. Pascale Drouet. Newcastle upon Tyne: Cambridge Scholars Publishing, 2005, pp. 3–16.

Kahn, Coppélia. *Man's Estate: Masculine Identity in Shakespeare*. Berkeley: University of California Press, 1981.

Kahn, Coppélia. *Roman Shakespeare: Warriors, Wounds, and Women*. London: Routledge, 1997.

Kant, Immanuel. *The Critique of Judgment*, trans. J. H. Bernard, 2nd edn rev. London: Macmillan, 1914.

Kantorowicz, Ernst. *The King's Two Bodies: A Study in Mediaeval Political Theology*. Oxford: Oxford University Press, 1957.

Kearney, James. '"This is above all strangeness": *King Lear*, Ethics, and the Phenomenology of Recognition'. *Criticism* 54.3 (2012), 455–67.

Keller, Catherine. *Political Theology of the Earth: Our Planetary Emergency and the Struggle for a New Public*. New York: Columbia University Press, 2018.

Kenny, Anthony. *Aristotle on the Perfect Life*. Oxford: Oxford University Press, 1992.

Kerrigan, John. *Archipelagic English: Literature, History, and Politics (1603–1707)*. Oxford: Oxford University Press, 2008.

Kerrigan, John. 'Revision, Adaptation, and the Fool in *King Lear*'. In *The Division of the Kingdoms: Shakespeare's Two Versions of* King Lear, ed. Gary Taylor and Michael Warren. Oxford: Clarendon Press, 1986, pp. 195–239.

Kimmerer, Robin. *Braiding Sweetgrass: Indigenous Wisdom, Scientific Knowledge, and the Teachings of Plants*. Minneapolis, MN: Milkweed Editions, 2013.

King, Ros. *'Cymbeline': Constructions of Britain*. Burlington, VT: Ashgate, 2005.

Kirabaev, Nur and Olga Chistyakova. 'Knowing God in Eastern Christianity and Islamic Tradition: A Comparative Study'. *Religions* 11.675 (2020).

Klein, Jacob. 'The Stoic Argument from Oikeosis'. *Oxford Studies in Ancient Philosophy* 50 (2016), 143–200.

Kleinberg-Levin, David. *Before the Voice of Reason: Echoes of Responsibility in Merleau-Ponty's Ecology and Levinas's Ethics*. Albany: State University of New York Press, 2008.

Knapp, Jeffrey. *Shakespeare's Tribe: Church, Nation, and Theatre in Renaissance England*. Chicago: University of Chicago Press, 2002.

Knowles, Richard. 'Myth and Type in *As You Like It*'. *ELH* 33 (1966), 5–6.

Kolb, Laura. 'The Very Modern Anger of Shakespeare's Women'. *Electric Literature* 6 (February 2019), available at https://electricliterature.com/the-very-modern-anger-of-shakespeares-women/ (accessed 25 January 2023).

Kramnick, Jonathan. *Paper Minds: Literature and the Ecology of Consciousness*. Chicago: University of Chicago Press, 2018.

Kramnick, Jonathan. 'The Interdisciplinary Delusion: Saving Disciplines is the Only Way to Save Ourselves'. *Chronicle of Higher Education*, 2 November 2018.

Lancashire, Ian, ed. 'An Homilie on the State of Matrimony'. *Renaissance Electronic Texts* 1.1, University of Toronto, 1994, available at https://www.anglicanlibrary.org/homilies/bk2hom18.htm.

Lane, Julia. 'A Clown in Search of Ethics'. In *Comedy Begins with Our Simplest Gestures: Levinas, Ethics, and Humor*, ed. Brian Bergen-Aurand. Pittsburgh, PA: Duquesne University Press, 2017, pp. 163–84.

Langis, Unhae Park. *Passion, Prudence, and Virtue in Shakespearean Drama*. London: Bloomsbury, 2011.

Lanier, Douglas. 'Shakespearean Rhizomatics: Adaptation, Ethics, Value'. In *Shakespeare and the Ethics of Appropriation*, ed. Alexa Huang and Elizabeth Rivlin. New York: Palgrave Macmillan, 2014, pp. 21–40.

Law, Alex. 'Of Navies and Navels: Britain as a Mental Island'. *Geografiska Annaler. Series B, Human Geography* 87.4 (2005), 267–77.

Lear, Jonathan. *Radical Hope: Ethics in the Face of Cultural Devastation*. Cambridge, MA: Harvard University Press, 2006.

Lehnhof, Kent R. 'Relation and Responsibility: A Levinasian Reading of *King Lear*'. *Modern Philology* 111 (2014), 485–509.

Lehnhof, Kent R. 'Theology, Phenomenology, and the Divine in *King Lear*'. In *Of Levinas and Shakespeare*, ed. Moshe Gold, Sandor Goodhart and Kent Lehnhof. West Lafayette, IN: Purdue University Press, 2018, pp. 107–22.

Lehtonen, Kelly. *The Sublime and the Remaking of Renaissance Epic*. Toronto: University of Toronto Press, forthcoming 2023.

Lennox, James G. 'Aristotle on the Biological Roots of Virtue'. In *Bridging the Gap Between Aristotle's Science and Ethics*, ed. Devin Henry and Karen Margrethe Nielsen. Cambridge: Cambridge University Press, 2015, pp. 193–213.

Leo, Russ. *Tragedy as Philosophy in the Reformation World*. Oxford: Oxford University Press, 2019.

Leroy, Louis. *Aristotles politiques, or Discourses of gouernment*. London: Printed by Adam Islip, 1598.

Levin, Carole and John Watkins. *Shakespeare's Foreign Worlds: National and Transnational Identities in the Elizabethan Age*. Ithaca, NY: Cornell University Press, 2009.

Levinas, Emmanuel. 'Dialogue with Emmanuel Levinas'. In *Face to Face with Levinas*, ed. Richard A. Cohen. Albany: State University of New York Press, 1986.

Levinas, Emmanuel. *Le temps et l'autre*. Paris: Presses Universitaires Français, 1983.

Levinas, Emmanuel. *Nine Talmudic Readings*, trans. Annette Aronowicz. Bloomington: Indiana University Press, 1994.

Levinas, Emmanuel. *Otherwise than Being or Beyond Essence*, trans. Alphonso Lingis. Pittsburgh, PA: Duquesne University Press, 1998.

Levinas, Emmanuel. *Totality and Infinity: An Essay on Exteriority*, trans. Alphonso Lingis. Pittsburgh, PA: Duquesne University Press, 1994.

Lewis, Charlton T. and Charles Short. *A Latin Dictionary*. Oxford: Clarendon Press, 1879.

Lewis, Cynthia. 'Horns, the Dream-Work, and Female Potency in *As You like It*'. *South Atlantic Review* 66.4 (2001), 45–69.

Lewis, Rhodri. *Hamlet and the Vision of Darkness*. Princeton, NJ: Princeton University Press, 2020.

Lewis, Samuel L. 'The Perfection of the Heart. An Original Sangatha'. Murshid Samuel Lewis Archives, available at https://www.ruhaniat.org/index.php/major-papers/sufi-practices-ryazat/2247-the-perfection-of-the-heart--an-original-sangatha (accessed 25 January 2023).

Liddell, Henry and Robert Scott. *A Greek–English Lexicon*. Oxford: Oxford University Press, 1996.

Lily, William. *An introduction of the eyght partes of speche, and the construction of the same . . .* London: Thomae Bertheleti, 1547.

Lin, Erika T. *Shakespeare and the Materiality of Performance*. New York: Palgrave Macmillan, 2012.

Lippincott, H. F. '*King Lear* and the Fools of Robert Armin'. *Shakespeare Quarterly* 26 (1975), 243–53.

Lippitt, John. 'Is a Sense of Humour a Virtue?' *The Monist* 88.1 (2005), 77–92.

Lipsius, Justus. *Two Bookes of Constancie*, trans. John Stradling. London, 1595.

Littleton, Thomas. *Tenures in Englishe*. London, 1556.

Lodge, Thomas. *A Reply to Stephen Gosson's Schoole of Abuse in Defence of Poetry, Musick, and Stage Plays*. London, 1580. Renascence Editions, available at https://www.luminarium.org/renascence-editions/lodge.html (accessed 25 January 2023).

Loewenstein, David and Paul Stevens, eds. *Early Modern Nationalism and Milton's England*. Toronto: University of Toronto Press, 2008.

Longinus. *On the Sublime*, trans. W. H. Fyfe, rev. Donald A. Russell. In *Aristotle:*

The Poetics. Longinus: On the Sublime. Demetrius: On Style. Cambridge, MA: Harvard University Press, 1995.

Lowrance, Bryan. 'Marlowe's Wit: Power, Language, and the Literary in *Tamburlaine* and *Doctor Faustus*'. *Modern Philology* 111 (2014), 711–32.

Lucretius. *On the Nature of Things*, trans. Martin Ferguson Smith. Indianapolis, IN: Hackett Publishing, 1969.

Lupton, Julia Reinhard. 'After Sovereignty / *After Virtue*'. *SEL* 58.1 (2018), 205–17.

Lupton, Julia Reinhard. 'Birth Places: Shakespeare's Beliefs / Believing in Shakespeare'. *Shakespeare Quarterly* 65 (2014), 399–420.

Lupton, Julia Reinhard. *Shakespeare Dwelling: Designs for the Theater of Life.* Chicago: University of Chicago Press, 2018.

Lupton, Julia Reinhard. 'Shakespeare's Virtuous Properties'. In *Shakespeare's Things*, ed. Brett Gamboa and Lawrence Switzky. New York: Routledge, 2019, pp. 109–22.

Lupton, Julia Reinhard. 'Trust in the Theatre'. In *The Palgrave Handbook of Affect Studies and Textual Criticism*, ed. Donald Wehrs and Thomas Blake. New York: Palgrave Macmillan, 2017) pp. 155–81.

Lupton, Julia Reinhard and Donovan Sherman, eds. *Shakespeare and Virtue: A Handbook*. Cambridge: Cambridge University Press, 2023.

Machiavelli, Niccolò. *The Prince*, ed. and trans. Mark Musa. New York: St. Martin's Press, 1964.

MacIntyre, Alasdair. *After Virtue: A Study in Moral Theory.* Notre Dame, IN: University of Notre Dame Press, 1981.

MacIntyre, Alasdair. *After Virtue: A Study in Moral Theory*, 2nd edn. Notre Dame, IN: University of Notre Dame Press, 1984.

MacIntyre, Alasdair. *After Virtue: A Study in Moral Theory*, 3rd edn. Notre Dame: University of Notre Dame Press, 2007.

MacIntyre, Alasdair. *A Very Short History of Ethics.* New York: Macmillan, 1966.

MacKay, Ellen. *Persecution, Plague and Fire: Fugitive Histories of the Stage in Early Modern England.* Chicago: University of Chicago Press, 2011.

Magnusson, Lynne. 'Grammatical Theatricality in *Richard III*: Schoolroom Queens and Godly Optatives'. *Shakespeare Quarterly* 64.1 (2013), 32–43.

Maley, Willy. *Nation, State and Empire in English Renaissance Literature: Shakespeare to Milton.* New York: Palgrave, 2003.

Margalit, Avishai. *The Ethics of Memory.* Cambridge, MA: Harvard University Press, 2004.

Martindale, Charles and Michelle Martindale. *Shakespeare and the Uses of Antiquity: An Introductory Essay.* New York: Routledge, 1990.

Massi Dakake, Maria. '"Walking upon the Path of God like Men": Women and the Feminine in the Islamic Mystical Tradition'. In *Sufism: Love and Wisdom*, ed. Jean-Louis Michon and Roger Gaetani. World Wisdom, 2006.

Massumi, Brian. *Parables for the Virtual: Movement, Affect, Sensation.* Durham, NC: Duke University Press, 2002.

Matar, Nabil. *Europe through Arab Eyes, 1578–1727.* New York: Columbia University Press, 2008.

McCrea, Adriana. *Constant Minds: Political Virtues and the Lipsian Paradigm in England, 1584–1650.* Toronto: University of Toronto Press, 1997.

Merleau-Ponty, Maurice. *The Visible and the Invisible*, trans. Alphonso Lingis. Evanston, IL: Northwestern University Press, 1968.

Merton, Thomas. *A Thomas Merton Reader*, ed. Thomas P. McDowell. New York: Doubleday/Image Books, 1974, pp. 346–47.

Middleton, Thomas. *Thomas Middleton: The Collected Works*, ed. Gary Taylor and John Lavagnino. Oxford: Oxford University Press, 2007.

Mikalachki, Jodi. '*Cymbeline* and the Masculine Romance of Roman Britain'. In *The Legacy of Boadicea: Gender and Nation in Early Modern England*. London: Routledge, 1998, pp. 96–114.

Miles, Geoffrey. *Shakespeare and the Constant Romans*. Oxford: Clarendon Press, 1996.

Milton, John. *Paradise Lost*, ed. Alastair Fowler, 2nd edn. London: Longman, 2007.

Minton, Eric. 'Shakespeare Plays Popularity Index'. Shakespearances.com, available at https://www.shakespeareances.com/wherewill/Play_Popularity _Index.html (accessed 25 January 2023).

Miola, Robert S. *Shakespeare's Rome*. Cambridge: Cambridge University Press, 1983.

Miola, Robert S. '"Wrying but a little"? Marriage, Punishment, and Forgiveness in *Cymbeline*'. In *Shakespeare and Renaissance Ethics*, ed. Patrick Gray and John D. Cox. Cambridge: Cambridge University Press, 2014, pp. 186–210.

Mitscherlich, Alexander and Margarete Mitscherlich. *The Inability to Mourn: Principles of Collective Behavior*, trans. Beverley R. Placzek. New York: Grove Press, 1984.

Monsarrat, Gilles D. *Light from the Porch: Stoicism and English Renaissance Literature*. Paris: Didier-Erudition, 1984.

de Montaigne, Michel. *Complete Essays*, trans. M. A. Screech. London and New York: Penguin, 2003.

de Montaigne, Michel. *Les Essais*, ed. Claude Pinganaud. Paris: Arlea, 1992.

de Montaigne, Michel. *The Complete Essays of Montaigne*, trans. Donald M. Frame. Stanford, CA: Stanford University Press, 1998.

de Montaigne, Michel. *The Complete Works: Essays, Travel Journal, Letters*, trans. Donald M. Frame. New York: Alfred A. Knopf, 2003.

de Montaigne, Michel. *The Essays of Michaell de Montaigne*, trans. John Florio. London: Printed for Edward Blount, 1603.

Moretti, Thomas J. 'Misthinking the King: The Theatrics of Christian Rule in *Henry VI, Part 3*'. *Renascence: Essays on Values in Literature* 60.4 (2008), 275–94.

Morson, Gary Saul and Caryl Emerson. *Mikhail Bakhtin: Creation of a Prosaics*. Stanford, CA: Stanford University Press, 1990.

Moschovakis, Nicholas. 'Review of the Public Theater's Julius Caesar'. *Shakespeare Quarterly*, available at https://shakespearequarterly.folger.edu /web_exclusive/public-theater-julius-caesar/.

Mousley, Andy. *Re-Humanising Shakespeare: Literary Humanism, Wisdom and Modernity*. Edinburgh: Edinburgh University Press, 2007.

Munson Deats, Sara. '"Truly, an obedient lady": Desdemona, Emilia, and the Doctrine of Obedience in *Othello*'. In *Othello: New Critical Essays*, ed. Philip C. Kolin. New York and London: Routledge, 2002, pp. 233–54.

Murdoch, Iris. *The Sovereignty of Good*. London: Routledge, 1970.

Murphy Paul, Annie. *The Extended Mind: The Power of Thinking Outside the Brain*. Boston, MA: Houghton Mifflin Harcourt, 2021.

'Mute Swan Nesting and Breeding Habits'. The Royal Society for the Protection of Birds, available at https://www.rspb.org.uk/birds-and-wildlife/wildlife-gu ides/bird-a-z/mute-swan/nesting-and-breeding-habits/ (accessed 25 January 2023).

Narveson, Kate. 'Hexis (Habit)'. In *Shakespeare and Virtue: A Handbook*, ed. Julia Reinhard Lupton and Donovan Sherman. Cambridge: Cambridge University Press, 2023, pp. 61–2.

Nashe, Thomas. *The Works of Thomas Nashe*, ed. Ronald McKerrow. London: A. H. Bullen, 1904.

Nasr, Seyyed Hossein. *Knowledge and the Sacred*. New York: State University of New York Press, 1989.

Neely, Sol. 'Toward a Critical Theory of Laughter'. In *Comedy Begins with Our Simplest Gestures: Levinas, Ethics, and Humor*, ed. Brian Bergen-Aurand. Pittsburgh, PA: Duquesne University Press, 2017, pp. 99–121.

Nicholson, Catherine. *Uncommon Tongues: Eloquence and Eccentricity in the English Renaissance*. Philadelphia: University of Pennsylvania Press, 2014.

Nietzsche, Friedrich. *Untimely Meditations*, ed. Daniel Breazeale, trans. R. J. Hollingdale. Cambridge: Cambridge University Press, 1997.

Nixon, Anthony. *The Three Brothers*. London: 1607.

Nussbaum, Martha C. *Creating Capabilities: The Human Development Approach*. Cambridge, MA: Harvard University Press, 2013.

Nussbaum, Martha C. *The Fragility of Goodness: Luck and Ethics in Greek Tragedy and Philosophy*. Cambridge: Cambridge University Press, 1986.

Nussbaum, Martha C. *The Fragility of Goodness: Luck and Ethics in Greek Tragedy and Philosophy*, 2nd edn. New York and Cambridge: Cambridge University Press, 2001.

Nussbaum, Martha C. *The Therapy of Desire: Theory and Practice in Hellenistic Ethics*. Princeton, NJ: Princeton University Press, 1994; 2018.

Nussbaum, Martha C. *Upheavals of Thought*. Cambridge: Cambridge University Press, 2001.

Nussbaum, Martha C. 'Virtue Ethics: A Misleading Category?' *The Journal of Ethics* 3 (1999), 163–201.

O'Dair, Sharon. 'Who Did Kill Shakespeare?'. In *Shakespeare and the 99%: Literary Studies, the Profession, and the Production of Inequity*, ed. Sharon O'Dair and Timothy Francisco. Cham: Palgrave Macmillan, 2019, pp. 225–46.

Oksenberg Rorty, Amelia. 'The Place of Contemplation in Aristotle's *Nicomachean Ethics*'. *Mind* 87.347 (1978), 343–58.

Olmsted, Wendy. 'To Plainess is Honour Bound: Deceptive Friendship in *King Lear*'. In *Discourses and Representations of Friendship in Early Modern Europe, 1500–1700*, ed. Maritere López, Daniel T. Lochman and Lorna Hutson. London: Routledge, 2010, pp. 181–94.

Orgel, Stephen. '*King Lear* and the Art of Forgetting'. In Stephen Orgel, *Spectacular Performances: Essays on Theatre, Imagery, Books, and Selves in Early Modern England*. Manchester: Manchester University Press, 2011, pp. 101–8.

Orgel, Stephen. 'Shakespeare Imagines a Theater'. *Poetics Today* 5.3 (1984), 549–61.

Orwell, George. 'Lear, Tolstoy, and the Fool'. In George Orwell, *Shooting an*

Elephant: And Other Essays. New York: Harcourt, Brace and Company, 1950, pp. 32–52.

Palfrey, Simon. *Poor Tom: Living King Lear*. Chicago: University of Chicago Press, 2014.

Parker, Patricia. 'Preposterous Reversals: *Love's Labour's Lost*'. *Modern Language Quarterly* 54.4 (1993), 435–82.

Parker, Patricia. 'Romance and Empire: Anachronistic *Cymbeline*'. In *Unfolded Tales: Essays on Renaissance Romance*, ed. George M. Logan and Gordon Teskey. Ithaca, NY: Cornell University Press, 1989, pp. 189–207.

Parolin, Peter. 'Anachronistic Italy: Cultural Alliances and National Identity in *Cymbeline*'. *Shakespeare Studies* 30 (2002), 188–215.

Passannante, Gerard. *Catastrophizing: Materialism and the Making of Disaster*. Chicago: University of Chicago Press, 2019.

Phelan, Peggy. 'Reconstructing Love: *King Lear* and Theatre Architecture'. In *A Companion to Shakespeare and Performance*, ed. Barbara Hodgdon and William Worthen. Oxford: Wiley-Blackwell, 2005, pp. 13–35.

Pikli, Natália. 'Hybrid Creatures in Context: Centaurs, Hobby-horses and Sexualised Women (*Hamlet, King Lear, The Two Noble Kinsmen*)'. *Actes des congrès de la Société française Shakespeare* 38 (2020), 1–18.

Plato. *Complete Works*, ed. John M. Cooper and D. S. Hutchinson. Indianapolis, IN: Hackett Publishing, 1997.

Pliny. *Natural History*, trans. H. Rackham. Cambridge, MA: Harvard University Press, 1940; repr. 1997.

Plotinus. *Enneads IV.8: On the Descent of the Soul into Bodies*, trans. and commentary by Barrie Fleet. Las Vegas, CA: Parmenides Publishing, 2012.

Plutarch. *Consolatio ad Apollonium*. In *The Philosophie, commonlie called, the Morals written by the learned philosopher Plutarch of Chaeronea*, trans. Philemon Holland. London, 1603.

Plutarch. *Moralia*, trans. Philemon Holland. London: Arnold Hatfield, 1603.

Porter, Jean. 'Virtue Ethics in the Medieval Period'. In *The Cambridge Companion to Virtue Ethics*, ed. Daniel C. Russell. Cambridge: Cambridge University Press, 2013, pp. 70–91.

Preiss, Richard. *Clowning and Authorship in Early Modern Theatre*. Cambridge: Cambridge University Press, 2014.

Puttenham, George. *The Arte of English Poesie*. London: Printed by Richard Field, 1589.

Puttenham, George. *The Art of English Poesy*, ed. Frank Whigham and Wayne A. Rebhorn. Ithaca, NY: Cornell University Press, 2007.

Quiring, Björn. 'Curse'. In *Entertaining the Idea: Shakespeare, Philosophy, and Performance*, ed. Lowell Gallagher, James Kearney and Julia Reinhard Lupton. Toronto: University of Toronto Press, 2021, pp. 86–101.

Quirke, Stephen. *The Cult of Ra: Sun Worship in Ancient Egypt*. London: Thames & Hudson, 2001.

Quispel, Gilles. *Gnostica, Judaica, Catholica: Collected Essays of Gilles Quispel*, ed. Johannes Van Oort. Leiden: Brill, 2008.

Raber, Karen. *Animal Bodies, Renaissance Culture*. Philadelphia: University of Pennsylvania Press, 2013.

Raber, Karen. 'Equeer: Human–Equine Erotics in *1 Henry IV*'. In *The Oxford Handbook of Shakespeare and Embodiment*, ed. Valerie Traub. Oxford: Oxford University Press, 2016, pp. 347–66.

Raber, Karen and Karen Edwards. *Shakespeare and Animals: A Dictionary*. London: Bloomsbury, 2022.

Rawlinson, John. *Fishermen, Fishers of Men. A sermon preached at Mercers Chapell on Mid-Lent Sunday the 26. of March 1609*. 1609.

Redford, Donald B., ed. *The Oxford Essential Guide to Egyptian Mythology*. New York: Berkley Books, 2003, pp. 157–61.

Reynolds, Bryan. *Performing Transversally: Reimagining Shakespeare and the Critical Future*. New York: Palgrave Macmillan, 2003.

Rich, Barnabe. *My Ladies Looking Glasse*. London, 1616.

Richards, Jennifer. 'Assumed Simplicity and the Critique of Nobility: Or, How Castiglione Read Cicero'. *Renaissance Quarterly* 54.2 (2001), 460–86.

Roberts, Alison. *Hathor Rising: The Power of the Goddess in Ancient Egypt*. Rochester, VT: Inner Traditions, 1995.

Rosenberg, Jessica. *Botanical Poetics: Early Modern Plant Books and the Husbandry of Print*. Philadelphia: University of Pennsylvania Press, 2022.

Rosenberg, Jessica. 'Poetic Language, Practical Handbooks, and the "vertues" of Plants'. In *Ecological Approaches to Early Modern Texts: A Field Guide to Reading and Teaching*, ed. Jennifer Munroe, Edward J. Geisweidt and Lynne Bruckner. Abingdon: Routledge, 2016, pp. 61–9.

Rosenthal, Margaret. *The Honest Courtesan: Veronica Franco, Citizen and Writer in Sixteenth-Century Venice*. Chicago: University of Chicago Press, 2012.

Ruggiero, Guido. *Machiavelli in Love: Sex, Self, and Society in the Italian Renaissance*. Baltimore, MD: Johns Hopkins University Press, 2007.

Rumi, Jalāloddin. *Spiritual Verses: The First Book of the Masnavi-ye Ma'navi*, trans. Alan Williams. New York: Penguin, 2006.

Russell, Daniel C. *The Cambridge Companion to Virtue Ethics*. Cambridge: Cambridge University Press, 2013.

Russell, J. R. 'Hymn of the Pearl'. *Encyclopædia Iranica*, 2012, available at https://iranicaonline.org/articles/hymn-of-the-pearl (accessed 25 January 2023).

Sachon, Susan. *Shakespeare, Objects, Phenomenology: Daggers of the Mind*. New York: Palgrave Macmillan, 2020.

Sahih al-Bukhari 6416, trans. Dr. M. Muhsin Kahn, available at https://sunnah.com/bukhari:6416 (accessed 25 January 2023).

Sale, Carolyn. 'Eating Air, Feeling Smells: *Hamlet*'s Theory of Performance'. *Renaissance Drama* 35 (2006), 145–68.

Sale, Carolyn. '"The king is a thing": The King's Prerogative and the Treasure of the Realm in Plowden's Report of the Case of Mines and Shakespeare's *Hamlet*'. In *Shakespeare and the Law*, ed. Paul Raffield and Gary Watt. Oxford: Hart Publishing, 2008, pp. 137–58.

Salkeld, Duncan. 'Literary Traces in Bridewell and Bethlem, 1602–1624'. *The Review of English Studies* 56.225 (2005), 379–85.

Salkeld, Duncan. *Shakespeare and London*. Oxford: Oxford University Press, 2018.

Sanchez, Melissa E. *Queer Faith: Reading Promiscuity and Race in the Secular Love Tradition*. New York: New York University Press, 2019.

Sanchez, Melissa E. *Shakespeare and Queer Theory*. New York: The Arden Shakespeare, 2020.

Sanders, Eve Rachelle. 'Interiority and the Letter in *Cymbeline*'. *Critical Survey* 12.2 (2000), 49–70.

Sandler, Ronald and Philip Cafaro, eds. *Environmental Virtue Ethics*. Lanham, MD: Rowman & Littlefield, 2005.

Schimmel, Annemarie. *A Two-Colored Brocade: The Imagery of Persian Poetry*. Chapel Hill, NC: University of North Carolina Press, 1992.

Schimmel, Annemarie. *My Soul Is a Woman: The Feminine in Islam*. London: Bloomsbury, 2003.

Schimmel, Annemarie. *Mystical Dimensions of Islam*. Chapel Hill, NC: University of North Carolina Press, 1975.

Schmitt, Charles B. *John Case and Aristotelianism in Renaissance England*. Montreal: McGill-Queen's University Press, 1983.

Schneewind, J. B. 'The Misfortunes of Virtue'. *Ethics* 101 (1990), 42–63.

Schuon, Frithjof. *The Essential Writings of Frithjof Schuon*, ed. Seyyed Hossein Nasr. Amity, NY: Amity House, 1986.

Schwyzer, Philip. *Literature, Nationalism and Memory in Early Modern England and Wales*. Cambridge: Cambridge University Press, 2004.

Scott, Jonathan. *When the Waves Ruled Britannia: Geography and Political Identities, 1500–1800*. Cambridge: Cambridge University Press, 2011.

Scott, William O. 'Self-undoing Paradox, Scepticism, and Lear's Abdication'. In *Drama and Philosophy* 12, ed. James Redmond. Cambridge: Cambridge University Press, 1990, pp. 73–85.

Sebald, W. G. *Campo Santo*, trans. Anthea Bell. London: Hamish Hamilton, 2005.

Sedgwick, Eve. 'Paranoid Reading and Reparative Reading: Or, You're So Paranoid You Probably Think This Essay Is About You'. In *Touching Feeling: Affect, Pedagogy, Performativity*, ed. Michèle Barale, Jonathan Goldberg, Michael Moon and Eve Kosofsky Sedgwick. Durham, NC: Duke University Press, 2002, pp. 123–51.

Self, Lois S. 'Rhetoric and Phronesis: The Aristotelian Ideal'. *Philosophy & Rhetoric* 12 (1979), 130–45.

Seneca. *The Workes of Lucius Annaeus Seneca, Both Morrall and Naturall*, trans. Thomas Lodge. London, 1614.

Shaikh, Sa'diyya. *Sufi Narratives of Intimacy: Ibn 'Arabi, Gender and Sexuality*. Chapel Hill, NC: University of North Carolina Press, 2012.

Shakespeare, William. *As You Like It*, ed. Juliet Dusinberre. London: Bloomsbury/Arden, 2006, repr. 2014.

Shakespeare, William. *Cymbeline*, ed Valerie Wayne. The Arden Shakespeare, 3rd series. London: Bloomsbury Publishing, 2017.

Shakespeare, William. *King Henry V*, ed. T. W. Craik. London: Bloomsbury/Arden, 1995, repr. 2016.

Shakespeare, William. *King Lear*, ed. Stephen Orgel. New York: Penguin Random House, 1999.

Shakespeare, William. *Othello: A Revised Edition*, ed. E. A. J. Honigmann. London and New York: Bloomsbury Arden, 1997, 2016.

Shakespeare, William. *Richard II*, ed. Charles A. Forger. London: Bloomsbury/Arden, 2002, repr. 2014.

Shakespeare, William. *The Arden Shakespeare: Antony and Cleopatra*, ed. John Wilders. London: Bloomsbury, 1995.

Shakespeare, William. *The Arden Shakespeare: Hamlet, Revised Edition*, ed. Ann Thompson and Neil Taylor. London: Bloomsbury, 2016.

Shakespeare, William. *The Arden Shakespeare: Love's Labour's Lost*, ed. H. R. Woudhuysen. Walton-on-Thames: Thomas Nelson and Sons, 1998.

Shakespeare, William. *The Arden Shakespeare: The Taming of the Shrew*, ed. Barbara Hodgdon. London: Bloomsbury, 2010.

Shakespeare, William. *The Complete Works*, ed. Stephen Orgel and A. R. Braunmuller, The New Pelican Text. New York: Penguin, 2002.

Shakespeare, William. *The Complete Works of Shakespeare*, 5th edn, ed. David Bevington. New York: Pearson, 2004.

Shakespeare, William. *The New Oxford Shakespeare: Modern Critical Edition Online*, ed. Gary Taylor, John Jowett, Terri Bourus and Gabriel Egan. Oxford: Oxford University Press, 2016)

Shakespeare, William. *The Norton Shakespeare*, ed. Stephen Greenblatt et al., 3rd edn. New York: W. W. Norton, 2016.

Shakespeare, William. *The Oxford Shakespeare: The Complete Works*, ed. Stanley Wells and Gary Taylor (Oxford: Oxford University Press, 1986).

Shakespeare, William. *The Riverside Shakespeare*, ed. G. Blakemore Evans, 2nd edn. Boston, MA: Houghton Mifflin, 1997.

Shakespeare, William. *The Tempest*, ed. Stephen Orgel. Oxford: Oxford University Press, 1987.

Shakespeare, William. *Two Noble Kinsmen*, ed. Lois Potter. London: Bloomsbury/Arden, 1997, rev. 2015.

Shannon, Laurie. *The Accommodated Animal: Cosmopolity in Shakespearean Locale*. Chicago: University of Chicago Press, 2013.

Shannon, Laurie. 'Emilia's Argument: Friendship and "Human Title" in *The Two Noble Kinsmen*'. *ELH* 64.3 (1997), 657–82.

Shannon, Laurie. *Sovereign Amity: Figures of Friendship in Shakespearean Contexts*. Chicago: University of Chicago Press, 2002.

Shapiro, James. 'The Shakespeare Play That Presaged the Trump Administration's Response to the Coronavirus Pandemic'. *New Yorker*, 8 April 2020, available at https://www.newyorker.com/culture/culture-desk/the-shakespeare-play -that-presaged-the-trump-administrations-response-to-the-coronavirus-pan demic (accessed 25 January 2023).

Sharp, Jane. *The Midwives Book, or, The Whole Art of Midwifry Discovered*. London, 1671.

Sheerin, Brian. 'Making Use of Nothing: The Sovereignties of *King Lear*'. *Studies in Philology* 110.4 (2013), 789–811.

Shelp, E. E., ed. *Virtue and Medicine: Explorations in the Character of Medicine*. Philosophy and Medicine 17. Dordrecht: D. Reidel, 1985.

Sher, Antony. 'The Fool in *King Lear*'. In *Players of Shakespeare 2: Further Essays in Shakespearean Performance by Players with the Royal Shakespeare Company*, ed. Russell Jackson and Robert Smallwood. Cambridge: Cambridge University Press, 1988, pp. 151–65.

Shirilan, Stephanie. 'Shakespeare's Rabbinic Virtues'. In *Shakespeare and Virtue: A Handbook*, ed. Julia Reinhard Lupton and Donovan Sherman. Cambridge: Cambridge University Press, 2023, pp. 279–89.

Sidney, Philip. *An Apology for Poetry (Or The Defence of Poesy)*, ed. R. W. Maslen. Manchester: Manchester University Press, 2002.

Sidney, Philip. *Defense of Poesy* (1595). Renascence Editions, available at https://www.luminarium.org/renascence-editions/defence.html (accessed 25 January 2023).

Siemon, James. *Word Against Word: Shakespearean Utterance*. Amherst and Boston, MA: University of Massachusetts Press, 2002.

Simmons, William Paul. 'Levinas's Divine Comedy and Archbishop Romero's Joyful Laughter'. In *Comedy Begins with Our Simplest Gestures: Levinas, Ethics, and Humor*, ed. Brian Bergen-Aurand. Pittsburgh, PA: Duquesne University Press, 2017, pp. 123–39.

Simonds, Peggy. 'Platonic Horses in *The Two Noble Kinsmen*: From Passion to Temperance'. *Renaissance Papers* (1998), 91–101.

Sinfield, Alan. 'Cultural Materialism and Intertextuality: The Limits of Queer Reading in *A Midsummer Night's Dream* and *Two Noble Kinsmen*'. *Shakespeare Survey* 56 (2003), 67–78.

Skinner, Quentin. *From Humanism to Hobbes: Studies in Rhetoric and Politics*. Cambridge: Cambridge University Press, 2018.

Slater, Michael. 'Desdemona's Divided Duty: Gender and Courtesy in *Othello*'. In *Travel and Travail: Early Modern Women, English Drama, and the Wider World*, ed. Patricia Akhimie and Bernadette Andrea. Lincoln, NE: University of Nebraska Press, 2019, pp. 215–35.

Smith, Bruce R. *Phenomenal Shakespeare*. Oxford: Wiley-Blackwell, 2010.

Smith, Matthew James and Julia Reinhard Lupton, eds. *Face to Face in Shakespeare in Shakespearean Drama: Ethics, Performance, Philosophy*. Edinburgh: Edinburgh University Press, 2019.

Smith, William, ed. *A Dictionary of Greek and Roman Biography and Mythology*. London: c. 1873.

Snyder, Susan. *The Comic Matrix of Shakespeare's Tragedies*. Princeton, NJ: Princeton University Press, 1979.

Sokol, B. J. and Mary Sokol. *Shakespeare, Law, and Marriage*. Cambridge: Cambridge University Press, 2003.

Spenser, Edmund. *The Faerie Queene*. London, 1609.

Spinrad, Phoebe S. 'Dogberry Hero: Shakespeare's Comic Constables in Their Communal Context'. *Studies in Philology* 89.2 (1992), 161–78.

Spurgeon, Caroline. *Shakespeare's Imagery and What It Tells Us*. Cambridge: Cambridge University Press, 1966.

Staley, Lynn. *The Island Garden: England's Language of Nation from Gildas to Marvell*. Notre Dame, IN: University of Notre Dame Press, 2012.

Stallybrass, Peter. 'Patriarchal Territories: The Body Enclosed'. In *Rewriting the Renaissance: The Discourses of Sexual Difference in Early Modern Europe*, ed. Margaret Ferguson and Maureen Quilligan. Chicago: University of Chicago Press, 1986.

Stanwood, Paul and Lee Johnson. 'The Structure of Wit'. In *The Wit of Seventeenth-Century Poetry*, ed. Claude Summers and Ted-Larry Pebworth. Columbia: University of Missouri Press, 1995, pp. 22–41.

Stock, Timothy. 'How Humor Holds Hostage: Exposure, Excession, and Enjoyment in a Levinas Beyond Laughter'. In *Comedy Begins with Our Simplest Gestures: Levinas, Ethics, and Humor*, ed. Brian Bergen-Aurand. Pittsburgh, PA: Duquesne University Press, 2017, pp. 61–81.

Strier, Richard. 'Against Morality: From *Richard III* to *Antony and Cleopatra*'. In

Richard Strier, *The Unrepentant Renaissance: From Petrarch to Shakespeare to Milton*. Chicago: University of Chicago Press, 2011, pp. 98–149.

Strier, Richard. '*King Lear* and Social Security'. *Raritan* 40.2 (2020), 63–72.

Strier, Richard. *The Unrepentant Renaissance: From Petrarch to Shakespeare to Milton*. Chicago: University of Chicago Press, 2011.

Stroud, Matthew D. *Fatal Union: A Pluralistic Approach to the Spanish Wife-Murder Comedias*. Lewisburg, PA: Bucknell University Press and Associated University Presses, 1990.

Stroup, Thomas B. 'Cordelia and the Fool'. *Shakespeare Quarterly* 12 (1961), 127–32.

Tate, Nahum. *The History of King Lear* (1681), reprinted in *Five Restoration Adaptations of Shakespeare*, ed. Christopher Spencer. Urbana: University of Illinois Press, 1965.

Tave, Stuart M. *The Amiable Humorist: A Study in the Comic Theory and Criticism of the Eighteenth and Early Nineteenth Centuries*. Chicago: University of Chicago Press, 1960.

Tessman, Lisa. *Burdened Virtues: Virtue Ethics for Liberatory Struggles*. New York: Oxford University Press, 2005.

The True Chronicle History of King Leir. London, 1594.

Thompson, Ayanna and Laura Turchi. *Teaching Shakespeare with Purpose: A Student-Centred Approach*. London and New York: Bloomsbury, 2016.

Thompson, Catherine. 'Swan Population a Welcome Sight'. *Stratford Observer*, 8 April 2017, available at https://stratfordobserver.co.uk/news/swan-popul ation-a-welcome-sight/ (accessed 25 January 2023).

Tillich, Paul. *The Courage to Be*, 2nd edn. New Haven, CT: Yale University Press, 2000.

Tillich, Paul. *The Courage to Be*, 3rd edn. New Haven, CT: Yale University Press, 2014.

Todd, Margo. *Christian Humanism and the Puritan Social Order*. Cambridge: Cambridge University Press, 1987.

Tolstoy, Leo. *Tolstoy on Shakespeare: A Critical Essay on Shakespeare*, trans. V. Tchertkoff and I. F. M. New York and London: Funk & Wagnalls, 1906.

Topsell, Edward. *The History of Four-Footed Beasts*. London, 1658.

Traub, Valerie. 'The Homoerotics of Shakespearean Comedy'. In *Shakespeare, Feminism and Gender*, ed. Kate Chedgzoy. London: Palgrave Macmillan, 2001, pp. 135–60.

Turner, Robert Y. 'Slander in *Cymbeline* and Other Jacobean Tragicomedies'. *English Literary Renaissance* 13.2 (1983), 182–202.

Vernant, Jean-Pierre and Pierre Vidal-Naquet. *Myth and Tragedy in Ancient Greece*, trans. Janet Lloyd. New York: Zone Books, 1990.

Virno, Paolo. *A Grammar of the Multitude*, trans. Isabella Bertoletti, James Cascaito and Andrea Casson. Los Angeles, CA: Semiotext(e), 2004.

Virno, Paolo. *Multitude: Between Innovation and Negation*, trans. Isabella Bertoletti, James Cascaito and Andrea Casson. Los Angeles, CA: Semiotext(e), 2008.

Vitkus, Daniel. *Turning Turk: English Theater and the Multicultural Mediterranean*. New York: Springer, 2016.

Vives, Juan Luis. In *The Education of a Christian Woman: A Sixteenth-Century*

Manual, ed. and trans. Charles Fantazzi. Chicago: University of Chicago Press, 2000.

Wade, Jenny. 'Meeting God in the Flesh: Spirituality in Sexual Intimacy'. *ReVision* 21.2 (1998), 35–41.

Walker, Jessica. '"What should his sufferance be?" Protesting Injustice in Shakespeare's Venice and the Age of Black Lives Matter'. *Journal of American Studies* 54.1 (2020), 44–50.

Walker, Matthew. 'Aristotle on Wittiness'. In *Laughter, Humor, and Comedy in Ancient Philosophy*, ed. Pierre Destree and Franco Trivigno. Oxford: Oxford University Press, 2019, pp. 103–21.

Watson, Robert N. 'Protestant Animals: Puritan Sects and English Animal-protection Sentiment, 1550–1650'. *ELH* 81.4 (2014), 1111–48.

Wayne, Valerie. 'The Woman's Parts of *Cymbeline*'. In *Staged Properties in Early Modern English Drama*, ed. Jonathan Gil Harris and Natasha Korda. Cambridge: Cambridge University Press, 2002, pp. 288–315.

Weber, Samuel. *Theatricality as Medium*. New York: Fordham University Press, 2004.

Wells, Stanley. *Shakespeare and Co.* London: Vintage, 2008.

von Wied, Herman. *The Glasse of Godly Love, A brief and a plain declaration of the duty of married folks*, trans. Haunce Dekin. London: J. Charlewood, 1588.

Wildberg, Christian. 'Neoplatonism'. *The Stanford Encyclopedia of Philosophy*, ed. Edward N. Zalta (Summer 2019), available at https://plato.stanford.edu/archives/sum2019/entries/neoplatonism/ (accessed 25 January 2023).

Wilkinson, R. H. *The Complete Gods and Goddesses of Ancient Egypt*. London: Thames & Hudson, 2003.

Williams, Bernard. *Ethics and the Limits of Philosophy*. Cambridge, MA: Harvard University Press, 1984.

Williams, Bernard. *Shame and Necessity*. Berkeley: University of California Press, 1993.

Williams, Bernard and Thomas Nagel. 'Moral Luck'. *Proceedings of the Aristotelian Society* 50 (1976), 115–50.

Witmore, Michael. 'Eventuality'. In *Early Modern Theatricality*, ed. Henry Turner. Oxford: Oxford University Press, 2013, pp. 386–401.

Wood, Neal. 'Cicero and the Political Thought of the Early English Renaissance'. *Modern Language Quarterly* (1990), 185–207.

Woodman, Marion. *Bone: A Journal of Wisdom, Strength and Healing*. New York: Penguin Putnam, 2000.

Yoder, Audrey. *Animal Analogy in Shakespeare's Character Portrayal*. New York: Columbia University Press, 1947.

Zargar, Cyrus Ali. *Polished Mirror: Storytelling and the Pursuit of Virtue in Islamic Philosophy and Sufism*. New York: Simon & Schuster, 2017.

Zekrgoo, Amir H. 'Metaphors of Music & Dance in Rumi's *Mathnawi*'. *KATHA: The Official Journal of the Centre for Civilisational Dialogue* 8.1 (2012), 1–14.

Žižek, Slavoj. 'Hegel on the Future, Hegel in the Future'. *Philosophy Now*, available at https://philosophynow.org/issues/140/Hegel_On_The_Future_Hegel_In_The_Future (accessed 25 January 2023).

Index